The Year the Packers Came Back

ALSO BY JOE ZAGORSKI AND FROM MCFARLAND

*The NFL in the 1970s: Pro Football's
Most Important Decade* (2016)

The Year the Packers Came Back

Green Bay's 1972 Resurgence

JOE ZAGORSKI

Foreword by Mike Holmgren

McFarland & Company, Inc., Publishers
Jefferson, North Carolina

ISBN (print) 978-1-4766-7424-7
ISBN (ebook) 978-1-4766-3785-3

LIBRARY OF CONGRESS AND BRITISH LIBRARY
CATALOGUING DATA ARE AVAILABLE

© 2020 Joe Zagorski. All rights reserved

No part of this book may be reproduced or transmitted in any form or by any means, electronic or mechanical, including photocopying or recording, or by any information storage and retrieval system, without permission in writing from the publisher.

Front cover: Packers running back John Brockington (42) carries the ball against the Chicago Bears during a game at Lambeau Field on October 8, 1972, in Green Bay, Wisconsin (Focus on Sport/Getty Images)

Printed in the United States of America

McFarland & Company, Inc., Publishers
Box 611, Jefferson, North Carolina 28640
www.mcfarlandpub.com

To all Green Bay Packers fans
who diligently and unfailingly cheered
for their team throughout the 1970s

Table of Contents

Acknowledgments	ix
Foreword by Mike Holmgren	1
Preface	3
1. Misery, Draft and Trades	11
2. Potential Amidst Early Injuries	28
3. Statement Wins	40
4. A Vital Comeback	53
5. A Predictable Slump	66
6. Losing a Coach, Gaining a Perspective	78
7. A Team in Every Sense	97
8. The Late-Season Drive for Victory	115
9. The Pack Is Back	130
10. Losing Too Soon	152
11. Proud to Be a Packer	169
12. A Legacy Remembered	182
Appendix A: The Players	191
Appendix B: Roster and Statistics	206
Chapter Notes	213
Bibliography	238
Index	243

Acknowledgments

Just as the 1972 Green Bay Packers relied on teamwork to become successful, so too did I rely on teamwork to write and finish this book. There are many people to thank for the completion of this project, and they all lent something special to help make this story of the 1972 Packers get a rebirth of sorts in the following pages. Some of the folks who helped me out offered a multitude of information, while others helped me to obtain dozens of outstanding photos. Still others offered me an encouraging word of endorsement and a much needed pep talk. Each of the following people were vital to the final draft of this book.

Jon Kendle is the chief research historian at the Ralph Wilson, Jr. Pro Football Research and Preservation Center at the Pro Football Hall of Fame in Canton, Ohio. His help to me on numerous visits were extremely important. Thanks to Jon for his incredible willingness and selflessness to devote his valuable time to help make my research efforts so enjoyable and successful.

Eric Goska is a famous and studious pro football writer and historian in Wisconsin. He has written several books on the Green Bay Packers, and his impressive knowledge of the team's past was very important in helping me with the writing of this book. I referred often to his book *Green Bay Packers: A Measure of Greatness*, which is one of the most comprehensive books ever written about the entire history of the team. As in true Green Bay fashion, he went out of his way many times to help me, and this book is a direct reflection of his help.

There are few people alive who know Green Bay Packers history better than Cliff Christl, who is the Packers' official team historian. His help in giving me advice and obtaining photos from the Packers' photographic archives is much appreciated. Moreover, Cliff continued to keep me on the right track with research and the facts that this book required. All teams should have an official historian, but it is highly doubtful that any will be as knowledgeable as Green Bay's.

Chris Willis is the chief archivist and historian at NFL Films, and once again, his help was invaluable. I'm very grateful for the assistance he has given me over many years of research at NFL Films in New Jersey. Also a big assist to me at NFL Films is Todd Schmidt, who has a love for the sport that is very inspirational. T.J. Troup is a pro football historian and author who is currently residing in Kentucky, but spent many of his earlier years coaching football in California. He is a grand repository of football knowledge, and some of his quotes can be read throughout this book. Our discussions about the sport, its strategy, and its history, have been very helpful. Thanks so much, Coach, for contributing your information and insight!

Thanks to Evan Siegle and Sarah Quick of the Packers organization, for helping me obtain the headshot photographs for this book. Thanks to Tricia Gesner of AP Images for helping me obtain many of the action photographs which have enhanced these pages. Thanks to Beth Kimball of the Parkettes Alumni Foundation, who was very helpful to me in acquiring a great photograph for the chapter describing the first Packers game versus the Minnesota Vikings on October 29, 1972. Thanks also to Tyler Bouyer of Getty Images for his critical photographic help. I was also very fortunate to obtain many great photographs from the Vernon and John Biever estate in Wisconsin. As all longtime Packers fans know, both Vernon and John Biever were some of the greatest photographers in pro football and Green Bay history. Their collection of pro football photos over the years is both grand and iconic. Very important in my attempts to procure some of these outstanding photographs was Jim Biever, who did everything he could to make this project a success. Matthew Foss and George Bozeka were also a vital help to me in obtaining the wonderful Biever photographs. George also helped me obtain interviews.

This book honorably belongs to every Packers player from that incredible 1972 season. I was unable to interview all of them (some have already passed away). That is unfortunate because they *all* had a say in how the team succeeded in that memorable year. Fortunately, I was able to interview some of the players, and I am very indebted to them for unselfishly giving up their time to discuss a big year in their lives from over four decades ago. Some of the people that I questioned were not players on that team, but they nevertheless had a story to tell ... and I was more than glad to listen! Everyone that I conversed with gave me an insight that I could never have explored without hearing their stories. Thanks to John and Diane Brockington, Jim Carter, Scott Hunter, Bill Lueck, Dave Robinson, Chuck Lane, Robert Miller, and Jonathon Schmidt. These people offered their help in so many different ways. These ranged from interviews to scheduling to organizational help (John Brockington's wife Diane is a Hall of Famer when it comes to organization!). This book would be a mere shadow of its finished self were it not for the efforts of these wonderful people. John Brockington, Jim Carter, Scott Hunter, Bill Lueck, and Dave Robinson were my heroes as I grew up in the 1970s, and I was both thrilled and honored to interview them. The information and anecdotes that I received from them represents the best and most illuminating parts of this book. Thanks to all of them for their help and their friendship!

Thanks to Frank D'Agostino for giving me a great story about Packers head coach Dan Devine. Thanks also to the former Green Bay and Seattle head coach Mike Holmgren, for contributing an outstanding foreword for this book. Thanks to my friend Tom Edell for lending me his helpful information and his outstanding pro football knowledge. Thanks to my friends Calvin Wetzel, Marialice Wilson, and Matt Hudson for their timely and vital support. Thanks also to my longtime friend John Thorn. Most know him as America's foremost Major League Baseball historian and expert, but he also knows a heck of a lot about pro football history. And he was always willing to give me some inspiration when I really needed it.

Thanks to all of my fellow members of the Pro Football Researchers Association (PFRA). Over the last several decades, I have been very fortunate to soak up knowledge from PFRA stalwarts, Ken Crippen, Lee Elder, Mark L. Ford, John Grasso, John Hogrogian, John Maxymuk, Rupert Patrick, Andy Piasik, and Ivan Urena (among others). I never fail to learn new information and obtain new leads whenever I chat with these folks. Virtually all aspects of pro football history have been explored, diagnosed, studied, and written about by the many members of the PFRA. There are several chapters of this book that were greatly aided by their help and support.

Thanks also to a man whom I consider to be the greatest pro football writer of the past and current—and probably future—generation, Michael MacCambridge. His innate knowledge of the game and its history is second to none, and his willingness to lend me advice over the years is greatly treasured.

Last but never least, I would like to thank my late parents, Stephen and Natalie Zagorski, for inspiring me throughout my life, and for showing me by their many examples the value of hard work and dedication to the things and to the people that you love. They taught me to fall in love with my dreams, and then through hard work they showed me how to make those dreams become a reality. My love to the best parents ever ... always.

I hope that all of you who are reading this book will enjoy reliving the incredible story of the 1972 Green Bay Packers!

Go Pack Go!

Foreword
by Mike Holmgren

In 1972, the Green Bay Packers won the National Football Conference's Central Division championship. As it turned out, they were the only Packers team during the decade of the 1970s to do so. Many years later, that '72 Packers squad has been forgotten by many, and that is indeed unfortunate. They exhibited the same level of spirit, determination, hard work, and solid effort that all Packers championship teams have displayed over the years. They are definitely a special Packers team, and they were filled with overachievers.

Joe Zagorski's book about that team is a well-rounded account of that group of Packers players, and how they overcame many obstacles to win the NFC Central Division title. The 1972 Packers were not expected to win their division. In fact, they were not even expected to win much more than the four games that they won in the previous year. But win they did, and despite a lot of adversity, they had a collective desire to succeed in the tough "Black and Blue" division.

I was fortunate to coach the Green Bay Packers for seven years in the 1990s, and during that time, I was surrounded by the many great stories of the team's incredible past. From the era of Curly Lambeau, to the years of Titletown with Vince Lombardi, there was a certain sense of history and tradition that was a huge part of the town and its team. In the 1970s, the Packers did not win on a consistent basis. The 1972 Packers did become winners, however, and as such they hold a treasured place in Packers history.

During the time that I was in Green Bay, I can attest to how important the town considers the Packers. It is indeed a special moment up in Green Bay on Sunday afternoons in the fall and winter when the Packers win. When I told our players after winning Super Bowl XXXI in 1996, "As much as winning the Vince Lombardi Trophy means to anyone else in the league, it means more to us," I wasn't kidding. The Green Bay Packers are a pro football institution. They always strive for excellence, year after year, regardless of who is the head coach or his assistants, and regardless of which players form the Packers roster.

The 1972 Packers team that is detailed in this book made the same sacrifices that all Green Bay teams do every year. The players on that team made a commitment to each other, and they managed to win a division championship. That Packers team needs to be remembered, and Joe Zagorski's book represents a good step forward in making sure that they are remembered. The 1972 season was a great season to be a Packers fan, and it was a great year to watch the Pack come back.

Mike Holmgren won 174 games as a head coach for the Green Bay Packers (from 1992 to 1998), and for the Seattle Seahawks (from 1999 to 2008). He led the Packers to the Super Bowl XXXI World Championship in 1996 and to the NFC Championship in 1997. Holmgren also led the Seahawks to the AFC Championship in 2005. He earned two Super Bowl rings as an assistant coach and offensive coordinator for the San Francisco 49ers in 1988 and 1989 and was the president of the Cleveland Browns from 2010 to 2012.

Preface

On a recent visit to historic Lambeau Field in Green Bay, Wisconsin, I had the opportunity to take a tour of the impressive and picturesque facilities. Our knowledgeable tour guide regaled us with all of the popular stories of the Green Bay Packers' glorious past, from the founding of the team by the great Curly Lambeau, to the dynasty of Titletown built by the legendary head coach Vince Lombardi, to the championship exploits of quarterbacks Bart Starr, Brett Favre and Aaron Rodgers. But our tour guide also admitted a fact that struck me as somewhat odd and curious. "We don't talk about the 1970s here," was her response to a random question about the post–Lombardi era of the team.[1] I had always known that the decade of the 1970s was filled with failure for the Packers. But I also knew that 1972 was a special and memory-filled year for the team during that decade. It was the only year in the 1970s in which the Green Bay Packers won a division title and went to the playoffs. I always thought that the '72 team was worth remembering and celebrating, not just because they were winners, but because of the multitude of problems and unnerving situations that they had to endure during that successful season. This book is my attempt at reacquainting Packers fans (and Packers tour guides!) with a proud moment of their team's past, sandwiched in the midst of Green Bay's mostly forgettable results in the decade of the 1970s.

In retrospect, the team probably should not have achieved success in 1972. They struggled greatly in the offensive phase of the passing game, where they lacked quality starters and strong depth in both the wide receiver and quarterback positions. Their best tight end sustained an injury in the second week of the regular season and was lost for the remainder of the year. The team also had difficulty in decision making, particularly when it involved their head coach, Dan Devine, who had the innate ability to keep his players guessing and scratching their heads. He was perpetually aloof and unpredictable when dealing with his players on a personal level on any given week. Devine also made more than his share of what turned out to be bad decisions in play calling and game plan development, two of the most important factors in determining how well a coach and a team will do during the course of a game and a season. This book will analyze Devine's coaching decisions and statements throughout the 1972 season. It will also examine the players' positive and negative moments, in an effort to understand how the Packers managed to earn a division title in that incredible year.

Past and current professional football teams were and are comprised of many different personalities among the players on the roster. The same is true among NFL head coaches. Some are very analytical and strategic. Others are master motivators who can inspire their players to outstanding feats on the gridiron. Some head coaches wear their emotions on their sleeve, while others can be quite calm and collected while pacing the sidelines. Dan Devine turned out to be one of the most difficult head coaches for any grid athlete to play for in NFL history. Most accounts would label him as an enigma, due in large measure to the sheer unpredictability of what he would say or do in many situations. At times he would have very little to discuss, and he would say his words in a normal, collected voice. At other times, when out of the public eye, he would be boisterous and loud in tone, shouting and yelling to get his point across. Analysts and psychologists today might spend hours attempting to diagnose him, but, after reading many of his quotes, I suspect he just might attempt to diagnose *them*. Just by looking at him, one would probably describe Devine as a rather bookish, Poindexter type of coach. His dark-rimmed eyeglasses and his constantly tight-lipped countenance on game day, however, gave at least some visual evidence to the representation that he had far too many different items bouncing back and forth in his head. It appeared to most fans who watched him during the games that the clipboard-carrying Devine had everything well under control. However, the opposite was all too often true.

Most of the players who comprised the 1972 Packers roster would eventually discover that their head coach was out of his element in the National Football League. Devine achieved notable success as a head coach in the collegiate ranks. But in the NFL, Devine by most accounts bit off more than he could chew. The players on the Green Bay team of 1972 somehow managed to overcome Devine's indecision and baffling incompetence during many occasions throughout the year, however. The team also survived numerous injuries to key players to win the National Football Conference's Central Division title. It was a team and a year when the various personalities on the Packers would express moments of disgruntled anguish, look quizzically at each other and wonder what was going on, yet manage to achieve several incredible and inspirational victories.

In the annals of the National Football League's divisional championship teams dating back to the first playoff game in 1933, the story of the 1972 Green

Bay Packers is probably one of the most unusual of all time. The Packers had recently completed one of the most glorious decades of ultimate victory in NFL history during the 1960s, winning five world championships in the span of seven years. But they had fallen upon hard times immediately after the retirement of their legendary head coach, Vince Lombardi, following the glorious 1967 season. Devine succeeded Lombardi's hand-picked replacement, Phil Bengston, as Green Bay's head coach in 1971. Devine had experienced a good deal of success in coaching at the University of Missouri, where he went 93-37-7 in 13 seasons (and earned four bowl victories). As a direct result of his collegiate coaching achievements, he had justly earned layers of job security as a college coach, only to give it up in order to try his luck with the pros. But professional football was a much different game, and few were the college coaches at that time who scored immediate success in the NFL. Devine would certainly not be the exception. The Packers had finished Devine's inaugural season with a dismal 4-8-2 record, the worst mark for the club in the past 13 years. They had shown signs of talent and statistical improvement during the 1971 campaign, but those moments were brief and sporadic. Few diehard Packer Backers felt that the 1972 season would produce any better results, but surprisingly, that is exactly what happened.

The 1972 Packers managed to rise up off of the NFL canvas in the space of several months after the conclusion of the 1971 season. Certainly in the NFL there have been a multitude of Cinderella teams which have come from virtually nowhere to earn a playoff berth in NFL history. Indeed, many have overcome some very tough odds in order to accomplish such a feat. The 1972 Packers would fall into that category. Not many prognosticators and pro football media pundits felt that this team was going to contend for the division title, and given Green Bay's less-than-stellar record in the previous year, who could disagree with them? The 1971 season was a very misleading one for the Pack. The offensive, defensive, and special teams statistics in Dan Devine's first year at the helm of the team were indicative of a squad that should have finished with a much better won-loss record. Green Bay's offense scored 274 points in 1971, compared to the 196 points that they scored in 1970 before Devine arrived. The Packers also gained 634 more rushing yards in 1971 than they did in 1970. Devine's rushing attack in 1971 accumulated an incredible 115 first downs, amounting to 46 more than the 1970 Packers could accrue. Green Bay's pass protection was stellar in 1971, giving up only 18 quarterback sacks, compared to 43 in the previous year. But the 1971 Packers could account for only four wins. Why? What hurt Green Bay the most in the 1971 season was their inability to win several close games in the fourth quarter. Of the Packers' eight losses, three were by three points or less, and both of their tie contests could naturally have ended in victories with a successful field goal. Speaking of field goals and the kicking game, the 1971 Packers employed three different placekickers during the course of the season, and they could only account for a combined total of 14 field goals in 26 attempts.

Devine's defense in 1971 also regressed somewhat from the previous year. The Pack gave up 28 more first downs in 1971 than they did the previous season, and their pass rushers were only able to account for 19 quarterback sacks in 1971, compared to 32 in 1970. Devine knew that he was going to have to find a way to improve all aspects of his team, and to his credit, he did so by making intelligent use of two important options which were available to him: trading away older players who he may have felt were past their prime, and selecting quality rookies in the NFL draft to replace some of them.

The story of the 1972 Green Bay Packers begins with the day-to-day off-season decisions that Devine made to affect his roster, and ends under the microscopic lens of nationwide attention during the divisional playoffs. In between are important details of how a very young team with limited experience melded with a modest group of sagacious veterans, many of whom had tasted the former glory of past world championships, to recapture—if but for only a moment—a truly victorious season.

Those victories would not come easily. Devine was fully aware of the resonant shadow that Lombardi had cast on him, and indeed on all future coaches in the NFL. Perhaps in all likelihood it was an impossible task to live up to the standard set by a man that most pro football experts regarded—and still regard—as the greatest head coach in the history of the game. In retrospect, Devine's approach to trade away many Packer veterans from the 1960s was probably considered by most pro football authorities as his first mistake. Players such as Forrest Gregg, Lionel Aldridge, Doug Hart, Bob Jeter, Don Horn, Donny Anderson, Travis Williams, Jim Grabowski, and Dave Hampton were among those proven athletes who were targeted as expendable by Devine. Other veterans like Dave Robinson, Bob Brown, and Carroll Dale would—within a couple of years—follow this trend of former Lombardi men who were traded to other teams. Three of them would go on to play in three more future Super Bowls with their new teams.

Devine's actions were further perplexing, however, as his words and his decisions could not have helped but play mind games with the players on his team. A case in point came when Devine immediately benched future Hall of Fame middle linebacker and fan favorite Ray Nitschke, in favor of the young and inexperienced Jim Carter (just a year removed from the University of Minnesota), before the beginning of the 1971 season. Near the end of that season, however, Devine stated that Nitschke was (still) a hitter, and that he (Devine) "always had a warm spot in my heart for a hitter."[2] Yet despite his long history of hitting opponents (often and very successfully), and despite the fact that he was relatively healthy, Nitschke rode the bench for most of the final two years of his pro career (1971 and 1972). Nitschke would assert that he was still a better player than Carter, and that the better player at each position should always be the starter, regardless of his age. It did not take long for most of the older veterans on the 1971 Packers team to come to the conclusion—with this example as its most notable one—that their new head coach was playing favorites. The public at that time would never know this with any amount of definite certainty, however, nor would they hear much from the media in those years about how several players on the team harbored shared grievances against their head coach. The situation between Devine and his players throughout 1972 will be explored in greater detail in Chapter 6.

Devine differed from many head coaches in at least one respect. All new head coaches across the league are allowed to name their own assistant coaches, and Devine naturally followed suit. But Devine did not clean house with his assistants, even though that was one of his unstated goals with the leftover players on the team from the Vince Lombardi era. Devine instead decided to keep a few of the coaches from Phil Bengston's and (previously) Vince Lombardi's tenures, rather than getting rid of all of them. Perhaps he knew deep down that any assistant coach who learned from Lombardi had to have some qualities worth keeping around. The Packers players naturally had to quickly adjust to the new position coaches that Devine *did* bring in to Green Bay, and by most accounts, they did this very well. Devine added the likes of assistant coaches Don Doll (defensive backs), Rollie Dotsch (offensive line), and Burt Gustafson (linebackers) in 1971. Other new assistant coaches would eventually join the team prior to the 1972 campaign. They included Hank Kuhlmann (special teams), and John Polonchek (passers/receivers). Speaking of passers, the great Packers veteran Bart Starr served as a player-coach in 1971, and he eventually took over as quarterbacks coach in the following season. Longtime Green Bay defensive line coach Dave Hanner was named the team's defensive coordinator for 1972. The coaching staff was finally set as the team prepared for the training camp that summer.

The 1972 Packers also had to address the fact that most of their newer players had the stigma of inexperience as their most common denominator. The coaches and fans were going to have to get used to seeing youthful mistakes occur throughout the preseason and regular season. Those fans had in fact grown accustomed to that sight, however, as the previous few years had shown just how far Green Bay had fallen from their lofty heights during the 1960s, when they had won five NFL championships and the first two Super Bowls. From 1968 to and including 1970, the team had won a combined total of only 20 of 42 games. Devine could tell from reviewing the films of 1971 that his team was deficient in applying onto the field the basic fundamentals of tackling, blocking, and hustling. To address this, Devine was knowledgeable enough to instruct his assistant coaches to stress these basic principles of the game constantly to every player—even the veterans—all throughout training camp and the regular season. The results were noteworthy, as the Packers improved statistically in 1972 in many important categories. By the end of 1972, they were a fundamentally sound football team.

Offensive improvements came about with reclaiming a vital portion of Green Bay's recent past. The bedrock of the Packers' game plans of the 1960s was a strong, robust running game. Devine decided to build upon that one aspect for his team, beginning in 1971 with the drafting of 6-foot-1, 225-pound halfback John Brockington out of Ohio State University. Devine then upgraded his ground game in 1972 with the addition of 6-foot-1, 220-pound fullback MacArthur Lane, who came to the team in a trade with the St. Louis Cardinals. Both of these men would have been comfortable playing either fullback or halfback, and both would end up blocking for each other throughout their years in Green Bay. "I've watched Lane play for a while," admitted Devine. "Lane is a devastating blocker, what a guy like Brockington really needs. Your short side attack has to be good. He's big enough to pick up blitzes and he has a history of making long runs."[3]

Brockington won the league's 1971 Rookie of the Year award with his 1,105 yards rushing, tops in the National Football Conference. Brockington thus became the first NFL rookie since 1934 to eclipse 1,000 yards rushing in a season, and his 5.1 yards-per-rush average in 1971 was the best mark in the entire lNFC for running backs who toted the pigskin with at least 200 carries. In 1972, both Brockington and Lane would team up to form the most productive rushing attack in the team's history since the early 1960s, when Paul Hornung and Jim Taylor helped to make the Packers the most feared rushing duo in the NFL.

Several important trades and savvy draft choices led to an improved defense in 1972. To bolster the secondary, Devine selected blue-chip cornerback Willie Buchanon out of San Diego State University in the first round of the 1972 collegiate draft, and his presence on the field reaped immediate dividends for the team. Devine also traded with the San Diego Chargers to acquire veteran defensive back Jimmy Hill, who lent stability and wisdom to the group. Green Bay's newly-formed pass coverage, combined with an improved pass rush from a younger group of defensive linemen, would add up to one of the best seasons at stopping their opponents' passing attacks in the team's history.

Green Bay reached the playoffs in 1972, in spite of the turbulence caused by Devine's questionable decisions, which were present all throughout the season, and which will be explored in more detail in Chapter 6. In retrospect, it was a near-miracle that the team achieved as much as they did, considering all of the discord caused by their head coach. As you read through these pages, you will note a number of typical challenges which face every NFL team every season. Those challenges through the years have inadvertently served as a springboard to make some good teams great. But those similar challenges have also made some marginal teams worse. The 1972 Packers could have gone either way when faced with the normal and expected amount of challenges and issues. There were indeed quite a few moments when they had to deal with more than their share of difficulties. You will thus note and take account of those troubles, and in the midst of these pages, of Green Bay's constant search for success. You will also notice during the course of the 1972 season a multitude of big plays that the Packers pulled off, many of which seemingly came out of nowhere. The team coalesced through the cracks and crevasses of their concerns and troubles for positive solutions, as evidenced with the words and thoughts of several of their players. How they managed to find and obtain success in this season is quite impressive. The players offered critical and important responses to the challenging issues that they were faced with in 1972, and those answers and decisions led them to victory, a division title, and to a berth in the NFC playoffs.

It was the 1972 NFL season: a very special and unique season to be sure, and one that every Packers fan—and every Lambeau Field tour guide—should fondly remember today. It was the year that the Packers came back.

1
Misery, Draft and Trades

By the time that the final gun had sounded at Miami's Orange Bowl Stadium on December 19 to end the 1971 National Football League regular season, Green Bay Packers head coach Dan Devine had already known the steps that he needed to take in order to avoid a repeat performance of what he had just witnessed and experienced during the previous five months. Devine's first season at the helm of the Packers ended in a 27–6 defeat by the host Dolphins, a loss that concluded a dismal 4–8–2 season for Green Bay. Devine was not treading on unfamiliar ground, however. Few were the head coaches who enjoyed winning seasons in their first year of calling the shots for their professional teams. Devine knew full well at this point that the specter of his previous success as the head coach of the University of Missouri football team—where he established a winning program—was far behind him. The pros provided Devine a much different game, with its own set of distinct difficulties and challenges. He took the job in Green Bay because he wanted to experience a new challenge. "It's hard to tell what motivates people," Devine opined after the 1971 season. "Five years from now, I'd hate to wake up, shave, look at myself, and say, 'You chickened out.'"[1]

Devine and the Packers to their credit showed no signs of cowardice, but they did indeed struggle all throughout 1971. They made more than their share of mistakes, as the players and the pro game itself gave their new head coach the challenge that he had desired. Despite the failure of his first season at Green Bay, however, Devine stayed at least somewhat optimistic.

"It had to be the most frustrating year I've put in, I guess, and the most disappointing," Devine said after the Miami game. "But still, I'm certainly not discouraged. I've always analyzed myself as one who fought a little harder the tougher things got."[2]

Things definitely got tough right away for Green Bay in 1971. They could muster only two wins in the preseason, as Devine substituted his players on a constant basis, in the hopes of finding a formula which would develop some consistency on the field. Unfortunately for Devine and his team, that seamless formula geared to obtaining such consistency never really appeared throughout the preseason. Green Bay's 1971 regular season did begin with hopefulness, however, up in Lambeau Field on September 19. There is always plenty of promise for every NFL team at the onset of a new regular season. Every team takes their stance at the same starting line, and expectations spring eternal for all teams, even those who finish the previous year with a losing record. The Packers and their fans were aspirant that with a new head coach, Green Bay's fortunes would improve. But despite scoring 40 points on that rain-saturated opening day against the visiting New York Giants, the Packers gave up 42 points in their initial loss of the season. Once again, mistakes were plentiful, and those errors proved to be the determining factor in the contest.

Unfortunately for Green Bay, the game versus the Giants served as an accurate harbinger of what awaited the team during the 1971 season. It was a game where every good thing that the Packers did against their foes was usually offset by one and sometimes two (or more) bad things that happened to the Green and Gold. The loss to New York also saw a moment of pathos and pawky misfortune, as Giants offensive lineman Bob Hyland (ironically a former Packer himself) chased Green Bay defensive back Doug Hart out of bounds after an interception. Hyland accidentally plowed right into Dan Devine's knee. The rookie head coach sustained a broken leg in his first regular season game in the NFL, and was carried off the field on a stretcher amidst a smattering of good-natured cheers of sympathy from the Packer fans in attendance. Devine must have felt a sense of forlorn disgust as he rode in an ambulance toward a local hospital to get fitted for a cast on his leg. His team symbolically also wore a cast throughout all of 1971.

"We'd much rather win than lose, of course, but I'd just as soon do it easier than that," Devine with a dry wit suggested, as he grimaced while trying to walk with his crutches. "It's sort of the story of my life. I very seldom get to do it the easy way."[3]

The 1971 Green Bay season would go on from there, with the upsetting feeling that as the weeks went by, they would never earn a key victory or two which could have given them a solid dose of momentum and optimism. In the end, the Packers would eventually finish with a last-place divisional record. The next year, however, Green Bay would happily enjoy a trading of fortunes, as they would experience several more easier games than that unhopeful loss to the Giants in 1971. Moreover, the Packers would also achieve more moments of solidified play on both offense, defense, and special teams, throughout most of 1972.

Back in 1972, the annual NFL Draft of college players was usually held just shortly following the end of the previous season. Today, all NFL teams have four months to compile their collegiate scouting reports, conduct numerous player workouts, and probe and question hundreds of the nation's top recruits in the annual league combine and plenty of pro day events. Such was not the case in the early 1970s. When Coach Devine, player personnel director and head scout Pat Peppler, and the entire Green Bay scouting staff ended their 1971 season, there was virtually no time to lose. A determined and resolute effort was needed in order to compile the many volumes of data and information that the Packers' brain trust had to have in order to make quality selections, and they would have a large number of 16 players to select in the 1972 draft. That number is much more than the number of five to nine selections (on average) that pro teams have in the recent years of the draft. The Packers—along with the other 25 NFL teams at that time—simply had to work fast, with long hours being the norm as the draft approached. Green Bay had to obtain better overall college talent if they were to produce a more competitive team, and every minute of time spent studying scouting reports would be the most fundamental key to giving them a needed edge.

The 1972 NFL Draft of college players was held on February 1 and 2 at the Essex House in Manhattan, an upscale hotel overlooking New York City's Central Park. The NFL Draft of today is a big prime-time television extravaganza, but it was not always that way. A casual observer of the NFL Draft in the early 1970s would have seen a small table for each team, with the team names on raised placards sitting centrally on the tabletops. Those work stations in the cramped ballroom were filled with cigarette ashtrays, pots of coffee, old-fashioned dial telephones on each table, a simplistic wooden podium with the NFL Shield hanging in front of it a few feet away for Commissioner Pete Rozelle to announce the selections, and an overhead projector (like the ones we old-timers had in elementary and high school) which displayed the choices from each team on a six square foot screen. In many ways, the NFL Draft back in those days almost resembled a clandestine meeting, where savvy secrets were passed between team representatives like schoolchildren used to pass notes to their friends across the classroom, right under their teacher's nose. Speaking of noses, the cigarette smoke in the room was constantly wafting throughout the throng of league personnel people and newspaper reporters, no doubt ignited by the nerves of the selectors, whose psyche was invariably on edge. Jobs, careers and reputations were regularly at stake in this annual exercise of attempting to turn a losing team into a winning team. Each team owned anywhere from 10 to 20 choices back in the early 1970s on average, and each decision was weighed highly with pertinent factors of what each team needed the most (in the sphere of positions on the football field), and which college seniors were best apt and prepared to give them those necessities. The location of the NFL draft was readily accepted by all participants. Since the NFL's main office was located on Park Avenue in New

York City, the Big Apple was the natural setting every year during the 1970s for the annual draft. Sightseeing, Broadway and Times Square, and the wintery snow scenery were definitely not on the minds of the 26 football personnel departments, however.

Coach Devine and Pat Peppler were still thinking about possible solutions to the problems that 1971 produced for the Packers, as they paced the hallways of the Essex House just hours before their first selection. The areas of greatest and most immediate need as far as Devine was concerned involved his pass defense and his kicking game. In 1971, Green Bay gave up 2,301 passing yards and 21 passing touchdowns. These were not horrible statistics, but in order to become more competitive in the National Football Conference, Devine knew that those numbers had to decrease. When it came time for the Packers to make their first selection, a bona fide gem of a defensive back turned out to be available. Willie Buchanon was a standout cornerback from San Diego State University, and he was a prized gift that was waiting to be snatched. He was ranked by the vast majority of draft experts as a blue chip, can't miss prospect. Buchanon spent most of his senior year on college football fields across America doing two different things—knocking down opposing passes and intercepting them. As incredible as this statistic sounds, competing NCAA quarterbacks threw the ball just 46 times in Buchanon's direction during his entire senior season, and only 12 of those attempts were completed.

Head coach Dan Devine was at the center of the controversies that surrounded the 1972 Packers. He was a winning collegiate head coach, but according to most of his Packers players, he was in over his head as a professional head coach. Despite that opinion, Devine was named the NFC Coach of the Year in 1972 (courtesy the Green Bay Packers).

Devine's personnel aide in the congregation ballroom quickly wrote down Buchanon's name for Commissioner Rozelle to read aloud to the attending audience and the other representative teams, and in an instant, the strength of the Packers defense had received an immediate boost. "I think Willie Buchanon is going to help a lot," said Green Bay defensive coordinator Dave Hanner. "He's better right now than a lot of people who are playing regular in the NFL."[4]

Devine admitted that Buchanon would be named the team's immediate starter at left cornerback. "He's going to get his feet wet in a hurry,"[5] Devine said. The prevailing belief at that time in the league was for rookies to sit on the sidelines, gain some experience by watching film each week, and making the mistakes that he was destined to make on the practice field. Devine differed from this norm, particularly where a rookie of Buchanon's caliber was concerned. "He (Buchanon) will learn more in there (on the field) than he will on the bench," Devine asserted.[6]

Green Bay defensive backfield coach Don Doll was practically giddy with joy and anticipation when he learned that Willie Buchanon would be wearing the Green and Gold in 1972.

"He looks like he has all the qualities to be a starter," affirmed Doll. "He has great natural ability. He does as many different things well as anybody I've ever seen. He has a knack of coming off a receiver and going for the ball that is exceptional. And he catches the ball exceptionally well. He does it with ease. In fact, everything he does is effortless, and he's very, very coachable. But the big thing about him is that his attitude is so good. He's a talented young man with a bright future."[7]

The 1972 college draft was just beginning, however. As is the rule, the teams that finish the previous year with poor records get to make their selections before the teams that had achieved winning records. This decree was aimed at trying to give those losing teams a fair chance to become more competitive with the tougher teams, a principle that would in theory raise the competition level all throughout the league. The Packers somehow benefited from their woeful 1971 record by owning the rights to another rookie selection just a few minutes after Willie Buchanon was drafted. Besides the defense and the kicking game, one other important segment of the team that needed help was at the vital quarterback position. Future Hall of Famer Bart Starr would end his exemplary playing career in 1971, and even though he would stay on with the team as its quarterback coach, his on-field experience and abilities would be deeply missed. Devine had traded away quarterback Don Horn before the 1971 season began, leaving a void at that position. Horn was considered by previous head coach Phil Bengston (and many Packer fans) as the heir apparent to Starr's spot, but Horn was inconsistent, and Devine desperately needed consistency in his field general. Moreover, Horn did have some level of trade value, which greatly enticed Devine to send him to the Denver Broncos for defensive end Alden Roche. The Packers were needful of all kinds of players to fill voids in various positions, and the defensive end spot was one such position.

Devine then relied on his wealth of scouting reports, and he chose the standout quarterback from the University of Nebraska, Jerry Tagge, with his second pick in the 1972 draft. Tagge had guided the Cornhuskers to consecutive National Championships in both 1970 and 1971 before graduating. Tagge did benefit greatly at Nebraska by playing in the same backfield with the great wingback Johnny Rodgers, but what quarterback would not have? Nebraska head coach Bob Devaney featured Rodgers in his wishbone offense, and the results were outstanding to say the least. Rogers finished his collegiate career with 6,059 total yards and a Heisman Trophy. But to his credit, Tagge was a steady leader, and was named the Most Valuable Player in both the 1971 and 1972 Orange Bowl games (both Nebraska victories). He was also a big and strong quarterback at 6-feet-2, 220 pounds, which projected well to pro ball, and that was a point that may have swayed Devine's mind when making his choice.

For Tagge, it would be a most happy homecoming. He had spent his teenage years in Green Bay, and even sold concessions at Lambeau Field during his youth. "This (his being selected by Green Bay) has been my dream since I was a little boy," Tagge admitted.[8] He also had a colorful story to tell about his recollections of the Ice Bowl, the famous Green Bay victory over Dallas in the 1967 NFL Championship Game, where the frigid weather (13 degrees below zero at kickoff) made the game one of the most historic and iconic in NFL history. Tagge was an usher that arctic day at Lambeau Field, so he got a chance to freeze with the rest of the chilled fans who attended the game. As the contest wound down to under a minute, He decided to move down to the bottom row of the stands to get a closer look at the action. Tagge at this point felt the urge to get even closer than the seats in the stands, however. "I jumped over the railing just before that play (Bart Starr's famous quarterback sneak for the winning score) and was standing right on the sidelines at the goal line when Bart scored," Tagge recalled.[9]

Five years after that fateful day, Tagge would not have to climb over a railing to get on Lambeau Field's historic turf. The situation could not have been more ideal for him, as the Packers depth chart at the quarterback position was virtually void of a designated and confirmed starter. Tagge would end up competing for the job with former Alabama signal caller Scott Hunter, whose first year in the league (1971) did not produce enough positive results to keep Devine from drafting another quarterback in 1972. And even though the Packers did not utilize a wishbone offense, Devine felt strongly that Tagge, who was a quick learner and very mature for his youthful age, would quickly adjust to the pro set offenses of the National Football League.

The 1972 NFL Collegiate Draft was by no means over with the selection of Tagge to Devine's roster, however. Perhaps the most obvious need for Green Bay that was heard over the past several seasons was the call for an adequate placekicker. The Packers had lost no less than four games in 1971 because of missed field goals. A total of nine different men were used as a kicker from 1968 to the end of 1971, and none of them were consistent enough to be regarded as reliable. Devine, to his credit, would find the remedy to his team's kicking woes in the small town of Hillsdale, Michigan. Chester Marcol of Hillsdale College was considered by most scouts as the finest placekicking specialist in the nation. He blasted a 62-yard field goal while in college, and that successful kick put him on the placekicking map. He also attempted a 70-yard field goal that was kicked long enough, but was just wide of the uprights. But because most teams usually waited until the later rounds to obtain a kicker in the draft, he was naturally passed over by every team in the first round. But that did not mean that he was not courted by some teams.

"I was projected to be taken somewhere between the second and fourth rounds of the 1972 NFL Draft," Marcol recalled. "The Dallas Cowboys, Atlanta Falcons and New York Jets were among the teams that scouted me at Hillsdale but as far as I knew, the Packers never watched me kick, even though we played games just a few minutes away at St. Norbert and a couple hours up the road at Northern Michigan. The [Dallas] Cowboys called me the morning of the draft and there's no doubt in my mind they were going to call my name in the second round. But the Packers beat them to it."[10]

"I really wanted to go in the first round. But I wasn't too disappointed at having to wait."[11] Marcol's new roommate on the Packers—rookie quarterback Jerry Tagge—put matters into perspective with a timely quip. "Don't blame them [the scouts]," advised Tagge when discussing the draft with Marcol. "By the time they found Hillsdale [on the map], the first round was over."[12]

Devine broke with the accepted tradition of the day of waiting to late in the selection process to draft a kicker. He picked Marcol (who was born in Poland and who emigrated to America at the age of 16) early in the second round. Devine's decision to make Marcol the 34th overall pick in the draft would have immediate and remarkable results. Marcol connected on three straight field goal attempts from 47 yards out on his first day of spring practice with the Packers. On the second day of spring practice, he booted three straight field goal attempts from 52 yards out. From that moment on, Marcol was anointed as the team's starting placekicker. "He's going to kick the first kickoff of the season, the first field goal or the first extra point, whichever it is," Devine proclaimed.[13]

Devine's statement following Marcol's early success at practice was symbolic of the Packers' statement of purpose with the entire 1972 draft. The Green Bay decision makers left the extravaganza in New York City with a distinct feeling of optimism, and well they should have. The team was definitely on the rebound, selecting a total of 16 new players, and as far as Dan Devine was concerned, those Packer draft selections were proof that success was just around the corner. Green Bay had indeed made some noise in the draft, and it was a welcomed cacophony that resounded with the yells of hopeful and future achievements.

The town of Green Bay, Wisconsin, was a far cry, however, from the overpopulated throngs of people that Devine and his staff encountered in New York City for the 1972 NFL Draft. Green Bay during the early 1970s was still a small town by many people's standards, containing roughly 70,000 inhabitants. But it was a growing town, maybe not at the rate of a city like Milwaukee, but growing nonetheless. Blue color industries melded with numerous farming environments to comprise the life blood of Green Bay. Its citizens were hardy souls, accustomed to frigid temperatures in the winter. Today, the town is celebrated by the frozen elements that have—along with the Packers—made Green Bay famous over the past several decades. But back in 1972, however, the town's inhabitants were not really concerned all that much about the chilled operations of winter. They were used to wearing layers upon layers of clothing in order to stay warm. Rather, they were both curious and eager for a chance at redemption from their team's miserable defeats that they had witnessed from 1968 to 1971.

In his plan to gain that redemption and accomplish great things in 1972, Coach Devine felt that there was an obvious need for young talent to fill out the roster, and replace any and all veterans who were past their prime. No one, regardless of how esteemed or how reliable they were in the past, would be guaranteed of a place on the team in 1972. That was Coach Devine's mind set, and every veteran player knew it, especially when witnessing their friends on the team from previous years get their pink slips. It was a systematic purging, and seemingly unfair—at least to the older athletes—in its execution. A number of quality and still-productive veteran players at key positions were sent away and replaced with inexperienced rookies. But to his credit and taking all of his moves into consideration, Devine did manage to make a couple of key trades for veterans from other teams in the off-season, and some of those new players would eventually pan out successfully for the Packers.

The trades began in earnest in the spring. Devine swapped longtime defensive tackle Lionel Aldridge for San Diego safety Jim Hill on April 18. In order to get Hill, a three-year veteran out of Texas A & M-Kingsville, the Packers would have to sweeten the deal somewhat. Devine would also have to send the Chargers a third-round draft pick in 1974, but that was not considered too big of a price to pay to secure the services of a pretty good performer who would greatly help to solidify the Green Bay defensive pass coverages. Hill played in every game during his first three years in the league with the Chargers, and intercepted a total of nine passes during that time frame. He could play both cornerback and safety positions, and was quite serviceable anywhere in the defensive secondary. Devine would list Hill as his starting free safety, and it turned out to be a wise choice. According to the 1972 Packers Highlight Film, the defensive secondary "jelled almost immediately."[14] Hill would be a calming and reliable factor for the team as the season wore on. Longtime pro football author and historian T.J. Troup took a retrospective—but studious—look at Hill's NFL career, and lauded the safety for having undeniably "his greatest season in 1972."[15] Hill's veteran leadership would help the younger members of the secondary to learn the many strategical nuances of the pro game, particularly zone coverages, which are typically much more complicated to understand and execute in the professional ranks, as opposed to the college ranks.

Safety Jim Hill came to the team from the San Diego Chargers, and he immediately helped the Packers defensive backfield became one of the strongest units in the league. Hill intercepted four passes in 1972 (courtesy the Green Bay Packers).

But just as it appeared as if Green Bay's final roster was set, Devine made several more trades for veteran players just prior to the start of the regular season.

One such veteran was offensive tackle Malcolm Snider, who had suited up for the Atlanta Falcons for the past three years, and who was added to the Packers' lineup on September 6. To obtain Snider, Devine offered the Falcons the services of Dave Hampton, a quality Packer running back for the past four years. Snider was a major piece to a revamped offensive line in 1972, and he did much to solidify that unit. The dependable play from Snider was vital, mainly because someone had to cover up for one of the most puzzling and most criticized decisions in NFL history. Just prior to the first game of the regular season at Cleveland, Devine decided to transfer All-Pro offensive guard Gale Gillingham to the defensive line. The defensive line! More than just a few of Gillingham's teammates looked quizzically with their mouths wide open at each other when they heard of this news. John Brockington, the workhorse of the Green Bay rushing attack, and the man who most often benefited from Gillingham's bruising blocks, was aghast when he heard the news. "Are you kidding me?!? What the hell?!?" exclaimed Brockington.[16]

The ill-timed switch also baffled most fans and the local sportswriters.

Gillingham was regarded by many scouts and pro personnel people as one of the best offensive guards in the league. Packer historian Cliff Christl regarded Gillingham as "possibly ... even better than Jerry Kramer."[17] Christl was not alone in his assessment. John Brockington followed Gillingham's blocks for several years. He proclaimed that "Gillingham was the best ... and I mean no disrespect to the other members of our offensive line, but they will tell you this: That Gilly was a cut above ... he just was. He was strong. He was mean. He was athletic. And nobody wanted to mess with Gale Gillingham. In practice, if you made Gale mad, you had a long two hours, man. He would pound you into salt. He was that mean. [Former Packers offensive guard] Fuzzy Thurston once said, 'Gale's chest was as big as one of those Black Angus cattle' that he [Fuzzy] was raising [on his ranch]. Gale was young and he was talented. I've never seen anything like it. I used to watch game film and watch him [Gillingham] as much as I watched myself [on the film] ... because he would destroy people."[18]

Gale Gillingham was one of professional football's greatest offensive guards throughout his career in the 1960s and 1970s. His career, however, was inexplicably changed in a dramatic way by head coach Dan Devine just prior to the beginning of the 1972 season, when Devine switched Gillingham to a defensive tackle position. A knee injury shortly thereafter ended Gillingham's 1972 season, abbreviated the rest of his playing days, and probably ended any chance of Gillingham becoming enshrined in the Pro Football Hall of Fame (courtesy the Green Bay Packers).

Coach Devine's decision to move his star offensive guard to the defensive line practically and indirectly destroyed the remainder of Gillingham's pro career. In the decades since the 1972 season, several pro football experts and historians have mentioned the same belief to this author. Indeed, the ridiculousness of this roster switch is still one that so many years later is just too hard to believe. Keep in mind that Gillingham never played on the defensive side of the line of scrimmage all throughout college or in his previous seven years in the pros. "It was not a good move," Gillingham later admitted. "What was really ridiculous about it is was that we played six exhibition games back then, but Devine waited until the regular season to put me on defense. I started the [first] game with basically no practice time. I wanted to leave [Green Bay] but I was a team captain."[19]

To his credit, Gillingham stayed and

did his best to learn his new position, but his good luck, and seemingly the Packers' good luck, would run out on September 24. The Packers were playing the Oakland Raiders at Lambeau Field in their second game of the year, when Gillingham injured his right knee. The team lost Gillingham for the season, and also lost to the Raiders, 20–14. "I tore up my knee," Gillingham recalled. "Devine comes in [the locker room after the game] and said that he was planning to switch me back to offense. He knew it [his decision to move Gillingham to the defensive line] was a mistake, but it was too late."[20]

Several key decisions that did not work out well would in retrospect become a trademark of Devine's, and back in 1972, virtually no one on the team knew who would become the next victim of one of the head coach's roster moves. Devine threw caution to the wind and quickly resumed making trades. He decided to send veteran reserve quarterback Zeke Bratkowski to the Chicago Bears in September for a sixth-round pick in the 1974 NFL Draft. Bratkowski's big game experience would have been extremely helpful to the team's young quarterbacks (Scott Hunter and Jerry Tagge), but Devine sent him packing. Devine then traded away a second round draft choice in 1973 to the Dallas Cowboys for two players from their roster, punter Ron Widby and kick returner/defensive back Ike Thomas. Both Widby and Thomas were deemed expendable by the defending World Champion Cowboys. This fortunately turned out to be one of Devine's better acquisitions, as Widby would go on to record a 41.8-yard punting average, one of the best marks in the NFC. Thomas contributed quality speed to several facets of the special teams. He recorded a 27.2-yard average on kickoff returns in 1972, good enough for fifth-best in the conference.

Devine would be open to adjusting his roster and his depth charts throughout the season, an unusual irony considering his stubbornness on many other personnel and strategical instances with the team. A person giving an objective look at Devine's decisions during his tenure as Green Bay's head coach would have to admit that there were more bad decisions than good ones, but the good ones did much to help the team succeed, particularly in 1972. Enjoying success was not the focus of the team after the 1971 season ended, however, and there were no guarantees that Devine's off-season moves would be helpful or detrimental to the team as a whole. For better or worse, the 1972 version of the Green Bay Packers were now ready to take the field, with nothing but uncertainty to fall back on.

The preseason began in earnest with a 24–14 win against the Cincinnati Bengals at Lambeau Field. It was a fairly even game, but the Packer rushing attack was already showing signs of strength, even at this earliest of stages. Halfback John Brockington scored on a 2-yard run, and quarterback Scott Hunter also dove in from the Bengals' 1-yard line. Green Bay would accumulate 132 total rushing yards in the victory. What was somewhat puzzling about this game was the fact that Devine kept his starters playing throughout much of the second half. "He [Devine] had said before that he might play all 69 that he had in uniform," reported Glenn Miller of the *Madison* (Wisconsin) *State Journal*. "Devine did not do that. He kept the regulars in for most of the game, used a few of the acknowledged second-stringers—and won the game. Can you blame him? Maybe he already knows which ones he likes."[21]

It was about as optimistic of a beginning that the Packers and their fans could expect, as there were miraculously no injuries sustained to any of the starting players in the contest with the Bengals. Moreover, it is always good to get that first win, even if it is an exhibition win. Devine wanted the team to get an initial taste of victory, in the hopes that they would see that his way of coaching could be and would be successful.

The next preseason game produced a similar result. Devine and his charges traveled back to the place where they endured their final loss of the 1971 season, the Orange Bowl in Miami. Devine and the veteran players were still smarting from the drubbing that they received at the hands of the Dolphins the previous December, and even though this next game was an exhibition contest with no value in the standings, the Packer team as a whole really wanted some payback. Once again, Devine saw to it that his starters took snaps in most of the game, but in this contest, he allowed reserve quarterback Jerry Tagge much more playing time with the first unit. The Packers registered a 14–13 triumph over the Dolphins, thanks mostly due to a fumbled snap by Miami holder Karl Noonan on an extra point attempt. Keep in mind that Miami head coach Don Shula decided to play most of his substitute players in the second half, something that was normal for most pro coaches during the first few exhibition games. More good news for the Packers in this game at Miami came from the impressive production of John Brockington, who carried the ball for a respectable 77 yards in the first half against Miami's No-Name Defense.

The team's victory surge was derailed the following week, however, in a rather upsetting 20–3 loss inside the Houston Astrodome against the lowly Oilers. It did not matter who Devine put on the field in this game, as the Packers could scarcely register any momentum against a team that had won only four games themselves in 1971. The Oilers were doomed to win only once in the 1972 regular season, but on this evening, they played like a well-oiled machine (no pun intended), capitalizing on Packer miscues all game long. A successful Houston onside kick led to a 10–0 Oiler lead at halftime. Youthful Houston quarterback Dan Pastorini threw for two scores in the one-sided affair. Devine allowed more of his rookies to play in this game, and it showed. Green Bay's time of possession on offense was woefully under their norm. "Sure we had a lot of new people [in the lineup]," said a disgusted Devine in his analysis of the game, "but two or three won't be on it next week."[22]

Devine was true to his word, as several rookies were cut from the team following the Houston debacle.

The Packers' rivalry with the Chicago Bears is legendary, but besides playing each other twice during the regular season, the two adversaries also played each other in the 1972 preseason. There was no love lost between these two teams, even in the exhibition season, and the remaining rookies on both squads would receive their indoctrination right away in the midst of a tight struggle with their divisional rivals on August 27. The game was held in Milwaukee County Stadium, a venue where the Packers played two to three times each year during the regular season. Indeed, the fan base and support for the team spread all throughout Wisconsin, from large cities like Milwaukee and Madison, to smaller towns like Oshkosh, Sheboygan, Appleton, and Fond du Lac. Milwaukee thus served as a natural site for the Packers to visit in attempting to build up the fan patronage in Wisconsin.

This hard-hitting defensive contest with the Bears was tied at 7–7 with only 13 seconds remaining in the fourth quarter. In short, it was a typical Bear-Packer game, filled with bruising hits and more bruising hits. It was at this point that Devine's early selection of placekicker Chester Marcol in the recent NFL draft exacted its first profitable dividend. Marcol's 40-yard field goal traveled straight through the uprights of the goal post, setting off a jubilant celebration of Packer players on the field, and Packer fans in the stands. Clearly, this Packer team was hungry for a big comeback win over the hated Bears, even in the preseason. You would have thought the Green Bay Packers had just won the Super Bowl championship, with all of the excitement that Marcol's game-winning kick set off. At least the Packers now had what they had really needed for the past several years—a kicker with glowing potential, and accuracy from almost any distance. Green Bay's new kicker also possessed a great deal of trust in his own abilities.

"If I didn't have the most powerful leg in the league, I was in the top two or three," Marcol said years later. "I had a tremendous gift, and I was bursting with confidence. There wasn't a kick I didn't think I could make. Even if I missed, I didn't beat myself over the head because I knew there would be other opportunities."[23]

Green Bay was taking advantage of their opportunities during the hot Wisconsin summer of 1972. With a 3–1 record in the preseason, they were somehow standing better than most people thought they would at this early stage of the year. The win over Chicago was a great victory for the team, as is any conquest of the Bears. And even though it came in the exhibition season, it was still a cause for optimism, and that was something that the Packers definitely had lacked during much of the past four years.

But just as things were going on the upswing, a brutal 31–10 loss to the St. Louis Cardinals at Lambeau Field immediately followed the win over

Chicago. Virtually nothing went right against St. Louis, and after viewing the coaching films from the game, Devine was appalled by how poorly his Packers played. "[The game was] as bad as it initially appeared, because I hate to see so many little mistakes cost you so dearly," said Devine.[24] The Green Bay special teams committed four turnovers (including two fumbled punts), which directly led to 24 St. Louis points. "Veterans as well as rookies were guilty of breakdowns," Devine added. "It was a case of one team playing mistake-less football and the other team making a lot of mistakes. Some [of our] people were outmatched, but we think the kind of mistakes we made can be eliminated by hard work. We want to win this year, and the experience isn't there in a lot of places. So we just have to play even better."[25]

This was the first concrete message (about winning this year) coming from Devine that he thought, even before the regular season started, that a winning team in Green Bay was a distinct possibility. Was Devine an optimist? That was difficult to say. But winning brings about optimism among all coaches and players, and everyone involved with the team was certainly tired of enduring the pessimism of the previous four years.

The preseason in 1972 lasted a month and a half, and it was nearing its end for the Packers. Virtually every player on the squad at this point felt the extreme pressure to play better. Nobody on the team or the coaching staff wanted to see a repeat of the Cardinals game in the future. Devine had by this time whittled down the roster to the prescribed number of players, with only one final cut remaining. The 3–2 Packers would have one more preseason game remaining, this one coming in Milwaukee against the defending AFC West Champion, the Kansas City Chiefs. It would be one more chance for Devine's players to gather some semblance of momentum before heading into their first regular season game. A victory over the Chiefs would not be a cure-all for all of the perceived problems that the youthful Green Bay team was experiencing, but it would be another step in the right direction.

If there was an exhibition game that the Packers were ever predicted to lose, it would be this one against the Chiefs. Kansas City had won four of their previous five preseason games heading into Milwaukee County Stadium to take on Green Bay on September 9. But in what could only be described as a big upset, the Packer defense shut down Kansas City's offense in a 20–0 Green Bay win. It was the first time since 1962 that Kansas City had suffered a shutout defeat. Green Bay quarterback Scott Hunter threw for 127 yards in the game, which was his best yardage output of the preseason. Green Bay halfback John Brockington contributed a 22-yard touchdown run in the second half. The Packers defense dominated the line of scrimmage all game long, and it did so with the Chiefs' veteran starting quarterback Len Dawson playing well into the third quarter. It was a victory that the young Packers

Quarterback Scott Hunter receives instructions from quarterbacks coach Bart Starr during pregame warmups of an exhibition game versus the St. Louis Cardinals. Reserve Packers wide receiver Paul Gibson (No. 41) is also pictured at right (AP photo/Vernon Biever).

really needed heading into the regular season. It gave them a dash of confidence and assurance that they were on the right track.

Devine completed his roster decisions following the win over Kansas City. He knew that due to John Brockington's spectacular 1971 season, the Packers would be featuring the running game over the passing game. To change his rushing attack in a (hopefully) positive way, however, Devine decided way back on February 21 to trade running back Donny Anderson to the St. Louis Cardinals for MacArthur Lane. Anderson was a solid runner and many fans felt that he would be missed in the lineup. But Lane was an excellent pass receiver coming out of the backfield. He was also a very strong blocker and a power runner in his own right, much like Brockington. Moreover, Lane was a dependable runner, meaning that he stayed healthy for the most part and that he rarely fumbled the ball. The acquisition of Lane would go on to become one of the most important and successful trades that Devine would make in 1972.

As it turned out, the Anderson-Lane trade would be beneficial for both of those players, each of whom had dealt with a measure of bad blood towards their original teams. Anderson's problems came as soon as Devine became Green Bay's new head coach in 1971. "I would probably not have been back at Green Bay," Anderson said, "because there was a lot of animosity between Coach Devine and myself. That's why I'm very happy with the trade."[26] Lane—like Anderson—was despondent regarding his particular situation. Lane's problems were due to his contract issues with the Cardinals. In the early 1970s, it proved to be much more difficult to renegotiate a better contract, as the players' union was still in its formative stages, and it was certainly not the influential organization that it is today. "I had a little misunderstanding with the [St. Louis] management because I was playing without a contract," acknowledged Lane. "My frustrations came out."[27]

Devine also had frustrations regarding his team's offense. He hoped that the passing game would somehow offer at least a slight change of pace from the running game to keep opposing defenses honest. That did not happen throughout 1972, however. Green Bay had two young and fairly inexperienced quarterbacks (Scott Hunter and Jerry Tagge), and a very unimposing staff of receivers. The Packer pass catchers included veteran Carroll Dale (who was undoubtedly the most reliable of the group), rookie Leland Glass, second-year man Dave Davis, and journeyman Jon Staggers, who was acquired off of waivers from the Pittsburgh Steelers. None of these players struck much fear in any defense, but Hunter and Tagge would also have a strong tight end, the 6-foot-4, 235-pound Rich McGeorge from Elon, to throw to at the beginning of the 1972 regular season. Despite being a strong run blocker, McGeorge also had an excellent pair of hands as a pass catcher.

The Green Bay defense, however, was in a much better overall shape than the Green Bay offense. The defensive line had two quality defensive ends in Alden Roche and Clarence Williams, and two strong and durable defensive tackles in Mike McCoy and Bob Brown. Any four of those men—assuming that they could stay healthy—possessed the potential to make the Pro Bowl or possibly even achieve All-Pro honors. The linebackers were considered by most pro scouts as the weakest segment of the Packer defense, but that term is a misnomer of sorts, because they were really not *weak*, and they would get better as 1972 continued. Outside backers Fred Carr and Dave Robinson anchored the unit. They were fast, agile, and intimidating. The middle linebacker position was filled by Jim Carter, who started most games over the venerable and experienced Ray Nitschke. The backup linebackers included rookies Larry Hefner and Dave Pureifory.

Rounding out the team's defense in 1972 was the secondary, a unit which would become the surprise of the year in Green Bay. The quartet of starters Willie Buchanon, Ken Ellis, Jim Hill, and Al Matthews, with Charlie Hall, Butch Davis, Bob Kroll, and Al Randolph in reserve, would quickly become one of the best defensive secondaries in the entire league by the end of the regular season. Indeed, most of their opponents would throw the ball against them in decreasing numbers as the season wore on, and usually at their own peril.

Devine and his staff had worked hard to put together a strong roster for his 1972 Packers. Not all of the roster decisions were roundly applauded by the fans before the first regular season game, but most fans were willing to give Coach Dan Devine the benefit of the doubt. Like it or not, the new season was upon them. There was not much expectation for a winning season, but only time would truly tell if this year would be an improvement over the forlorn results of 1971 or if it would produce just more of the same.

2
Potential Amidst Early Injuries

The 1972 Packers preseason failed to offer any substantial context clues as to how well the team would perform in the regular season. Sure, there was more optimism generated amongst the team thanks to four wins and only two defeats in the summer exhibition season, but as any pro football fan can tell you, the preseason is much different than the regular season. Many teams have miserable exhibition outings, only to excel when the games count in the fall, and vice-versa. What did occur in the 1972 Packers preseason was a mixture of good decisions by head coach Dan Devine, and a seemingly equal mixture of bad (or ridiculous, if you will) decisions by Devine.

The Green Bay players tried their best not to think too much about Devine's decisions, however. They were too concerned with their own performances, in the meeting rooms watching and digesting films, and when they were out on the practice field and on game day versus their opponents. Like many pro squads, the rookies on the Packers roster were making the multitude of the mistakes, mainly because it was their first taste of professional football. It was only natural for them to mess up the most, much more so than the more seasoned members of the squad. The preseason, however, is the time for all players, regardless of their amount of experience, to make some mistakes. But even though the preseason games do not count in the standings, you still had to play well. If you were a rookie, you did not want to make any miscues during the preseason (or anytime for that matter), as it could guarantee you a ticket home. Coach Devine would—like all NFL head coaches—be handing out some of those tickets, in order to reach the 40-man active roster limit (as it was in 1972).

Devine's 1972 regular season roster was filled with a majority of younger players, and with a small mixture of older and more experienced leftovers from the Lombardi era. Devine knew that he could not cut every player who suited up for Vince Lombardi ... at least not right away. But that was his hope and plan, and it was an unceasing motivator for him. Devine wanted to cultivate his own team with his own players.

"He [Devine] was paranoid about Vince Lombardi's people," remembered All-Pro outside linebacker Dave Robinson. "He told us one time at a meeting that the worst thing about coaching the Packers was the fact that each day you would come to work, you've got to drive down the street that's named for another coach [Lombardi Avenue]."[1]

The Packers would begin the 1972 regular season on a street away from home, however, at Cleveland's Municipal Stadium, in front of a capacity crowd of 75,771. The weather was as close to perfect as it could be for northern Ohio—a cloudy sky with 81 degree temperatures and 16 mile-per-hour winds, which amounted to merely a favorable breeze next to Lake Erie. Green Bay's opponent would be the tried and tested Browns, a mostly veteran team which showed up as a commonly-seen entry in the NFL playoffs. The Browns finished the 1971 season with a 10–4 record, good enough for first place in the AFC Central Division. Cleveland was used to winning, and there was no reason to expect that they would not continue that trend in 1972. They had plenty of experienced players on their roster, but somewhat incredibly, that experience did not make an appearance on this day against Green Bay. The Browns were (like the Packers) having a problem at the all-important quarterback position, unsure of who would be their starter. They eventually wanted their prized youngster, Mike Phipps out of Purdue, to take over the reigns as their signal caller. But Cleveland head coach Nick Skorich did not yet believe that Phipps was ready to be named as his starter, so he stuck with his oft-injured veteran, Bill Nelsen, as his first string quarterback. As it turned out, both quarterbacks would see action on this day against the Green Bay defense, and luckily for the Packers, both would have below-average outings.

There is something special about opening day in pro football, even if your team is the visiting club. Hopefulness envelops the attitudes of most teams on opening day, as the desire to win for every player reaches a fever pitch just before the first kickoff of the new season. For Dan Devine and his team, a sense of nervous anticipation mixed in with the basic belief that in 1972, overall improvements in many phases of the game were in the offering. The team had suffered through a difficult opening day in 1971 (a 42–40 loss to the New York Giants), and Green Bay definitely wanted to avoid a repeat of that performance against the Browns. As with most opening games, no one was absolutely sure which positive or negative facets of the team would have an impact on strategy and scoring. Nor could they know which of their players would perform up to (or exceed) their capabilities. But they could not worry about that now. Ready or not, the 1972 regular season—one of the most unique in Green Bay history—was set to begin.

Outside linebacker Fred Carr (No. 53 at left) withstands a straight arm from Cleveland Browns running back Leroy Kelly in the Packers' 26–10 victory in the first game of the regular season on September 17 (AP Photo/Vernon Biever).

The Packers dealt with a pretty even first half, as they showed potential and somehow stayed even with the Cleveland club. Three plays elapsed in the first quarter when Devine's draft decisions paid an early dividend. Rookie cornerback Willie Buchanon stepped in front of Cleveland wide receiver Frank Pitts and intercepted a Bill Nelsen pass at the Browns' 33-yard line. Buchanon then eluded several attempted tackles and ran out of bounds with his prize 11 yards further downfield. The young defensive back proved to be a quick study when it came to utilizing the proper technique.

"I think I had a pretty good [training] camp," surmised Buchanon. "I was pretty well set with the defensive keys because we used almost the same thing in college, so it wasn't too big an adjustment. I was well coached in college. We ran pretty much a pro type offense and defense. All I had to do after I came here [to Green Bay] was learn different techniques and terminology. I felt fairly secure [out there today versus Cleveland and during the preseason games]. For example, I played with my outside leg up [forward] in college. Here [in the pros] I play with my outside leg back. It takes some getting used to."[2]

2. Potential Amidst Early Injuries

Second-year Green Bay quarterback Scott Hunter was getting used to being the team's starter at his position. He was once again named by Devine as the starter for this game, mostly due to his extra year of pro experience over rookie Jerry Tagge. It did not take long at all for Hunter to figure out the Cleveland defensive schemes. He capitalized on the gift of Buchanon's interception by leading the Packers to their first touchdown a few snaps later from the Cleveland 23-yard line. Like most teams, the Packers had a few plays that always seemed to work well, regardless of what a defense would do to recognize it and stop it. One of those "pet" plays for Green Bay's offense involved their tight end Rich McGeorge, who would run a down-and-out pattern, running across the field from the strong side of the formation (the side where the tight end takes his stance) to the weak side. While McGeorge ran his pattern, Hunter would first fake a handoff to fullback MacArthur Lane, who was running a sweep to the right.

Tight end Rich McGeorge was greatly missed by the Packers offense, thanks to a season-ending injury that he suffered in the second week of the 1972 regular season. Had McGeorge stayed healthy throughout 1972, the Green Bay team passing statistics would undeniably have been more prosperous (courtesy the Green Bay Packers).

The flow of the backfield and the blockers would then move to the opposite direction from the one that McGeorge was headed to. Hunter would then stop on a dime and throw the ball against the motion of the play, where a wide open McGeorge—who jogged behind the Cleveland linebackers completely unnoticed—would wait all alone for the pass. The play worked to perfection against the Browns, as McGeorge caught the ball with no defender near him at the Cleveland 17-yard line, then easily pranced untouched into the end zone for a 6–0 Green Bay lead. Chester Marcol booted the extra point.

"Rich McGeorge was one hell of a football player," proclaimed star Green Bay halfback John Brockington. "We called him 'Magic Mick,' because he caught the ball so well. He was a tremendous tight end."[3] Packers signal caller Scott Hunter certainly liked to use McGeorge's talents. According to Hunter, McGeorge was a very important player in the Green Bay lineup.

"In those days, you used the tight end a lot," admitted Hunter, who finished the Cleveland game by completing seven passes in 17 attempts for 150 yards. "You used them in critical situations, on second and third downs. Also, you used them to beat up the other guys [your opponents]. You get that ball to Rich [McGeorge], who weighed 235 pounds, and those 195-pound safeties didn't like to take on guys like that downfield in the open. I would always make a point of getting the ball to him. When I was a rookie, as much as I could, early in the game, I would let him [McGeorge] beat up those other guys.

"Rich was a basketball player at Elon. He knew how to get open. He was one of those guys who was a perfect tight end. If he was covered on his lefthand side by the strong safety or a linebacker, I would just throw it to his righthand side. And like a center in basketball, he could bump the guy and then catch the ball on his righthand side. He had that kind of bigness."[4]

Cleveland was accustomed to playing "big" themselves, however, and they displayed their competitiveness by quickly coming back following McGeorge's touchdown. Placekicker Don Cockcroft kicked a 21-yard field goal to open the scoring for the Browns. Then Cleveland's special teams struck for a score in the second quarter when defensive tackle Jerry Sherk blocked a Marcol field goal attempt. Second-year Browns cornerback Clarence Scott picked up the bouncing ball and sprinted 55 yards down the sideline for a go-ahead touchdown. "I kicked it too slow and too low," Marcol commented.[5] "It wasn't the way I'd envisioned starting my professional career. But I was done missing."[6]

Marcol's youthful bravado in the wake of his first blocked kick seemed to inspire his teammates. It was now time for Green Bay to show how well they could retake the lead, which was the mark of any good team ... of any contending team. Marcol began that process by kicking his first official career field goal from 41 yards out. He also managed to launch each one of his kickoffs that day through the Cleveland end zone for touchbacks. Then Hunter and McGeorge once again found success, this time just before halftime. On a play that was

The Green Bay kicking game was a veritable joke from 1968 to 1971. Then in 1972, rookie placekicker Chester Marcol was selected by the Packers in the college player draft. Marcol came into the league with high hopes, and he responded in a big way by leading the entire NFL in scoring in 1972 (courtesy the Green Bay Packers).

similar to their first quarter touchdown, Hunter once again faked a handoff to Lane, turned around to look downfield, and once again found McGeorge standing all by himself. McGeorge cradled Hunter's perfect pass in the end zone, and the Packers had reclaimed the lead, 17–10.

Only the Packers would score in the second half, and all of the scores would come from Marcol's foot. The "Hillsdale [Michigan] Hammer," as he was nicknamed, Marcol kicked three more field goals, giving him a total of four in the game, and the Packers prevailed, 26–10. It was a very important opening game for Green Bay, as it proved that they could play well and defeat a perennial playoff team. McGeorge and Marcol were the stars of the victory, and both reveled in their successes. McGeorge even helped a teammate become somewhat prophetic with his results.

"Al Matthews [Green Bay safety] predicted this, you know," said McGeorge of his success. "At the pre-game meal this morning, he told me he dreamed last night that I would catch a lot of passes today."[7] McGeorge would end up only catching two passes, but they both had the ultimate effect in the Cleveland end zone. "We had intended to stress McGeorge today," admitted Green Bay head coach Dan Devine after the win, "in our general, overall game concept, partly because we hadn't thrown to him much in the exhibition season."[8]

Marcol connected on four of his six field goal attempts, as he quickly proved the worth of Devine's selection of the rookie placekicker in the draft. Even after getting his first attempt blocked and returned for a Cleveland score, Marcol came right back. "You can't think about the one that was blocked," Marcol said. "If I had been thinking about that one, I probably would have missed the next four too. All of Ron Widby's holds were good too. He has real good hands and that makes a lot of difference. Ron's an old basketball player."[9] Marcol's efforts tied him with former Packer greats Paul Hornung and Jerry Kramer for a team record with the most field goals made in a single game. The Packers win in the opener was a team goal that was happily realized.

"You always like to get off to a good start," Devine said, "and with the schedule we have this year, I think it is important that we get off to a good start."[10]

The team statistics from the Cleveland game were indicative that Green Bay did indeed start the season on a positive note, and even though it was still very early in the year, they were quickly becoming a better team than what was seen at this stage in 1971. The Packers defense gave up only 62 rushing yards against the Browns for a 2.7-yard average-per-rush. Premier Cleveland tailback Leroy Kelly could manage only 26 ground yards against the Packers on 13 carries. Green Bay's pass defense also did outstanding work, intercepting three Cleveland passes, and limiting Browns quarterbacks Bill Nelsen and Mike Phipps to a combined 14 completions in 33 attempts.

Green Bay's obvious strength was its ground game, and the results in this category against Cleveland were suggestive of the good beginning to the 1972 regular season that Devine hoped for. John Brockington rushed for 83 yards, and fullback MacArthur Lane added 45 more. Those results would fortunately be repeated many times throughout the year. This first game gave the team a very important boost of energy, enthusiasm, and optimism at this earliest platform of the season. All NFL teams like to win their opening game, and Green Bay was no different. But this first win against the Browns proved that the Packers had taken a good first step, and that at least some of Coach Devine's decisions (i.e., drafting Chester Marcol and Willie Buchanon) had achieved an initial sign of positive results.

The win over Cleveland was at least partially due to the play calling knowledge of former Packer quarterback and icon Bart Starr, who was signaling plays into the offensive huddle from the bench. With Starr's acumen on their side, the final score could have and indeed should have ended with an even greater margin of victory for Green Bay. A brief and simple misstep cost the Packers another touchdown. Scott Hunter possesses a sharp memory of many of the events from his pro football career, and he retells the colorful story here:

"The epitome of the first game is what Bart Starr meant to me and the offense, calling the plays and coaching me," said Hunter. "The Browns punted in the first half ... I think it was the second quarter. The ball rolled dead [inside our 1-yard line]. We were thinking of running a wedge play with [John] Brockington just to get a yard or two. Then there's a TV timeout. And on comes Leland Glass our wide receiver [into the huddle]. And he says that Bart says to run a play-action pass. I'm literally at the back of the end zone and I'm waiting back there during the TV timeout. The Browns had a little fence there and all these Browns fans were yelling at me ... they saw my name on the back of my jersey. 'Hey Hunter you bleep bleep.' I put my hands up to try to quiet them down [chuckle]. And then in my best southern accent I said, 'Y'all are really gonna like this next play!'

"I came out and faked the ball to John and then looked up. The split end [Glass] would run a curl [pattern] and suck up the cornerback [Cleveland's Ben Davis] and the free safety [the Browns' Thom Darden]. MacArthur Lane [Green Bay's fullback] would run out into the flat with the linebacker [Cleveland's Billy Andrews] chasing him. Then he [Lane] would turn upfield on a 36 × Circle Takeoff. Mac turned up and he was wide flat open. I hit him and he's going down the sidelines for a 99-yard, 2-feet, and 11-inch touchdown. It was going to go down into the record books, but he shifted the ball from his right to his left hand and barely stepped out of bounds right on the 50-yard line right in front of the Browns bench. He goes down there [to the end zone] and scores and the referees call it a touchdown, but the Browns are all yelling and pointing [to the ground]. One official saw the white [sideline] dust come up, so they brought it back to the 50. But what a great call by Bart!"[11]

Salient pro football author T.J. Troup referred back to that play, and he brings to mind the outstanding play selection coming from the Packers sideline in the decisions made by their former and eventual Hall of Fame quarterback.

"Starr did enough in his play calling early in that year to put the fear factor into the minds of the opposing defenses," Troup explained. "Once that play succeeded for about 50 yards, all opposing defensive coordinators took notice. They all realized that MacArthur Lane could peel out of the backfield, sprint down the sideline faster than any outside linebacker, make the catch, and run for a lot of yards. The defenses from the other teams now had to worry that this could happen to them. It was all part of the genius that is Bart Starr."[12]

Starr's play calling also emphasized the team's powerful rushing attack, and it provided enough punch to keep Green Bay's offensive drives alive in Cleveland. The Packers accounted for seven rushing first downs against the Browns. But would the Green Bay ground game be strong enough to do the same against their next opponent? The Packers would be playing their home opener against the Oakland Raiders, a brawny and successful team that they had faced only once before. In Super Bowl II, the Packers defeated the Raiders 33–14, but both squads had changed the personnel on their rosters quite a bit since that famous meeting in January of 1968. The Raiders had grown wiser in experience since their loss to Coach Lombardi in Super Bowl II, while the Packers had diminished in overall experience with the inclusion of more younger players. Both Oakland and Green Bay had new head coaches as well. John Madden was at the helm for the Raiders, and the Lombardi regime had been passed on to Phil Bengston, and then to Dan Devine. No one was really quite sure how this second matchup between these two interconference foes would turn out. The second game of the 1972 season would list Green Bay as decided underdogs to Oakland, but the contest would eventually become a very close and hard-fought affair.

The first quarter featured quick scoring by both teams. Oakland's first drive lasted 13 plays and ended with a 43-yard field goal by the NFL's oldest player, George Blanda, who was participating in his 23rd pro season. Green Bay responded quickly, thanks to their rushing attack. John Brockington culminated a six-play drive with a 1-yard burst for a touchdown. A key play in that scoring drive was a 33-yard reception by Brockington, who veered out of the backfield to catch Scott Hunter's perfect pass.

The waning moments of the first quarter would produce the game's most controversial play, the result of which would eventually account for the winning points in this contest. The Packers were driving deep into Raider territory for another score when from the 3-yard line, Hunter pitched the ball to fullback MacArthur Lane, who was running a sweep to his right. Lane never did get a full grasp of the ball, and it dribbled out of his hands and into the Oakland end zone. Raiders safety Jack Tatum picked the ball up and sprinted 104 yards down the sideline for a touchdown, which broke a 49-year-old record by George Halas of the Chicago Bears, who returned a fumble 98 yards for a touchdown against the Oorang Indians on November 4, 1923. Against the Raiders, several Packer players stopped moving after Lane dropped the ball, as they believed that the play was nothing more than a muffed lateral, a play where the ball cannot be advanced by either team. But the referees did not blow a single whistle, and Tatum had no contention to the Green Bay end zone.

"I just took off," Tatum admitted after recovering the ball. "I thought they [the Packer players] might have been closer than they were behind me."[13]

The fans in the Lambeau Stadium stands were in a state of perplexed confusion. Some got a better look at the play than others, but most were owning a profound moment of disarray. What just happened? Was this play legal? Was it a forward pass and if so, why was a referee's whistle signaling an incomplete pass absent following the action? Practically all of the Green Bay fans shared an incredulous look amongst themselves, as their bewilderment concerning what they had just witnessed was incredibly also shared with the Packers' brain trust.

"I'm just trying to understand this rule," said Devine after the game.[14] The Packers head coach had addressed the media with an official NFL rule book in his hands, and he proceeded to read the section that pertained to fumbled laterals. "We feel maybe it could have been a dead ball in the end zone," opined a dejected Devine.[15] A few days after the game, NFL Supervisor of Officials Art McNally confirmed Devine's belief. The play should have been ruled a muff, not a fumble, and therefore could not have been advanced by Tatum. Because Tatum recovered the ball in the end zone, the Raiders should have been awarded a touchback at their own 20-yard line, and seven points should have been erased from Oakland's point total.

Unbelievably, even some of the Raiders defenders agreed with Devine. Oakland defensive back George Atkinson stated that Lane "never had control of the ball. He was bobbling it and I strip-tackled him. I pinned his arms up high and the ball went out. Then I laid on him so he couldn't get up, and when Jack went past me I knew they'd never catch him."[16]

Then following a brief moment of introspection, another Green Bay coach offered his opinion. "You can't advance a muff," stated Packers defensive coordinator Dave "Hog" Hanner, "but they [the officials] felt he [Lane] had the ball and had taken several steps with it."[17] Lane himself was in obvious disagreement with the call made by the referees. "I looked at the ball and all of a sudden, it wasn't there," said Lane after the game. "The next thing I knew I was being hit. I never had full control of it [the ball]."[18] After watching the play on film, it appeared that Lane in all likelihood just took his eyes off of the ball, and instead for just a brief instant looked forward to the goal line and to an approaching Oakland defender, safety George Atkinson.

Scott Hunter's opinion was representative of most of his teammates. "Nobody [on the team] knew that [rule]," Hunter said. "I didn't know that, [and] nobody on our sidelines knew [that rule]. I don't think anybody on the Raiders sideline knew [that rule]. It was one of those things in the rule book that nobody ever pays any attention to until it happens. And I thought that I had made a bad pitch [to Lane]. Devine for some reason was running up the field and he wanted to run an option near the goal line. But it really wasn't an option. I was just to go out there and freeze the strong [side] linebacker [Oakland's Phil Villapiano] and pitch [the ball] to Mac [Lane]. Devine just wanted his play to work, and that was his play. So I go out there and pitch, and I thought that I made a bad pitch, but it was right there in the basket, and he [Lane] just muffed it."[19]

The blown call did not take the starch out of the Packers offense, however. Brockington managed to burrow into the end zone once more for a 1-yard score in the second quarter, giving Green Bay a 14–10 lead going into halftime. But the Oakland defense made some necessary adjustments and shut out the Packer offense during the entire second half. Another field goal by Blanda and a 1-yard touchdown run by Oakland's Charlie Smith gave the Packers their first loss of the season by a score of 20–14. Smith's score was set up by a questionable pass interference call against Packer cornerback Willie Buchanon, which placed the ball at the Green Bay 1-yard line.

In describing the pass interference play, Buchanon felt that he was wronged by the officials. "If anything, he [Biletnikoff] pushed me. I had both hands up, going for the ball, so how can I push him?[20] In my opinion, it wasn't interference. I knew he was outside of me on the play and I knew there was no way he could get inside of me. And I was looking right at him until I saw him look back for the ball. When I saw the ball was coming inside, I just played the ball.

"I went up with both hands. With his being that close, there may have been contact. But how can I push him when I've got position on the ball? I was really the receiver on the ball. If anybody interfered on the play, he did. Both of us had a right to the ball. I've got a right to raise my hands for the ball. And that's what I was doing. I was going for the ball. I saw the ball in the air and I went for it."[21]

Green Bay safety Jim Hill was near Buchanon when the play was developing, and he had a good view of what went down. He naturally corroborated his teammate's version of the play. "I took a quick look as the ball was coming down," Hill recalled. "From what I saw, Willie was inside and in front of Biletnikoff. There's no way he [Buchanon] could use his hands when he's in front of a receiver. That's the way I saw it."[22]

Naturally, Biletnikoff disagreed with Buchanon's and Hill's versions of the play. "I had him beat and I came around him," said the crafty receiver with the texture of fresh airplane model glue on his hands and fingers. "He [Buchanon] pushed me."[23]

Adding to the defeat at the hands of the Raiders was the unwanted specter of a bunch of untimely injuries to eight important Packer starters. This might have been the most important result of the game. Among the wounded were Rich McGeorge and Gale Gillingham, both of whom suffered what would later be determined season-ending knee injuries. Quarterback Scott Hunter hurt his back. Offensive guard Bill Lueck aggravated a previous shoulder injury. Star halfback John Brockington sustained a pinched nerve in his neck. Cornerback Ken Ellis sprained an ankle, and offensive tackle Francis Peay hurt his knee.

"This kind of thing has to hurt you," said Devine in referring to the injuries. "We had to go with a lot of inexperienced people. In the end, we had two rookies fielding punts. But I'm proud of the way we were able to bounce back from so many things."[24] Oakland head coach John Madden concurred with Devine. "They [the Packers] were hurting today, but they're tough," said Madden. "They're really improved and they'll give a lot of people problems."[25]

Green Bay's problems were now quite visible for Dan Devine to observe and deal with. Their 1–1 start to the 1972 regular season could easily have been a 2–0 start, and probably should have been. But the Packers had no time to dwell on their misfortune from the Oakland game. On tap was a visit from the defending World Champion Dallas Cowboys. In spite of their new rash of injuries, Devine's players would not have difficulty in getting prepared to play a team as good as Dallas. Two players on the 1972 Green Bay roster—Ron Widby and Ike Thomas—were both members of the Cowboys team that won Super Bowl VI just several months before. Widby and Thomas would naturally be very excited to play against their former team. The upcoming game against Dallas would provide a bona fide early measuring test to see just how good the Green and Gold really were.

Tough opposition would seemingly provide the framework for Green Bay's 1972 schedule, as the Packers would be saddled with the fourth-toughest slate of opponents in the league that year, based upon their opponents' winning percentage (.579) from 1971. The Pack would play five different teams in 1972 that made the 1971 playoffs. So far, they had defeated one of those playoff teams (Cleveland), but only time would tell how well they would fare against the others. Realistically, splitting your first two games in the NFL

2. Potential Amidst Early Injuries

with one win and one loss is not that bad. No one wins a division title during the first month of the season, and neither would Dan Devine's team. But the other NFC Central teams (Minnesota, Chicago, and Detroit) that Green Bay had to contend with in 1972 had built strong reputations over the years on being tough, competitive teams. Because of this, it was universally felt that the Packers were going to have quite a few tough and competitive games on their schedule.

Green Bay's good fortune in assessing their current fight in the NFC Central Division lay in the fact that they now had the tough horses on offense that they needed to control the ball for longer periods of time. Both Brockington and Lane knew that opposing defenses would be paying them plenty of attention, but as we shall see, that did not matter. Those two runners were determined to get their yards from scrimmage, and they would get them any way that they could. That fact would naturally benefit the team's defense, which would not be required to be on the field for longer periods of time, as they were during the 1971 season. When the Packer defense *was* on the field, they would show a lot of people as the season wore on just how much they had improved, especially in the categories of pass defense and overall consistency.

Their first two contests (versus Cleveland and Oakland) would give Coach Devine and his players a fairly clear indication of how strong a team the Packers were destined to become. Barring any more unforeseen future injuries, Green Bay appeared to be a tougher team (on paper and on the field as well) in 1972 than what they were in 1971. An improved won-loss record would serve as one important and obvious gauge with which to measure the success of the 1972 Packers. A winning record would also serve as proof around the league that they had taken a critical step forward in the very competitive National Football Conference's Central Division. Given that feeling of future optimism, Green Bay now had a goal to strive for, namely winning their next game against the Dallas Cowboys, as they continued their challenging regular season schedule.

3
Statement Wins

The tough loss against Oakland served as a vivid reminder and an obvious example of what had happened to the Packers team since their glory days in the 1960s. Injuries, missed opportunities, a lack of overall experience, and the general decline in the efficiency of the offense's passing attack left the Green Bay squad in a rebuilding stage that all teams go through at one time or another. But there were some positive facts to observe as the team prepared for their upcoming meeting against the Dallas Cowboys. For one, the season was still very young, with plenty of time to make adjustments and improvements. For another was the fact that the Packers were still at this young stage of the regular season tied for first place in the NFC Central Division with the Detroit Lions and the Minnesota Vikings. Green Bay's 1–1 record at this infant point of the campaign was identical to their beginning ledger from the previous year.

Packers head coach Dan Devine was not an overtly emotional man, but he was also not much of an optimist either. He never seemed to get too excited over a win. At times, however, he would tend to get too depressed over a defeat. The loss to the Raiders was very early in the season, and that was to Green Bay's benefit. So it was not truly accurate to say that Devine was unconcerned about losing to Oakland in a close, competitive game. But he was more pragmatic than he had been in 1971, and he would continue to be so during the first few weeks of 1972. Devine had a full year in Green Bay under his belt, and that included a full year to observe how *his* draft selections were faring. As far as the early weeks of September were concerned, the Packers were showing at least some level of improvement by beating Cleveland and by hanging tough with Oakland for four quarters. That was a positive and noteworthy sign for the team, and a good and secure place for Devine's frame of mind.

Going into the game against Dallas, it is important to note for those who are unfamiliar with the Packers' history, that the Green Bay Packers were not just Green Bay's team in the 1970s. They were also Wisconsin's team, and more accurately, Milwaukee's team in particular. The Packers played a few of their "home" regular season games each year at Milwaukee's County Stadium. It was mostly due to financial reasons, as Milwaukee is a much larger city than Green Bay, and its television marketing potential far outdid that of Green Bay's. Moreover, when County Stadium opened in 1953, it had more seating capacity than Lambeau Field. The Packers would typically play two to three of their seven regular season home games each year at County Stadium in the early 1970s. The Packers were not the only tenants of County Stadium, however, as the Milwaukee Brewers major league baseball team played all of their home games there. The stadium was thus configured as a baseball stadium for most of the year. When the Packers played there, the end zones were laid out extremely close to the stands, because there simply was not enough room between the third base foul line and the right field fence for any more spacing distance to be had. It is also interesting to observe that both of the football bench areas were stationed along the same far sideline, allowing for better viewpoints for the fans who occupied the lower rows of seats along the first base line.

The Packers would play their initial County Stadium game of 1972 in week three against the Cowboys. Dallas entered the game undefeated at 2–0, but in their early victories over Philadelphia and the New York Giants, the Cowboys "played down" to the level of their sub-par opposition. It is also significant to recall that the Cowboys at that time were being led by their second string quarterback, Craig Morton, who was filling in for injured starter Roger Staubach. Morton was a long-time starter for the team, however, before losing that designation to Staubach midway through the 1971 season. Morton would certainly not be phased by the pressure of taking over the reins of the defending world champions. Indeed, Morton would eventually go on to lead the Cowboys back to the playoffs in 1972. Dallas could not take Green Bay for granted, however. The Packers had defeated the Cowboys in six of the previous seven meetings between the two clubs.

"The Cowboys and the Packers were a different kind of rivalry," explained Green Bay's Scott Hunter. "We kinda knew how to beat those guys. Our older guys knew how to beat them, and they kinda told us younger guys how to do it. They [the Cowboys] only featured four [offensive] plays ... five at the most. They had their fancy wide receivers and their pretty socks ... we made them earn every damn inch that they got.

"When we were on offense, we would just run the shit out of them. Just get after their ass and go right at them. You know [Dallas middle linebacker] Lee Roy [Jordan] wasn't a big guy. He was a great player, but he wasn't a big guy. If you got on Lee Roy, he didn't have a chance against a 265-pound or a 270-pound guard. And Cornell Green, their strong safety, was a [former] basketball player."[1]

The Packers' third game of the '72 season began as a defensive struggle, which was not really that uncommon in the early 1970s in the NFL. Most of the rules at that time were spread out evenly to aid both offenses and defenses in equal amounts. The hash marks (inbounds lines denoting the placement of the ball on every down) were moved closer to the middle of the field in 1972, and that change resulted in much more ground yardage being recorded all across the league from previous years. But it was not until 1978 when the league's competition committee really inlayed a few radical changes in the rules, and the benefitting offenses would produce much more yardage production and scoring among all of the pro teams. Beginning in 1978, offensive linemen were allowed to grasp the jerseys of opposing defensive linemen, provided that their grasp remains in the sphere of their left shoulder to their right shoulder. Even more noticeable were the new rules governing defensive backs. In 1978, they were no longer allowed to hit a wide receiver after the receiver ran more than five yards past the line of scrimmage.

In 1972, however, good defenses could still dominate many games. The Dallas Cowboys had such a good defense, as evidenced by their 24–3 win over the Miami Dolphins in Super Bowl VI, which ended the 1971 NFL season. But the Green Bay Packers were working diligently at developing a strong defense themselves, and the result of their week three game against Dallas would prove that they were achieving a similar level of success as the Cowboys on the defensive side of the ball.

Dallas was first to get on the scoreboard with a 46-yard field goal off the foot of placekicker Toni Fritsch, which culminated the Cowboys' first offensive drive of the game. On their next possession, however, the Dallas offense got an unwanted taste of the much-improved Green Bay defense. Dallas quarterback Craig Morton threw a dart for wide receiver Bob Hayes, but he threw the ball just a little too high for the leaping Hayes to grasp it. Green Bay safety Al Matthews snared the tipped pass for a timely interception. Matthews' play seemed to put an immediate halt to the Cowboys' momentum. Green Bay placekicker Chester Marcol converted a 44-yard field goal for his team, tying the game at 3–3. But Marcol was certainly a work-in-progress project, at least in the early stages of his rookie season. He missed a chip shot field goal on the Packers' next possession, as the ball thudded off of the goal post upright from a mere nine yards out. Marcol would end the game making three field goals, but missing three as well.

The second quarter provided more fortunate breaks for Green Bay, however. A fumble by Dallas running back Calvin Hill deep in Cowboys territory, which was recovered by rookie Packers cornerback Willie Buchanon, led directly to the first touchdown of the contest. Green Bay running back John Brockington was planning on running a simple off-tackle play to his right from the Dallas 2-yard line. But Cowboy middle linebacker Lee Roy Jordan

Tailback John Brockington (No. 42) and quarterback Scott Hunter (No. 16) chat on the sidelines at Milwaukee during the Packers' 16–13 victory over the Dallas Cowboys on October 1. Both men were playing in their second pro year for the Packers (© Vernon J. Biever Photo).

was executing a force into the Packer backfield. Brockington instinctively darted away from the diving Jordan, who filled the open hole in the line about as well as any linebacker could. Brockington then benefited from an outstanding kickout block by his running mate MacArthur Lane, who sealed off Dallas safety Cornell Green from making the tackle. Brockington—who would finish the game with 91 yards rushing on 26 attempts against the Doomsday Defense—thus saw daylight, and he pranced into the end zone for the score.

Scott Hunter describes Brockington's score in this manner: "So we get down there [near the west end zone] of the old Milwaukee County Stadium infield," recalled Hunter. "You know the [Major League Baseball's] Brewers were still playing, so the infield was still there. I look down there and Cornell Green is by himself over there, and we're in a slot left [a formation where the slot receiver—the receiver in between the last player in the formation and the outside wide receiver—is situated on the left side of the ball]. I audible from a Brown to a Blue [formation], which brought [Packers running back] Mac [Lane] back to the weak side [the side without a tight end lined up next to an offensive tackle], and of course Cornell Green is all by himself, and he knows what's coming [laughter]. I handed the ball over to Brock [John Brockington], and Mac came up and got [Cornell] Green right up under his shoulder pads. If John hadn't scored—he just walked into the end zone—and they hadn't whistled the play dead, Mac would have put Green into the third row behind the third base seats [more laughter]."[2]

Brockington made no pretense to nimbleness and/or hesitation when he had a football in his hands. He was a perfect type of running back for the perfect decade. He simply plowed through the line of scrimmage and dragged many a defender for several yards before help arrived to finally tackle number 42. It was a scene replayed in game after game during the early 1970s ... John Brockington gaining yardage bit by bit. It was power football at its basic best. Legendary Packer head coach Vince Lombardi's "Run to Daylight" philosophy of gaining yardage would have been custom made for the former Ohio State running back.

Brockington's style of running differed greatly from another Packers running back who did play for Lombardi, the veteran superstar Donny Anderson. The two quickly became good friends in 1971 (the only year that they played together, because Anderson was dealt to the St. Louis Cardinals in 1972), and Brockington learned quite a bit in a short amount of time from a guy who had a very contrasting running style than that of himself. He also learned how to make the most of constructive criticism from his coaches to be able to judge and improve upon his own rushing performances.

"I liked off-tackle plays better," explained Brockington. "Because at Ohio State, I never ran sweeps. Donny [Anderson] was a great sweep runner, because Donny had patience and I didn't. Donny could hang out there and wait for a hole to open. In 1971 we were playing the Lions. We run a sweep, and I'm running behind Gale Gillingham's block, and I cut inside. I get caught in the wash [of defensive players], and I get dropped before I reach the end zone. So the game ended up in a 13–13 tie. We get back the next day and we're watching films, and that play comes up. [Assistant coach] Rollie Dotsch says, 'John, John ... if you had stayed outside we would have had a touchdown. We would have won this game.' And I'm looking at him [Dotsch] and I'm thinking.... Gale hits this guy ... flattens him. If I would have just stayed with Gale a little longer, I could have walked into the end zone for a touchdown. Gale just demolished the [forcing] defensive back.

"That's what I loved about [assistant coach] Red Cochrane, because he was a [former] running back. He said, 'John, *never* run outside of a block. If you do that, 99 percent of the time you're going to get caught. This time it just didn't work out for you. But I am not going to coach you to run outside of blocks.' And I felt awful because Gale destroyed the guy, and I wasted his block. But Donny Anderson, man he had the patience, and he'd wait for Gale to make his block, and *then* he [Anderson] would make his move. Donny was a great sweep runner, because he had the patience to wait. I made my yards by running straight upfield."[3]

The obvious differences between Brockington and Anderson—or between Brockington and anyone else—did not really register on anyone's mind as the game against Dallas wore on. The Cowboys drew closer to the Packers on the scoreboard with a 9-yard field goal by Fritsch on the final play of the second quarter. Fritsch's kick culminated the longest and best Dallas offensive drive of the game, and their momentum would continue into the early stages of the second half. Cowboys running back Walt Garrison put an exclamation mark to the end of his team's initial drive of the third quarter when he bowled over Packer safety Jim Hill en route to a 10-yard touchdown run right up the gut of the Green Bay defense. Dallas now appeared to have taken over control of the momentum and the game as a whole. The fight to regain the lead from the defending champs would now be even tougher for the Pack than acquiring it in the first place. The time was now at hand for a classic gut check.

No one can accurately define what it is that changes the course of a season for any one particular team. Indeed, the "turning point" of a season is a phrase so overused these days, that it really has lost its effectiveness and possibly even its meaning. A typical Packers fan could observe the 1972 season and probably pick out three or four potential "turning points" of that year. It is somewhat hard to argue that a turning point in a season could be found as early as the third game of a 14-game schedule. Nevertheless, the first moment where the Packers were faced with a bona fide gut-check stood in front of them in week three, and they were symbolized by the royal blue stars on the side of their silver helmets.

The historic character of the Green Bay Packers that was forged in triumph during the previous decade under Coach Lombardi somehow managed to return at this moment. The team could fold under the pressure of the Dallas defense, but they did not. Coach Devine's offense immediately responded to Garrison's touchdown with a scoring drive of their own. Kick returner Bob Hudson performed his specialty to the tune of a 55-yard kickoff return, giving Green Bay instant quality field position with which to aid the Packer offense. Chester Marcol quickly booted a 26-yard field goal to tie the game at 13–13 midway through the third quarter. Now the game was up for grabs, and one big play could determine the outcome. The Green Bay defense had been able to make several big plays throughout the contest. Their defensive line had penetrated the Dallas pass pocket four times in the game for timely sacks, and their defensive backfield chipped in with three key interceptions. Safety Al Matthews contributed two of those thefts, one of which early in the fourth quarter led to a 22-yard Marcol field goal, which returned the lead to the Packers, 16–13.

"We gave them a lot of stuff," lamented Dallas head coach Tom Landry, reflecting on the multitude of mistakes that his offense had made on this day. "Our turnovers were the key to the game."[4]

The Cowboys were not going to be easy to put away, however. They had two more drives in the final quarter, but the Packers defense somehow held strong and delivered another big play when it counted the most. Craig Morton rolled to his right with 1:52 left in regulation and threw across the middle for wide receiver Bob Hayes. But rookie Green Bay cornerback Willie Buchanon stepped in front of Hayes and intercepted the ball. Buchanon then proceeded to break for the sideline and sprinted downfield for 26 yards, breaking a pair of diving arm tackles by Hayes and Walt Garrison along the way. He was eventually knocked out of bounds at the Cowboys' 2-yard line by Dallas offensive tackle Ralph Neely to ice the game. The Packers' had somehow miraculously prevailed, defeating the defending world champions, 16–13.

"This has to be our most important win," said Dan Devine after the game. "We played awfully well up at Minnesota last year, but we didn't win. One game doesn't make a season, but it sure is nicer to be 2–1 than 1–2. The one thing we stressed all week was avoiding offensive turnovers. We [the

Defensive tackle Bob Brown hits Dallas Cowboys quarterback Craig Morton during the Packers' 16–13 victory over the defending world champion Cowboys (AP Photo/Vernon Biever).

coaches] preached it until they [the players] were sick of hearing it. We didn't feel we could stay with this club [Dallas] if we made mistakes. [We're now] tied for first place [in the NFC Central Division]."[5]

A big factor in the big win over the Cowboys was the overall outstanding play of the Green Bay defense. Seldom-used veteran defensive tackle Vernon Vanoy came out of obscurity to record three quarterback sacks in the game. It would turn out to be the greatest game in Vanoy's brief three-year pro football career.

"I was lucky," said a gleeful Vanoy from inside a joyous Green Bay postgame locker room. "You've got to be lucky to get three sacks in a game. Bob Brown was the key. He cleared out a whole side of their line so that I could get in."[6]

Brown would later be named an All-Conference defensive tackle following the 1972 season, and his performance in the Dallas game against one of the best offensive lines in the league was undeniable proof of his surge to greatness. In describing Vanoy's sacks, Brown related that they all came as the result of a basic switch between the defensive tackle and the defensive end, known as a stunt.

"It's what we call a tackle stunt," described Brown. "I pinch down and keep the center and guard in, blocking me. Then Vernon loops right behind me and goes on in. Sometimes we work it the other way. We've used it in other games. I don't know why the Cowboys had so much trouble picking it up, but I'm sure glad they did."[7] Packer safety Al Matthews was equally as glad, for his teammates and for himself. "Anytime you get a great rush, the quarterback has to get rid of it [the ball] in a hurry," Matthews said. "It's the first time I ever had two interceptions [in one game]."[8]

The upset victory over the Cowboys would serve as the first consummate sign that the 1972 Packers had become markedly improved over the performance of the 1971 Packers. Also improving was the confidence of their younger players, many of whom were new to the NFL scene, and many of whom were extremely new to winning at the professional level. According to veteran center Ken Bowman, "This was a big game for a very young team. I don't think some of the new men on this club thought deep down that they could win, or that they belonged on the same field with Dallas."[9]

The goal now following one of their biggest victories in years was to find a way to win consecutive games, or a string of games. Fortunately for Devine, he did not have to do too much motivational speaking to his charges following the Dallas win. The Packers were next scheduled to play their long-time divisional rivals, the hated Chicago Bears. The rivalry with the Bears, which was and still is the league's oldest rivalry, had similarities to college football rivalries such as Yale versus Harvard, Michigan versus Ohio State, and Army versus Navy. Both the Bears and the Packers had been hitting each other hard on gridirons in America's Midwest since pro football's infancy in the early 1920s. By the time that the 1972 NFL season began, the Bears owned a 54-44-6 all-time edge over the Pack. Even if the Packers had lost 12 of their 14 regular season games, their season would still be considered by many inexorable Green Bay fans as quite successful if their two victories came by the means of defeating Chicago. The same was true with many diehard Bears fans, most of whom acknowledged that a great opportunity for overall improvement for their team in the standings would occur after Vince Lombardi retired from coaching the Packers.

The NFL Central Division was a very competitive division in the early weeks of the 1972 season. Practically any of the four teams (Minnesota, Green Bay, Detroit or Chicago) could possibly win the title, given a lucky break here and there, and minimal injuries to their rosters. The history of the division saw the Vikings winning first place from 1968 to 1971. The Packers were in reality just a shadow of their former selves during those years. They were competitive at times, but they were not champions anymore. Things were about to change in 1972, however. The result of the game against Dallas the previous week proved that Devine's team could become a bona fide factor in a championship chase. This first meeting with the Bears on October 8 would be an early indication of how far Devine's team had come since their multitude of failures of 1971.

Green Bay ran out onto Lambeau Field on a sunny and windy day, and after two different exchanges of possessions, took an early lead against Chicago with just less than five minutes remaining in the first quarter. Bears running back Jim Harrison took a handoff from quarterback Bobby Douglass and ran to his right on an outside sweep. Veteran Packers linebacker Dave Robinson sliced into the Chicago backfield and hit Harrison hard at the Bear 23-yard line, thus dislodging the ball from Harrison's grasp. Green Bay defensive end Clarence Williams arrived on the scene a sec-

Defensive end Clarence Williams was known as the "Big Cat" for his 6-foot-5 height. He was one of the team's best pass rushers. Williams contributed three sacks of Minnesota quarterback Fran Tarkenton in the game that clinched the NFC Central Division title for the Packers on December 10 (courtesy the Green Bay Packers).

ond later, picked up the bouncing ball at the 21-yard line, then outraced Douglass to the Chicago end zone. The Packers had grabbed the all-important early lead.

The Bears finally put together an offensive drive early in the second quarter, and it was a pretty good one. It lasted for 13 plays, but it fizzled at the Packers' 5-yard line, when Harrison fumbled the ball again. Fortunately for him, he recovered the ball this time, which permitted Chicago placekicker Mac Percival to salvage three points with a 12-yard field goal.

"I can't say why it is we don't move the ball in the first quarter," surmised Bobby Douglass. "We're still a young team and I guess we're apprehensive out there early in the game. Another thing is that we're doing things offensively this year which we haven't done before. The [Packers] have a great defense, no question about it. They're just big and tough."[10]

The Green Bay offense was big and tough too, but they were still being challenged by the Chicago defense. Just before the two-minute warning, the Packers put together a 70-yard touchdown drive to increase their lead. Big plays in the drive were a 25-yard pass over the middle from Scott Hunter to rookie wide receiver Leland Glass, and a couple of key first down runs by running backs MacArthur Lane and John Brockington. But the biggest play was the touchdown itself, a 48-yard bomb from Hunter to third-year wide receiver Jon Staggers down the far sideline. On that play, Hunter intended his pass to go to second-year wide receiver Dave Davis, but Chicago cornerback Joe Taylor deflected the ball at the Bears' 12-yard line. Staggers was wisely trailing the play, and he dove for the deflected ball and caught it before it bounced off of the turf at the Chicago 9-yard line. Staggers then bounced up quickly and pranced into the end zone. The Bears were incredulous as to how Staggers was able to make the play. They were not the only ones.

"I don't know how he does it," remarked Packers head coach Dan Devine, "but Staggers always seems to come up with the big play."[11]

Green Bay was still not done scoring in the first half, however. The Packer defense quickly forced three downs and a punt from the Bears offense. Two quick passes from Hunter to Brockington moved Green Bay's offense deep into Chicago territory. Chester Marcol was called on to connect on a 26-yard field goal, which he successfully did. Green Bay entered their locker room at halftime with a 17–7 lead over their arch-rivals.

To their credit, the resilient Bears fought back hard in the second half. This was a divisional rival, after all, so even the most optimistic Packer Backer would probably predict that Chicago would play more competitively in the second half. Bear pride and dignity demanded it. The Bears culminated a nine-play drive early in the third quarter with their initial touchdown of the game. With the ball at the Green Bay 2-yard line, Chicago running back Cyril Pinder took a handoff from Douglass, broke a tackle from Packer safety Al

Matthews (who was forcing on the play), then squeezed into the end zone. Packer defenders Jim Carter, Willie Buchanon, and Jim Hill simultaneously met Pinder and tackled him, but Pinder managed to cross the goal line just prior to the collision.

Chicago's offense was just getting warmed up, however. Momentum was on their side as they drove back into Green Bay territory late in the third quarter. A missed 48-yard field goal by Mac Percival on the second play of the fourth quarter did little to stem the surging Bears. Following a Packer punt, Douglass—who would finish the game with 45 rushing yards—surprisingly threw across the middle of the field for flanker George Farmer, who was all alone as he caught the ball 16 yards downfield. Farmer then streaked for 30 more yards until he was driven out of bounds at the Green Bay 8-yard line. The Packers were fairly certain that the Bears would stick to their ground game this deep in Packer territory. They were correct in that assumption. Three runs by Harrison, Don Shy, and Pinder placed the ball at the Green Bay 2-yard line. It was now fourth down. A field goal would pull the Bears to within four points of the Packers. Chicago head coach Abe Gibron decided to try one more run, this time on a veer option play by his quarterback. Douglass took the snap, ran to his left, outraced Green Bay outside linebacker Fred Carr, and just barely made it into the corner of the end zone. The game was now tied at 17–17 with less than 10 minutes to play.

"I've always said Douglass was a good quarterback, even before I became a pro coach," admitted Devine. "There are football experts who say quarterbacks can't run in the NFL. They should come out here and try coaching in a game like this."[12]

The 6-foot-4, 225-pound Douglass was annually derided by many "experts" as nothing more than a misplaced fullback. His statistics in 1972 would somewhat lend credence to that belief, as Douglass would rush for a then-record for pro quarterbacks with 968 ground yards (and a 6.9 yards-per-rush average). His 1,246 passing yards during the same year would prove that Douglass was much more feared as a runner than as a passer. Nevertheless, Packers quarterback coach Zeke Bratkowski, who had retired as an active player and had rejoined the team as a mentor to young signal callers Scott Hunter, Jerry Tagge and Frank Patrick, concurred with Devine. "He [Douglass] has great natural ability," admitted Bratkowski.[13]

Green Bay's offense had displayed virtually no ability to move the ball in the second half. The game whittled down to the five-minute mark, and both teams realized that whoever was able to score next would probably emerge as the winner. The Packers had the ball at their own 27-yard line, and in what could best be described as a nerve-wracking march to glory, they succeeded. Scott Hunter first passed for 11 yards and a first down to tight end Len Garrett. A seven-yard pass to John Brockington was next, and it was followed up by a 15-yard completion to Jon Staggers. The Packers were finally putting together a good drive when they needed it the most. But at the Chicago 40-yard line, their drive almost ended. Green Bay fullback MacArthur Lane sprinted through the line of scrimmage and fumbled the ball, causing a gasp to echo throughout the patrons at Lambeau Field. Lane was able to recover his own fumble, however, and still managed to gain six yards in the process. Lane's good fortune was followed up with three more Packer rushing attempts and two more incomplete passes, leaving the team with a fourth-down situation at the Bears' 30-yard line. Chester Marcol was called on to kick a crucial 37-field goal, which he successfully did, giving the Packers a 20–17 lead with just 30 ticks left on the clock.

Marcol remembered the ensuing kickoff with as much pride as any other kick of his pro career. "I had to kick into the teeth of a strong, swirling wind, which was blowing twenty-five miles per hour and gusting into the mid-thirties, if not higher," recalled Marcol. "Though there wasn't much time left in the game, there was enough time for the Bears to move into position for a tying field goal. Their kicker would have the wind at his back—if I got off a bad kick. Ron Smith, the Bears' Pro Bowl returner, was waiting for the ball at the fifteen-yard line; normally, he would have been standing on the goal line. He was a dangerous returner, and the last thing I wanted to do was allow [him] to field the ball at the twenty-yard line, make a few cuts, and give the Bears good field position.

"I psyched myself up as I prepared to kick off. I stared at Smith and said, 'Chester, you are going to kick this one over his head and he's going to have to run backward to pick it up, and by then our coverage guys will be all over him and the game will be over. I put everything I had into the kick and the ball exploded off my foot on a line drive. It cut through the wind like a hot knife through butter, sailed over Smith's head, and actually hit the crossbar [of the goal post]. Never in my life, before or after that day, did I kick a football harder or more perfectly."[14]

Nevertheless, the Bears were extremely resilient. Three completed Douglass passes against the fatigued Packers defense netted 36 yards. On the game's final play, Mac Percival narrowly missed a 51-yard field goal, and Green Bay survived by a score of 20–17, boosting their record to an impressive 3–1, good enough for a first-place tie in the NFC Central Division with the Detroit Lions.

"You've got to win this kind of a game to be in a race we're in," said Devine from a relieved Packers locker room. "I'd rather not have to do it the hard way—but I'm glad to have it anyway. It was a great win."[15] Bratkowski added that "We anticipated the kind of game they [the Bears] played."[16]

Also anticipated were the mistakes that a young team like the Packers made in this game. Len Garrett caught a beautiful 55-yard scoring pass from

Scott Hunter in the second quarter, but offensive guard Malcolm Snider was penalized for holding, which wiped out that touchdown. Green Bay's offense also committed four fumbles, two of which were recovered by Chicago.

"I just can't explain them [the bobbles]," said Devine. "They just happened. A lot of little things hurt us."[17] Devine then focused on the positive factors in the game. "Our offensive line really protected [quarterback] Scott [Hunter], but he did a good job of throwing the ball."[18]

Over the course of the first four games of the 1972 season, the Packers offense accounted for only 76 points, the lowest output for all first-place teams in the National Football Conference. But their defense had limited their opponents to a mere 60 points during the same time span, which amounted to giving up only 15 points per game. So Devine and his assistant coaches were getting used to taking the good with the bad. But they had no time to worry about the statistics from their first four games. Their next contest would provide the Packers with yet another tough division rival, and that game would be televised in front of a national audience for all of America to witness.

4
A Vital Comeback

The Packers were slated to play in their only *Monday Night Football* game of the season on October 16 in Detroit's Tiger Stadium. The host Lions were also 3–1, and their offense was quickly becoming one of the more talented offenses in the league. They had a quality rushing attack, led by halfback Altie Taylor and former Heisman Trophy winner Steve Owens. They also had a good passer and another excellent runner at the quarterback position in Greg Landry. Catching passes were Ron Jessie and Larry Walton, both of whom could be depended upon to make clutch catches on both short and deep routes. Added to all of those weapons was one of the best tight ends in the entire NFL in future Hall of Famer Charlie Sanders. The Detroit defense was also quite formidable, with stalwart veterans such as linebackers Mike Lucci and Charley Weaver, and quality defensive backs Lem Barney (another future Hall of Famer) and Mike Weger. It was becoming fairly evident that the Packers were not going to have any "easy" games on their 1972 schedule.

Green Bay quarterback Scott Hunter was well aware that the Lions would be crowding the line of scrimmage in this contest. Even though Hunter had his best passing game of the year against the Bears the previous week, Detroit knew that the Packers' main strength was its rushing attack. Virtually every opponent that Green Bay faced in 1972 was more inclined to ignore Hunter's throws, and instead focus on trying to stop the likes of runners John Brockington and MacArthur Lane. Some of their opponents made their formulas work against the Packers offense, but many more were unable to stop Green Bay's ground attack, regardless how hard they tried to do so. One of Dan Devine's strategies that seemed to succeed more often than not was his willingness to stick with what was working. For example, if Brockington was running well, Brockington would get the majority of the carries. But if Lane was gaining more yards, he would be called on to tote the pigskin with an increasing number of attempts. The team was definitely not a selfish team. You never heard any man complain about not being used enough in the scheme of things. The objective for all good teams was to win, regardless of how that was achieved. The 1972 Green Bay Packers were just such a team.

As with most close and competitive games in the National Football League, the team that makes the least amount of mistakes usually emerges as the victor. The Packers were well aware of this, and certainly they did not want to make any major miscues, especially early in the game versus the Lions. But that is exactly what they did. Following a missed field goal attempt by Detroit placekicker Errol Mann, Green Bay's Scott Hunter tossed an interception on the Packers' third offensive play of the contest. Detroit cornerback Lem Barney stepped in front of Hunter's pass, which was intended for Green Bay wide receiver Leland Glass, and returned the ball to the Packers' 30-yard line.

"You know, you can look at all the movies there are of someone like Lem Barney, and he doesn't look the same as he does on the field," admitted Hunter. "You have to see the defenses in action before you can recognize them and know what's going to happen."[1]

Detroit did not waste the field position, and in eight plays, they would score the game's first touchdown. On a play very similar to Bobby Douglass' touchdown run against the Packers from the previous week, Detroit quarterback Greg Landry ran to his right on a veer option play from the 2-yard line and made it into the end zone.

Detroit's 7–0 lead would last into the early stages of the second quarter, when they quickly added to it. The Lions culminated an eight-play drive when Mann booted a 12-yard field goal, giving Detroit a 10–0 advantage. Less than three minutes later, the Packers would see things go from bad to worse. Green Bay fullback MacArthur Lane had throughout his career owned a reputation of not fumbling the football very much at all. On this evening, however, that reputation took somewhat of a hit—as did Lane himself—and his ensuing fumble was recovered by Detroit linebacker Wayne Walker at the Packers' 25-yard line. The veteran Walker toted the pigskin another 14 yards until he was corralled at the Green Bay 11-yard line. Three plays later, Detroit halfback Altie Taylor sliced into the end zone from a yard out, and the Lions owned a seemingly insurmountable 17–0 lead. Green Bay had hoped to make as little mistakes as possible in this game against a tough division rival. But well before halftime, the Packers had committed two key turnovers, which directly led to both of the Lions' touchdowns. Despite that fact, one Green Bay player remained confident.

"I'm kind of happy we started slow," confided Packers fullback MacArthur Lane to a group of reporters following the game. "Because when you play catch-up and you do it [namely succeed at catching up], you gotta be a good team."[2]

The Green Bay offense needed to make some good adjustments to their game plan in the midst of their deficit, but what they really needed to do as fast as possible was eliminate their turnovers. Virtually all of their drives up to the midway point of the second quarter were short in duration and minimal in yardage gained. The Packers would abruptly change that trend when they took over at their own 19-yard line following the second Detroit touchdown. Scott Hunter finally completed a pass, a short screen to Lane. It is important to note that the bullish Lane was not your typical fullback. He had good speed and moves to go along with his pounding blocking ability. On the screen play, Lane proved too fast for a diving attempted tackle by Detroit defensive end Jim Mitchell. He then sprinted untouched downfield until Detroit defensive back Wayne Rasmussen finally chopped down the steaming setback at the Lions' 39-yard line. Lane's 41-yard catch-and-carry represented only the second first down for the Packers in the game. A 7-yard run by Lane ensued, followed by a 16-yard burst off tackle by John Brockington, which gave Green Bay another first down. Devine then called Lane's number twice in succession, and he responded on a sweep to the right for nine yards, and a three-yard smash up the middle for another first down.

Following a sack of Hunter by Detroit defensive end Larry Hand, the Packers quarterback got back on his feet, fastened his chin strap, and

Head coach Dan Devine and quarterback Scott Hunter follow the action on the sidelines at Detroit. Hunter would go on to throw the winning touchdown pass in the Packers' 24–23 come-from-behind victory over the Lions on *Monday Night Football* on October 16 (© Vernon J. Biever Photo).

responded favorably on the very next play. Hunter threw a dart to Green Bay wide receiver Jon Staggers, who caught the pass for 10 yards, and who was immediately tackled at the Lions' 1-yard line. Hunter finished off the nine-play drive by bootlegging to his right, following a great block by right guard Malcolm Snider, and eluding a diving arm tackle by Detroit defensive back Mike Weger. Once he got past Weger, Hunter jogged untouched the rest of the way into the end zone for the Packers' first touchdown of the game. It was a vital score, as it stopped the Lions from imposing their will on the Packers for at least this moment in the game. Green Bay's sense of relief, optimism and momentum then got an added jolt when with time waning in the first half, Detroit quarterback Greg Landry threw across the middle for his wide receiver, Earl McCullough. Landry threw the ball too hard, however, and the ball ricocheted off of McCullough's arms and right into the hands of Green Bay safety Jim Hill, who returned the ball 21 yards to the Packers' 37-yard line. Green Bay failed to score again, but at least their defense was able to stop the Detroit offense at a key moment of the game, a moment where if the Lions had scored again, the contest might have been for all intents and purposes declared over. The Lions took a 17–7 lead into halftime.

Momentum is a fickle thing in pro football, and virtually no player or coach can predict when it will appear or disappear. Just as quickly as the Packers gained it near the end of the first half, they would once again lose it early in the third quarter. A short Detroit drive culminated with a 45-yard Errol Mann field goal, which increased the Lions' lead to 20–7. Green Bay would get those three points back several minutes later from the foot of Chester Marcol, who finished an 11-play Packer drive with a successful 34-yard field goal. Green Bay now trailed Detroit by a score of 20–10, but they could ill-afford to continue to trade field goals with the Lions. The Packers needed to stop Greg Landry's offense, and possibly even more importantly, they needed to come up with some big plays to secure the momentum and keep it on their side, all while obtaining a lead on the scoreboard.

The Lions managed to obtain one first down before they had to punt with just over a minute left in the third quarter. What ensued was perhaps the most important single play during the entire 1972 season for the Packers. Out of the many hundreds of plays that occur for any team during the course of a single season, it is often very difficult to state that one particular play is the most important of all. At least in retrospect at the end of the 1972 season, it appeared to many observers that such a significant and indeed such a crucial play for Green Bay occurred in this *Monday Night Football* game against Detroit. It was definitely a play that meant the most to the Packers' chances to win this game, and to surge ahead in the divisional standings.

Detroit punter Herman Weaver did not have a chance to perform his specialty until this moment of the game, and his first punt was a moment that he and the Lions instantly regretted. Weaver's strong kick spiraled 46 yards, where Green Bay cornerback and punt returner Ken Ellis fielded the ball at his own 20-yard line. Ellis immediately broke to his left, dodged a diving attempted arm tackle by Detroit's Mickey Zofko, then sped past reserve Lions tight end John Hilton and defensive tackle Herb Orvis near the sideline. Ellis then slightly dashed inside to evade Herman Weaver's attempted tackle. From there, it was a sprint to the end zone, and Ellis outraced reserve Detroit defensive back Charlie Potts to score. It was a spectacular 80-yard punt return for a game-changing touchdown, courtesy of one of the best punt returners and best overall athletes that Green Bay had during the early 1970s. The Packers, who were behind in the first half by a score of 17–0, were now only trailing by three points at 20–17, with one full quarter remaining to be played.

"I saw John Hilton [of the Lions] coming at me and I figured if I could get by him I would go all the way," said Ellis. "I knew Hilton's speed and he underestimated mine. Hilton came down and had me hemmed in. But for some reason he went for my inside move. After I started retreating I saw my men were forming a wall. I knew I could go all the way."[3]

As the season wore on, it was clear that Ellis' return marked a definitive turning point in the fate of the 1972 Packers. Detroit was stuck in the current

Ken Ellis is seen just moments after he crossed the goal line on his 80-yard punt return at Detroit. Ellis's score turned the game and possibly the season around for Green Bay. Reserve Packers running back Perry Williams (No. 31) is also in the photograph (© Vernon J. Biever Photo).

moment, however, and they accepted two main facts: One was that their prized momentum was squarely in the hands of their foes, and the other was that they knew that their slim lead was shaky at best. Another strong offensive drive was needed by Detroit, and fortunately for the them, that is exactly what they got. Twelve plays and 38 yards later, Errol Mann outdid himself (his previous kick was good from 45 yards out) when he booted a 51-yard field goal, which increased the Lions' lead to 23–17 with under 10 minutes to play. The momentum was now at least somewhat back in Detroit's grasp. One more defensive stop by the Lions would virtually seal up the victory and first place in the NFC Central Division for the boys in the Motor City. Green Bay had made the game competitive up to this point. They had erased an early deficit, and they had positioned themselves to get to within a touchdown of the lead late in the game. Coach Devine wanted his squad to be known not just for its toughness and for its unwillingness to quit, however, but also for its ability to come from behind and actually win a tight contest. On this evening, both of Dan Devine's desires would be realized.

Green Bay's offense received Detroit's kickoff with just under six minutes left to play in this nail-biting contest. They had the ball at their own 17-yard line, a full 83 yards away from a touchdown and victory. The Packers wasted no time. Hunter zinged a pass over the middle to wide receiver Carroll Dale for 21 yards. It was Dale's only reception of the game, but it proved to be a good start to a game-winning drive. On the next play, Hunter completed an 11-yard pass to wide receiver Jon Staggers. Halfback John Brockington was called on for the next three straight plays, the first two of which were short runs, and the third play coming when he snared a 7-yard pass from Hunter, which gave the Pack yet another first down. Then it was MacArthur Lane's turn. The burly Lane carried the ball on the next three plays for three short gains, but combined they gave Green Bay one more first down. By this time, the Packers were situated at the Detroit 28-yard line, and the two-minute warning was looming ahead. A screen pass to Staggers and another short run by Brockington resulted in still another Green Bay first down. The Lions defense was now in full panic mode, and they were reeling. They had been unable to stop the Packers offense during these final exciting minutes of the game, and their failure to do so would be manifested fully on the following play.

Devine and assistant coach Bart Starr agreed on a pass play featuring rookie wide receiver Leland Glass, who was silent up to this point in the game. Glass was told to run a simple down-and-out pattern, and he would be quarterback Hunter's primary target on the play. Devine and Starr figured that because Glass was not used much at all during the night, the Lions defense would ignore him now. The Detroit defender who would be guarding Glass was four-year cornerback Rudy Redmond. If anyone on the Lions' veteran-laden roster would be fooled by the strategy, Redmond would probably be the man. The Packers threw caution to the wind, and Hunter threw the ball to Glass, who ran his pattern well. Call it luck or call it genius, but whichever you call it, Redmond played well off of Glass, just as Devine and Starr had hoped that he would. The extra free space was just what Glass needed to make his cut and head for the sideline in the Lions end zone. Glass caught the ball and just barely got both of his feet down for the score, and the entire Green Bay bench area went wild. Chester Marcol's extra point conversion gave the Packers their first lead of the night, 24–23, with just 1:54 left on the clock.

Rookie wide receiver Leland Glass averaged 17.4 yards per reception in 1972. Glass caught the winning touchdown pass in a 24–23 victory over the Detroit Lions (courtesy the Green Bay Packers).

"I think I made a pretty good move on Redmond, one of the best I've ever made," admitted Glass. "I went in—faked in—and he [Redmond] went for it. Then I made my move out and the pass was there."[4]

Detroit received the ensuing kickoff, but kick returner Ron Jessie could only bring Marcol's booming kick out to his 19-yard line. Detroit quarterback Greg Landry knew that throwing the ball was his only option, but he was unsuccessful. A key sack by Packers defensive end Clarence Williams combined with three Landry incompletions to finish the game. Green Bay had somehow managed to prevail in this incredible gut-check encounter with the Lions, 24–23.

"We just kept plugging away until things started to go right," described Devine after the game. "A large majority of the players played ... like I'd like them to play, as far as effort is concerned. If fact, I'm very proud of what our people did. To come from behind in a game like this really raises our confidence. But I'm not saying we didn't have confidence in ourselves before this game. We know we had a good team and this [game] reinforces that. We always thought we could win it [the NFC Central Division title]. Now we know we can win it."[5]

Ken Ellis, one of the big heroes of this contest, concurred with his head coach. "We're in front [of the division] now and nobody's going to catch us," Ellis predicted.[6]

Ellis was not alone in his beliefs. The defensive secondary was certainly a key reason why the Packers were doing so well during the first month of the 1972 season, and by this time of the year, the secondary was getting better and more proficient at stopping the opposing passing attacks with each successive game. What's more, each of the members of the quartet of cornerbacks Ken Ellis and Willie Buchanon, and safeties Jim Hill and Al Matthews, felt that the moment was now at hand where they were beyond any stage of doubt as to their abilities. The Green Bay defensive secondary would *definitely* achieve a great deal of success in 1972.

"We thought they'd be ready in a couple of years," admitted Coach Devine. "*They* decided they'd be ready now."[7]

They all had their own unique talents. Author Don Kowet described Hill as "the traffic cop, calling out defensive formations and hints. Matthews earned recognition as a brutal tackler. Everyone began to notice the unit's speed, its youth, [and] its rare ability to anticipate each other's moves and help each other out. By the end of the season, Buchanon was the defensive Rookie of the Year, and Ellis made several All-Pro squads."[8]

According to Green Bay defensive backfield coach Don Doll, the four young men wasted little time in getting to know each other and in getting to know how to help out each other. "Through some weird luck, these four guys hit it off like no other group I've ever seen," said Doll. "They became instant friends, real buddies. On or off the field, when they're together, they become one person with four heads, eight arms and eight legs."[9]

Noted pro football historian and author T.J. Troup has intensely studied many facets of the 1972 Packers. His astute comments regarding the team's defensive secondary confirm that almost anything that could go right for them, did go right for them, and that the stars all aligned to produce one incredible season for each of those four athletes.

"The Green Bay defensive sec-

Rookie cornerback Willie Buchanon was the final piece to the puzzle in one of the best defensive secondaries in NFL history. Buchanon intercepted four passes in 1972, and it was not long before opposing quarterbacks started to avoid throwing the ball near his area on the field (courtesy the Green Bay Packers).

ondary intermixed their man-to-man and zone coverages so well, that guys like Matthews, Hill and Ellis had the best season of their careers in 1972," Troup said. "They rolled [or rotated] their zone coverages to the strong side of the field [the side where the tight end lined up], and left the cornerback on the weak side alone to play man-to-man against the wide receiver opposite him. They naturally could not do this on every play, but when they did use it, they succeeded beyond anyone's expectation. They studied their opponents' tendencies very well, and they knew where the most favorable matchups across the line of scrimmage would be found. They knew that [cornerback] Ken Ellis could handle a particular receiver by himself, which allowed the other three defensive backs to focus their attention to the other side of the field. The Packer coaches had known by 1972 that they had a really talented player in Ellis. They knew that he could handle his opponent man-to-man. When they got Willie Buchanon in the draft, they realized as early as by the end of summer training camp how far ahead he was in his abilities over most of the veteran cornerbacks already in the NFL. Buchanon's learning curve was very short, and he quickly became reliable enough to also [like Ellis] handle wide receivers man-to-man.

He [Buchanon] also became outstanding enough in many of the other aspects of successful cornerback play, like forcing a running play and making tackles.

"Because of the play of Ellis and Buchanon, the safeties—Al Matthews and Jim Hill—really had great career years in 1972. Hill had some decent years while he played in San Diego, but when he came to Green Bay and teamed up with Ellis and Buchanon, it really allowed him to do more back there in the secondary. He could all of a sudden do more freelancing ... to take a few more chances ... because he knew that his two cornerbacks had their receivers covered adequately enough. That 1972 season was a spectacular year for the Packers defensive secondary, because they worked so well together ... they blended their talents so well together ... from the beginning of the year to the end of the year."¹⁰

Al Matthews provided the 1972 Packers with steady and consistent play from his strong safety position. He was always around the ball, and he was called upon to support the outside linebackers on many opponent sweep runs, which he did rather well (courtesy the Green Bay Packers).

Scott Hunter was very happy that the defensive secondary was excelling. He knew that the defense, thanks in large part due to the performance of the defensive backs, was keeping the opponents' scores low, which was very important in helping the Packers come from behind and pull out a close victory, as they had done at Detroit. Hunter—like most of his teammates—also felt that the Green Bay defensive secondary would (barring any unforeseen injuries) be a force to be reckoned with for the remainder of the 1972 season. But the youthful Hunter was naturally more concerned with his own progression as a starting quarterback in the pros. His recollections of that Monday night game against the Lions involved his observations along the sidelines, as well as some testing moments for himself ... with some good plays spackled in for good measure. All of Hunter's dropbacks into the passing pocket would center upon his own unique "battle within a battle" against one of the greatest defensive backs in NFL history. Hunter broke down the victory versus the Lions in this way:

"The whole season pivoted on that [first] Detroit game," Hunter said. "We were down 17–0. They [the Lions] were all jumping up and down on their sideline. You know the old Tiger Stadium ... both teams were on the same side of the field for the television camera angles. And they're all jumping up and down on their side of the bench, rah rah ... and giving us your typical signal of the middle finger and all. And then Kenny Ellis runs a punt back 80 yards for a touchdown. We had other big plays, but I think the Lions might have held us off if we had not gotten [Ellis'] return.

"Then we get the ball back with about five or six minutes to go on about our 20-yard line, and I hit about six [passes] in a row. Then [wide receiver] Leland Glass ran what they call a post corner [route] against Lem Barney. He [Barney] had picked one off from me earlier in the game. I went over to the sideline [after that interception] and I was a little disgruntled. [Assistant coach] Bart [Starr] said, 'Hey, you threw a good pass. That's *Lem Barney*!' So to get that touchdown [the winning score to Glass] and come back and win that game, 24–23 ... that was special. I say that was the game that turned our whole season around. Our season pivoted on that comeback win."[11]

In dissecting the win at Detroit, Hunter's successes and struggles went hand in hand with each other. He deserved the praise for the game-winning drive and for throwing the game-clinching touchdown pass. And to be honest in assessing his overall performance on that night, Hunter certainly could not totally be blamed for Lem Barney's thievery of his first quarter interception. According to longtime pro football writer Tex Maule, "Leland Glass had taken a few stutter steps before angling to the sideline, and Barney correctly read the stutter and cut in front for the interception."[12]

Scott Hunter was starting to become a good NFL starting quarterback. He was beginning to complete more and more key passes, for both short and

4. A Vital Comeback 63

Quarterbacks coach Bart Starr and quarterback Scott Hunter talk in the Packers locker room while drinking Coca-Colas. Both men were former quarterbacks at the University of Alabama, and in 1972, both men could list starting a playoff game for the Packers on their list of shared accomplishments (© Vernon J. Biever Photo).

long distances, in every type of situation, and against any type of defense. It was a maturation process that all quarterbacks go through, particularly if they stay in the game for any decent amount of time. The win over the Lions was a performance that head coach Dan Devine was hoping to see when he drafted Hunter in the 1971 NFL Draft.

"Hunter was the first man that I drafted on my own," admitted Devine. "We were drafting right after I had taken the job [in early 1971], and I moved his name over from the list of players to be drafted down the line and put it up when we came to the sixth draft choice. He had all the qualities you look for in a quarterback. He set up quickly and well, and he threw well. So when he was still available in the sixth round, I took him. Scott is a fine quarterback."[13]

Assistant coach and quarterback coach Bart Starr did not agree with Dan Devine on too many aspects of football coaching and strategy, but he did agree with the Green Bay head coach on his assessment of Hunter. "I never really had to work with Scott on fundamentals," said Starr during the early stages of the 1972 season. "He had all that already when he came to us.

I've seen rookie quarterbacks who practically had to start from scratch. Some of them didn't even know how to set up or how to release the ball. But Scott was polished technically. Scott's a bright man and he has a good mind."[14]

Hunter was certainly happy to have a fellow University of Alabama alum serving as his mentor at Green Bay. Starr played for the Crimson Tide during his collegiate years (1952–1956) and in time, he was destined for the Pro Football Hall of Fame, as he piloted the Packers to five world championships in the span of just seven years.

"Working with Bart was like reading an encyclopedia," Hunter proclaimed in 1972. "Every day I turned over a new leaf and learned something different. That's still true. I guess I'll be turning over leaves for the rest of my life and never get to the end of the book. Bart refined everything [for me]. Nobody can teach you to throw [however]. You can throw the ball or you can't. That's something you got or you ain't got."[15]

One thing that the Packers definitely did have at this stage of the season was confidence, thanks mostly to securing a couple of big victories. Devine previously described the Packers' win over Dallas as his team's most important. But in reality, the win at Detroit on *Monday Night Football* did more to help the Packers in their drive for a potential playoff spot than did the triumph over the Cowboys. In the aftermath of the come-from-behind win over the Lions, Devine altered his opinion. "We're a pretty emotional team," Devine said. "Dallas was a big win for us, but this one [against the Lions] is bigger. I think that you've got to prove to yourself that you can come from behind and win."[16]

Devine was correct in making such a statement. Until a football team can eliminate a fairly large deficit on the scoreboard late in a game and notch a victory over a good opponent, a potential playoff opponent, the feeling of overall improvement cannot truly and completely be felt among the members of that team. The Packers had now felt such a feeling, and it—by virtue of their win at Detroit's Tiger Stadium on October 16—was a feeling that all of the players in Green and Gold wanted to keep experiencing more of.

One member of the 1972 Packers was at this point of the season holding firmly onto a cautiously optimistic opinion, however, about the progress of his team, which now sported an impressive 4-1 record. Green Bay offensive guard Bill Lueck was seen walking off the field at Tiger Stadium, arm-in-arm with center Ken Bowman and former Packer All-Pro guard Jerry Kramer, who just happened to be in attendance on that night. Lueck sported a most telling wide smile on his face, in the wake of the team's impressive victory over their divisional rivals.

"I definitely thought that we could win our division and go on from there," admitted Lueck. "The dream is always to win the Super Bowl. But also, we didn't want to get too far ahead of ourselves. My best friend on the team was Gale Gillingham. He and I talked often about trying to keep focused. All of us ... [offensive tackle] Dick Himes, Ken Bowman ... the whole offensive line ... we needed to stay focused, and not to get ahead of ourselves. You can win three or four or five games in a row, but if you don't stay focused, you may lose all the rest of them. We just tried to support each other, and look forward to the next game, and not take anything for granted. I remember back in that day, when you played a game against a losing or a supposedly inferior team ... those were the teams that ended up kicking your butt. You weren't prepared, and you were [probably] looking past them. We all wanted to avoid that."[17]

The victory over the Lions gave all of the Packer players the feeling of at least some measure of confidence, in their team and individually as well. There was a noticeable perception that this team could achieve some pretty special things, especially if they just continued to do the things that they were already doing. The older veterans on the squad had not experienced that level of success since the Lombardi era, and the younger players on the roster had seldom enjoyed the fruits of a stunning come-from-behind triumph. All of the players on the team, however, knew that they were not going to be taken for granted anymore by any upcoming opponent that they faced for the rest of the 1972 season. What was now left for Green Bay to accomplish was to prove how well they could keep winning, and how long they could stay on top of the NFC Central divisional standings.

5
A Predictable Slump

Only one team in modern NFL history has never felt the sting of losing at least once during the course of a year. That team was the 1972 Miami Dolphins, a team that had a perfect season, earning an incredible 17-0-0 record. Every other great team achievement in the NFL, and every superb individual accomplishment during that year—including the highlights of the Green Bay Packers—would pale in comparison to the exploits of the undefeated Dolphins. Whether a loss comes in the midst of a string of victories, or whether several losses are piled together or separated apart over the course of a couple of months, no player, coach, team employee, ball boy or fan ever enjoys losing a game in the NFL. The 1972 Dolphins would not experience that type of suffering. The 1972 Packers, unbeknownst to them as the season neared the midway point, were unfortunately about to for the second time.

Green Bay had compiled a very impressive 4-1 record to start the 1972 season, a record that left them all alone in first place in the NFC Central Division, and a record that they were quite proud of. But the team under head coach Dan Devine's leadership did not become complacent. They knew that the year was far from over, and they also knew that their division was still a very competitive one, with every team still in the running to win the "Black and Blue Division." The NFC Central had earned that "Black and Blue" moniker because of its overall rugged, physical, and extremely hard-hitting style of play amongst each of the four teams that comprised that division. Moreover, the Green Bay players also felt that any team in the league could beat any other team in the league if the conditions were ripe for an upset to occur.

That knowledge makes what happened to the 1972 Packers in their next two games (in the latter part of October) stand out as a vivid example of a common football mystery. Why does a seemingly superior team somehow lose to an undeniably inferior team? It has occurred literally hundreds of times since the NFL was formed in 1920, and the reasons for it are many.

Most observers would probably describe the phenomena with the familiar phrase of "playing down to the level of your opponent." Green Bay was scheduled to play the Atlanta Falcons at Milwaukee County Stadium on October 22, 1972. The Falcons were sporting a winning record at 3–2, but they were not considered to be contenders for the NFC Western Division crown. Indeed, Atlanta would complete the 1972 regular season with a mediocre 7–7 record, which was good enough for a second place finish in their division. The Falcons were one of those teams that every other team had to be concerned about, however. Atlanta was capable of springing an upset on any of their opponents. Moreover, they had a lot of very good athletes on their roster, and some of those players were quite familiar with the Packers.

Dave Hampton had previously played for Green Bay from 1969 to 1971, and was a quality runner and kick returner. Coach Devine decided to trade him to Atlanta, however, just prior to the start of the 1972 season, for offensive guard Malcolm Snider. Devine could make that swap for several reasons. One, he needed to build up his offensive line, because he had lost All-Pro guard Gale Gillingham to an ill-advised switch to the defensive side of the line of scrimmage, and then to Gillingham's subsequent season-ending injury. Snider would definitely be a big help on the Packers' offensive line. Two, Devine also knew that he had recently obtained a much-needed running back in the form of one MacArthur Lane from St. Louis, which made Hampton somewhat expendable.

Finally, Devine knew that he could only carry so many halfbacks in his lineup, and he felt that he had some better ones than Hampton still in Green Bay. Like most traded players, Hampton would be playing the game against his old team in week six of the 1972 season with a chip on his shoulder, feeling at least to some degree that he never really got enough of a chance to be the premier running back for Devine in Green Bay. In 1971, Devine decided to give the majority of the carries to his super first-year halfback John Brockington, who responded with 1,105 rushing yards and a Rookie of the Year award. Hampton for his part would go on to have several very good seasons for the Falcons, and he would definitely give his best effort whenever his new team played against his former team.

"I truly don't think I got a fair chance here [in Green Bay]," admitted Hampton. "But that's no sour grapes because I'm happy where I am now [in Atlanta]."[1]

But the reasons for losing a game that you are expected by most observers to win are seemingly more numerous than one can count. Unpredictable factors such as turnovers, penalties, controversial calls from the referees, etc., were just some of the elements that could produce an unexpected defeat. As was the case, all of the above occurred in Green Bay's game on October 22 against Atlanta. But the most visible cause for the result may have been the elements themselves, namely the bad weather.

There was an ominous symbol of worry that befell the Packers as they went through their pre-game warmups. A deluge of rain started to come down, and the showers continued throughout the game. The field would instantly turn into a quagmire. Because Milwaukee County Stadium was primarily a baseball park, the infield dirt turned into a muddy mess in no time. The grounds crew members were busy throughout the afternoon spreading sand all over the puddles of rainwater. It was about as uncomfortable of a playing surface as any player could hope for. Yet the Packers, with their stronger rushing attack, were expected to be able to handle the miserable playing conditions better than the Falcons. Such was not the case, however. Atlanta would dominate the game in factors such as time of possession, total first downs (19 to 10), total offensive plays (71 to 45), and first downs passing (10 to 4). Dave Hampton got the last laugh for his trade from Green Bay to Atlanta during the off-season by rushing for a game-high 93 yards on 30 carries.

"Somebody said Dan Devine said I wasn't durable enough to carry the ball a lot," Hampton said after the game. "I think I proved myself [today]."[2]

It is important to note that no Green Bay player or coach would blame the poor weather conditions for the loss, however, as the blame really belonged to every player. This was a very winnable game for the Packers that was lost in so many different ways.

It started out like Green Bay was going to handle both the elements and the Falcons in the first quarter. The Packers' first drive of the game lasted for 10 plays and ended with a 44-yard field goal by Chester Marcol. Green Bay then recovered a partially deflected Falcons punt on Atlanta's first offensive series of the contest. The ensuing great field position at the Falcons' 24-yard line would quickly result in another Marcol field goal, and Green Bay owned a 6–0 lead as the first quarter expired.

Midway through the second quarter, the Packers would strike again for another score. Although they were not moving the ball close to the Atlanta goal line, Green Bay's offense was getting close enough to give Marcol another shot at three points, which he delivered upon. The "Polish Prince" as he was sometimes called by the press, booted another field goal from 35 yards out, and the Packers were now ahead by a score of 9–0 as halftime neared.

Despite their lead, a fearful sense of worry enveloped the Green Bay sideline, and there was a very good reason for it. The Packers had been unable to score a touchdown, and that futility would haunt them by the game's end. Had just one of their offensive drives ended in the Atlanta end zone, Green Bay would have had enough points to prove victorious. But unbeknownst to them in the second quarter, Devine's team had already scored all of the points that they would register on this day. It would be left to the Packer defense to somehow keep the Falcons off of the scoreboard. As the first half wound down, it proved to be too difficult of a task for them to achieve. Atlanta's offense embarked on the most impressive drive of the game late in the second quarter. A total of 14 plays in the mud and wet grass ended when fullback Art Malone dove over left guard from the 1-yard line to pull the Falcons closer at 9–7, just seconds before halftime. The game's momentum had thus changed in only a few minutes.

The third quarter would feature only one score, a 24-yard field goal off the foot of Atlanta placekicker Bill Bell, which gave the Falcons their first lead of the game, 10–9. A controversial roughing the passer penalty on Green Bay linebacker Fred Carr preceded Bell's kick. Carr's infraction also cancelled a big interception on the same play at a key moment of the game by Green Bay safety Al Matthews. That penalty flag certainly surprised Carr. "I hit him [Falcons quarterback Bob Berry] just as he released the ball," explained Carr after the game.[3]

It was noticeably clear by this time of the afternoon that this would not be a high-scoring contest. This would be a battle of attrition, where every mistake would be multiplied in the eyes of everyone watching this struggle, and where every good play might end up becoming a game-winning play. This was a struggle where the punters on both teams might have the biggest say in deciding the victor, as field position could become the most important factor in determining a winner or a loser. Turnovers would also be a noteworthy divisor in this game. A fumble by Green Bay quarterback Scott Hunter deep in Packers territory in the third quarter gave the Falcons an excellent chance to boost their lead. Hunter would in retrospect accurately describe the game as "a mudfest."[4] Unfortunately for Atlanta, Bill Bell missed the ensuing field goal attempt for his team following Hunter's fumble from 38 yards out, and the score remained unchanged. Bell would go on to miss a total of two of his three field goal attempts in this game. Added to those misses was the fact that the Falcons' running backs were also not immune either from fumbling the wet football.

With 4:34 left in the fourth quarter and with the score still situated at 10–9 in favor of Atlanta, an untimely fumble by Malone was recovered by Packers defensive end Clarence Williams at the Falcons' 37-yard line. In spite of all of their previous mistakes and missed opportunities, Green Bay could still somehow manage to win this game. Three straight runs by John Brockington placed the ball at the Atlanta 31-yard line with two minutes remaining. Chester Marcol, who had made all three of his previous field goal attempts, would be called upon once more, this time from 39 yards out, to give Green Bay what would be the relief of securing an incredible victory. The snap from the wet ground by Packers center Ken Bowman was right on target, and Ron Widby's hold on the sloppy turf was perfectly fine. Marcol's kick seemed to be solid enough, and it had plenty of distance. Unfortunately for Marcol, the ball was hit with an inauspicious gust of wind at the worst possible time, and it sailed just wide to the right of the upright. The Falcons held on for the final 1:55 to post a 10–9 win. The loss for the Packers was palpable and disconcerting for everyone involved. It was sudden, abrupt, and no player or coach on the team expected it, especially considering how well the squad had been doing prior to this game.

"I really didn't feel as though there was any real pressure on that last kick," said a dejected but composed Marcol following the loss.[5] "Mud can be impossible. I suppose if I had missed a 50 yarder on a dry day, I'd say wind. Right now, I'd say mud.[6] There was nothing different about the last field goal than any of the other three [which he made]. I did slip a little, but just really didn't kick it square like I wanted to. I had to kick from a spot on the muddy infield of the stadium's baseball diamond, [but] I don't think the weather affected me. I can't blame the rain, the snap, or the holder. It just tailed away a little bit."[7]

Marcol's teammates rapidly came to his aid after the unexpected loss to the Falcons. "He's going to win a lot of games for us," said mammoth defensive tackle Mike McCoy. "Heck, he has already. This loss wasn't his fault. I hope this doesn't hurt his confidence."[8] McCoy's partner on the defensive line—veteran Bob Brown—was also discussing Marcol in favorable terms. "I just thought he'd put it [Marcol's final field goal attempt] through the uprights," admitted Brown. "I was sure of it. But then he missed one today. That doesn't take anything away from the fact that he's matured into a fine young kicker. I had trouble with the footing out there near the end, and I'm sure he had trouble, too. But I still have complete confidence in Chester Marcol and in our kicking game."[9]

Green Bay head coach Dan Devine was not as diplomatic as his placekicker and the rest of his players, however. The various factors of turnovers, controversial referee calls, and missed opportunities that all played a part in Green Bay's second loss of the 1972 season—which dropped them into a first-place tie at 4–2 with the Detroit Lions—would all be addressed in one degree or another by Devine after the game. But it was his bitter opinions about the men who officiated the game against the Falcons that drew the majority of Devine's ire.

"I never argue with an official," explained Devine. "When I'm sure I'm right, I state my case. Every time I've done that in this league the movies have proved I'm right. I haven't been proven wrong yet. I'm batting 1.000, but it doesn't do you any good on Wednesday to say you should have won, when the guy [actually the league office] admits he [the referee] made a mistake."[10]

Devine was not just referring to the supposed late hit by Packers linebacker Fred Carr in the Atlanta game which cost Green Bay an interception and which would eventually result in the game-winning field goal for the

Falcons. His comments also touched on the botched fumble/muffed lateral by his fullback MacArthur Lane in the loss to Oakland in the second week of the season. That particular play proved to be the difference in the Raiders' 20–14 victory over the Packers. That muff/fumble was also a play in which representatives of the league office admitted a few days later that the referees had made the wrong call, costing Green Bay a chance to win the game. Devine was not finished with his bitter invective, however.

"I've got a bunch of guys battling their guts out trying to win a championship," remarked Devine following the loss to Atlanta. "Then they run into this kind of malarkey [the apologies from the league office stemming from the controversial calls]. It's not fair to them and it's not fair to my coaches. If I'm a poor sport, then I guess that's the way it is. I'm a poor sport."[11] Devine at this time knew well enough that such criticism of the referees would usually result in a monetary fine, imposed upon him by NFL Commissioner Pete Rozelle. "I think I probably said too much about it already," admitted the Packers head coach.[12]

It is important to note that a big reason why the Falcons were able to beat the Packers on this day was by imitating some of the basic running elements from Green Bay's typical game plans. Atlanta ran the ball constantly, and did it effectively enough to hold on to the ball for 36 minutes and 25 seconds of elapsed game time. The Packers could keep the ball for only 23 minutes and 35 seconds, which was the least amount of time of possession that their offense would accrue for any game in 1972. That lack of time on offense was detrimental to their chances of scoring more than nine points against the Falcons. It was—and still is—all very simplistic in theory. If you do not possess the ball, you will not score points.

Despite narrowly losing to the Falcons, however, the Packers were not without their laurels. Green Bay's overall improvement from this stage in 1971 was obvious to see. "One big reason for the improvement [at Green Bay] is having [Bart] Starr on the coaching staff," proclaimed former Packer Dave Hampton. "The offense is more disciplined. No one knows the Green Bay system as well as Bart. With him on the sidelines, it's a source of confidence."[13]

Standout and future Hall of Fame Atlanta defensive end Claude Humphrey would go on to agree with his teammate. Humphrey praised the exemplary efforts of the Packers' rushing attack after his team's 10–9 win over Green Bay. "Lane and Brockington block for each other so well, and they're both halfback-type fullbacks," said Humphrey. "Brockington would rather run over you than around you. He doesn't care about juking you. He makes you tackle him."[14] Atlanta head coach Norm Van Brocklin would add that "The Packers come off the wall at you. We had to pack all the pads we had for this trip [to Milwaukee]."[15]

Earning generous accolades from their opponents was nice, but the

Green Bay players and coaches were certainly not thinking about garnering complements at this stage of the 1972 season. They had just failed to claim a game against Atlanta that they definitely should have won, and that fact alone was very upsetting to the team. The Packers could partly attribute their two losses in their first six games to flukes, and even the casual observer could admit that the team was just hit with a decent dose of bad luck. But the losses to Oakland and Atlanta could also have been blamed on the Packers' own untimely mistakes. A stronger effort to hold on to the ball with a stronger grip, or to become just a little more consistent in the kicking game, were identifiable remedies to the team's recent miscues.

But the overall situation did not get any better for Green Bay in the following week. In fact, their forlorn state of affairs was compounded by a near-repeat of the Atlanta fiasco. The Packers would once again be at home for their seventh game of the regular season. This time, Lambeau Field would be the site for their week seven contest against the defending NFC Central Division Champions, the Minnesota Vikings, who were surprisingly mired in the midst of a last place 2–4 record. The beginning of Wisconsin football weather made its initial appearance of the season, as the temperature dipped to below 40 degrees, and the overcast skies would return for the second

The NFL experimented on several occasions throughout the 1970s by inviting cheerleading squads from opposing teams to cheer for their team at visiting stadiums across the league. The Minnesota Vikings cheerleaders, known as the Parkettes, enjoyed their opportunity to cheer their Vikings on to victory over the Packers in Green Bay on October 29 (courtesy the Parkettes Alumni Foundation).

straight week. But unlike the previous game in Milwaukee versus the Falcons, this contest against the Vikings seven days later in Green Bay would be minus any drops of rainfall.

Notwithstanding the cloudy weather, a new entity of the lovely nature would be making an appearance at Lambeau Field on October 29, and that entourage would be the Minnesota Vikings cheerleaders, known as the Parkettes. Someone in the Packers' front office got the bright idea that inviting your opponents' cheerleading squad to Green Bay might bring about some reverse psychology and help the fortunes of the home team. The Packers back then (and to this very day) did not have a full-time cheerleading squad, as they preferred instead to invite local high school girls to cheer on the sidelines. The Parkettes would stay along the Vikings' sideline all during the game, and the reverse psychology would turn out to work ... in reverse. Those young ladies somehow brought the Minnesota team the good luck that the Norsemen needed.

The game began eerily similar to the Atlanta contest from the week before. Green Bay struck quickly on their first offensive drive, which lasted for 12 plays and took eight minutes and two seconds off of the game clock. It ended short of the Vikings' end zone, however (just like the Packers' first drive in the Atlanta game). Green Bay's Chester Marcol successfully kicked a 41-yard field goal to salvage at least some points from the offense's initial effort, and the Packers led, 3–0. The Green and Gold surge would fortunately continue a few minutes later, however, when Minnesota halfback Oscar Reed was hit hard by Green Bay middle linebacker Jim Carter, fumbled the ball, and Packers safety Jim Hill made the recovery at the Vikings' 42-yard line. Six plays later, Green Bay was situated at the Minnesota 6-yard line, where they faced a third-and-goal predicament. All but one of the previous six plays from scrimmage were runs. The Vikings' defense expected a pass from Scott Hunter, but what kind of pass? Green Bay head coach Dan Devine was getting sick and tired by this time of having to settle for a field goal (as he did on several occasions during the previous game versus the Falcons), but he also knew that he could ill afford to come this close to the Minnesota goal line and not obtain at least a field goal. Devine decided to call for one more pass. Veteran wide receiver Carroll Dale would be the primary target, and the route that Dale would run would be an simple down-and-out pattern. As it turned out, Dale was guarded by Nate Wright, a quick and able second-year cornerback, but also a somewhat inexperienced one. Wright should have played Dale much closer than he did, and Dale took advantage of his adversary's lack of savvy. Scott Hunter's pass to the near corner of the end zone was high enough for Dale to catch it, but too high for Wright to get a hand on it. Dale leaped to snare the ball, and managed to come down with both of his feet in the end zone. Green Bay now owned a 10–0 lead with 59 seconds left to play in the first quarter.

The second quarter was a difficult one for both teams. Green Bay's offensive output was curtailed sharply by the stalwart Minnesota defense, which limited the Packers to just two first downs and a missed 43-yard field goal attempt by Marcol. The Vikings offense accrued seven first downs, but they also committed two fumbles, both of which were recovered by the Packers. Minnesota was able to register a 22-yard field goal by placekicker Fred Cox with 14 seconds left in the first half, however. Green Bay led at halftime, 10–3.

Minnesota quarterback Fran Tarkenton had a decade's worth of experience over what Green Bay quarterback Scott Hunter possessed. That gulf of an experience level would turn out to be very beneficial for the Vikings during the second half. Tarkenton knew by this time that this game would go to whichever team made the fewest offensive mistakes. He also knew that he would keep his throws in the high percentage range, preferring to throw short passes in places where his receivers would be the only ones who would have a chance to catch them. Tarkenton finished the game by completing 13 passes in 22 attempts for 192 yards. Most importantly, the veteran signal caller would throw zero interceptions.

Hunter was not so fortunate, however. He would begin what would become the worst half of statistical football in his pro career by throwing the first of his four interceptions. With less than three minutes elapsed in the third quarter, Hunter tried to throw a pass to Dale on a play that was very similar to his touchdown pass to Dale in the first quarter. This time, however, Minnesota safety Jeff Wright played Dale tighter than Nate Wright had done earlier. Jeff Wright's interception at the Vikings' 47-yard line would not result in any points for Minnesota. But the next time that they got their hands on the ball, the Vikings offense would have its best drive of the game. Tarkenton mixed his short passes and some key runs by halfback Ed Marinaro expertly, and with a little over five minutes remaining in the third quarter, veteran Minnesota fullback Bill Brown burrowed into the Green Bay end zone from one yard out. The game was now tied, 10–10.

"It has constantly been little things all year that seem to have turned the tide on us," said Green Bay head coach Dan Devine in a contemplative mood after the game. "Our inexperience showed. We just didn't get the big play. This is still the game of big plays."[16]

To their credit, the Packers offense revived itself with one big play. Hunter completed what would be the longest pass of the game for either quarterback, a 48-yard bomb down the far sideline to Carroll Dale. But just as soon as Hunter appeared to be moving his offense, two successive incompletions ended any hopes for a Green Bay touchdown on this drive. Chester Marcol did manage to give the lead back to his team, however, by booting a 34-yard field goal. The fourth quarter began with Green Bay owning a slim 13–10 advantage.

That tenuous edge vanished with 4:11 elapsed in the fourth quarter. Minnesota's Fred Cox kicked a 32-yard field goal, tying the struggle at 13–13. That deadlock would survive for only 43 more seconds. On first-and-10 from his own 22-yard line, Hunter sent Packers setback John Brockington down the far sideline, where he appeared to be wide open. By 1972, the Minnesota defense had a roster of veterans with experience. Free safety Paul Krause was one such veteran, and he stepped in front of Brockington, intercepted Hunter's pass, and returned it 32 yards for a go-ahead touchdown. Krause just barely beat Green Bay offensive guard Malcolm Snider into the end zone, while the Vikings' Parkettes leaped and cheered with joy along the sideline.

Quarterback Scott Hunter (No. 16 at right) manages to get a pass off against onrushing Minnesota defensive tackle Alan Page (No. 88) during the Vikings' 27–13 win over the Packers (Vernon J. Biever via AP).

"We were in blitz coverage [and] I was working an in-and-out with the strong safety and my job was to take the inside," described Krause. "The receiver [Brockington] started inside and then broke out. I just happened to get in front of him."[17] Brockington lauded Krause's effort. "I never saw him coming," admitted the shocked setback. "He just came out of the clear blue sky [which was actually grey] and picked it off. There was no way I could catch him since I was backing up and he was heading the other way. It was a super interception."[18]

Minnesota now had their first lead of the game at 20–13, but neither team could gain a first down during either of their ensuing possessions. The Vikings were winning the battle of field position, however, as evidenced by punter Mike Eischeid's 55-yard punt, which was downed by Minnesota special teams player and reserve wide receiver Jim Lindsey at the Green Bay 2-yard line. The Packers were still stuck on the same yard line on third down. Hunter dropped back into his end zone and threw for setback MacArthur Lane. The pass ricocheted off of Lane's hands at the Green Bay 11-yard line. Minnesota outside linebacker Wally Hilgenberg was running behind Lane, when to his surprise, the deflected ball flew right into his hands at the 14-yard line. Hilgenberg proceeded to weave his way toward the Packer goal line, and thanks to key blocks by Minnesota defenders Gary Larsen, Roy Winston, and Bobby Bryant, he reached it. Green Bay's Leland Glass and Bill Lueck tackled Hilgenberg, but the veteran linebacker had already fallen into the end zone. It was the game-clinching score.

Scott Hunter's final pass of the day occurred on the next series, when he threw down the middle of the field, where Minnesota outside linebacker Roy Winston intercepted with 2:16 left on the game clock. The Vikings offense took it from there and used up the remainder of the time, as Minnesota prevailed in what was a must-win game for the Norsemen, 27–13.

"We've had that backs-to-the-wall feeling for the last three games," admitted Minnesota quarterback Fran Tarkenton. "We just had to have this one, especially against Green Bay."[19]

Hunter recalled the disheartening turning point of this game, and he was man enough to take the blame for it. "I blew the game," admitted the Green Bay quarterback. "We were playing well, but I led Paul Krause over there with my eyes when I was looking for John [Brockington] on a B Flat Up. He [Krause] intercepted the pass and ran it in for a touchdown. You know, we're in a position to beat those guys [the Vikings]. We're playing them nose to nose, and I just made a mistake."[20]

After the game, Dan Devine displayed an infrequent moment of support for his quarterback, but he still managed to somewhat deride the members of his defense. In describing the Krause interception, Devine said, "I thought the ball was thrown well, but it was a big play by Krause. We didn't get the big plays from the defense like they [the Minnesota defense] got."[21]

The Packers had thus lost two straight games, finishing the first half of the 1972 regular season with a 4–3 record. Perhaps the only good thing to come from this was the fact that the night after Green Bay's loss to the Vikings, the Detroit Lions also lost to the Dallas Cowboys on *Monday Night Football*. Green Bay and Detroit were now after seven weeks back in a first place tie with each other in the NFC Central Division. "I don't feel we're out of it," said Dan Devine, referring to his team's hopes for a title. "It's going to be an interesting race now."[22]

Coach Devine nevertheless had to feel some level of angst with the team's second straight loss. They were experiencing their best start since the Lombardi era, and then all of a sudden, they had hit a brick wall. Most football games can be won or lost by mistakes. The proper thing to say after a tough defeat is to praise your opponent, and more often than not, every team does that. But the Packers needed to look inward at their effort during the previous two weeks as well. The honest assessment of the losses to Atlanta and Minnesota involved their own mistakes. Untimely turnovers formed the core of the Packers' miscues, but a simple missed field goal cost the team a predictable win over the Falcons. Devine's players had to somehow determine what they needed to do in order to stop the losses, and resume with winning.

Green Bay's star running back, John Brockington, was realistic and at the same time optimistic following the team's two-game losing streak. "You're really upset when you lose," said Brockington, "but we were winning up until that point. So it wasn't that bad. It was a two-game setback, but we knew that we could bounce back from it."[23]

Brockington's positive thinking was fortunately shared by the vast majority of his teammates, and as we shall see, that was vital in helping the Packers deal with their future contests. One final note regarding the loss to the Norsemen: The Minnesota Vikings cheerleaders—the Parkettes—who seemed to have brought such good luck to their team on October 29, 1972, have not been invited back to Lambeau Field since.

6
Losing a Coach, Gaining a Perspective

There would be two teams in the NFL that would be fortunate enough to win their conference titles and compete against each other in Super Bowl VII. It would take a combination of the physical health of most of their starting players, combined with key strategical decisions from players and coaches alike on game days throughout the regular and post-seasons, in order to become one of those two conference champions. It would also take a lot of positive chemistry among the men on any team to win enough games to climb to the summit of pro football. All of these factors would be equally important in order to achieve the greatest victory of all—a win in the Super Bowl. Assuming that most teams will be attacked sometime during the course of a season by the relentless factors of untimely injuries, game day mistakes (i.e., fumbles, interceptions, missed field goals, etc.), poor play calling from their head coaches, their offensive and defensive coordinators, and possibly from their quarterbacks, a lack of physical strength and endurance, and the specter of the growing pressure to produce positive results on the field and to win, and you have more than enough detrimental components going against your team. All of those factors almost seems to be an assurance of registering more defeats than victories for any team during the path of a long NFL season.

The pressure to succeed affects different people in different ways. Some people are better able to handle large amounts of pressure, while some are not. When a pro football team begins a season with a 4–1 record, as the 1972 Green Bay Packers did, pressure seems to be almost nonexistent to the casual onlooker. Losing, however, will impel the wraith of pressure to re-emerge on the scene in a most visible fashion. Players and coaches who stay in the NFL for a number of years will eventually have to face pressure, regardless of their record or their level of achievements. How they handle it says much about the character of each individual. How did the Packer players handle their

6. Losing a Coach, Gaining a Perspective

two-game losing streak going into the mid-season stage of their 1972 schedule? How did their coaches handle it? Just as insightful was how well the Green Bay players and coaching staff handled success. Did they become complaisant? Did they get too overconfident? The 1972 Packers—probably more than any other NFL team in memory—had to rally around and support each other during both their wins and their losses. The internal strife and untimely confusion that was caused by their head coach—which will be addressed in this chapter shortly—forced the players to become unselfish professionals in the truest sense of the term.

The team's attitude revealed much about how the players felt about each other. Although many were new to the Packers' roster, the camaraderie on the squad was simply outstanding right from the onset of the season. The feelings that the men on the 1972 Packers had for each of their teammates could probably be best described as a faithful friendship, and as a promise to have each other's back. Such sentiments served as a very important foundation for the team, and it was evident and visible by observing the huge amount of confidence that the players had in each other. That confidence transferred to victories on the football field. The players who comprised the Green Bay lineup in 1972 were solid and united. It was almost as if these young men and these older veterans, many of whom had just recently met each other, had blended together magically and astonishingly right from the very first handshake. Just as the team started to win, so too did the positive feelings of the players gel and grow almost immediately, as they became more and more familiar with each other.

"I've told people over the years, that the magic of that team ... the greatness of that team ... was the oneness," expressed quarterback Scott Hunter in a contemplative interview many years later. "I was the weakest link, because I was a second-year quarterback. I wasn't a five, or six, or seven-year veteran, you know. I was the weakest link. I mean it was so much oneness on that team. Everybody was together. Defense, offense ... everybody was friends. We all went and had dinners together and so forth. It was just a wonderful team from that standpoint of oneness."[1]

Hunter's fellow backfield buddy, star running back John Brockington, concurred with the sentiments of his quarterback. "On some teams in this league, you have everybody bitching at everybody else," Brockington said in 1972. "On this team we don't have that. On a lot of other teams there's friction, but not here. You know you are going to make mistakes at times and so is the other fellow. But nobody yells at you. We pull like dogs together, then we go out and have a good time. We dig each other. That's the kind of team it is."[2]

As it turned out, the players *had* to stick together with each other. This was because they played for a head coach who stunningly changed his attitude and his actions almost on a regular basis, which forced the players to adjust on the fly, sometimes on a week-to-week basis. Green Bay head coach Dan Devine was both inwardly and outwardly sickened by the close losses to the Falcons and the Vikings, and he had seemingly reached his limit of patience and restraint following those two games. Conversely and somewhat identically, the Packer players had also reached their limit of patience and understanding with Coach Devine.

In any organization or business, the person who is at the top of the company ladder, be his or her designation listed as owner, boss, CEO, upper management head, or head coach, sets the tone for his or her employees, students, or players. That person sets an example—a good or a bad example—for everyone else to follow. This has been the case ever since America has had a structure of learning and working. A pro football team is no different. The head coach and head decision maker for the 1972 Green Bay Packers was Dan Devine. His assistant coaches and his players would be expected to learn from him, obey him, and follow his lead. That is how any business in America works.

But there was a problem. What happens when the head coach is obviously in over his head, incapable of doing his job properly? What happens when the head coach displays to his underlings many moments of sheer incompetence, or extends many bad examples of poor preparation and faulty decisions? What happens when the head coach displays and delivers angry tirades and insults, or humiliates his players in front of many of the other players? Does anyone stand up to him and contradict him? Should not the assistant coaches do so? Where does the courage to do the right thing and basic common sense merge into decisions and actions by the rank and file? Where would that sacrifice come from? What would the high price be for telling Coach Devine that he was wrong? Would a player be cut from the team for doing so? Who would want to risk losing their job? The vast majority of the players from that era did not make anywhere near the high salaries that today's NFL players make. Standing up to Devine to voice their opinions of him and his skewed approach to the team, to the players, and to the game itself would very possibly incur his wrath. A benching would be a definite result, assuming that the player who stood up to him was not cut from the team outright. Would the head coach then telephone many of his contacts around the league and tell dozens of other decision makers across the NFL not to sign the player who stood up to him? Was there a remedy to this depressing and discouraging problem that the players faced?

No one on the 1972 Green Bay roster knew the answers to those questions, but you can bet that many of them thought about the problem regularly. They might have even dreamed about telling Coach Devine what their true feelings were regarding him during the course of that season. Some may have even aspired to actually make their voice be heard, regardless of the consequences. Some players just kept their mouths shut and tried to ignore what Devine was saying and doing. Others just shook their heads in disbelief. Some players probably felt that the assistant coaches should have interceded for them, but none of them really did. For whatever reason, they too did not (at least as far as could be discovered) confront Devine about his decisions and his attitudes. Perhaps they were fearful of the supposed blacklisting (similar to what the players might have faced) that might be labeled against them by Devine, should they stand up and confront him.

On paper at the beginning of the year, the leadership of this team from the head coach pointed to the misfortune of nothing more than another losing season for the post–Lombardi Packers. The fact that this team succeeded beyond anyone's expectations made the story of the 1972 Green Bay Packers so unique and so incredible, considering all of the difficulties that they had to endure with the decisions and the actions of their head coach. In all of the history of pro football, there are few teams—if any—that have had as many unfortunate problems and distasteful situations with their head coach as what the 1972 Green Bay Packers had to deal with.

Undoubtedly the one Devine decision that stood out as a hallmark of the category of utter ridiculousness involved his plan at the latter part of the preseason for the Green Bay offensive line. The Packers possessed one of the best offensive guards in the pro game in Gale Gillingham. Yet despite that fact, Devine had the unbelievable notion that by moving Gillingham to the defensive unit, he (Gillingham) would instantly become an All-Pro on the other side of the line of scrimmage. Pro football had by the 1970s already become a game with specialized talent, and asking a player to play from one side of the ball to the other was simply ludicrous. Gillingham was a professional and a team leader, and he knew that all of his teammates were looking up to him to set a positive example. So Gillingham sucked up his pride and moved to defense under Devine's instruction. It was certainly not what the big guard wanted to do, but he did it anyway, in a constructive effort at leading by example. The result as we now know was disastrous, as Gillingham suffered an injury very early in the season. He was eventually moved back to his old offensive guard position by Devine, but he would never be the same All-Pro that he was prior to 1972 after he returned from his injury. Chalk up another Coach Devine decision that failed to pan out.

The decisions involving the defensive secondary were also Devine's. But in a rare exception of pure and realized good luck, both Devine and the team were blessed with extremely beneficial fortune overnight. Devine took a risk with a new set of four starting players, two of them were brand new to the team (Willie Buchanon and Jim Hill). He then made the decision to move his other two defensive backs (Al Randolph and Ken Ellis) to different positions. One might be able to credit those moves to good luck as well, but in reality, Devine made the decision to move Randolph and Ellis. If you want to blame Devine for his bad decisions, it stands to reason that you also have to praise him for his good decisions.

Unfortunately for the Packers, Devine's good decisions in 1972 were few in number. And in a luckless vein, it is the bad or the wrong decisions that Devine made during that season that still resonates with the players from that team. Devine's big mistakes seem to stand out the most to those men all these years later. When you discuss the 1972 season with them, they inevitably end up mentioning one miscue or another that had their head coach's handwriting all over it. One of the important reasons why some of the players fault Devine was not actually Devine's fault, however. It is because they (and virtually everybody else associated with the sport) felt that it was naturally very difficult for a college head coach to go right into the pro head coaching ranks. Back in the 1970s, that practice was not too common, and even though you see more of it decades later, you still rarely see evidence of a successful college coach achieving instant success as a head coach in the NFL.

Superstar running back John Brockington became the first man in NFL history to earn over 1,000 yards rushing in each of his first three years in the league. Brockington averaged 73.4 yards rushing per game in 1972 (courtesy the Green Bay Packers).

"I think that he should have stayed right where he was [at the University of Missouri]," admitted John Brockington. "And that's not a bad thing. He wanted a different kind of athlete, not a guy who was 26 or 27 or even 32 years of age. These guys [here in Green Bay] were seasoned pros, and they don't take kindly to college coaches telling them what to do. Dan was exactly that. We soon found out that this guy [Devine] was not up to the task. He wasn't watching film, he wasn't learning the game the way that he should. Devine was an egomaniac. You know it was all about him. He was very strange. He would say things like 'If I had to start a football team, I would start it with so and so.' And so and so was never a Green Bay Packer. He said that more than once. And at that time there was probably more Green Bay Packers in the Hall of Fame than any team in the league.

"But he [Devine] was never a Packer. It was almost like he wanted to replace Lombardi's image in Green Bay. Well you can't do it. Because Lombardi came on at a time that they [the Packers] were woeful, and won three championships in a row, five altogether and two Super Bowls. You're not going to replace a guy like that. You have to do your own thing. And that's what Mike Holmgren did. Holmgren didn't try to replace Lombardi. He *embraced* Lombardi, because that town *loves* him [Lombardi]. The stadium is on Lombardi Avenue for crying out loud. Holmgren did his own thing."[3]

Throughout the history of the game of pro football, comparing coaches has always been something that fans, players, the media, and even other coaches have done on an annual basis. In Green Bay Packer history, *nobody* was going to be compared to Vince Lombardi, and there is a very good chance that no one ever will. Despite that fact, Devine may have subconsciously felt that he could replace Coach Lombardi in the minds of Packer fans. Naturally, he was never able to do that.

"A player personnel director came to me one time and told me that Devine said to him that he [Devine] didn't want to hear that Lombardi shit or the Lombardi name mentioned anymore in this locker room," said Hall of Fame Green Bay linebacker Dave Robinson. "That's just the way he was. Nobody wanted to be around Devine. We won in spite of him. After '72 they had a sign that said 'Everything's Fine with Devine.' He [Devine] got rid of everybody. There were only a few of the Lombardi people that he kept. He just cleaned house with everybody else."[4]

And almost instantly, the Packer players noticed that there were other coaches that Devine could never be compared to as well. John Brockington related several stories to prove that belief:

"I only had two other head coaches before Devine," recalled Brockington. "One in high school, Mo Finkelstein, who was a hell of a football coach, and Woody Hayes [at Ohio State University]. And I can tell you right now, with Woody and Mo, we never went into a football game thinking that we could lose it. And I remember that they would say to us, 'Here's how we are going to beat this football team. This is how we're going to do it.' By Thursday [two days prior to game day], they would say, 'Okay, the hay is in the barn.' By Friday [the day before game day], they would say, 'Okay, the nail is in their coffin.' Every week from my freshman year to my varsity [senior] year, we would hear that ... the hay is in the barn, the nail is in their coffin. And we *believed* them [Mo and Woody]. He was *Woody Hayes* ... if he knew that we were going to beat this football team, then that's what we were going to do. I get to the Packers, and we have this weak-kneed coach [Devine] talking about 'We're not as good as this or that football team' or 'We're going to have to play the best game that we have ever played to win.' What the hell?!? Even if we are not as good [as our opponent], don't tell us that! Make us believe that we are better [than our opponent]! He [Devine] was just the worst. I've never seen a coach like that in my life! That playoff game [against Washington] was the coup de grace [see Chapter Ten for details on the December 24, 1972, NFC Divisional Playoff game between Green Bay and Washington].

"One time Mac [MacArthur Lane] and I led the conference in rushing [1972]. At one point Devine said, 'If I had to pick two backs [to start a team with], I would pick Joe Moore and Jimmy Harrison.' [Author's note: Joe Moore and Jimmy Harrison were both running backs who played for the Chicago Bears. They both played for Devine at the University of Missouri. Neither ever gained more than 622 yards rushing in any single year during their brief pro careers.] I thought, oh my gosh! Can you believe that crap?!? And we [left that meeting] and went to practice. Mac and I would hit the two-man [blocking] sled and try to turn that damn sled upside-down.

"And then you know what that little chump stain [Devine] did? So we go back to [training] camp for the 1973 season. The first team meeting over at St. Norbert's College [where the Packers spent their summer training camp during those years]. And this joker [Devine] comes out with his little pink cardigan sweater and his slacks, and he has three roles of films in his hands. And he says, 'You guys think you're so good? You think you're so good [center Ken] Bowman? You think you're so good [guard Gale] Gillingham? You want to see these films? You want to see these films from last year's playoff game?' We should have told him, 'Yeah, let's see the film! Let's see them! Let's see how you [Devine] kept us running the same play against a five-man [defensive] line when all we had to do was pass [the ball].'"[5]

Speaking of game films, another story about how Devine's honesty (or lack of such) during his Packer years had one man scratching his head in disbelief. It is a recollection from former Packers assistant coach Bob Schnelker, and it proved that even the other coaches were aware that the head man in Green Bay was probably not the caliber of man that should have been in that particular position.

"Dan Devine knew nothing of X's and O's," asserted Schnelker after 1971. "One time I and our film guy [Al Treml] handed Devine some game films in those old tin film roles. But we suspected that Devine was not even watching the films. So we stuck some toothpicks on the inside rims of the cans, so that when the cans were opened, the toothpicks would fall out. We wanted to see if Devine was watching the films. If he did, there would be no toothpicks in the can, because they would have fallen out. So we asked Devine if he watched the films that we gave him, and he claimed that he did watch those films. But when he handed the tin film cans back to me, the toothpicks were still there!"[6]

Whether or not Dan Devine possessed honesty as his trademark trait could certainly be questioned. But one thing that he definitely had that was beyond question was his ego. Many of his former players have called him an "ego-maniac." Some of Devine's feelings and beliefs were in retrospect hard for anyone to believe, considering what was actually happening back at that time.

"I don't always say a lot at practice—it varies from day to day and week to week—but I've always been on top of everything going on out on the field," said Devine.[7] In reality, many of his players and most of the assistant coaches would disagree with those particular assessments from their head coach. When asked about how Devine coached the team, Green Bay offensive guard Bill Lueck, who was one of the more even-tempered and analytical members of the squad, commented that it was more appropriate to ask "how he *didn't* coach the team. I would agree with my teammates," Lueck continued. "If we would have had a decent coach ... [pause] ... I hate to be critical of Dan, but from the moment that he first came to his first training camp, he was in over his head."[8]

Verbal and vivid proof of Devine being "over his head" in coaching pro football could be gleaned from listening to some of his own misinterpreted words. One of Devine's statements was actually meant to inspire his players, but it unfortunately had the opposite effect.

"I had seen better overall scrimmages, many, many better ones [than what he was seeing in Green Bay], while I was a college coach. Better blocking, better tackling—not by everybody, but overall."[9]

All too often, however, such statements (which were repeated by Devine to the Packer players on a regular basis) did little more than increase the bitter feelings that his players had for him, and the contempt that they had for him as well.

One particular player certainly had the authentic credibility to complain about Devine. Former All-Pro and eventual Hall of Fame outside linebacker Dave Robinson had experienced the highest of highs as a member of the Lombardi-led Packer World Championship teams during the 1960s. Now he was playing in 1972 for

Veteran outside linebacker Dave Robinson was the glue that held the Packers linebacking corps together in 1972. Robinson was a team leader who often stood up to head coach Dan Devine, which resulted in an occasional benching and his eventual ticket out of Green Bay. Robinson would be enshrined in the Pro Football Hall of Fame in 2013 (courtesy the Green Bay Packers).

a head coach who was definitely his own man with his own unpredictable mind set. His memories of his brief time with Coach Devine (in 1971 and 1972) reveal his own obvious perceptions and feelings of disdain for the man.

"We talk about Vince [Lombardi] giving those inspirational speeches. Devine never did that. He just stood there," recalled Robinson. "One year, the Bears had the number one draft pick from Missouri [where Devine served as head coach prior to coming to Green Bay]. I think he was a fullback. He came down the kickoff team and made one hell of a tackle. He really did. Dan Devine stopped the film and said, 'See that? That kid right there is going to be All-Pro someday. That shows how good he is. When I came here [to Green Bay], I wanted to draft him in the first round, and they [the other Packers coaches and front office advisors whom Devine was pointing at] talked me into drafting you, John [Brockington]. When this kid [the Chicago player in the film] makes All-Pro, you better be on the same team and not embarrass me.'"[10]

Besides humiliating John Brockington with such a statement—a man who most experts would agree was the best running back to wear a Packers uniform during the entire decade of the 1970s—Devine also exhibited his lack of understanding about what it took to play in the NFL. Sometimes, despite all of the report gathering, film study, and a wealth of interviews of a potential recruit from his former coaches and teammates, scouting a college player can amount to little more than a guessing game. Scouts who fail to evaluate players properly and successfully will usually not be scouts for very long. Nevertheless, it is not uncommon for head coaches to ignore the advice of his scouts, especially if the head coach gets a special "feeling" about a player that he wants on his roster bad enough. Dave Robinson continues the story of the player that Devine wanted instead of John Brockington, but at the last minute decided not to select:

"Well, that kid couldn't play dick," Robinson bluntly confirmed. "Recently they wrote an article in Arkansas where they named the worst pick of each [pro] team, and he was the Chicago Bears pick as the worst they ever had.

"When Devine made a mistake, the whole team suffered. We were playing the Chicago Bears and somebody [on the Bears] had a long kickoff return. Devine comes into the meeting room and shows us the Missouri highlight film. On the highlight film, Missouri kicks off against Kansas, the returner drops the ball and gets wiped out at the five-yard line. Then Dan says, 'That's the kind of tackling that I want on our kickoff team.' And somebody on our team said, 'We aren't tackling that bum. What would that [Missouri] team do against Gale Sayers?' Devine got upset [with that remark]."[11]

Some of Devine's mistakes were small-minded and sometimes personal. If he disliked a player for even a minor reason, he probably disliked that player for as long as he was a player. Unfortunately, his attitude toward any one player was quite visible to the other players on the team. And what was even more unfortunate, Devine would often openly ridicule that player in front of everyone else on the team, despite how everyone else felt about that particular player. Even though he did not realize it, Devine was cultivating an "Us versus Him" outlook that the Packer players were certain to recognize and hold strong to. Such actions and statements by Devine—whether wittingly or unwittingly—boosted the feelings and the bond of togetherness among all of the players on the 1972 Green Bay roster.

For example, if Coach Devine found out that a certain player that he had issues with was having his family come in to Wisconsin from out of state to watch him play, he (Devine) would intentionally bench that player just prior to that upcoming game. That occurrence happened at least once to linebacker Dave Robinson.

"I got the tickets, but I told my family not to come, because I wasn't starting," Robinson recalled. "They [Robinson's family] said they didn't care if I played or not, they wanted to come and have a good time and spend the week. As it turned out, I got the game ball for that week [the game against the 49ers on November 5, 1972]. The next week we go down to Chicago. My family [also] went down to Chicago, and after the game they got back on the highway and drove down to New Jersey [where they resided]. I had another good game ... a really good game. And I got another game ball. I got two game balls back-to-back. We went back in [to the locker room] after the [Chicago] game, and he [Devine] has this big speech. He says, 'Well, game balls are so important, I don't think anybody should get two game balls in one season.' I raised my hand. I said, 'Coach, I agree with you, because I already got mine.' The whole team broke up in laughter. Anytime Devine said stuff like that, I used to cut him down, because I couldn't stand him."[12]

The confrontations between Devine and his players soon got to be somewhat predictable. Coach Devine was always comparing his current professional team to his previous college team. Anyone sensible who knows anything about the sport knows that there is no legitimate comparison. Pro teams were (and still are) much better than college teams. The pro teams had the benefit of more years of experience and coaching. Most pro players were bigger, faster, and stronger than most college players. Nevertheless, Devine kept comparing the two levels of play, often deriding his current Packer players.

"He [Devine] came in once," Robinson recalled, "and said 'This team [the Packers] is nothing. The greatest team I ever had was my 1969 Missouri team. That was one of the finest teams ever ... the Orange Bowl team. You guys are too young to remember.' I said, 'No coach, I remember that team. You went to the Orange Bowl against Penn State [Robinson's alma mater] and you lost that game because you had 12 men on the field.'"[13]

Despite his own faults and failings (even from his days as a head coach at the University of Missouri), Devine still somehow had the audacity to call into question his own players' integrity and honesty. It sounds somewhat remarkable and quite hypocritical, considering how often Devine was less than honest with his team and his assistant coaches. Dave Robinson remembers the following incident:

"He [Devine] was always talking about his undefeated Missouri team," Robinson said. "He said, 'You guys are too young to remember them.' I said, 'Coach, I played against you as a nose tackle at Penn State. I whooped your asses so bad, they [your players] wrote me in on the all-opponent team.' He stopped questioning me when I said this stuff. The next day Devine says to me that he called and found out that I did make the all-opponent team. I said, 'Yeah I made it. I had your center bleeding like a stuck hog.' Three times during that game [Penn State versus Missouri], the referee had to call time out because they wanted to check my forearm pad, because they thought I had metal in my forearm pad."[14]

The 1972 Green Bay Packers players did manage to dominate several teams, much in the way that Dave Robinson dominated Dan Devine's Missouri team during his college years. But it was not easy. The Packers worked hard to become a stronger team than they had been in the past several years. They dedicated themselves to become a better team, a more intelligent team, and a more opportunistic team. They made their own breaks on the field, then took advantage of many of them to score points and gather victories. They were underdogs in most of the games in which they played perennial playoff teams, yet they also managed to upset most of those opponents in 1972.

Irrespective of this fact, Dan Devine was getting increasingly upset at his players, especially when the team lost to Atlanta and Minnesota in consecutive weeks at mid-season. It was exactly at this stage of the year where the players needed a more understanding and a more optimistic head coach. Instead, they had to deal with a head coach who cultivated nothing to them but negativity. Dave Robinson felt that this was a critical time in the season, for it really tested the players' resolve. It also displayed to the men what kind of head coach they had.

"We knew we had a good team," Robinson said. "Dan Devine was probably one of the worst coaches that I ever played for, in high school, college or pro. We [the players] were not really happy with Dan. Around mid-season in that 1972 season, probably after the depressing loss to the Falcons, Dan Devine came into the meeting room and said, 'I'm done with this team, and I want nothing to do with them.' He told Bart [Starr], 'You and the other [assistant] coaches take this team. I don't want nothing to do with them.' When Dan Devine left this team alone, we went something like 6–0, and ended the season with 10 wins. Bart Starr and Hog Hanner really coached the '72 team."[15]

Green Bay offensive guard Bill Lueck offered concrete corroboration of Robinson's recollections regarding the scene where Dan Devine "left the team alone" at the midseason mark of 1972. "Yes, I do [remember it]," Lueck confirmed. "That's exactly the way I remember it."[16]

The word *quit* is a powerful word. Practically no ambiguity can accompany it. On the topic of Dan Devine, however, there is plenty of ambiguity to go around. He was indeed a complicated man. To say that Dan Devine "quit" on the team at mid-season was probably a stretch. More accurately, Devine in all likelihood took more of a backseat when it came to designing the weekly game plans, calling plays, and the like. This was probably true after the team's unexpected and depressing loss to the Falcons on October 22. Naturally, the media continued to interview Coach Devine before and after each succeeding game, and no mention of anyone "quitting" was ever discussed. But for some unknown reason, he just stopped coaching in the same manner that he coached in the early part of the season. Green Bay team historian Cliff Christl knows that there are various points and counterpoints on the issue. Taking all known opinions into consideration, he feels that the questions over time regarding the Packers head coach were a mixture of Devine's competency, and his understanding of his own role on the 1972 team.

"I think two of his strengths were hiring good people and delegating," opined Christl. "And so [Dave] Hanner and [Bart] Starr probably were given more leeway in their jobs all season. If he [Devine] had quit, then was he a coach in name only in 1973 and 1974? I find it hard to believe that he did [quit]."[17]

It is important to note that neither the newspaper reporters nor the fans knew anything about Devine relinquishing the majority of his coaching duties to Bart Starr and Dave Hanner (as ascribed by several Packer players) in the middle of 1972. The over-saturated media elements that we see in today's day and age were just not so prevalent in 1972. A 24-hour-a-day pro football television channel was still several decades away from its inception. The overall lack of constant news on the teams left much room for doubt as to what was really going on during a typical week during a season. In regards to the Green Bay head coach, there were simply two frames of mind: Those who were pro–Devine, and those who were anti–Devine. As the years have gone by, the numbers of the anti–Devine contingent have increased, while those in the pro–Devine faction have decreased. One has to doubt if Devine really cared how he was going to be perceived by the press or the public, back in 1972, or even several decades later.

Dave Robinson was definitely in the anti–Devine camp. He went on to explain something more illuminating about the former Green Bay head coach and his abrupt methods toward the team.

"What he [Devine] couldn't understand was that in college, every year you have a whole new team," Robinson explained. "In pro ball, a guy is going to sit there and look at you for 9–10 years. In college, you can tell a kid, 'You suck. You're probably one of the worst guards I've seen.' But when you get into pro ball, where it's only 13 teams in a conference [author's note: In 1972, both the AFC and the NFC were comprised of 13 teams each. Today, each conference has 16 teams], and where only 28 people out of 400 million can do what you do ... that's one thing you can't tell a pro player ... you suck."[18]

Scott Hunter never outwardly told his head coach that he (Devine) "sucked." But Hunter could not ignore the unmistakable signs of incompetence and failure that permeated many things that resulted from Coach Devine's words and actions. A quarterback on any team naturally receives more attention from the head coach than any other player on the team. Hunter would be the perfect source to discover what was going on in Devine's mind during the season of 1972. Many of Hunter's remembrances involved the examples that he noticed about Devine on a strategic level.

"Calling plays would not have been Coach Devine's expertise," Hunter recalled. "We all knew that Coach Devine had a tough time getting up on the blackboard and putting [drawing] 11 players up [author's note: Only 11 players are allowed on the field for each play, on offense or on defense]. Sometimes he would get 10, and sometimes he would get 12. He wasn't a guy that was all about detail, if you know what I mean."[19] Hunter's teammate, offensive guard Bill Lueck, also saw Devine struggle in the team's strategical meetings. "He [Devine] couldn't draw plays on the blackboard correctly," Lueck remembered.[20]

Some of the problems and differences that the Packer players noticed between themselves and their head coach were psychological in nature. Dan Devine, like any head coach, wanted to be a winner and a champion. But he allowed insecure factors such as jealousy, animosity, and overall ignorance to impede his relationships with his players and with the other assistant coaches on the team. In short, this situation was a very difficult one for the team to deal with. Similarly, it would also be a difficult situation for the players to ignore and to continue to play their best.

"Yeah, Dan Devine was jealous of everybody," Hunter remembered. "You know, I played for [University of Alabama] Coach [Paul 'Bear'] Bryant, and Coach Bryant would stand on the sideline and he'd say, 'Why do you want to do that? The last time it didn't work. Well, do you think it will work this time?' You always defended yourself. You had an idea. You told him what you wanted to do, and you made a case for it. And he'd say, 'All right by God, go out there and do it!' And that was Coach Bryant. Well with Coach Devine ... that didn't work so well with him."[21]

The Packers public relations director in 1972 was Chuck Lane, and he was the conduit between the team, Devine, and the media. Even he eventually came to realize the truth in how the players felt about Coach Devine.

"I think quite frankly that there were very few [players] that did like him [Devine]," admitted Lane in a 2016 interview. "It might have been people with Missouri connections, because he was very clannish with players that had played for him [at Missouri]. But by and large, I don't know many players that were really that excited about him [Devine]. Initially they [the press] were very enthused about him, but then it kinda fell apart shortly after that. I don't know where they [the press] got their information, but I think a lot of them doubted his capabilities. Devine really didn't know that much about x's and o's [offense and defense], and certainly not in pro football. He was more of a figurehead.

"And here's the difference between college and pro football: In college, his assistants did most of the recruiting. He [Devine] did the closing when he went to the recruit's house. But he had no idea what was going on."[22] Later on following his years with the Packers, Devine became the head coach of the University of Notre Dame football team. While there, according to Chuck Lane, "Devine had his assistants do the work for him. And he also had Joe Montana [the eventual Hall of Fame quarterback and four-time Super Bowl Champion with the San Francisco 49ers] sit on the bench. That tells you about what he [Devine] knew about player evaluation."[23]

Running back MacArthur Lane was evaluated quite high by Devine when he traded for him prior to the 1972 season. But Lane did not enjoy the best of coaching during his first four years in the league. He had endured the coaching regimes of Charlie Winner and Bob Hollway in St. Louis during that time span, and neither of those two men could inspire the Cardinals to obtain a playoff berth. The Cardinal teams that Lane played for from 1968 to 1971 showed moments of progress and promise, but many more moments of mediocrity and failure. When he was sent to Green Bay in a trade for running back Donny Anderson, he welcomed the change in scenery. Little did he know that what he got with the Packers was another head coach (Dan Devine) who would be more difficult to deal with than either Winner or Hollway ever were. But he also became a member of a roster filled with outstanding teammates in Green Bay, each of whom welcomed him with open arms. It certainly did not take long for Lane and the rest of the team to embrace each other. And Lane's talents would soon be evident for all to see. The team definitely had a stronger offense with Lane in the backfield. And the victories in Green Bay started mounting up.

Winning football games on a regular basis was the byproduct of the great relationships that were formed on the 1972 Packers. MacArthur Lane knew what basic ingredients were needed to build a winning football team, having seen firsthand what was lacking in St. Louis. It was a foundation built with a mixture of great team camaraderie and chemistry, a total sacrifice to the game and to all of the other players on the team, and an intense desire to win from everybody on the team. Those traits are generally accepted in pro football as the major requirements for any also-ran team to eventually become a winning team. How did this particular Green Bay team jell so quickly? How did they—almost overnight—go from a losing team one year to a division champion the next? Clues to this answer can be found in Lane's description of the attitudes of all of his teammates. It was primarily due to how the Packer players felt about each other. Those winning feelings could thus have been reiterated by every man on the team.

"The atmosphere has to be right to have a winning ball club," Lane pronounced. "I'm convinced of that. These cats love each other. That's what it takes. I'll bet if you started something with one of these guys, all of these cats could jump on you.

"John [Brockington] and I like each other and I think everybody on the team likes each other. We had to find each other out at the start, our weaknesses and our strengths, and we had to rely on each other. This is just a great bunch of people."[24]

All of the goings-on within the team in 1972 were certainly not in the public eye at that time. The public would hear and read about the good things, such as the great camaraderie on the team, as confirmed by MacArthur Lane. But the difficulties with Coach Devine were an internal problem, and the players were honest and loyal enough to keep what was truly happening "inside the locker room." Dan Devine, as head coach, was naturally going to get interviewed by the press much more often than any of his players or his assistant coaches. After taking into account all of the players' feelings about their head coach, one has to figure that if Devine could have gotten away with it, he would have restricted the media's access to every one of his players and his staff. It would have been entirely within his nature to do so.

Some of Devine's quotes to the media sound quite magnanimous, as he at times would praise his players in the press, and at times he would also be critical of his own coaching abilities. You might even think after reading some of these statements that he was a very modest man as a head coach ... indeed a very understanding man.

"Loyalty is the best word that I can use to describe this team," said Devine about his players near the end of the 1972 regular season. "Loyalty to each other, loyalty to the coaches."[25] Well, the players definitely were loyal to each other and to the assistant coaches, but it is debatable as to how "loyal" they were to Coach Devine. "I was disappointed in the way I coached last year [in 1971]. I did a few things differently this year. But we were dedicated."[26]

Devine certainly did do a few things differently than what he did in his rookie year in 1971. He made many more trades to alter his roster, and most of those trades turned out to benefit the team. Again, if you give him criticism and blame for his poor decisions, you should also be willing to give him praise and credit for his good decisions. "I don't know when I've had a more cohesive staff than this one we've assembled for 1972," Devine stated. "I really feel this staff works together extremely well."[27]

Well, they pretty much *had* to work well together. The assistant coaches were similar to the players, in that they also were at odds with the way that Devine was running the show. But also just like the Packer players, there was little that they could do about the situation.

Devine's own opinion regarding how well he was doing as a pro head coach could have been deciphered by looking at the team's won-loss record. That is a natural gauge of success even in today's NFL. If a team wins a lot of games, the head coach will usually get plenty of credit and good press. Devine certainly knew this, and maybe that was what was driving him in 1972. He certainly felt optimistic regarding his abilities just prior to the start of the 1972 season.

"I just think that I myself am going to do a better job of coaching," said Devine. "I feel my best job ever will be coming up this year. I don't feel like I did a very good job last year [in 1971]. But I feel now that I'm capable of doing a good job."[28]

Devine possessed this goodly amount of optimism because of the seeming revolving door of Packer players from 1971 to 1972, each of which he was responsible for. Devine was not shy about making numerous trades, and he was certainly willing to get rid of veteran players, many of whom were held in beloved status by the Green Bay fans. "I guess what I've [been] saying is that, eventually, you have to get people who think like you. When you inherit a team, you're going to convert a few and there are a few who aren't going to be converted."[29]

Resistance among some of the older Green Bay players did result. Devine was definitely not going to tolerate much of that. Veterans like Donny Anderson, Lionel Aldridge, and Dave Hampton were each sent to other teams in rapid fashion. Former Green Bay defensive back Bob Jeter once complained about Devine moving an off-season training session to the searing hot summer sun of Arizona. Devine proceeded to trade him to the Bears in less than a week. Packer legends such as Willie Wood, Elijah Pitts, Zeke Bratkowski and Doug Hart had each seen enough of Devine's act to hasten their own retirements prior to the start of the 1972 season (or shortly thereafter, in the case of Bratkowski). It was business as usual for Devine.

"I think we've made progress in conversions," admitted Devine. "I really sense that the squad wants to be cooperative—that they want to do what the coaches want them to do and are going to do it to the very best of their ability."[30]

One Packers player proved the old adage that there is an exception to every rule, however. Reserve Green Bay offensive tackle Francis Peay had played for Devine as a collegiate at the University of Missouri. Somewhat expectedly, Devine displayed a loyalty to the seven-year veteran in 1972. Peay responded in kind, going as far as to even praising his former college coach.

"He's pretty mild mannered, but he can burn you," Peay asserted when describing Coach Devine. "He can burn you, but he won't scare you. I couldn't be happier [being here in Green Bay]."[31] Peay recalled a story that Devine told to Peay and his Missouri teammates just prior to a big game at the Air Force Academy in Colorado Springs. Ironically, it involved another big game from Devine's past, also against the Air Force Academy. "He's really a master psychologist, and I mean a master," said Peay of Devine. "The night before that game, he told us about the first Missouri team he took to the Orange Bowl. When they got to the Orange Bowl, they found the door to the dressing room locked. He [Devine] said, 'We didn't wait. We went right through that door!' And the next day, we got to that Air Force Stadium, and don't you know it—*that* door was locked! I've never been sure he [Devine] didn't lock it himself, just to get us up."[32]

Make no mistake, Dan Devine was a disciplinarian. He probably would not admit that were he still alive today, but the opinions of his former players and even his own previous remarks bear out that fact. In his never-ceasing effort to rid his Packers team from the shadow of Vince Lombardi, Dan Devine may have been more like Lombardi than he would like to acknowledge. "I've been raising my voice all my life," Devine once admitted tersely. "I don't know how to coach *without* raising my voice."[33]

So there was a confusing situation that the Packer players had to deal with. On one hand, their head coach was an introspective man, realizing and admitting his own shortcomings. "I'm going to be wrong some of the time," Devine would say during 1972.[34] At other times, he would be angry at his own players, and he would openly discuss his desire to get rid of many of them. According to author Bob Rubin, Devine believed that there were some slackers on his team, and that they "were ex–Packers just as soon as Devine could get rid of them."[35]

Part of the title of this chapter pertaining to "losing a coach" is a misnomer of sorts. It would not happen for the Packers until after the 1974 season, when Devine left Green Bay to become the head coach at Notre Dame University. In reality, Devine was rarely "with" the Packers in any real sense of the word. He was not the kind of coach that the players could go to with a question, or with a problem, or even with an idea on possible strategy. Also on a truthful vein, many players on the 1972 Green Bay squad would have wished for another man to be their head coach. Who could blame them? They may have wanted a man who possessed flexibility and understanding

6. Losing a Coach, Gaining a Perspective

in his mind set, and a man who did not exhibit the ego that Dan Devine certainly did. They actually had a man on their staff who already owned those positive traits, and his name was Bart Starr. But Starr would not assume the role of Green Bay head coach until 1975. The Packer players in 1972 had to play the cards that they were dealt, and for better or worse, the dealer of those cards was Dan Devine.

A question naturally comes to mind: Could this team have achieved winning a division title if it did not have a head coach like Dan Devine? For example, how well would the Packer players do if they had labored for another head coach who was not so difficult to deal with? How well would the 1972 Packers have succeeded if the players did not feel the instant need to blend so closely together as one unit like they had to under Devine? You could make somewhat of a case that MacArthur Lane, John Brockington, Scott Hunter, Dave Robinson, and the rest of their teammates might not have had the same level or amount of inspiration if Devine had not been their head coach. And inspiration is a very important factor to winning pro football games, and it can come from many different directions. Indeed, many Green Bay players were "inspired" to show their head coach just how wrong he was whenever he insulted them or humiliated them in front of their teammates. Some of those players badly rectified the smug Devine comments by ramming their helmets and shoulder pads into their opponents every autumn and winter Sunday afternoon in 1972. They wanted to take out their frustrations regarding Devine on the opposing teams, and in the brutal "Black and Blue Division," that rage and anger initiated and caused by their head coach might just have been the secret ingredient to winning all of those games. In that respect, and by using the simple barometer of winning games regardless of how it was done, Dan Devine might have actually been good for that 1972 Packers team.

Looking at this situation with a completely open mind, and at the risk of speaking heresy and having those former Packer players from that season wholeheartedly disagree with this theory, Devine might have been the most inspiring head coach in the NFL that year, albeit in a fashion that few coaches would prefer to emulate. If the ending that you want to happen is to win and become a division champion, who really cares about how you achieve that goal? As long as you attain it, the means should not matter all that much. It was the successful ending that mattered most. Pretty simplistic in thought is this bottom line reasoning, and probably not accepted as factual by the players and the assistant coaches at the time. But it is a hypothesis that bears mentioning over the span of almost 50 years later, if only to jar the memories of those who were there, and to get them to ponder how things were done— and how their victories were accomplished. Perhaps that is the most important memory that those players and assistant coaches can hold fast to so many years later ... that they won a division title in the midst of continual chaos from their head coach enveloping so many of their efforts back then. Because of that unique and indeed unusual situation, they deserve to be remembered in the NFL history books. Although they were not one of the two teams to make it to Super Bowl VII, the 1972 Green Bay Packers faced a much more difficult challenge than either the eventual AFC Champion Miami Dolphins, or the eventual NFC Champion Washington Redskins. In that respect, the 1972 Green Bay Packers still managed to achieve substantial and noteworthy success by the end of the season.

7
A Team in Every Sense

The dates of October 22 and October 29 marked a couple of important turning points for the 1972 Packers. The team had just lost a rain-soaked game to the Atlanta Falcons in Milwaukee County Stadium by the narrowest of margins, 10–9 (on the 22nd), and a disappointing 27–13 defeat to the Minnesota Vikings at Lambeau Field (on the 29th). Very few things went right for the team in either of those two games. Green Bay was now at a crossroads in the middle of their season. In order for the Packers to stay competitive in the NFC Central Division race, they would have to put a quick end to their two-game losing streak. Unfortunately for Green Bay, their next opponent was no push-over. The San Francisco 49ers were a veteran team that challenged every opponent with their dynamic offense and their stalwart defense. They had participated in the previous two NFC Championship games, but like the Packers, they too were stuck in a struggling phase of their schedule. The 49ers owned a 3–3–1 record going into their November 5 game against the Packers, but it was not unchartered territory for them. They were faced with unexpected losses in each of their past two seasons, yet they had put together much-needed winning streaks, which enabled them to make it to the playoffs in both 1970 and 1971.

The game would be played in Milwaukee, and it marked the third straight home game for the Green and Gold. It also marked the third and final contest that would be played at Milwaukee County Stadium in 1972. The remainder of Green Bay's home games would be played at Lambeau Field. The biggest key to victory for the Packers going into the struggle with San Francisco would involve the play of the Green Bay offense, a unit which had scored only 22 total points during their previous eight quarters of action. "What do we have, one touchdown in two games?" asked Packer fullback MacArthur Lane of some nearby reporters. "That's no good. It seems like every time we get a good lead we get lax. I like to win games 35–10 once in a while. We're sticking together, but we aren't scoring. I just can't figure it out."[1]

Figuring things out usually involved making a change or two, or sometimes even more. One big change that was made was geared to alleviate the lack of point production problem, and it was a change that stemmed from the aforementioned turning points of the previous two games. Green Bay head coach Dan Devine had—for unknown reasons—decided to abdicate his game-planning roles on offense. In short, he gave his quarterbacks coach Bart Starr all of the rights and responsibilities to develop the game plans. Starr was already calling all of the plays on the offensive side of the ball, but now Devine would leave Starr alone for the rest of the year to sink or swim on his own. In retrospect, it may have been the most unselfish thing that Devine—or indeed any NFL head coach—had ever done. The thought that he trusted Starr enough to give him the complete reins to the offense was certainly a smart gesture, as Starr had carefully built a stellar reputation for himself as one of the most intelligent quarterbacks in league history. But for Devine, a man whom many players would consider as a person with a huge ego, this was certainly a major departure in routine. Many of the offensive players noticed the change in philosophy almost immediately, and most of them were glad for the change. The stories of how Devine came to his decision were simply conjecture, and nothing more. But they probably were due to the anger that he felt after losing those two straight winnable games to the Falcons and the Vikings.

Bart Starr followed up his legendary career as the championship quarterback for Green Bay during the Vince Lombardi era by serving as the quarterbacks coach for the 1972 Packers. Starr's efforts in tutoring young quarterbacks Scott Hunter and Jerry Tagge were vital in helping the team win the NFC Central Division title in 1972 (courtesy the Green Bay Packers).

Veteran outside linebacker and Hall of Famer Dave Robinson remarked that Devine's criticism of the team after the losses to Atlanta and Minnesota "were making the team angry."[2] The insults that the coach spoke to his players, whether they were intended to inspire them to play better or not, made some of the players push the envelope in their responses to him.

"He [Devine] had idiotic statements all the time," Robinson recalled. "He and I didn't get along very well.

He told us, 'You guys [the Packer players] couldn't beat the Little Sisters of the Poor.' [Green Bay defensive end] Clarence Williams leans over and whispers in my ear, 'Who are the Little Sisters of the Poor?' I told him, 'I don't know, but they must have one hell of a fullback.'"³

A sunny and clear 50 degree day greeted the fullbacks and all of the other players for both the 49ers and the Packers at Milwaukee County Stadium on November 5. The Green Bay offense once again scored first, just as they had done during the previous two games. Midway through the first quarter on a third-and-1 situation, offensive coordinator Bart Starr called for a play out of his own glorious past. The Packers' legendary quarterback had often thrown a long pass on a short yardage situation, assuming that the opposing defense would not be expecting it. It often succeeded, sometimes even when the opposing defense was looking for it! He told current Packer quarterback Scott Hunter to try the same type of play from the San Francisco 48-yard line midway through the first quarter. Hunter faked a play-action handoff to fullback MacArthur Lane, who then laid a crushing block on blitzing San Francisco outside linebacker Skip Vanderbundt. Green Bay setback John Brockington slipped unnoticed out of the backfield and ran a straight fly pattern down the middle of the field. Hunter lofted the ball downfield and into the waiting arms of Brockington, who caught it cleanly at the 49ers' 30-yard line, then ran untouched into the end zone. There was absolutely no San Francisco defender anywhere within a 15-yard radius in any direction around Brockington.

"From the films we knew how their safety [Mike Simpson] played in short yardage situations," explained Brockington. "Their cornerback [Bruce Taylor] has to go with our wide receiver [Leland Glass]. That leaves me with a linebacker [Frank Nunley] at best, and on a long pass there is no linebacker who is going to stay with me."⁴

That play actually almost did not happen. Hunter and Starr were both on the same page, but Starr and head coach Dan Devine were definitely not in sync. Hunter described the unique misunderstanding between the two coaches on the play with the following rendition:

"Well that [play] was a fourth down and about a foot to go," recalled Hunter. "As I heard the sideline conversation, Bart said to Devine, 'You want to go for it?' Devine said, 'Yeah.' But Bart wasn't talking about going for the foot. He was talking about throwing a play-action pass and going for the touchdown! Somebody out there said, 'Tell him [Hunter] to run Red Left, Fire Red Left, Fire Mid Play-Action Pass, Fire Red Left, 49 B Fly Inside.' It was a great call. He [John Brockington] came out of there [the offensive backfield] and he was wide open. [49ers linebacker] Skip Vanderbundt ... he was back in the backfield with me [laughter]. It was all I could do was to make sure [that the pass was on target] ... because John wasn't the best receiver.

He once told me as a rookie [in 1971] one day after practice, 'I just caught more passes [at practice at Green Bay] than I ever did at Ohio State [Brockington's alma mater].' I said, 'You mean in a game?' He said, 'No ... in the whole four years that I was there [laughter].' I just kinda floated it [Hunter's pass to Brockington versus the 49ers] out there and thought, 'Don't drop this.' He [Brockington] caught it like Jerry Rice [more laughter]."[5]

San Francisco's offense answered back quickly. A nine-play drive was culminated by speedy and shifty 49ers halfback Vic Washington, who ran a sweep to his right from the Green Bay 2-yard line and plowed over the goal line for the tying score.

One of the great talents of Bart Starr was his ability to sense what was needed at just the right time. Another one of his innate football skills was his knowledge of what talents each player on the team brought to the field. Starr knew that Green Bay's star halfback—John Brockington—was not being utilized as much by this stage of 1972 as he was the previous year. Once Starr held firm the reins of the offense, he knew that he would have to make amends for that situation. Starr would end up giving Brockington 24 carries against San Francisco, and the charging rhinoceros responded with 133 yards (a 5.6 yards-per-carry average) and three touchdowns (two rushing and one receiving). Brockington's 133 rushing yards represented the most that he would account for in a single game in 1972.

One of Green Bay's most successful running plays was a rollout draw play, a play where the opposing defense is lured into the offensive backfield, only to over-run the avenue that the ball carrier uses to reach daylight and open spaces. Coach Starr called for one such play from the San Francisco 30-yard line late in the second quarter. Brockington waited patiently in the backfield for Hunter to drop back and hand him the ball. Brockington quickly found an open alley off of his left guard Bill Lueck, then charged straight for the 49ers' goal post. San Francisco linebacker Skip Vanderbundt and defensive back Jimmy Johnson both grasped onto Brockington at the 5-yard line, but the surging halfback dragged both of them over the goal line.

"When I get that close [to the goal line], there's no way I'm going to be stopped," remarked Brockington. "When the hole opens up and the adrenalin comes, you just start smokin'."[6] Green Bay center Ken Bowman insisted that deception and familiarity were both important factors in the success of the play. "It's something you set up with the rollout pass," confided Bowman. "Until they [the opposing defense] get a look at the quarterback rollout, they aren't going to go for it."[7]

There was no further scoring in the second quarter. Green Bay's 14–7 halftime lead over the 49ers was not new. They had held halftime leads before earlier in the season, only to lose them later in some of those games. Against San Francisco, the Packers team as a whole knew that another such failure—

such as what happened to them against the Falcons or the Vikings—would probably end any chance that Green Bay would have of remaining in first place in the NFC Central Division standings (depending upon how the Detroit Lions fared in their contest against the Chicago Bears on the same afternoon). The Packers were thus determined to hold their lead against the 49ers, and if possible, to increase it. Enter John Brockington once again. The second-year halfback from Ohio State really helped Green Bay start the third quarter off in a positive way by finishing up a seven-play scoring drive with a 14-yard touchdown run. That play started out as just another draw play, but this time, Brockington broke to his left and dashed to the corner of the end zone. He surged through attempted tackles by 49er defenders Skip Vanderbundt and Mike Simpson. Finally, San Francisco outside linebacker Dave Wilcox tackled Brockington a little too late as the two tumbled across the goal line. The Packers now held a strong 21–7 advantage with just 5:01 elapsed into the third quarter.

"The coaches did a good job at halftime," said Devine after the game. "The coaches came up with a few runs, a few passes, and said, '…this is what we go with.' They [the Packers offense] stuck with it—despite my trying to foul 'em up."[8]

The Packer scoring surge would continue just four minutes later, when Green Bay placekicker Chester Marcol booted a 35-yard field goal to increase his team's lead to 24–7. Some old habits are hard to break, however. From this point on, it appeared to most onlookers as if the Packers started to let up, much as they did against the Falcons and the Vikings. But such was not the case, however. The 49ers did not participate in the previous two conference championship games by not making comebacks in games that they appeared to be defeated. San Francisco head coach Dick Nolan was very good at making adjustments, and as the third quarter waned, Nolan's adaptations started to take effect, especially on offense. Nolan instructed his second-string quarterback, Steve Spurrier (who was in the starting lineup in place of injured veteran signal caller John Brodie), to start throwing the ball more often on deeper pass routes. Spurrier, who won the Heisman Trophy in 1966, complied immediately.

"We had planned to pass against the Packers," Nolan admitted after the game. "But not that much. But the score dictated that we had to pass."[9]

San Francisco started moving the ball through the air, and the personnel on the Green Bay sideline began to feel a little uneasy about their situation. Packers linebacker Dave Robinson related the following personal story in a 2014 interview:

"Halfway through the season, my family is coming in to Milwaukee to see me play against the 49ers. I went out to try to get tickets, but could only get two per person. Devine gets wind that I've got my family driving in from

New Jersey, and decided to start Jimmy Carter at outside linebacker [Carter was usually a middle linebacker]. Dave "Hog" Hanner, our defensive coordinator, said that [such a decision] wasn't the case. I told Hog, 'Hey Hog, I love ya' but the grapevine is awful strong.' Just before the game Hanner comes through the locker room cursing, 'Goddamn sons of bitches!' Hanner tells me that 'he [Devine] is going to start Jimmy Carter. I want you [Robinson] to stand right next to me. If there's any trouble, you're going in right away.' I said okay. He [Devine] gets up in front of the team and says, 'Ray Nitschke has done so much for this team, he deserves to start. We can't bench Jimmy Carter. He's been filling in so well for Ray. So Carter starts in place of Robinson on the outside.'

Defensive coordinator Dave "Hog" Hanner is rightfully credited with producing one of the best defenses in the entire NFL in 1972. The Packers defense in 1972 allowed only 226 points (courtesy the Green Bay Packers).

"The 49ers notice that I'm not in there, so they start audiblizing [changing the plays at the line of scrimmage]. They started at their own 20 yard line and get down to our 20. Hanner tells me to get in there. So I go running into the huddle. 'Big Cat' Clarence Williams says to me, 'Thank God you're here!' I said, 'Cat, check it out. They [the 49ers] think I'm hurt. They're going to be running at us.' They ran three straight plays at us, and we held them on all three plays. They ended up kicking a field goal."[10]

Robinson's guile and experience certainly was needed by the Green Bay defense against the 49ers on this day, but his early absence from the starting lineup did not just go unnoticed by the San Francisco offense, however. The media outlets were equally as curious as to why the star outside linebacker began the game on the sidelines. That situation seemed to get almost as much attention in the post-game Packers locker room as did any specific play in the contest. Head coach Dan Devine claimed that the decision was merely an attempt to counter the strengths that the San Francisco offense showed on film.

"We just tried to start a good lineup against the things we thought they [the 49ers] might do at the start of the game," explained Devine. "It [Robinson's first half benching and his return to action in the second half] was a coaching decision."[11] As with every other Devine statement, one has to draw their own conclusions.

That 49ers' field goal made the score 24–10 in favor of the Packers as the fourth quarter began. By this time, coach Nolan realized that audibles were not needed ... but long passes were. The 49ers quickly scored a touchdown on the second play of the fourth quarter, when Spurrier hit star wide receiver Gene Washington (who was no relation to the Minnesota wide receiver with the same name) for a 62-yard score. The play, which made the score 24–17 in favor of Green Bay, was originally designed as a simple down-and-in pattern, with Washington being the primary receiver. But because Washington's route on this particular play was designed for the receiver to run downfield for more yardage than usual before making his cut towards the middle of the field, San Francisco's offensive line would have to hold their blocks for several more seconds than what they usually would have to do, should a shorter pass pattern have been employed. As fate would have it, the Packers' defensive secondary decided to use a rotating zone coverage on this particular play, meaning that one, two, three, or all of their defensive backs were moving (or rotating) towards a particular zone on the field. The specific zone on that play was rotating away from Washington. Both he and Spurrier noticed it within a couple of seconds after the snap of the ball. Washington was all alone as he caught Spurrier's perfect pass at the Green Bay 25-yard line. He then adjusted his direction on a dime and sprinted down the middle of the field untouched for the touchdown. The trailing Green Bay cornerback, Willie Buchanon, appeared to be the main player at fault for the easy 49ers' score. But as is often the case in zone coverages (and this play was no different), placing the blame on any one player is frequently foolhardy, because usually more than one thing will be needed to go wrong for such an easy score to develop.

"Don't blame Willie [Buchanon]," said fellow Green Bay cornerback Ken Ellis in assessing the strategy and execution behind Washington's long score. "It was just a heck of a play by Washington. He is going to beat a lot of people."[12] Packers' safety Jim Hill concurred with Ellis. "Even with their number two quarterback in there, San Francisco is still the number one passing team in the league," explained Hill. "That speaks for itself. You aren't going to contain receivers like Washington all day."[13]

What turned out to be Gene Washington's first score of the afternoon "really bothered" Buchanon. "But what made me feel good was everybody came over to me and said, 'That's one of those things and they're going to happen to you. Let's go back and play our defense.' Bob Brown [the huge Green Bay defensive tackle] came up to me and said, 'You're still my man.' That helped me, to know they [Buchanon's teammates] weren't down on me."[14]

Green Bay head coach Dan Devine was not down on his rookie cornerback either. He just realized and acknowledged very little drop off in the 49ers' success through the air. "I've always had a lot of respect for Spurrier," proclaimed Devine. "He can kill you with his passes."[15]

A 40-yard Chester Marcol field goal increased the Packers' lead to 27–17, but Spurrier kept throwing the ball, and kept completing the majority of his throws. He would end the day with 317 passing yards and two touchdowns, the second of which occurred six plays after Marcol's field goal. Once again, it was Gene Washington on the receiving end of a Spurrier scoring pass, this one coming from 34 yards out. It was also quite similar to Washington's first touchdown, as he ran a down-and-in pattern. This time, the Packers' defensive backs adjusted quicker to Washington's route, but Spurrier's pass was a very accurate dart which his wide receiver caught in stride. Green Bay safety Al Matthews belted Washington at the 1-yard line, but the elusive pass catcher tumbled into the end zone. San Francisco now trailed by only three points, 27–24.

"They threw a couple of touchdown passes on us, sure, but in the second half all they were doing was throwing," said Green Bay safety Jim Hill. "We're only human, but it did not sag us or break us. If anything, it made us more determined than ever to come back with the big play."[16]

There may not have been anymore big plays for the Green Bay offense in this game, but perhaps the most important Packer drive of the contest came right after Washington's second touchdown. Ironically, it was a drive that did not result in any points scored, nor did it gain much yardage, but it ate up over three minutes of the game clock late in the fourth quarter. By the time that Green Bay's Ron Widby was called on to punt, San Francisco would have only 37 seconds left in the game with which to drive 80 yards for the winning touchdown. They were unable to do so. The Green Bay secondary had finally seen all they needed to see of Steve Spurrier's tosses, and with the struggle in its final moments, one of their members finally and emphatically came up with a game-deciding play. Spurrier threw an incompletion on first down, and on second down, he once again attempted to connect with star San Francisco wide receiver Gene Washington. Green Bay cornerback Ken Ellis timed his approach perfectly, stepped in front of Washington, picked off Spurrier's arching pass, and streaked down the far sideline 28 yards for the clinching score. The Packers had thus ended their two-game losing streak with a resounding 34–24 triumph over the 49ers.

"When you put the ball up that many times, I knew sooner or later we'd get the big play," admitted Green Bay safety Jim Hill, who was referring to Spurrier's 37 pass attempts.[17]

According to the hero of the hour Ken Ellis, he had nothing to lose by going for the interception. "The ball I intercepted was hung," described Ellis.

"He [Spurrier] was hanging them all day and we should have had more interceptions. It was no gamble. They [the 49ers] were out of timeouts and we knew he would have to throw out of bounds or go for the long one. I saw it [the ball] all the way and I had the position. If I couldn't get it, he [Washington] wouldn't have either."[18] John Brockington was watching the action with the rest of the offensive unit from the Packers' sidelines, and he knew that the game was won as soon as Ken Ellis came down with the prized pigskin. "The defense was due for the big play," Brockington said. "When Kenny caught it [Spurrier's ill-fated pass], it was Katie bar the door man, because when Kenny catches one, no one's going to catch him."[19]

The media did catch up with head coach Dan Devine after the game, however, and recorded several of his opinions on a variety of topics, especially those involving his team's preparation for the 49ers, along with his sentiments of the game. "We had the simplest game plan we have had all season," Devine admitted, "and [we ended up] scoring the most points. We got some big plays. Of course, so did they [the 49ers]. It would be kind of nice to keep a lead once and not have to worry [about possibly losing it late in the game]."[20]

In discussing Scott Hunter's 48-yard touchdown pass to John Brockington in the first quarter, Devine acknowledged, "Bart [Starr] sent in the play. He sent in all of them. However, it was a play that Rollie [Dotsch, a Packers assistant coach] came up with during the week [author's note: it is highly doubtful that Devine would have authorized that play in that specific situation. As a result, Devine decided to put a magnanimous spin on his remarks, rather than admit his own ignorance concerning the play that was actually called.]. I don't want to point out people. This was a victory by 40 men—and my coaches."[21]

Perhaps the one player who benefited the most from the game against San Francisco was veteran linebacker Ray Nitschke, a holdover from the

Veteran middle linebacker Ray Nitschke served the Packers in a supporting role in 1972 despite his desire to remain a starter. Irrespective of his unaccustomed role on the bench, he often spent time as an undeclared coach for the team's linebackers unit. Nitschke was enshrined in the Pro Football Hall of Fame in 1978 (courtesy the Green Bay Packers).

Lombardi era. Nitschke was the proud owner of five world championship rings, but in 1972, he was forced to swallow his pride and serve the team as a knowledgeable and sagacious bench warmer. But the seasoned warrior finally saw a quarter of action against the 49ers, and he viewed it as a welcomed change from watching the game from the sidelines.

"Maybe a little rusty, but it felt good to play," admitted Nitschke after the game. "I'm not pleased playing a quarter, though, but that is not my decision. I expect they [the fans] remember the glory years, but it sure makes me feel good inside to know that I have been appreciated. I have always felt I can still play this game, but I haven't had much opportunity."[22] Devine was furthermore quoted as saying prior to the game, "Ray Nitschke [still] likes to hit people."[23]

The hitting would continue the following week when the Packers traveled to Chicago to take on their most hated rival, the Bears, who were owning up to a depressing 3-4-1 record at this point of the season. When these two teams meet, however, all team records were—and still are—ignored. This game would be tough ... indeed all of the contests filling out the rest of the Green Bay schedule would be so. The Packers had played most of their first eight games at home. They would now have to play five of their final six regular season contests on the road, including the next three straight. It would be a true test for a team that was striving to better its current 5-3 record.

Green Bay's offense began their meeting with Chicago on November 12th in the same way that they had begun many of their games this year ... with a quick moment of success. A fumbled snap by Bears punter Bobby Joe Green at the Chicago 24-yard line led directly to the first score of the game. Green Bay halfback John Brockington ran right up the gut of the Chicago defense for 12 yards. Brockington, whose nickname was the "Crazed Camel," took another handoff from quarterback Scott Hunter on the following play, and broke an attempted tackle just past the line of scrimmage by Bears defensive back Charlie Ford. Brockington then ran swiftly to daylight on his right, and proceeded to bowl over Chicago defensive backs Jerry Moore and Craig Clemons to reach pay dirt. "We jumped off quickly," said Brockington. "But the Bears never fold. They just stick to their game plan and patiently come back at you."[24]

The Bears—as Brockington witnessed—wasted no time in answering Green Bay's initial score. Chicago quarterback Bobby Douglass mixed his own bootleg runs with some runs by running backs Don Shy and Jim Harrison to drive 79 yards down the field in eight plays. Reserve Bears halfback Cyril Pinder made the most of his only carry of the game by rushing four yards off right tackle to score the tying touchdown. Green Bay defensive backs Jim Hill and Charlie Hall met Pinder at the goal line, but Pinder's momentum carried him over.

The score was now knotted at seven apiece, but Green Bay's special teams was now ready to make one of the biggest plays of the game. Packers kick returner Ike Thomas found a hole on his right and sprinted 89 yards down the far sideline, where he was finally tripped up by Cecil Turner at the Chicago 11-yard line. Green Bay quarterback Scott Hunter dove into the Bears' end zone a few plays later from the 1-yard line to reclaim the lead for the Packers, 14–7. It would be Hunter's lone moment of glory, however, as he would have one of his worst outings of the year in this game. Hunter would have two fumbles, two interceptions, and incredibly zero completions in this game. A head-on hit by Chicago defender Jimmy Gunn knocked Hunter out of the affair with a slight concussion. "Hunter wasn't hurt seriously, but I guess he couldn't play," said Coach Devine.[25]

Regardless of Hunter's lack of productivity, the Packers somehow managed to take a 17–3 lead over Chicago as both teams went into their halftime locker rooms. But the situation was not good for Dan Devine's ball club. The Bears were beating them at virtually every statistical category. The Green Bay offense would end up accounting for only eight first downs and 163 total yards in the game. Reserve Packer quarterback Jerry Tagge was needed to take over for Hunter in the second half. Tagge, who was just a rookie with hardly any playing experience, only completed four passes in seven attempts. But he did not throw an interception, and that fact would be very important in order for Green Bay to keep a hold of the lead. Tagge also managed to set up Chester Marcol for two more field goals in the second half.

"Tagge did an excellent job considering it was his first NFL appearance," admitted Devine. "I'm totally satisfied with his play."[26] So was Tagge himself. The young quarterback was called on to pull a victory out for his team, and he delivered. "You know, you sit around wondering if you're a good quarterback or not," Tagge said. "But you have to be patient and ready when the opportunity comes. I kept telling myself to calm down and be alert. We've come a long way, and I didn't want to blow it."[27]

"They [the coaches] didn't tell me at halftime whether I would play in the second half. I thought maybe Scott [Hunter] would come back. I did some good things and some bad things, but five good plays don't always atone for three bad ones."[28]

While it was true that Tagge missed hitting a wide open tight end Pete Lammons for a score in the game, he did produce enough positive plays to keep a couple of Packer drives alive in the second half. Green Bay wide receiver Carroll Dale proclaimed that "under the circumstances, Tagge did a fine job. He has a lot of zip on his passes."[29] Perhaps the most positive factor that Tagge brought to the offense was his ability to keep his teammates focused enough on scoring at least *some* points in the final two quarters. "Our [offensive] line did a great job of picking up the blitzes for me and giving me enough time to read the Bear defense," Tagge said. "You really don't know what you can do until you play. It felt good to play. I am ready any time. I always prepare myself like I was going to play 60 minutes."[30]

The Bears would draw closer to the Packers late in those 60 minutes when Douglass, who ended the day with 68 yards rushing on 12 carries, burrowed into the Packers end zone from the 1-yard line. Chicago now trailed by only six points at 23–17. The Bears definitely had the momentum at this stage of the game, and when they got the ball back again with a little more than a minute remaining, they began another sustained drive down the field. A vital defensive play by a veteran Packer linebacker, however, would decide the issue. Dave Robinson noticed an outside rush lane that was left unprotected, and that lane led directly into the heart of the Chicago passing pocket. Robinson did not waste an instant when he surged through the gap and hit Douglass on his blind side, jarring the ball loose. Green Bay defensive end Alden Roche fell on the football, and the game was over.

"We were in a 6-1 defense," explained Packers defensive tackle Mike McCoy, "and on that Robby [Dave Robinson] has the option to go on in [the pass pocket] if an avenue develops. That time it did. We can contain him [Bobby Douglass] if he runs. You just have to stay in your lane to rush him and get off the ball. We just got together and decided we had to stop him. Everybody [on the Packers defense] was talking a lot, reminding each other of what we had to do. It's a lot better than going it alone. It keeps you alert."[31]

Robinson's alertness came more out of a perceived necessity than anything else. "I had to do something because on one of their other drives, I stole the ball and then couldn't hold onto it," Robinson said. "We blitzed a little more [today] than usual. We are not a blitzing team, as you know, but we have great respect for Douglass."[32]

Another Packers linebacker agreed with Robinson. "The thing we have to prevent is a long pass," explained Jim Carter. "Douglass may not be a great percentage passer but he has a great arm. You can't let him get off a bomb."[33]

The Packers had lost in every category to the Bears, but they prevailed on the scoreboard, 23–17, giving them a 6-3 record. It was a game that could easily have gone to the Bears, were it not for one key play or another. "I really think the breaks evened out today," assessed Devine. "We got some, but they [the Bears] had two big ones on one of their drives—an interception that we missed and a play that was blown dead when we recovered a fumble."[34]

Devine's counterpart, Chicago head coach Abe Gibron, was naturally more upset with the final result. "It's a shame when you beat a team and lose," Gibron stated after the game. "We handled them [the Packers] physically. We didn't win but as long as we remain physical, we'll be okay. We made mistakes and put our offense under the gun."[35]

"I'm not the least concerned about the statistics," opined Devine. "I knew we were in trouble at times but I also know we kept getting out of it."[36]

Green Bay's Chester Marcol appeared to be in trouble as well, at least while he was kicking off. "On every kickoff I made, [Bears reserve running back] Gary Kosins came right for me," said Marcol. "He obviously was trying to put the wood to me—to soften me up. But I was able to dodge him. The Bears do it to every kicker in the league, I guess. So I was expecting it. You can expect anything from the Bears. But from my point of view, it just makes you want to do better."[37]

The most famous player on the Bears roster also tried to rattle the young Packers kicker. But instead of hitting Marcol, the future Hall of Fame middle linebacker Dick Butkus just tried to play some mental games with him.

"Just before my last field goal attempt, Dick Butkus came way out of his way to throw me off," Marcol confided. "I had a little scuff mark [on the artificial surface of Chicago's Soldier Field] to mark the spot where I intended to kick from. Butkus came over and rubbed the mark away. He never said a word ... he just rubbed it with his shoe."[38]

Butkus' effort proved futile, however, as Marcol made the field goal anyway. Green Bay was making some noise in the NFC Central Division standings by this time of the 1972 season. They were improving in many phases of the game, and the rest of the teams in the league were taking notice of that fact. On the same day that the Packers held on to sweep Chicago in their regular season series, the Detroit Lions were narrowly defeated by Minnesota, 16–14. Green Bay now owned a full game lead over the 5–4 Lions, and their young placekicker was a big reason as to why. Marcol, who had now defeated the Bears with three straight game-winning field goals (one in preseason and twice in the regular season), would receive a piece of paper immediately following the most recent Packers win over Chicago. It was an unsolicited telegram from an unnamed Bears fan. All the telegram said was: "Dear Chester: Go back to Poland."[39]

Devine's squad was not scheduled to cross the Atlantic Ocean for their next game, however. And to their relief, they did not expect to have too much trouble with their next opponent, the Houston Oilers, whose 1–8 record made them the worst team in the league, at least as far as overall standings were concerned. But the Packers had seen how their previous overconfidence could result in defeat, particularly in the loss in week number six to the Atlanta Falcons. Despite this knowledge, Green Bay had to address the fact that their offense could not sustain itself with a good showing one week, and a poor showing the next. Their offensive statistics in the recent Bears game lent credence to the belief that the Packers were not moving the ball efficiently, regardless of who was the quarterback. Chicago limited the Green Bay rushing attack to 123 yards on 34 carries, resulting in a 3.6-yards-per-carry average.

Green Bay's explosive ground attack was used to achieving better results. Chicago head coach Abe Gibron realized by this point in the 1972 season that if you managed to stop or at least slow down the Packers' runners (Brockington and Lane), you will subsequently force Green Bay to beat you by the pass, something that the Packers had been struggling to do all year. Houston's youthful defense would try to emulate the Bears' efforts, but alas, they just did not have the overall talent or the experience to do so.

This would mark the Packers' first ever regular season meeting inside the famous Houston Astrodome, at that time described by many sportscasters as "the Eighth Wonder of the World." Green Bay in the early 1970s played very few games on artificial turf fields, and even fewer inside domed stadiums. The Oilers in 1972 were the only team in the NFL that year that played their home games in a domed stadium, but their poor record was convincing evidence that most of their opponents were able to defeat them under their roof. The Packers would be one such team on November 19, 1972. The game started as if it would be a defensive struggle, however. Neither team managed to score any points in the first quarter, and it was the Houston offense which accumulated four first downs against only one for the Green Bay offense.

In Green Bay's previous game at Chicago, a very important 89-yard kickoff return from Ike Thomas led directly to a big touchdown for the Packers. Indeed, the special teams were often overlooked by many coaches all across the league in the 1970s, and yet it was the special teams which often produced one or two key plays to earn many victories. Against the Oilers, the Green Bay special teams had once again played a prominent role. They undeniably had their best game of the year, and their eye-catching plays resulted in two big touchdowns. It started midway in the second quarter, when the Houston offense was bogged down at their own 25-yard line. Oilers punter (and also their starting quarterback) Dan Pastorini boomed a 60-yard missile off of his right foot, which drove Green Bay punt returner Jon Staggers way back to his own 15-yard line. Staggers noticed immediately that Pastorini had out-kicked his coverage, however, and that fact gave Staggers plenty of time to size-up his return lanes. He quickly broke to his left and then headed upfield, where he revved up a full head of steam, which enabled him to break a half-hearted arm tackle by Houston's Willie Alexander. Staggers was now alone as he was streaking down the sideline. He saw Pastorini closing in on him about 15 yards in the distance, but he also observed two of his own teammates—Fred Carr and Tommy Crutcher—drawing a bead on Pastorini. For added emphasis, and just to make sure that Carr and Crutcher were aware of Pastorini's presence, Staggers pointed his finger at the potential Oiler tackler. Carr and Crutcher leveled Pastorini at the Houston 38-yard line, and from there, Staggers was home free to the end zone to complete his 85-yard scoring return. Packers 7, Oilers 0.

"When I got around the corner, all I saw were white shirts," described Staggers. The visiting Packers wore their white jerseys that day. "It was a great wall. It was set up perfectly. You try to get outside [of] their [the opposition's] containment. And I was able to do that."[40] Coach Devine was certainly pleased with the play. "You have to have those [returns]," Devine insisted. "It was a really beautiful return. And our guys hustled to set up the runback, which also helped. Jon Staggers also is a pretty good punt return man. He's faster than he looks."[41]

Unfortunately for the Packers, Staggers' dynamic play seemed to wake up the Houston offense. The Oilers immediately put together a 12-play, 80-yard drive, and none of the plays went for more than 15 yards. It was a grind-it-out slowly and methodically type of drive, and it culminated with a 1-yard touchdown run from journeyman halfback Paul Robinson to tie the game at 7–7. Houston's offense had rarely showed any punch or fight all throughout the year, but Robinson's score proved once again that Green Bay could ill-afford to slacken off against even the lowliest of teams.

Time was now waning in the second quarter, and it appeared as if both teams would settle for a tie going into their halftime locker rooms. Enter the Green Bay special teams once again. The Packers took quite a risk with but 34 seconds remaining on the clock, and facing a fourth-and-2 situation from their own 32-yard line. Green Bay punter Ron Widby was expected by virtually everyone inside the Astrodome to just kick the ball out of danger and into Houston territory, where the Oilers would presumably just finish the first half with a basic play or two until the clock ran out. But instead of that, Widby surprised the vast majority of the inhabitants in the Astrodome. He received the snap from center, and standing calmly at his own 18-yard line, he threw the ball down the near sideline for reserve wide receiver Dave Davis, who was standing all alone at his 39-yard line. Davis caught the ball cleanly and ran downfield, where he quickly broke a tackle by Houston safety John Charles at the

Punter Ron Widby came to the Packers in a trade with the Dallas Cowboys. He was a steady and consistent leader throughout the 1972 season. Widby also completed two key passes in 1972 (courtesy the Green Bay Packers).

Oilers' 45-yard line. Davis then broke towards the middle of the field, where he found plenty of open AstroTurf, so much so that no Oilers player came anywhere near him as he crossed the goal line to complete the spectacular 68-yard play. The Packers had shocked their opponents and took a 14–7 lead into halftime.

"We gambled and lost," admitted Houston rookie head coach Bill Peterson. "They gambled and won. We rushed everybody but one man trying to block it. Then we missed a tackle. You've got to give them [the Packers players and coaches] credit."[42]

The way the modest Ron Widby described his throw to Davis, you would think that he possessed the skills of a starting NFL quarterback. "It's an entirely different feeling," said Widby in front of a what was probably the most reporters hovering around his locker after a game than he had ever seen before. "I'm confident I can kick. But passing. It's a little different. Also, if you throw it on third down and it's incomplete, it doesn't matter so much. But if it's incomplete on fourth down and they're going to get the ball at your 32-yard line, that's something else. As soon as I looked up, I saw Davis was wide open. So I just floated the ball to him [Davis]. I just laid it out there. It was a wobbly pass. They [Houston's defense] rushed 10 men a lot. Jim Carter [the Packer fullback on the play] would have called it off if the Oilers changed their alignment. It [Widby's touchdown pass] was a big thrill to me. It was even more of a thrill to watch Dave run after he caught the ball. He made a great run."[43]

The Packer passing game was rarely a threat to any defense all season long, but perhaps that is why the play worked so well. No one expected it. Even the recipient of the pass was shocked at how wide open he was on the play. "All I was thinking about was catching the ball and getting a first down," admitted Davis. "But things went well and I got more than that. I went down 3–4 yards and waited. I wasn't worried about what kind of pass Ron was throwing. I was just worrying about catching it. And it [Widby's pass] was there. I hadn't picked my speed up. [Houston safety John] Charles was coming up and I knew I had to make a move on him. He got a hand on me but he couldn't hold me. From there on, it was a footrace."[44] A race that Davis won, and the Packers were back in front on the scoreboard.

Davis' play seemed to affect both teams in the third quarter in similar ways, as neither team was able to score any points during that frame. Houston did manage to begin the longest drive in the game by either team late in the third quarter, however. The 16-play marathon drive ended with a 13-yard field goal by Oiler placekicker Skip Butler. Houston's deficit was now narrowed to just 14–10. Fortunately for the Packers, the Oilers would not get any closer, as Green Bay's defense did not allow Houston to obtain another first down for the rest of the game.

Then the Packers' offense finally made amends for almost a full game of lethargy. Houston's defense had keyed on stopping John Brockington every time he touched the ball, and they were quite successful in doing so. Brockington would account for only 49 yards rushing on 15 carries.

"They [Houston] know who he [Brockington] is," said Packers fullback MacArthur Lane, "and they put pressure on him."[45] But while concentrating on stopping Brockington, the Oilers completely failed to pay much attention to the other runner in the Green Bay backfield. Lane would end the day with 126 yards on the ground on 16 carries, for an incredible 7.7 yards-per-rush average. It was a superb run by Lane midway through the final quarter that gave the Packers an important insurance score, and which for all intents and purposes signaled the ninth loss of the year for the Oilers.

It started out as a basic sweep to the right, with three offensive linemen—tackle Bill Hayhoe and guards Bill Lueck and Malcolm Snider—pulling to one side to provide interference for the runner. It was the most famous offensive play from Green Bay's illustrious past, seen in all its glory during the Vince Lombardi era of the 1960s—the Packer power sweep. This 1972 adaptation of the power sweep did not have Paul Hornung and Jim Taylor toting the pigskin, however. The new Packer power sweep employed charging bulls MacArthur Lane and John Brockington, and it was nonetheless very potent, just as the 1960s version had been. From the Houston 36-yard line, Lane took a handoff from quarterback Scott Hunter and followed his pulling blockers to the right towards the sideline. But Lane's peripheral vision immediately noticed a slight gap in the middle of the Oiler defensive line. He reacted instantly, and broke toward the sliver of a hole that he saw out of the corner of his eye. It was a wise decision. Lane ran with breakneck speed against the flow of the play, leaving several Oiler defenders flailing at air. The only Houston player who had the

Running back MacArthur Lane contributed greatly to Green Bay's offensive output. He came to the Packers in a trade from St. Louis, and he immediately proved his worth. Lane rushed for 821 yards and led the team in receptions in 1972. He was also a great blocker, opening many holes for running mate John Brockington (courtesy the Green Bay Packers).

slimmest of chances of stopping him was defensive back Willie Alexander, but Lane beat him to the end zone flag. Green Bay now owned a 21–10 lead.

"You never know where a play will open up," admitted Lane. "You just run with your eyes open and you run for daylight ... or your life. John [Brockington] screened a guy out on the play, which was a sweep, and [guard] Bill Lueck stepped up in the hole. I left him there and [wide receiver] Leland Glass made a heckuva block that made the play."[46] Dan Devine had noticed that Lane would sustain a pinched nerve late in the game, but he was not too concerned about the situation. "There is no way a guy can play like he [Lane] does and not get a pinched nerve."[47]

With the game virtually won and with 4:14 left on the clock, the next Houston play from scrimmage officially completed the vanquishing of the Oilers in their Astrodome. Veteran Green Bay defensive tackle Bob Brown, who would make the All-Pro team in 1972 for the first time in his career, stunted to the outside and ran past Houston's left offensive tackle, Tom Funchess [author's note: A stunt occurs when two or more defensive linemen switch pass rush lanes at the snap of the ball in an effort to confuse one or several members of the opposing offensive line]. Brown met Oiler quarterback Dan Pastorini in the Houston end zone, and dropped him for a safety. The Packers ran out the last few minutes of the game, and were the proud owners of a 23–10 victory and a 7–3 regular season record, good enough for the team to remain all alone in first place in the NFC Central Division.

Special teams coach Hank Kuhlmann was awarded a game ball by the team for his planning on the fake punt, which resulted in Dave Davis' touchdown reception, and for his work all week long with the punt return team. That work produced huge dividends with Jon Staggers' long scoring return. "It [being given a game ball] was the biggest thrill of my coaching career," admitted Kuhlmann after the victory. "I feel good about it because my guys have pulled together and hustled and given everything they've got. They work hard at it, and they take pride in what they're doing."[48]

The prideful Packers were now gelling as a team. They had just completed a three-game winning streak, the second time that they had accomplished such a feat in 1972. They did not play their best brand of football during the past few weeks, however, but they had persevered when they needed to the most. They had moved into the top spot in their division, and they were in charge of their own destiny as the final month of the regular season drew near. Their destiny, however, was still undetermined, and the other teams in the NFC Central Division (the Bears, the Lions, and the Vikings) were certainly not about to make things easy on the Packers if they could help it.

8
The Late-Season Drive for Victory

The Green Bay Packers were in the midst of accumulating a string of wins midway during the 1972 regular season, and it was appearing that their hopes for a postseason berth were coming closer to becoming a reality. They knew, however, that they had put together a streak of victories at the beginning of the year, only to go into a two-game losing slump in October. Now in late November, the excitement of earning a wildcard spot in the playoffs—or even a division title—had narrowed down to the final four games of the season.

The Packers were determined to a man to avoid a detrimental lack of focus as they prepared for the remaining opponents on their ledger. Despite their 7–3 record, their most recent victory over the Houston Oilers was not really a true indicator as to how well Green Bay could play, especially when faced with a foe which possessed a really determined and aggressive defense, and a very productive offense. The Oilers certainly did not fit the bill in those categories. The Packers would get to meet just such a strong team in the 11th week of the season, however. Unfortunately for the Green Bay players and coaches, their victory binge would hit an untimely road block on November 26, when they traveled to the nation's capital to take on the 9–1 Redskins. Washington had a roster filled with the oldest players in the league, but those veterans exhibited and delivered a wealth of experience and big plays all throughout the season. The Redskins by this stage of 1972 only needed one more victory to claim a spot in the playoffs for the second straight year, and that impetus alone was enough to make them even hungrier than usual when they took on the Packers.

Despite being underdogs, Green Bay actually began the contest by making a big play on defense, right on Washington's first play from scrimmage. The Redskins' prominent and productive halfback Larry Brown took a handoff from veteran quarterback Billy Kilmer and ran for seven yards off left tackle. Packer outside linebacker Fred Carr was a step too late to tackle Brown, but he was rangy and agile enough to take a swipe at Brown's football-toting arm. Brown never really had a good grip on the pigskin, and Carr's play dislodged the ball from Brown's grasp. Green Bay middle linebacker Jim Carter recovered the fumble at the Redskins' 34-yard line. It was a play which gave the Packers an instant jolt of momentum, but that momentum would be wasted in just three more downs.

The Washington team as a whole was nicknamed "The Over the Hill Gang," in honor of the accumulated average age of their players (28), which was several years above the league average. The Redskins were known for their experience, and for their abilities and their willingness to use that experience in crucial situations all year long. In this instance against the Packers, their defense decided to make a quick strategical adjustment. The Redskin coaches realized after watching game films how much the Packers relied on their running game, a fact that was certainly not so secretive anymore among coaches all across the league. To combat this, the Washington defense sported five defensive linemen on the line of scrimmage instead of the usual four. That strategy forbade Green Bay's offense from making a first down on their first series. It is interesting to note that Redskin head coach George Allen only used the five-man defensive front several times in the early stages of this game. He would use it much more often in the first round of the NFC playoffs (see Chapter 10). Then to officially put an official end to the early Packer scoring opportunity, Redskins defensive tackle Ron McDole blocked a 33-yard field goal attempt by Packers' placekicker Chester Marcol. A golden chance for Green Bay to score first in this game was quickly eliminated, and as this contest neared its end, those three missed points would come back to haunt the Packers in a big way.

Although the Green Bay offense was stymied on their first series of the game, so too was the Washington offense. The Packers' defense would limit the Redskins' offense to just 43 yards gained on four possessions in the first quarter. Green Bay's defense improved quite a bit during their recent three-game winning streak, and they were out to prove on this day that they could stop one of the best offensive units in the league. The Packers defense would force the Washington offense to punt the ball away after their third consecutive possession, and that change of pigskin ownership would lead to the game's first score. The Packers special teams—with the help of punter Ron Widby—had pushed the field position increasingly into the favor of the Green Bay offense. So much so, in fact, that Chester Marcol was given another chance to give his team the lead, which he managed to do. Marcol's 51-yard field goal (his second one of the season from that distance) with 5:29 left in the first quarter boosted the Packers to a 3–0 advantage. The second quarter would see a dramatic change in the game's momentum, however.

8. The Late-Season Drive for Victory

Green Bay quarterback Scott Hunter was not having a sterling season in 1972. He had a very good game against San Francisco at mid-season, but since then he had struggled against mediocre defenses. Against a stalwart and experienced defense like Washington's, Hunter would not enjoy the best of outings. He threw a second quarter pass for a wide open Carroll Dale along the near sideline, but he lofted the ball too high. By the time it descended, tiny Redskins cornerback Pat Fischer (5-foot-9, 170 pounds) arrived to break in front of Dale and intercept the ball. Fischer's play led directly to the first touchdown of the game. Washington tailback Larry Brown made up for his earlier fumble by running a sweep to his left and diving into the Green Bay end zone from two yards out for a 7–3 Redskins lead.

It was at this point that Green Bay head coach Dan Devine decided to bench Scott Hunter and replace him with rookie signal caller Jerry Tagge. The abrupt change shocked virtually everyone on the Packers team, including both Hunter *and* Tagge. At least that is what was believed by most observers at the time. When asked to discuss the matter after the game with reporters, Hunter remarked to them, "not a chance. I'm afraid of what I might say."[1] Green Bay running back John Brockington was also asked about the incident. He was only a little more informative than Hunter. "Was I surprised?" repeated Brockington to the media. "Nothing on this team surprises me anymore. Sometimes I wonder if they [the coaches] know what they are doing. I've probably said too much already."[2] Brockington's post-game comment served as one of the first outward public remarks by one of the Green Bay players in 1972 on the effects of head coach Dan Devine's decisions, and on the responding confusion with the coaching situation on the team.

In reality, Hunter was benched because of an injury he sustained just prior to this first meeting with the Redskins. Many years later, Hunter described the accidental nature of his injury, which involved a simple oversight by some of the noncombatants.

"They [the Packers maintenance staff and grounds crew staff] had taken [what was known as Coach] Lombardi's Tower [a coaching observation tower] off the practice field, and they had not covered up the depression [in the ground where the tower once stood]. I was running between the fields [during a practice session earlier that week] and I stepped in that six-inch-deep hole. It was like dropping off the face of the earth. Man, my back was *killing* me in that [first] game [at Washington]. I had [Packers wide receiver] Carroll Dale just wide open down the sidelines, and as I was halfway through my delivery, my back had another sharp pain. I underthrew it, and [Redskins defensive back] Pat Fischer intercepted it. I just told Bart [Starr], 'Man, Bart, I can't get it out there. I just can't put my back into it.' They put [backup quarterback] Jerry [Tagge] in there, and I think he did a pretty good job."[3]

Jerry Tagge was as prepared as he could be to go into the game at a moment's notice, but he was certainly not ready for what a veteran defense like Washington's would throw at him. The Over the Hill Gang decided to blitz the young Tagge at least once every series, and always coming from a different player in a different location, in order to keep the rookie quarterback guessing. The Green Bay brain trust on the sideline decided to keep Tagge upright by having him utilize his running game even more than usual for the majority of his plays. Tagge would throw the ball only 14 times in the game, and he would only complete a woeful three passes in two and a half quarters of action. To say he was a bit flustered at dealing with the Redskins' pass rush was an understatement.

"It was only the second time I had ever played," remarked Tagge. "He [Coach Devine] just told me to go in and I went in. I saw the blitzes and I kind of panicked. All I wanted to do was sustain a drive. We needed it badly."[4]

Fortunately for Tagge and the Packers, the Green Bay running game was enjoying at least some level of success, particularly in between the 30-yard lines. Washington's defense—like most defenses—keyed on John Brockington, which left fullback MacArthur Lane more opportunities to transport the ball. Lane responded with 71 yards rushing on 17 carries. Brockington could only muster 42 yards on 16 carries, but his efforts served as an important change of pace and variety in order for the Packers to move into scoring range near the end of the second quarter.

It was the Redskins offense, however, which would be the next to move into scoring position. Quarterback Billy Kilmer connected with journeyman wide receiver Roy Jefferson on consecutive plays for 13 and then 10 yards. Washington running backs Larry Brown and Charlie Harraway then contributed a total of 19 more yards on the ground. From the Green Bay 25-yard line and with the Packers defense thoroughly confused as to what player to focus on next, Kilmer threw down the middle, where tight

Rookie quarterback Jerry Tagge came to Green Bay in 1972 with a championship pedigree from the University of Nebraska. He helped the team pull out two important wins in the latter part of the 1972 regular season. He was one of the biggest and strongest quarterbacks in the NFL in 1972 (courtesy the Green Bay Packers).

end Jerry Smith was running free. Smith had beaten Green Bay safety Al Matthews, and he caught Kilmer's perfect pass in the end zone for a score. It was only the third touchdown pass that the Green Bay defense had permitted all season long.

With just slightly less than two minutes left until the conclusion of the second quarter, the Packers' offensive unit had to establish some sort of drive, in order to (primarily) keep the Redskins from scoring again. In order to achieve this goal, Coach Devine and Assistant Coach Bart Starr decided to employ a couple of gadget plays at this time, and both worked. The first came on a on a surprise 10-yard pass from Lane to Brockington. The second came on a reverse to wide receiver Dave Davis for seven yards. Lane also added a 9-yard run on the drive, and then Washington cornerback Pat Fischer was penalized 15 yards for pass interference against Green Bay wide receiver Jon Staggers near midfield on the following play. The Packers' Chester Marcol booted a 37-yard field goal with 23 seconds left in the first half to trim the Redskins' lead to 14–6 going into halftime.

The third quarter featured a bone-jarring hitting fest between both teams. It started out well for Green Bay, as Ike Thomas returned the second half kickoff 40 yards. But neither team could sustain a drive long enough to score. Washington could account for only one first down in the third quarter, which was identical to what they accomplished in the first quarter. The Redskins looked like they might add to their lead, but placekicker Curt Knight missed a 49-yard field goal when the ball thudded against the goal post. Such futility was shared by the Green and Gold, however. On one of the few moments where Tagge had enough time in his passing pocket, his bomb deep downfield landed perfectly in the hands of his wide open wide receiver, Dave Davis. This play—had it succeeded—would have easily resulted in six points. But Davis dropped the ball, and another valuable Packers scoring opportunity was wasted.

Despite Green Bay's earlier mistakes, however, a determined effort by MacArthur Lane early in the fourth quarter did result in a Packers touchdown. From the Washington 6-yard line, Lane ran a sweep to his right, when he notice a small hole to his left. He immediately cut back against the Robert F. Kennedy Stadium turf and rocketed upfield. The Redskins defense quickly noticed Lane's maneuver and closed in to fill the hole. Lane dove for the goal line and flew over it. He was hit while he was still in the air and he fumbled the ball, but his fumble occurred after the ball had crossed the goal line while it was still in Lane's grasp. The Packers were now just one point behind the Redskins at 14–13.

Earlier in the third quarter, Green Bay cornerback Ken Ellis injured his shoulder and was removed from the game. Ellis' injury was indeed very detrimental to the Packers' chances of winning this contest, as his replacement,

Ike Thomas, simply could not duplicate the success that Ellis had enjoyed at the cornerback position. Washington quarterback Billy Kilmer quickly noticed the Packers' lineup substitution, and he immediately began throwing the ball in Thomas' direction, in the hope of taking advantage of his inexperience. Kilmer led his team on an 11-play drive which consisted of six runs and five passes. All five of those passes were thrown against Thomas, and all five were completed. Roy Jefferson caught two of those passes for 30 total yards, and fellow wide receiver Charley Taylor caught the other three for a total of 31 yards. Taylor's final reception on this drive was a 5-yard lob from Kilmer for a touchdown. It gave Washington a 21–13 lead midway through the fourth quarter.

"They [the Redskins] worked over Ellis' replacement [Ike Thomas] pretty well," admitted Coach Devine after the game.[5] Kilmer concurred with Devine's statement. "It kind of looked like I was picking on Thomas," said Kilmer, "...but anybody who tries to cover Charley Taylor one-on-one has a tough job."[6]

To their credit, the Packers put together one more scoring drive in the waning moments of the game, but it was not enough to secure victory. Chester Marcol kicked one more field goal for the Packers, this one coming from 39 yards out, to make the final score 21–16 in favor of the Redskins. Had Marcol connected on the field goal attempt that he had blocked in the first quarter, the Packers would have needed only one more field goal to win, and they could possibly have gotten into his range once more before the game's final gun. This struggle at Washington was an excellent chance for Coach Devine's team to prove that they belonged in the upper echelon of winning teams in the league, but they could not pull it out.

Following the game, the Redskin players and coaches had nothing but praise for the way the Packers battled them so valiantly. "I think we're going to be facing them [the Packers] in the playoffs," predicted the soon-to-be prophetic Billy Kilmer. "I think they are the strongest team in their division [the NFC Central]. There isn't a weak link in the lineup, except maybe at quarterback."[7] Washington head coach George Allen had accolades aplenty to bestow upon his opponent from the post-game locker room. "Green Bay is quite a football team," said the ennobling Allen. "They are about as physical a team as we have played all year. Maybe somewhere along the line we will be going against Green Bay again. This is a very improved Green Bay team. Dan Devine and his staff have done a real fine job."[8]

Dan Devine was not thinking about his "fine job" while answering reporters' questions after the loss, however. Instead, virtually all of the inquiries involved the benching of quarterback Scott Hunter. Instead of taking individual responsibility for the decision to sideline Hunter, Devine went another route, preferring instead to get some Green Bay assistant coaches involved in the decision-making process, whether that was what actually happened or not.

"Obviously the coaching staff thought we had a better chance of winning the football game by making a change at that point [early in the second quarter]," explained Devine.[9] This excuse gave every knowledgeable media member in the locker room a quizzical expression on their faces. How could he (Devine) and his coaches know that Hunter would not be able to have a better second half? How could Devine and his coaches assume that Jerry Tagge would do a better job than Hunter? Did Devine and his coaches think about the effect on Hunter's confidence from the benching? Did Tagge start to assume that he would be a relief pitcher for the remainder of the season? The fact is that the media simply did not know about Hunter's injury from several days before the game, when he stepped in a divot on the Packers' practice field. Had they known this, they would certainly have understood that putting Tagge in the huddle was the only viable option left for Devine. In the midst of all of these perplexing questions was Hunter and his health. Would he be fit enough to play in the next game? Would his back have healed enough to play in *any* further games during the remainder of the 1972 season? Only time—and the hopeful success from a lot of heat compresses and analgesic balm ointments to Hunter's back—would tell.

The loss to the Redskins put the Packers back on another crossroads of sorts in their 1972 journey. Green Bay was now 7–4 with three games remaining. They could ill-afford to lose any more games if they had hopes of making the playoffs. The loss to Washington also meant that the Packers were now once again tied for first place in the NFC Central Division with the Detroit Lions, who just happened to be their next opponent. Detroit had crushed the New York Jets on Thanksgiving Day, 37–20. They were having a very good season, and they had earned seven victories prior to their final meeting of the season with the Packers. Moreover, they would be going into their next game with the benefit of three more days' recovery/practice time, simply due to the break that they received from their schedule. But there was one important question mark that haunted Detroit, and that involved a somewhat soft 1972 schedule. They had only faced two teams in 1972 that were in the 1971 playoffs, and they lost both of those matchups (against Dallas and against Minnesota ... twice).

A repeated question mark also now surfaced at this time for Devine's crew, and this particular inquiry did not have anything to do with Scott Hunter's injury. It involved the general psyche of the team as a whole. Which Green Bay squad would show up against Detroit? Would the team that lost consecutive games to the Falcons and Vikings meet the Lions for their second meeting of the year, or would the team that put together two different three-game winning streaks make another appearance? One thing was for certain:

The game against the Lions at Lambeau Field on December 3 would be the final home game of the regular season for the Packers in 1972. To a man, they knew that they would have to make the most of it. They did possess an advantage in the conference standings, however, in the fact that their own destiny could be determined by themselves, and not by another team winning or losing. If Green Bay won their final three games, they would make the playoffs in the NFC. It seemed simple enough, and it amounted to just taking things one game at a time.

Another big factor for the team to consider going into the game versus the Lions would be the health of defensive backs Ken Ellis and Jim Hill, both of whom had been injured in the previous loss to the Redskins. Ellis' dislocated shoulder was considered to be just a sore shoulder by some, but it was still tender going into Green Bay's second game against Detroit. Hill had a leg injury, which some termed as just a little more discomforting than a charley horse. Both men were determined to play, however, regardless of their physical condition.

"Ken told me last Monday he was going to play," Hill related. "And I told him I was going to play. I believed him and he believed me."[10] Ellis had the strength of his convictions. His team needed him, and he knew it. The time once again arrived for playing the game for self sacrifice, something that many members of the 1972 Packers would display to each other all season long.

"It's pretty tough to keep a guy out of the game at this time of year," said Dan Devine. "It was up to Ellis to convince the doctors he was in shape. Wanting to play was his decision. It was mine to decide whether he could help the team. I think he made his [decision] last Monday. Maybe even Sunday. I made mine 10 minutes before game time."[11]

Ellis agreed with his coach's assessment. "They [the Packers physicians] were afraid I might need an operation if I reinjured the shoulder. I said fine, but I've got from February to July to recover. Even if they said I couldn't play, I probably would have

Cornerback Ken Ellis was one of the best coverage players in the NFL due to his propensity for clutch plays. He was also a key player on several of the Packers special teams. He was named to the All-Pro squad in 1972 (courtesy the Green Bay Packers).

gone against them. It should be a ball player's decision. It's his future. And it [the shoulder] never hurt a bit today [he said, wearing a grin]. If I could be of any help, I should play now."[12]

Ellis' and Hill's level of play would inspire their teammates all during the game. Such inspiration would be needed by the Packers, because the temperature at kickoff was listed at eight degrees Fahrenheit, with a wind chill factor that made the temperature feel like two degrees below zero. Those conditions were enough to test the mettle of any football player. The frozen puffing breaths of every man on the field and every fan in the stands that day at Lambeau Field was a memorable and unmistakable sight, and it called to mind memories of the Ice Bowl, the famous 1967 NFL Championship Game at the same venue, where Coach Lombardi's Packers weathered 13 below zero degree temperatures and the Dallas Cowboys to win another league title. The cold weather in the second Lions game in 1972 was therefore not new for a December afternoon in eastern Wisconsin. But just because it was typical, that did not mean that it was any more welcomed by the athletes on the frozen field. Green Bay quarterback Scott Hunter was by 1972 getting adjusted to the northern winters, and he had recovered well enough from the previous week to start the game against Detroit. Even though he had played his college ball in the warm temperatures in the deep south at the University of Alabama, Hunter was savvy enough to realize how he could help his team win in these frigid Wisconsin conditions. The main components to Hunter's plan simply involved taking his time, and letting the outdoor elements do the rest.

Quarterback Scott Hunter experienced his best pro season in 1972. His ability to secure some big wins in tough games helped the Packers immensely. Hunter's mediocre passing statistics in 1972 fail to take into account the team's weekly game plan, which was centered around Green Bay's ground game (courtesy the Green Bay Packers).

"We win the [opening coin] toss, and of course [we elect] to take the ball," Hunter described. "It's eight [degrees Fahrenheit] at kickoff. So anyway, we're moving the ball down the field, and we're making five [yards] here, six [yards] there. I'd complete a short pass here, then John [Brockington] runs for five, then Mac [Lane] runs for seven. I'm looking up and the game clock is ticking off, then I'm looking over at the Lions [defense], and they're beating their hands together, stomping their feet trying to stay warm. Then I look over at their offense on the sidelines and [I see Detroit quarterback] Greg Landry walking around, trying to stay warm. That time clock is ticking, and we held the ball for I think 10 and a half minutes on that [opening] drive [author's note: Green Bay's offense actually used up 9:01 during their first drive of the game]. And it was 20 minutes [elapsed] on your wristwatch clock! And then we kick a field goal! All we get is a field goal out of it!

"When I saw those Lions stomping around over there, I was just going to slow that thing [the game clock] down. Bart [Starr] would send in a play, and I would wait for 15 seconds before I would call it in the huddle. I would wait a while, and let that frost settle in with them [the Lions] for all it was worth. The guys in our huddle never knew what I was doing. They never had any idea what I was doing. They'd be looking at me, and I'd be looking around, looking up, looking over there at the Lions, and then call the play. Coach [Paul 'Bear'] Bryant [at the University of Alabama] had taught me that ... how to watch the other team. You know at Alabama, where it's hot, and they [the other team] were worn out in the fourth quarter. You're watching them, and if they [your opponent] are dying because of the heat, you make them die a little more [by speeding things up]. In this game [against Detroit] you make them die because of frosty [and you slow things down]."[13]

Green Bay's Chester Marcol completed Hunter's prolonged drives with three consecutive field goals in the first quarter for a 9–0 Packers lead. The Lions would possess the ball for only five plays from scrimmage in the entire first stanza. A key turnover late in the first quarter to boost Green Bay's lead was a fumble by reserve Detroit running back Mickey Zofko, which was recovered by reserve Packers safety Bob Kroll. Marcol added his third field goal just a little more than a minute later.

The scoring for the home team would increase in the second quarter, as the Packers finally found their way into the Detroit end zone. Detroit quarterback Greg Landry threw a pass to his left side, but Green Bay's not-so-injured cornerback Ken Ellis made his first big play. Ellis stepped in front of the intended receiver and intercepted the pass, returning it to the Detroit 23-yard line. Interceptions were becoming somewhat of a rarity for Ellis, because most quarterbacks had learned by this time of the season that the Packers' cornerbacks were having a year for the ages.

"When you have good corner men like we have in Kenny [Ellis] and Willie [Buchanon], your interception rate tends to be lower, because your opponents have to be more conservative with their game plans, knowing they can't pick on any particular player," explained Packer safety Jim Hill.[14]

Five plays after Ellis' interception, John Brockington plowed over right

8. The Late-Season Drive for Victory

guard for a yard and a touchdown. The Packers' lead now swelled to 16–0. But good things were just getting started for the home team. Another big play later in the second quarter led directly to the second Green Bay touchdown, and it was probably the biggest theft of this game. Detroit halfback Altie Taylor was heading upfield for 12 yards when he met Green Bay linebacker Fred Carr in a collision that put an abrupt end to Taylor's progress. But Carr did more than just make the tackle, however. He also reached into the small space between Taylor's left arm and his chest, and swiped the ball out of the running back's grasp. It was indeed a pickpocketing effort that would make any polished convenience store robber beam with admiration and envy.

"He [Taylor] was carrying it loose and high," described Carr after the game. "I saw that as I was going in for the tackle, so I thought I might as well go for the ball. I stole it from him once last year too."[15]

Fred Carr was one of the most dynamic Green Bay linebackers during the decade of the 1970s. He was equally adept at destroying an opponent's running game as their passing game. Often the target of opposing double teams, Carr was named to the All-Conference team in 1972 (courtesy the Green Bay Packers).

Three plays after Carr's thievery, the Packers would score another touchdown. It was one of those plays that was definitely not drawn up on the chalkboard as it actually occurred. Scott Hunter would step back into his passing pocket, and seeing no one open, he stepped up to avoid the Detroit pass rush and an attempted arm tackle by Lions defensive end Larry Hand. He then noticed an open lane to his right, and he figured that the time for hesitation had ended. Hunter ran for the goal line, picked up a key block by John Brockington, then tumbled over a diving Detroit safety Mike Weger and into the end zone for the score. The Packers now owned an insurmountable 23–0 lead going into halftime. The Lion offense would account for only 35 total yards and only one first down all throughout the first two quarters.

Green Bay's advantage on the scoreboard got even more comfortable in the early moments of the third quarter, when Ken Ellis ignited the team once again. Detroit quarterback Greg Landry once again was trying to throw a pass to his left in Lions territory, when Packer linebacker Jim Carter leaped

The Green Bay offensive backfield at work during the Packers' 33–7 rout of Detroit on December 3. Pictured are quarterback Scott Hunter (No. 16), running back MacArthur Lane (No. 36, carrying the ball), and blocking back (No. 42), John Brockington (AP Photo/Vernon Biever).

8. The Late-Season Drive for Victory

Quarterback Scott Hunter and offensive play caller Bart Starr talk strategy on the sidelines at Minnesota on December 10. The strategy that both men discussed was good enough to help produce a 23–7 triumph over the Vikings, thereby securing for the Packers the NFC Central Division championship (© Vernon J. Biever Photo).

high to tip the ball. No one knows what direction where a ball will fly to (or its trajectory) after it gets tipped by anyone. Practically 99 percent of the time, however, a thrown ball will change its direction—at least somewhat—as soon as someone tips it. That is exactly what happened on this specific Landry pass. The ball flew over intended receiver Altie Taylor and into the arms of Ellis, who was in the right place at the right time, and who returned it 40 yards to the Detroit 10-yard line. Two plays later, John Brockington ran through a big hole up the middle for eight yards and his second rushing touchdown of the game. Everything was going right for Green Bay, more so now than at any other point of the 1972 season. It was easily their most dominating performance of the year. The Pack now owned a 30–0 lead, and Coach Devine began to replace his starters with replacements, some of whom were making their initial appearances of the season.

"You know football players, always greedy," acknowledged Brockington, who was replaced by reserve halfback Perry Williams. Brockington ran for 86 yards in the game, while Williams would go on to add 57 yards rushing himself. "But I might have gone back out there and got hurt. And we've got Minnesota coming up."[16]

Even several third string Packer players saw action. One such player was reserve running back Dave Kopay, who contributed 30 yards rushing on five carries. "Man, I never had so much fun in my life," Kopay admitted.[17] Green Bay head coach Dan Devine confirmed that sometimes a highly successful outing like the one that the Packers were experiencing against Detroit on December 3 was not that unusual. Indeed, virtually everything that Green Bay tried to do on that day met with success. "This will happen to a football team," Devine said. "We play aggressively and things went our way. Sometimes you get a day like that."[18]

The Packer scoring surge was not finished, however. Chester Marcol added his fourth field goal of the day, this one from 36 yards out, with 5:48 elapsed in the fourth quarter. Despite the desire for a shutout, the Packer defense was unable to keep the Lions out of their end zone. Substitute cornerbacks Charley Hall and Ike Thomas were in the lineup during the final quarter, and they allowed Detroit wide receiver Ron Jessie to get wide open with just three seconds left in the game. Jessie caught reserve Lions quarterback Bill Munson's arching pass over his shoulder for a 29-yard touchdown, which made the final score 33–7 in favor of the Packers.

"We were thinking shutout," admitted massive Green Bay defensive tackle Bob Brown, "and were a little disappointed not to get it, but Detroit is hard to hold for a whole game. We knew that this is the team we had to beat if we are going to think playoffs, and it made us pick up our defense. Detroit can strike you anytime."[19]

The scoring strikes of the Packers in this game against the Lions were the best of the whole season, and everyone on the team reveled in the glorious win. "The difference was the early breaks," explained veteran Green Bay linebacker Dave Robinson. "We got the upper hand and then we could predict what Detroit was going to do because the score dictated it."[20] The score got increasingly detrimental to what the Lions were trying to do all game long. "We never had a chance," admitted Detroit head coach Joe Schmidt, whose offense could muster only six first downs on 34 total plays all game long. "Our defense never got a rest and the offense was never out there long enough to get our game plan going."[21]

Ken Ellis' game plan was to simply survive for 60 minutes. It turns out that he did much more than that, as his two interceptions and one fumble recovery would attest. His comments following the victory reverted back to his health, and to his decision to play on this frostbitten Sunday.

"As far as I was concerned, I never doubted I would play," Ellis confided to the members of the press corps. "It [my shoulder] took a lot of treatment and a couple of prayers at night. I didn't know if I would be able to stand the pain. I had some guys give me [physical] shots during practice [in the week prior to the Lions game] to see if I could take it. But I progressed a little each day. And there's something about game day, walking in there [the locker room] and seeing all those uniforms spread out."[22]

Packer safety Jim Hill also survived the second game with the Lions. "The leg stiffened up a little bit in the cold," Hill said. "I didn't dare sit down when I was on the sidelines for fear it would stiffen more. I was always by the heater."[23]

Statistically speaking, the Packers amassed 310 total yards in the game, including 19 first downs. Green Bay owned the ball for 72 offensive plays from scrimmage. Green Bay's defensive statistics were impressive but misleading, as the vast majority of Detroit's success came late in the fourth quarter when the Packers had many second-stringers in their lineup. Packer punter Ron Widby only punted once in the game, and the team's motivation to keep the pressure on the Lions was evident all the way to the end. "Sometimes we have had a tendency to let down after getting a lead," said veteran Green Bay center Ken Bowman. "There was no letdown today."[24]

The Packers now owned an 8–4 record, which was good enough for sole position of first place in the NFC Central Division. The Lions and the Minnesota Vikings now both possessed a record of 7–5, and all three teams had just two games remaining in the regular season. Even though Green Bay was in the driver's seat, anything could still happen.

"It's been like this all season," said Coach Devine. "Now, the big game for us is next Sunday. Playing Minnesota at Minnesota is enough of a challenge not to get too excited about anything else, like beating the Lions. And Detroit isn't out of it yet."[25]

Green Bay linebacker Dave Robinson, who rarely agreed with anything that Devine had to say, would at least concur with him on his statement. "I could enjoy this win a lot more if I didn't know that Mr. Francis Tarkenton and the Vikings are waiting for us up in Minnesota next Sunday."[26]

The potential for a playoff berth was now more of a reality than ever before for the 1972 Packers. All it would take would be a focused effort by every man on the team. The trick was to keep their minds and their thoughts on the next opponent, and to somehow stay healthy heading into week 13. Green Bay could now at this exact place and time practically taste a division championship.

9
The Pack Is Back

The clutch victory over the Lions turned out to be just the remedy that the Packers needed in order for them to exorcize the past demons of a potential slump at the absolute worst time of the 1972 season. Green Bay was now down to the end of the year, and because of their stellar performance in many of their first 12 games, the Packers had given themselves an excellent chance to claim the NFC Central Division championship. If they would win their final two games, they would be division champions. As things turned out, the Detroit Lions would suffer an untimely 21–21 tie at Buffalo in the season's 13th week. This meant that a Green Bay victory over Minnesota on December 10 would clinch the NFC Central title for the Packers.

Some measure of good fortune was present for the Packers heading into their grudge match with Minnesota. The frigid temperature in the recent game versus Detroit would be replicated up in Bloomington, Minnesota, where Metropolitan Stadium stood and where the second meeting of the year between the Vikings and the Packers would be held. So there was no possibility of a shock to their collective systems when the Green Bay players emerged from their locker room and onto the frozen field up in Minnesota, because they had become at least somewhat acclimated to the frozen conditions during the previous week. This rematch with the Vikings would turn out to be the coldest regular season NFL game of the decade of the 1970s, however, with the temperature on that vibrantly sunny day stuck on a not-so-balmy zero degrees, and which included a wind chill factor of negative 18 degrees. Despite this, there was no real or imagined advantage for the Packers on this day, as the Vikings were used to playing in this arctic environment. It would become a test of wills in these elements, and a test of which team wanted victory more.

It would also be, however, a test of attire. Several Packers coaches, including head coach Dan Devine, wore a one-piece padded green and gold set of vinyl coveralls, which with sweatshirts and long johns underneath, would provide the wearer with the warmest of cold weather clothing that was available at that time. They were the type of coveralls that one might see people wearing in the Alaskan or Yukon bush environs. They unveiled those coveralls in the Lions game on December 3, and they apparently liked them so much that they wore them in Metropolitan Stadium for their 13th game of the regular season. The Green Bay players certainly could not wear those coveralls during the game, but most of them would wear plenty of layers of clothing under their uniforms. They would also try their best to obtain some sort of an advantage on the sidelines over the Minnesota players. You see, Vikings head coach Bud Grant always refused to allow heaters near his team's bench, in the uncommon belief that his players would psyche-out their opponents by showing that the Norsemen did not need any heaters, and that they were unaffected by the cold weather. Dan Devine did not share Grant's superstition. Devine made sure that several heaters were available to his players all game long.

One particular Green Bay defensive back might have indiscriminately provided the reason for Devine's decision. Rookie cornerback Willie Buchanon utilized some measure of psychological nerve and savvy to persuade his head coach into taking some precautions in order to deal with the cold weather.

"The week before [the second Vikings game] I had convinced Coach Devine to let us wear gloves [versus the Detroit Lions], which up to that point only quarterbacks were allowed to do," Buchanon recalled. "I gave him the spiel about being a poor California boy who had never played in this kind of stuff, and he reluctantly gave in. I had two interceptions that day. After that, more and more guys started wearing gloves."[1]

Devine thus had viewed the positive effects of taking precautions in cold weather games, as the win versus the Lions attested. But the Packers head coach was just getting warmed up (pun not intended). Thanks to Buchanon's big plays against the Lions while wearing gloves, Devine felt that such performances could be replicated if his players managed to keep their hands and bodies warm enough. So Devine would allow all of his players in the game at Minnesota to keep as warm as possible with gloves and with the use of propane sideline heaters along the Green Bay bench area. It was another type of heater that caught Buchanon's attention right from the outset, however.

"I remember the first time that I walked out on that frigid field," said Buchanon. "Some guy was driving something what looked like a big lawn mower, with flames shooting out to melt the field."[2]

The field quickly froze right back up again once those mobile propane heaters were removed from the gridiron. It was the stories of how they dealt with the cold weather which the Packer players remembered most about that game, even almost five decades later. Such accounts are in many ways similar, depending upon which player was retrieving them back from his memory. Yet they were also unique, much as each player was (and is) unique. Take Packers running back John Brockington, who recalled the following gem of an anecdote:

"It was awfully cold that day," remembered Brockington. "On the way to the stadium, Charlie Hall, who was my roommate at the time, was reading a newspaper, and he starts cracking up. I said, 'What's going on?' And he says, 'Listen to this [as he reads from the newspaper]: Minnesota head coach Bud Grant has elected not to have heaters along his sidelines, because he felt that if there were heaters along his sidelines, his players would not be concentrating on the game, and they would be trying to get back to the heat. Green Bay head coach Dan Devine has elected to have heaters on his sidelines, because many of his ballplayers were not of the ruddy, Scandinavian types [laughter].' I had never heard it put that way. We were cracking up."[3]

One of the Packer players—starting quarterback Scott Hunter—would incredibly try to out-psyche Grant and the Vikings by using some reverse psychology. Hunter decided not to wear a sweatshirt under his white Green Bay jersey, hoping that his opponents would see that the cold weather was no big deal for him. The frigid temperature on that afternoon and his chattering teeth, however, eventually made Hunter aware of his miscalculations, and when he emerged from the halftime locker room, he was wearing a white sweatshirt beneath his jersey, just like the rest of his teammates.

"I thought that I was going to be a tough guy," Hunter recalled. "I'm going to go out here [at Metropolitan Stadium] and be a tough guy. You know I was in the National Guard, and they had a cream that you could rub on any exposed skin. I had some of that stuff and I swabbed it all over. It worked well through most of the first half, then it started to wear off, and I started to get cold. I went into the locker room [at halftime] and told our equipment manager Bob Noel to find me something to wear [underneath my jersey]. I don't care what it is [laughter], as long as it covers my arms."[4]

The Vikings had adequately covered the Packers earlier in the year in Green Bay, 27–13, so they were considered the favorite to also win this second game between the two divisional rivals. But the pressure would be situated more on Minnesota's shoulders, as they were the defending division champions, and they were a full game behind Green Bay at this stage of the schedule. Even so, the Packers would still have to stay as focused as possible on their mission. Earlier in the week, the word "poise" was written in big letters on a blackboard in the Green Bay locker room. "I don't know who put it there, because it was ahead of me [coming in to the locker room on that particular day]," said Coach Devine. "But I was happy to see it. It's certainly one of my favorite words."[5] The Packer game plan would center on a level of poise that would make minimal mistakes. "Before the game we told ourselves 'no fumbles, definitely no fumbles,' and we didn't give them [the Vikings] any," said John Brockington.[6]

It would be Charlie West of the Vikings, however, who would fumble the opening kickoff deep in Minnesota territory, and although West recovered his fumble, having the Vikings start their first play from their own 7-yard line must have given the Packers a solid jolt of early momentum. Nevertheless, any optimism that the Green Bay defense might have had was quickly dissipated just a few plays later, when veteran Minnesota quarterback Fran Tarkenton threw deep down the middle for his star wide receiver, John Gilliam. It would turn out to be Gilliam's only catch of the day, but it was good for 43 yards to near midfield. Unfortunately for the Vikings, they could not go any further. In fact, they went backwards a little when Packers defensive end Clarence "Big Cat" Williams looped into Minnesota's offensive backfield and sacked Tarkenton to end the Viking drive. Williams would contribute a total of three of the four sacks of the Minnesota quarterback throughout the day.

"I want to get to the quarterback more," declared Williams. "If I do that, it will help the team as well as help me. I want to keep continuous pressure on the quarterback. I like this [Green Bay] defense, because it's more of a penetrating defense."[7]

No team could penetrate their opponents' end zones in the first quarter, however, as the game evolved into a series of punts, a fumbled punt return by Green Bay's Jon Staggers, and a missed 40-yard field goal attempt by Viking placekicker Fred Cox. The Packers offense was unable to earn a single first down in the first quarter, and that was certainly due to the well-earned reputation of the Vikings defense, which was still one of the most stingy in the entire NFL. If the "Purple Gang"—as the Minnesota defense was called—would keep this up, things could turn out to be pretty bad for Green Bay on this day.

Things indeed did get worse for the Packers early in the second quarter, when their own defense made a crucial mistake. A long Tarkenton bomb was intended for Minnesota wide receiver John Henderson, but it landed incomplete just a few yards ahead of his strides. Green Bay right cornerback Ken Ellis slightly bumped into Henderson as the ball descended 39 yards downfield, however. A referee's yellow hanky lofted down to the rock hard field, and the resulting penalty gave the Vikings a first down at the Packers' 22-yard line. "I thought he pushed me," said Ellis. "I don't know for sure. Somebody said they thought our feet got tangled up, but I'll have to see the film to be sure."[8]

Two plays later, Tarkenton looked pretty sure of himself as he threw over the middle to crossing tight end John Beasley, who rambled 13 yards for a first-and-goal at the Green Bay 7-yard line. On third-and-goal from the 1-yard line, Tarkenton handed the ball off to his other tight end Stu Voigt, who ran behind the line of scrimmage on an end around. Voigt somehow managed to dive into the corner of the Packer end zone, just beating Green Bay left cornerback Willie Buchanon to the flag. Minnesota had drawn first blood, 7–0.

    The Packers' offense was experiencing frustration all throughout the first half of this crucial game. The appearance of the Green Bay players puffing the cold smoke out of their frosty breaths gave some onlookers the impression that they were not as comfortable on this day as they were the previous week, when they played and defeated the Lions in similar weather conditions. At times, the Packers were successful in moving the ball, and at other times they struggled to even gain a first down. Moreover, when they did manage to get within scoring range, one break or another went against them. Green Bay's Chester Marcol was just short on a 45-yard field goal attempt midway through the second quarter, and a few minutes later, even more mistakes befell the Pack. With 3:04 left on the second quarter clock, Green Bay began its best drive of the game so far, starting at their 28-yard line, and lasting for 15 plays. The promising drive ended with zero points, however, as Minnesota safety Paul Krause intercepted a Scott Hunter pass right in front of the Vikings' goal line. This play was very frustrating for Green Bay, because they had managed to move the ball all the way down to the Minnesota 3-yard line. Certainly a field goal at the very least should have been the outcome. But three straight passing plays were inexplicably sent in from the Packer sideline, and Krause's interception was the unfortunate result. With power runners like John Brockington and MacArthur Lane, the idea not to run the ball in for a touchdown made little sense to most people watching the game. It hardly seemed possible that Green Bay Assistant Coach and Quarterback Coach Bart Starr would not have called for at least one running play at that moment on the field. But whoever was to blame, or even if the polar outdoor temperature itself was to blame, the Packers were behind 7–0 at halftime.

    Green Bay quarterback Scott Hunter was not really dismayed or discouraged by his team's deficit, however, as he went back into the locker room to warm up and to prepare for the third quarter. His feelings from many years later had him recalling his confidence in his team's ability to come back strong in the second half.

    "In that first game [against Minnesota on October 29], I knew that we had the better team," Hunter proclaimed. "In the second game, I didn't want to make any mistakes, and give our defense a chance to work on [Minnesota quarterback Fran] Tarkenton and that Minnesota offense. Willie [Buchanon], Kenny Ellis, all those guys back there [in the Green Bay defensive secondary] … you know they were *good*. So if I don't make any stupid errors or mistakes on offense, we've got a chance to win the game. That's what I said at halftime. It's 7–0. Okay. So what?"[9]

To a man, the rest of the Packers players felt the same way that Hunter felt. They were losing the game, but only by a touchdown, and they were not being dominated in any phase of the game by the Vikings. In fact, Green Bay's biggest foe as they returned to the field for the start of the third quarter was not the Vikings, or even their own mistakes. Rather, it was the frozen weather conditions and the unthawed playing field.

"It was so cold, you had to find an old cleat mark [on the field] to put your cleats in," remembered Brockington. "They [the grounds crew] were trying to heat the field up with heaters, but you couldn't do anything on that field. We were like stuffed dogs. We had on thermals under our uniforms. We had plastic [bags] over our toes. We had some frostbite cream that didn't do a damn thing for you. You had your plastic bag over your foot, then you put your sock on over that. And I'm telling you ... by the second half, you couldn't feel the bottom of your feet! The conditions were really awful in the second half. After halftime, the field was as hard as a rock. I slipped twice because of it, making cuts. Some guys got frost-bitten in that game and still have it to this day! It was a brutal game."[10]

Both Brockington and his backfield mate MacArthur Lane were held to a combined total of 56 rushing yards in the first half, a mark that was well below their average. If the Packers were to make a comeback in this contest, at least one of those runners was going to be needed to increase their production in the second half. As it turned out, both men would, and in a very big way. It started with Lane on the first Green Bay drive of the third quarter. On third down from the Packers' 25-yard line, Lane ran a typical sweep to his right, with Green Bay offensive linemen Bill Hayhoe, Malcolm Snider, and Bill Lueck all pulling to their right. But just as he had done so many times before, Lane noticed a small hole to the left out of the corner of his eye. He made an abrupt cutback and glided into the seeping daylight, where he gingerly pranced into the open field, virtually ignoring a couple of Viking defenders who tried to flail at him with their arms. "I just saw a little crack and went for it," Lane remembered. "Sure I ran fast. Man, there are 11 players on the other side, and when you've got the ball, they all want you."[11]

Lane's run ended 37 yards later, when he was driven out of bounds by Minnesota defensive backs Paul Krause and Charlie West. According to Lane, he was able to adapt to the frozen playing surface better than most of the other Packer players.

"It wasn't so bad out there," admitted Lane after the game, who unlike John Brockington, experienced few problems on the gelid turf. "The field was in pretty good shape. We had to score and we had to move the ball and eat up the clock. My old reliable shoes came through. I changed to them at halftime. I think everybody did. My hands didn't even get cold for awhile. Today I really ran for that daylight, just like in Lombardi's days."[12]

Running back MacArthur Lane carries the ball at Minnesota. Quarterback Scott Hunter is at left. John Brockington is shielded by Minnesota's Roy Winston (No. 60). Lane gained 99 yards rushing in this game, a 23–7 triumph over the Vikings (© Vernon J. Biever Photo).

The late and legendary Packer head coach Vince Lombardi would have been proud of what the Green Bay runners and the Packers as a whole did in the second half of this game. First off, they capitalized on Lane's run by scoring a few plays later on a 36-yard field goal by Chester Marcol.

"I hit that first one pretty well, and it went straight," assessed Marcol. "But the ball doesn't carry very far in this cold air. I think maybe 42 yards was the limit today, and then you had to hit it very well."[13]

The Packers then did another thing very well. They caused and then took advantage of a Minnesota turnover, which really changed the course of the contest. Veteran Minnesota running back and special teams player Bill Brown cleanly fielded a bouncing Marcol kickoff, and he adroitly returned it 27 yards up the middle of the field to the Vikings' 46-yard line. Great field position to be sure, but it was wasted a couple of plays later, however, when Brown fumbled a pass that he caught in the left flat after being hit by Green Bay safety Al Matthews. Packers outside linebacker Fred Carr was right on the spot, recovering Brown's fumble on one bounce, then showing off some of his stellar open field moves. Carr broke a low tackling attempt by Brown, then brushed away a sideswiping arm tackle by veteran Minnesota left offensive tackle Grady Alderman. Carr ended up being tackled 26 yards downfield by Viking left offensive guard Ed White at Minnesota's 28-yard line.

"I finally got one, and it couldn't have come at a better time," said Carr. "Both Matthews and I were converging on Brown and when Al hit him, the ball popped loose."[14]

The Green Bay offense did not waste the good field position. Three runs by Brockington and one by Lane set the ball down at the Vikings' 1-yard line. Packer quarterback Scott Hunter finished the drive successfully by diving above the line of scrimmage and holding the ball over the goal line. Minnesota linebacker Wally Hilgenberg could not reach Hunter's mid-section to tackle him, but after the referee's whistle, Hilgenberg grabbed Hunter's head with his arms. He then twisted Hunter's helmet—which at this time was still connected to Hunter's head—from the left to the right and then back again, just for good measure. Needless to say, Hilgenberg was quite upset that his team had just lost the lead. Green Bay now owned their first advantage of the game, 10–7.

"You don't practice something like that," Hunter said of his quarterback sneak for a score in this important contest, "it's just natural. Ever since I've started playing football, in high school, in college, and here in the pros, I've always been instilled with the idea of getting ready for the big games. I think the whole team was ready."[15]

The Packers' good fortune in this big game would continue on the ensuing kickoff. Viking wide receiver and kick returner John Gilliam misplayed Marcol's kickoff, and the ball bounced off of Gilliam's chest. He recovered the muffed pigskin, but was quickly tackled by Green Bay special teams cover men Bob Kroll and Charlie Hall at the Minnesota 14-yard line. Five plays later, Gilliam would be involved in another Vikings miscue, and it would directly lead to even more misfortune for his team. Fran Tarkenton got good protection from his offensive line as he dropped back to pass on a second-and-9 situation from the Minnesota 32-yard line. Tarkenton's throw over the middle hit Gilliam in his hands, then bounced off of them. Packers safety Jim Hill immediately hit Gilliam, and pulled him away from his forlorn attempt at trying to reach and grab the ball again. At this precise moment, Green Bay cornerback Willie Buchanon was in the exact right place at the exact right time. Buchanon trailed the flight of the ball, which landed perfectly in his hands. The rookie pass thief then ran the ball back 25 yards to the Minnesota 28-yard line.

According to noted pro football historian and author T.J. Troup, "nobody could tell where Buchanon was *supposed* to be on that particular play. It left me believing that the Packer defensive coaches were confident enough in the rookie [Buchanon] by this time of the year to let him act on his own instincts. He [Buchanon] probably read what both Gilliam and Tarkenton were trying

Rookie cornerback Willie Buchanon heads upfield at Minnesota with the first of his two interceptions against the Vikings. Minnesota's John Beasley (No. 87) gets blocked by a Packer at right. Buchanon was named the NFL's Defensive Rookie of the Year in 1972 (© Vernon J. Biever Photo).

to do, and positioned himself in the absolutely perfect spot on that play to make the play that he did."[16]

"We were playing them [the Vikings receivers] close," explained Buchanon after the game. "On one of my interceptions, I was with Gilliam every step of the way. On the other, Jimmy [Hill] really gave Gilliam a shot and I was right there. I was surprised to see that ball coming to me. But Jim hit him so hard, the ball just popped out. We were in a zone on the play and I had a deep coverage. I have to be as deep as the deepest receiver, in that situation. So when Tarkenton threw, I just went over that way [to Gilliam's area]. I know we had our momentum going after that interception."[17]

That Packers' momentum continued and in fact grew stronger four plays later from the Vikings' 3-yard line, when MacArthur Lane took a handoff from Scott Hunter, broke an attempted tackle by All-Pro Minnesota defensive end Carl Eller, and trotted into the end zone, holding the ball aloft for another Green Bay touchdown. The Packer running plays were starting to achieve increasing amounts of success. "We got used to what they [the Vikings defense] were doing, their stunts and stuff like that," said Lane.[18] Green Bay's lead now blossomed to ten points at 17–7.

The third quarter ended several plays later with another Buchanon interception. On that play—which originated from the Minnesota 40-yard line—Tarkenton once again benefited from quality pass protection by his offensive line. He decided to throw deep down the far sideline for setback Dave Osborn, who circled out of the backfield and headed straight for the goal line. Buchanon stayed a step ahead of him, however, and caught the ball at the Vikings' 18-yard line. Buchanon actually dropped the ball right after he caught it, and to the naked eye, did not hold on to it long enough for it to be considered anything but an incomplete pass. But Back Judge Bob Rice was slightly behind the Packer cornerback, and he ruled that Buchanon came down with the ball for a legal interception. Things were really going good at this particular time for Green Bay, even in the eyes of the officials.

This fact was confirmed early in the fourth quarter when a punting fiasco proved that this was definitely going to be the Packers' day after all. The longest Green Bay drive of the game was extended three separate times due to Viking penalties, specifically penalties on All-Pro Minnesota defensive tackle Alan Page. On fourth down from the Packers' 40-yard line, Page ran into Green Bay punter Ron Widby. The error gave the ball back to the Packers, but three downs later, they had to punt again. Widby's punt landed in the Minnesota end zone for a touchback, but Page was penalized for offsides. The five yards of penalty yardage was not enough for a Green Bay first down, however, so Widby had to punt again. Against all reasonable Las Vegas odds, the referees once again penalized Page for offsides, and that penalty yardage was enough to give the Packers a first down on the Minnesota 40-yard line. Page was quite miffed before his third consecutive penalty. After it, he erupted in spoken and animated displeasure. In what was one of the finest examples of poor sportsmanship in pro football history during the 1970s, Page screamed at the officials and threw his helmet 10 yards downfield in disgust. Jim Marshall, the venerable Minnesota defensive end who was one of the most dignified leaders on the team, tried his best to calm Page down. His forlorn efforts were ignored by Page, however, who pushed Marshall out of the way, and who was intent on voicing his opinion to the referees. Another Vikings defensive player retrieved Page's helmet and handed it back to him. Page immediately threw it across the field again. A referee took out a note card and supposedly wrote down some of the key phrases that the disgruntled defensive tackle had vocalized on the field during those tense moments. A Minnesota urban legend which was never confirmed publically has it that Page told the official where he could shove his note card. Hint: That particular location involved an important and vital part of the referee's lower anatomy. Then Green Bay linebacker Jim Carter added his two cents worth to the verbal discourse:

"When he [Page] was called offside the first time," Carter conveyed, "he told the referee 'I was not offside, you blankety-blank.' And I said to the umpire: 'He can't call you a blankety-blank.' Then Page called me that. On the very next play the umpire called the same thing [offsides penalty] on Page. I think he [the umpire] was still mad about what Page said to him on the previous play."[19]

The ensuing plays would mark the completion of this incredible 15-play drive, a drive that used up an astounding 9:18 of the fourth quarter. The Packers could only get as far as the Minnesota 34-yard line, but not to worry. Chester Marcol once again booted a field goal to increase Green Bay's lead to 20–7 with just a little more than five minutes left in the game. It would now take a miracle for the Norsemen to score enough points to tie or to win. Such a miracle would become impossible on the Vikings' next offensive series. From the Minnesota 39-yard line, Tarkenton overthrew wide receiver John Henderson. It was now Ken Ellis' turn to be in the right place at the right time. The Packer cornerback easily caught the ball, then ran clear across the field with his prize. He was finally tackled by John Gilliam 23 yards later near the sideline, and this final Vikings turnover gave Green Bay great field position to add yet more insurance to their lead.

"Our defense just went out there and played some ball, like we should be playing," admitted Green Bay star rookie cornerback Willie Buchanon. "We were aggressive, we flew around and we made the big plays."[20]

Packers middle linebacker Jim Carter would add that the defensive plan was "to cut off the [Vikings'] run, make them pass, and then intercept. We wanted to get Tarkenton to pass and then pick 'em off with our great deep backs—Willie [Buchanon], Kenny [Ellis], Jimmy [Hill] and Al [Matthews]— we figured we'd get the ball."[21]

MacArthur Lane got the ball again, and he proceeded to run for another touchdown, but it was called back when reserve tight end Len Garrett was detected holding on the play. Once again, Marcol contributed another field goal, this one a chip shot from just 10 yards out. It made the final score Packers 23, Vikings 7. The Green Bay Packers had finally ended four years of postseason drought. They were the crowned new NFC Central Division Champions.

Green Bay's dominance in this game was resounding and overwhelming to say the least, especially in the second half. The Packers possessed the ball for 13 of the 15 minutes in the fourth quarter. You could make a pretty strong case that the fourth quarter of this game was Green Bay's most dominant 15 minutes of the entire decade of the 1970s. It was a beautiful thing to see for fans who enjoy smash mouth football—a team with a singular purpose of shoving the ball down the collective throats of their favored opponents. It was a scene of vibrant glory, and it was indeed the most glorious highlight of the 1972 Packers season.

According to noteworthy pro football author T.J. Troup, assistant coach Bart Starr deserved to share in the glory. "Starr maximized the talent of a good offensive line throughout the 1972 season," Troup observed. "You could see how well they did in that game at Minnesota. Starr did not care that his offense was going up against the intimidating Purple Gang. He kept his foot on the gas pedal and kept running the ball, and that plan eventually wore those Vikings down."[22]

Starr employed simple traps and draws, then intermingled them with a timely sweep or two, and then offered a few robust and vividly brutal power thrusts into the heart of the Vikings defensive line. The result was forceful and indeed mighty offensive football. Scott Hunter ran those plays to perfection. It was almost as if the Packer blockers and runners were taking all of their frustrations that had bit into them throughout the entire season, and blasted them straight into the chests of the Minnesota defenders. For aficionados of throwback running game football strategy, the second half of the contest at Minnesota on December 10 was simply beautiful to behold.

Conversely, Green Bay's defense limited Minnesota's offense to just 13 plays in the third quarter, and only five plays in the fourth quarter.

"There was no sense trying to fool us," observed veteran Packers linebacker Dave Robinson. "We knew Tarkenton had to throw. We changed a few of our keys around, but the main thing was that we were able to put pressure on them, to make them play into our hands.[23] I've been in Green Bay for 10 years and never seen anybody tackle [sack] Fran Tarkenton three times in one game, but Big Cat [Packers defensive end Clarence Williams] did it today.[24] The odds of us winning the division were 100–1 back in July. But whoever fixed those odds never stood in one of our huddles."[25]

The Green Bay offensive huddle featured the pride and joy of the Packer offense ... their running game. That unit certainly stepped up in this crucial matchup. Both John Brockington and MacArthur Lane were limited to subpar first halves, but both would excel in the second half. Lane finished with 99 yards rushing on 19 carries, for an outstanding 5.2 yards per carry average. Brockington contributed 114 more ground yards of his own, which put him over 1,000 yards rushing for the second straight year. Brockington thus became the first man ever in NFL history to rush for at least 1,000 yards in each of his first two seasons.

"The championship overshadows my getting 1,000 yards for the second year in a row," said Brockington as he thawed out after the game. "I wasn't aware of 1,000. I was thinking of getting first downs, eating up the clock and getting closer to that goal line."[26]

One of Brockington's runs that got his team nearer to the Minnesota goal line was indicative of the desire of the big back to earn yardage, all the while demonstrating the symbolic power of the Packer rushing attack. On

Halfback John Brockington (No. 42) cuts upfield at Minnesota. Packers quarterback Scott Hunter (No. 16) is in the background. Brockington rushed for 114 yards in this game, which clinched the NFC Central Division Championship for the Packers (© **Vernon J. Biever Photo**).

that particular play, Green Bay quarterback Scott Hunter handed the ball off to Brockington on a misdirection play (a play where Hunter and most of the other members of the offense runs in one direction, and Brockington as the ball carrier runs in the opposite direction). Brockington charged through a wide hole, picked up at least 10 yards of steam, and bowled over Vikings safety Paul Krause, who was credited with "making the tackle." Krause got back to his feet a few seconds after Brockington did. That particular play still gets quite a laugh all these years later when being discussed by Scott Hunter.

"So the clock runs down to four or five minutes to go [in the game], and they [Minnesota] are obviously beaten," Hunter recalls. "I'm running John [Brockington] left and John right. We needed to build up some yardage for him so he could go to the Pro Bowl and get his bonus [laughter]. So on one play he goes running down the field and there is nobody but Paul Krause and him [Brockington]. You know Krause wasn't a tackler, he wasn't a tough guy. He just sat back there and picked up trash. All John had to do was give him a chip. John could have easily just stuttered and chipped him [Krause] and gone on in and scored a touchdown. But John looked at him and lowered

As time winds down to a division championship, Green Bay quarterback Scott Hunter stands alongside head coach Dan Devine (AP Photo/Vernon Biever).

that shoulder, and there wasn't nobody but him and Krause. And it [the collision] looked like a garbage can that had been hit by an 18-wheeler [laughter]. And John winded up stumbling over him [Krause] as he ran over him [continued laughter], or else he would have scored [more continued laughter]. We're on the airplane [coming home after the game], and John told me 'I did that for you Scottie' [Hunter offers nearly a minute of hearty laughter].

"I talked to Paul [Krause] many years later, and he said, 'I still remember it [the collision with Brockington]. I saw him coming and I said, 'oh no.' There was nothing to hit there but shoulder pads and thigh pads. He [Brockington] was 6-foot-1, 225-pounds, and all muscle."[27]

Predictably, the humble Brockington shared his success after the game by praising those who made it possible.

"The [offensive] line really fired out," Brockington said. "It all just came together. We really believe in ourselves now.[28] We've been talking about this [winning a championship] ever since July, when we were doing those doggone up-downs on the grass. But those drills are paying off now."[29]

A couple of Brockington's teammates reflected after the game on what the victory meant to them. Scott Hunter's feelings concerning the contest were more of redemption than anything else. He really wanted his teammates to believe in him and in his abilities, especially when considering his previous outing against Minnesota.

"After that first game against the Vikings, when they intercepted me four times, I kind of wanted to redeem myself today in the eyes of some of our players."[30] Packers safety Jim Hill reveled in the aura of the victory. "I get a lump in my throat just thinking about it," said Hill of the win. "I don't know how long it'll be before I start crying. Today I'm so happy I feel like I died and went to heaven."[31]

The glory of winning a division title was certainly not to be considered identical to going to heaven, but the feeling of euphoria after beating the Vikings at their own outdoor igloo was noticeably enjoyed equally by every player and coach. The scene inside the warm post-game locker room at Metropolitan Stadium would be a special memory for all of the men in Green and Gold, and their words accurately depicted their joy at coming so far in so short a time since head coach Dan Devine took over the helm in 1971. Far from the egomaniac image that he had projected for the past two years at Green Bay, even Devine proved that after discussing some successful elements of his team's strategy, a glorious victory could also bring out some graciousness and magnanimous praise from him for his players.

"What we did in the second half is the sign of a good football team, and one that wants to win," said Coach Devine as he thawed out after the game. "We played better than we did in the first half. We got the key defensive plays to put us into field position.

"I really believed we could win all along. I know we were a last-place team, but to hell with that. All 26 coaches think they have a chance of winning, and we certainly did. This team has been very receptive. The players have done everything I've asked of them, and to the best of their ability. They deserve to be champions. We've beaten the good teams, we beat Detroit twice, beat Chicago twice, and we split with the Vikings. We've also beaten Dallas and San Francisco. I always have high expectations. I'd say we belong where we are. We deserve the [division] championship."[32]

A couple of Packers players were overjoyed for this moment of victory, but for different reasons. Long-time veteran linebacker Ray Nitschke had experienced all of the great memories of being a champion while playing for Coach Vince Lombardi in the 1960s. The win over Minnesota marked a moment where he could—for at least one brief moment—relive those winning feelings again. Five-year veteran MacArthur Lane was experiencing his first year of victory in 1972 with the Packers. He spent his first four years in the league languishing with the St. Louis Cardinals, a perennial also-ran team.

"It's great to be associated with a winner again," said Nitschke. "There's no better feeling. It's great to be a part of this with these young men."[33]

An epic moment of pure joy and victory. As Green Bay head coach Dan Devine is carried off the field following the Packers' 23–7 win at Minnesota, tight end Pete Lammons (No. 86), quarterback Scott Hunter (No. 16), and running back John Brockington (No. 42) celebrate their NFC Central Division title (AP Photo/Vernon Biever).

Nitschke did not see much action in this, his final NFL season, but playing in the division-clinching win at Minnesota would be a celebrated moment in his legendary 15-year career. Lane, on the other hand, had been one of the most relied-on Packers all throughout the season. "Not bad for a day's work," assessed the burly but tired fullback. "I'm all beat up. Your old body starts to go down at this time of the season. Figure out how many times I've been hit.[34] But it's that time of the year. You don't think about that when you're playing for all the marbles. I'll come out of it with a lot of rest in the off-season. I've been waiting for this for five years. It means so much to everybody. So few guys around the league are able to appreciate something like this.[35] You could see this thing coming together ever since the beginning of the year."[36]

The victorious moment as the final gun sounded was crystalized in memory as an oft-repeated highlight from NFL Films. Although he was derided by most of his squad, Coach Devine was carried off the field by several of his players, and that epic scene became the ultimate visual moment of the team's success that was captured in time in 1972. "If you're happy like that, you do happy things," commented Brockington when referring to his coach's victory ride. "To overcome so many things and beat that team. That's the first time that we had ever beaten the Vikings since I was there. That victory was big."[37]

The poise that had been nothing more than just another word on a blackboard had now been indelibly written into the hearts and minds of all of the Packer players. They could now lay claim to the poise of a champion. With puffs of their breath spewing forth like a chugging freight train (as it had all afternoon long), the Green Bay Packers ran off the frozen field triumphant. They had somehow managed what most people thought was impossible. They had won a division title in one of the most trying seasons in the team's storied history. They had won a championship in the "Black and Blue Division" amidst disagreements and disorders with their head coach, and with a lot of new players in their starting lineup. Dan Devine would later be named NFC Coach of the Year, mostly due to Green Bay's winning record and their brand new division title. The trophy honoring him for this award resides under glass to this day in the Packer Hall of Fame and Museum at Lambeau Field. After the big victory over the Vikings, the Packers were honored by an estimated 5,000 Packer Backers upon their return to Green Bay at the Austin-Straubel Airport later that evening. Those fans were gleefully displaying "We're Number One!" signs in green and gold. A pep band even braved the cold temperatures to play some victory songs. Nothing less would have been expected by the diehard Packer fans, who were now celebrating a winner once again. All of Wisconsin and all of Green Bay could now say in unison that the Pack was back.

Green Bay's final game of the 1972 regular season would be in New Orleans on December 17, and it would serve as an award of sorts for all of the Packers' hard work and success during the past several months. The Saints had won only twice all season long, and even though Green Bay would be resting many of their starters, New Orleans would once again be regarded as underdogs. This contest would be akin to a one-week vacation, from the development of the game plan to the playing of the game and everything in between. The Packer players would not be taking this contest as seriously as any of their previous 13 games, and it would show. Green Bay played down to the level of their opponents, especially in the second half. The Packers could not really be faulted for their lackadaisical attitude in preparing for the Saints and playing in this game. Green Bay had already clinched their division, and nothing could be gained in the standings with a win over New Orleans. The Packers' playoff opponent in the divisional round of the postseason tournament (Washington) was already determined prior to Green Bay's contest with the Saints. While it was true that several individual and team records could be achieved with good statistical outings for Green Bay in New Orleans, that was hardly the team's focus. It would just look better and feel better amongst the players, coaches, and fans alike to finish with 10 wins instead of nine. In order to get those 10 victories, the majority of the starting Packer players would end up playing most of the first half, in the hopes of piling up enough points to obtain a big lead. Then the second-string players would come on in and help the team coast in the second half. The initial part of that strategy happened as planned.

"It was a strange game," admitted Green Bay head coach Dan Devine. "It's the type of game in which both teams played real well at times and real bad at times."[38]

The bad that Devine alluded to was evident in a total of five blocked kicks throughout the game between both teams. There were not a lot of turnovers in the contest (the Saints committed two, and the Packers committed none), but there were enough strange plays in this matchup to make it interesting.

A sunny, 39-degree day greeted the teams, in what could certainly be described as a perfect day in December to play football. Most every player on the Green Bay team would admit that it was a welcomed change from the frigid climates of the previous two weeks. The Packers would wear their home green jerseys in this game, and the Saints would wear their white jerseys. As is a long-standing pro football rule, the home team gets to decide which color jerseys (light or dark) they want to wear, and the visiting team is required to wear an opposite color jersey. New Orleans as the home team decided to wear their white jerseys, so for the only time in 1972, the Packers wore their traditional home colors (green jerseys) as a visiting team. The game would be played in old Tulane Stadium, which since the previous year now employed an artificial turf playing surface. It would mark the third and final time in the 1972 regular season that the Packers would be playing on the colorful and clean fake grass.

The unusual look of Green Bay wearing their dark jerseys at a visiting venue was just the beginning to the aforementioned strangeness of this game. It all started in a predictable way, however, with Chester Marcol lining up to kick a 48-yard field goal in the first quarter. Then the strangeness took over. Marcol's kick was blocked by Saints linebacker Joe Federspiel, and from then on, virtually everything else in the contest settled into an outlandish pattern. Green Bay punter and kick holder Ron Widby picked up the bouncing ball and immediately looked downfield for a potential receiver. He quickly spotted reserve linebacker Ray Nitschke, who was undoubtedly the most unlikely player on the field to catch a pass, and who was relegated to playing on special teams in order to experience at least some game action. Widby threw for Nitschke, who made an extraordinary grab of the low pass at the Packers' 49-yard line. Nitschke then turned around and discovered that there was plenty of running room in front of him, so he ran as fast as his 35-year-old body would permit. He picked up a couple of key shielding blocks, and was eventually tackled by New Orleans safety Tommy Myers at the Saints' 7-yard line.

"I made my block and I heard the thud of the ball being blocked," recalled Nitschke. "I looked back to see where the ball was, and saw Widby running around. I motioned to him a little and I'm glad he saw me. The next thing for me to do was to get open. I concentrated on the ball. It's a reaction type of thing. I just wanted the first down, until I saw the left side open. Widby is the one who made it go. He's played quarterback, and [he] throws a nice spiral. It was a big thrill. You hope there's some way you can contribute, and it's great to get the opportunity. I want to contribute any way I can."[39] In a rather humorous vein, Green Bay assistant coach Rollie Dotsch claimed, "I'll bet Ray Nitschke never thought he'd be our leading receiver [in the game]."[40]

For his part, Widby modestly downplayed his role. "Ray made a heck of a catch," Widby stated. "I think the pass was low. Chester [Marcol] would have been eligible [to catch the pass] too, but I didn't see him [smile]. He probably was buried somewhere."[41]

Green Bay quarterback Scott Hunter was buried himself five plays later, but his entombment took place in the opposing end zone. From the New Orleans 1-yard line, Hunter took the snap from center and followed right tackle Dick Himes through a small hole and under a horde of Saints tacklers. Hunter had crossed the goal line, however, and the Packers took a 7–0 lead.

The second quarter featured more good fortune for Green Bay. Following a 34-yard field goal by Marcol, the Saints lined up for a field goal attempt of their own. New Orleans placekicker Happy Feller probably wished that his fate would not include getting a kick blocked like Marcol, but that is exactly what happened. Willie Buchanon of the Packers stormed into the Saints backfield and grazed the booted ball with his hand. Green Bay defensive end Clarence Williams scooped up the pigskin and started upfield, when all of a sudden he recognized a friendly face 15 yards into his run. Buchanon had caught up to the man they called the "Big Cat," and Williams lateraled the ball to the Packer rookie defensive back. Buchanon started this play, and a few seconds later, he finished it. His 57-yard return for a touchdown (he actually got credit for all 57 yards, even though he only carried the ball 42 yards following the lateral he received from Williams) down the sideline served as undeniable proof that to win this crazy game, a team sometimes needed more good luck than skill in the execution of their game plans. It also proved that Happy Feller was not too happy of a fellow, at least not as happy as his counterpart in Green and Gold, Chester Marcol.

In describing his scoring return, Buchanon's interpretation validated the accuracy of the age-old adage about football. It is indeed ... *a game of inches*.

Buchanon and the Packers benefited from being exactly where he needed to be to achieve the absolute greatest benefit of the play.

"Freddie Carr came down hard on the up-block and that cleared the way for me [to rush the kicker]," Buchanon said. "I had a clear shot at the ball. I felt the ball hit my hand, but I didn't get as much of my hand on the ball as I wanted or it wouldn't have even gone forward. Clarence got the ball and I was going to block for him. Then I yelled, 'Cat.' Clarence saw me and tossed the ball to me. After that it was an easy footrace."[42]

Green Bay owned a 17–0 lead as halftime neared, and things were looking good. Just then, however, a brief moment of Packer carelessness produced a New Orleans touchdown. Ron Widby was back to punt in his own end zone when New Orleans defensive end Richard Neal got good penetration. Green Bay linebacker and (on this play) blocker Jim Carter moved to address the threat of Neal possibly blocking the punt, but Carter inadvertently and accidentally got in the way of Widby's kick. The ball bounced off of Carter's back, and landed right in front of Neal, who fell on it uncontested in the Green Bay end zone for a score. The Saints were now back in the game, trailing by a 17–7 score at halftime.

"When [Richard] Neal came rushing in, I took a few steps to the right side," Carter recalled. "And the ball hit me low in the back. It was dumb, and it shouldn't have happened."[43] Packers head coach Dan Devine concurred with Carter's sentiments when appraising not just Carter's mistake and Neal's freak touchdown, but the entire contest as well. "Some of it was carelessness," assessed Devine in regards to the sloppy play. "It was not my favorite kind of game to play—or watch."[44]

The second half saw mass substitutions by the Packers, and more mistakes as well. It started off well enough for Green Bay, however, right from their very first possession of the third quarter. Second-string Green Bay quarterback Jerry Tagge ran an option play to his right from the Saints' 1-yard line. He scored standing up, which re-instilled the Packers' 17-point lead at 24–7. New Orleans responded immediately afterward when Saints quarterback Archie Manning found setback Bill Butler on a 9-yard touchdown pass. Butler was actually not the primary or even the secondary receiver on the play. He stayed in the backfield to block and was knocked down in the process. When he got back up on his feet, he saw Manning scrambling to avoid the Green Bay pass rush. Butler ran a few yards downfield when Manning noticed him. The two connected for the score to pull the Saints closer at 24–13, but New Orleans had botched the extra point conversion attempt, so the Saints remained 11 points behind the Packers as the third quarter ended.

Chester Marcol then added two more field goals for the Packers midway through the fourth quarter, but it was his two blocked field goals earlier in the game which ended his hopes for a league record. Jim Turner, who in 1968 was a placekicker for the New York Jets, owned the all-time pro record from that year with 34 successful field goals. Marcol ended 1972 with 33 field goals. He also ended 1972 as the league's leading scorer with 128 points. Long-time Packers public relations director and team historian Lee Remmel once told Marcol that he "doubted any rookie, other than the great wide receiver Don Hutson, made a bigger impact on the Packers than [Marcol] did in 1972."[45]

"If I let it [not getting the league field goal record] bother me, I'd miss all of them," admitted Marcol. "I always forget the ones I miss. Anyway, one of the blocked field goals led to a touchdown for us [Hunter's quarterback sneak in the first quarter for Green Bay's initial score]."[46]

Marcol's performance was even more incredible when one considers that the average distance of his field goals in 1972 was 33.8 yards long, a mark that was better than any other placekicker in the league. Marcol would by season's end be named the United Press International's Rookie of the Year.

One final Saints score, coming on a 10-yard rollout pass from Archie Manning to New Orleans wide receiver Dave Parks against reserve Green Bay defenders, made the final score 30–20 in favor of the Pack. The two Saints touchdown passes in this game kept the Green Bay defense from also setting a new league record for the fewest touchdown passes allowed in one season, set by Minnesota in 1970. The Vikings had permitted only six scoring tosses in that year, and the 1972 Packers conceded just seven touchdown passes.

"It would have been nice to have had the record," said star Green Bay rookie cornerback Willie Buchanon, "but going into the playoff games means a heck of a lot more. All I can say is that we're 10 and 4."[47]

The victory at New Orleans marked a rather strange end to an outstanding regular season for the Packers. Coach Devine still was unsure what to make of the win, but one can tell that he was fairly glad to have won the game amidst all of the mistakes. "It was just a case of not putting everything together," Devine inferred. "It was a kind of scrambled effort. Our defense did well in the first half. In the second half, our special teams did a good job and our offense was moving the ball. We had a good effort."[48]

Green Bay would need a really good effort if they were to be successful in the playoffs. New Orleans defensive end Richard Neal may have anticipated and predicted the Packers' chances best, however, when he was asked by reporters how well he thought Green Bay would do in the playoffs. "If they [the Packers] make the same amount of mistakes in the playoffs as they did today against us," Neal said, "they would have two chances: slim and none."[49]

The 1972 regular season was now over, and it ended for Green Bay with the success of a division championship and a playoff berth. The reasons why the 1972 Packers won games centered on their strong ball carriers. According to the research-oriented pro football historian and author T.J. Troup, there was never any second guessing as to who represented the strength of the offense. The running back duo of John Brockington and Mac Arthur Lane were expected to do a lot for the team, and they did just that, compiling a total of 1,848 yards rushing in 1972. The statistical comparisons with the AFC rushing trio of Miami's Larry Csonka, Mercury Morris, and Jim Kiick were obvious to many. A team's ground game was considered by many as their pride and joy back in the early 1970s.

Nevertheless, some performers continually shed at least some degree of light on the 1972 Green Bay regular season. For example, the punt return squad did incredibly important and outstanding work. Green Bay punt returners such as Jon Staggers and Ken Ellis (and others) brought the ball back on punts with much determination, and always striving to obtain even one more yard. That meant that the Packers offense often started many of their drives in decent (or good) field position. Green Bay also did not throw the ball that much, but when they did, they were quite effective. Packer quarterbacks and their targets rang up just over 15 yards per completion, meaning that every Green Bay completion moved the sticks downfield for many first downs. Finally, the place-kicking prowess of Chester Marcol was simply superb. Marcol connected on 33 field goals, and he was successful on over 68 percent of his field goal attempts. Coach Devine had a weapon that he would rely on to give his team three points, even if his offense could barely get the ball past midfield.

Such statistics were indicative of how improved this Packers team was from those of the past few years. Only time would tell, however, if the 1972 Packers could keep winning in the NFL playoffs.

10
Losing Too Soon

The 10-4-0 Packers were now the proud owners of the NFC Central Division title, their first championship of any kind since they won Super Bowl II in 1967. They had surprised many of their opponents during the 1972 regular season. As a result, Green Bay had earned the right to travel to Robert F. Kennedy Stadium in Washington, D.C., where they would play the Redskins in the first round of the NFC Divisional Playoffs on December 24. There was an excited feeling of optimism that was running through the ranks of the Packer players heading into the postseason tournament. The rookies and the younger players on the team were enjoying their very first visit to the playoffs, while the older veterans (many of whom had played for Vince Lombardi and who were still somehow on Coach Devine's roster), were gleeful that they had garnered at least one more shot at greatness. To a man, the players—regardless of their age—did not care who they were playing in the upcoming playoffs. They were all just simply happy to be there.

Washington had won the NFC Eastern Division title with an outstanding 11-3 record, the best mark in the conference. The Redskins were a team that had a roster filled with older players, quite a few of whom were over the age of 30. Their head coach was George Allen, a firm believer in trading away his collegiate draft choices to many different teams, in order to obtain more experienced veteran players from those teams. Despite the fact that many of these men were slower than most younger players in the league, the experience of Allen's men more than made up for their lack of speed and quickness on the field, at least in 1972. They became known to pro football history as "The Over the Hill Gang," and they were enjoying the success of their most legendary season of the decade.

In preparation for this playoff game, both teams made important adjustments to their game plans. But one adjustment had nothing to do with the players themselves. Green Bay head coach Dan Devine had at this time decided to take the play-calling duties away from assistant coach Bart Starr, who had helped the team immensely during the entire regular season. Starr's football intellect as a former quarterback was legendary, and his knowledge of how to get the most out of the players on the Packers offense was vital in their drive to the 1972 playoffs. Devine's decision was inexplicable to most of his players and to most of his assistant coaches. Starr refused to publically denounce Devine's methods and play calling, but that was not surprising. Starr was always one of the most humble, likeable, and kind men who ever played or coached pro football. It would be completely out of his character to speak out against the head coach. In the many years since 1972, some of the players and front office people, however, were willing to dissect and discuss what happened to the team just prior to their playoff game at Washington. The odds against a Packer victory over the Redskins were somewhat long, and the untimely decision by their head coach to resume calling plays on offense would not improve those odds one single bit.

The Packers and the Redskins had met earlier in the regular season on November 26 at Washington, and it was a game that did not turn out the way that Green Bay had hoped. The Packers had kept that contest close, however, and were very capable of winning it. A key injury to cornerback Ken Ellis of Green Bay gave the Washington offense an opportunity to take advantage of a few second half pass routes that were not available when Ellis was in the game. The Redskin air attack had thus accounted for the winning touchdown in a 21–16 victory for George Allen's team. Ellis would fortunately be on the mend, however, and would be starting for the Packers in the upcoming playoff game.

During that earlier meeting, Allen decided to employ a unique (unique for 1972 that is) five-man defensive front line for the first few plays of the game. The coach's main reason for doing so was preliminary in nature. The Packers were—by the day of their first contest with the Redskins—being regarded by many onlookers as a potential NFC playoff team. Allen risked no stone unturned, so he diligently prepared for almost any circumstance (and any team with a winning record), regardless of who his foe would be in the postseason. He wanted to see how Green Bay would alter their strategy when five Washington defensive linemen were used, as opposed to the usual four-man line. That savvy move represented a separate game within a game, and it clearly demonstrated just one example of the football genius of George Allen. The results of the new defensive alignment back in their November encounter were inconclusive, however, depending upon whose opinion you believed.

"We couldn't do anything against it," admitted the Packers' John Brockington.[1] "We used it in the first game against them a couple of times," recalled Allen, "and it didn't do too well, but we won anyway."[2] Veteran Green Bay outside linebacker Dave Robinson experienced the strategy from a different viewpoint:

"Dan [Devine] made some serious mistakes," Robinson remembered. "One of which was when the Redskins had a five-man [defensive] line [in the first meeting between the two teams]. Gale Gillingham our guard said [to Devine before the playoff game], 'Dan, what are we going to do if they [the Redskins] run this five-man line against us? We don't have any plays against it.' Dan Devine said, 'Don't worry about it. They wouldn't dare run that against us.'"[3]

Despite their excitement, there was also some feelings of tentativeness and uneasiness among most of the Packer players and coaches going into their playoff match. You could call it a common perception of nervousness, and it accompanies any young football team (past or present) playing in their first playoff game in years. One young Packers player was showing no signs of pre-game jitters, however. In fact, Green Bay quarterback Scott Hunter felt even more confident going into the playoffs than his head coach and virtually anyone else wearing Green and Gold. Hunter was even projecting the Packers' possibilities for success *after* their playoff meeting at Washington.

"There's a little bit of thinking going on before that [divisional playoff] game," admitted the second-year signal caller. "We were the last team to beat the [Miami] Dolphins in 1972 in an exhibition game. [Author's note: The Packers had defeated the Dolphins in Miami's Orange Bowl Stadium in the second week of the 1972 preseason.] And you know in those days, you played six exhibition games. The Dolphins played all of their first-string guys for four quarters [author's note: The Dolphins did in fact substitute some of their starting players for their second and third string players in the second half of this game], and we played all of our first-string guys for four quarters. We beat them 14–13, but we just didn't beat them. I remember that we were physically much stronger up front, offensively and defensively. We were rolling over [Miami middle linebacker Nick] Buoniconti.

"My thoughts are, we'll beat the Redskins this time. Then we would get the Cowboys, who had beat the 49ers [in the 1972 NFC Divisional Playoffs]. We would likely get the Cowboys up in Green Bay the next week, in another Cold Bowl [author's note: Hunter was referring to the famous 1967 Ice Bowl game, where the Packers defeated the Cowboys for the NFL Championship in 13-degree below zero weather at Lambeau Field], and we would beat their ass again, even worse than we did the first time [on October 1]. And then we would go play Miami [in Super Bowl VII], and we wouldn't let [Miami quarterback Bob] Griese and [Miami wide receiver Paul] Warfield on the field ... we'll keep their ass on the sideline. We would run up and down the field on that small Miami defense. And that's the way you win a Super Bowl."[4]

Hunter's optimism was a breath of fresh air for the Packers. His confidence was a positive sign, even though many of his teammates (and Hunter included) had never played in an NFL playoff game before. The postseason fervor and excitement would indeed be a new feeling for those younger Green Bay players. They were pumped up and ready to prove to the Redskins (and indeed to the rest of the NFL landscape) that they belonged in the 1972 playoffs. Even the coaching staff started to feel a higher level of excitement going into the playoff game at Washington. "We knew that we had a team that could win," admitted Coach Devine. "We knew it in July when training camp started."[5]

An overcast day featuring 38 degree temperatures greeted the throng of fans at RFK Stadium. Those folks were about to watch the first home playoff game in Washington, D.C., since 1942. It did not take long for those fans to tell that this would be a defensive battle. Neither team could score in the first quarter, as both defenses were shutting down the opposing offenses. The hitting was some of the hardest that either team had seen all season long. Playoff football is famous for that, and it has been that way for years.

Washington quarterback Billy Kilmer could certainly attest to the increased ferocity of the hits being distributed. On a specific play in the first quarter that symbolized this whole game, Kilmer just barely got a pass off and was simultaneously hit by Green Bay defensive ends Alden Roche and Clarence Williams, both of whom were looping around the outside edges of the Redskins' pass pocket. Roche hit Kilmer first in the small of his back, and you could see—and some could even hear—Kilmer's back snap in half like a tree branch. A fraction of a second later, Williams planted his helmet in the quarterback's jawbone in a not-so-gentle manner. Kilmer decided to not wear a chinstrap in this game (he rarely wore one throughout his career), and that was a decision that he instantly regretted when he woke up a few minutes later. The striking of Kilmer's head (courtesy of Williams) dislodged the quarterback's headgear. As he fell to the hard dirt that was described as "turf," Kilmer's head bounced off the ground not once but twice.

"Boy, did the lights go out for a while," admitted Kilmer.[6] He needed help from the trainers to stand up and walk off the field, but to his credit, the courageous signal caller did not miss a play on offense. Kilmer's gutsy performance was well documented over the length of his 16-year career, and the Roche-Williams hit that he sustained in the 1972 playoffs provided yet one more example of the courage of Billy Kilmer. He ignored his fuzzy head, and remarkably stayed in the game. Several minutes later in the second quarter, Kilmer would inspire the Redskins to obtain the lead, but they would have to come from behind to obtain it. That is because of what the Packers offense did midway in the second stanza of this divisional playoff tilt.

Scott Hunter spearheaded the most productive Packers drive of the game when he hit on several key passes to get his team deep into Washington territory. His pass over the middle to veteran wide receiver Carroll Dale gave Green Bay a much needed first down. Then a 23-yard strike down the far

Defensive end Clarence Williams (No. 83) brings down Washington Redskins quarterback Billy Kilmer in the playoff game at Washington on December 24. Packers defensive tackle Bob Brown (No. 78) is on the ground at the bottom left of the frame (© Vernon J. Biever Photo).

sideline from Hunter to young wideout Jon Staggers—who had beaten Redskin cornerback Mike Bass—placed the pigskin at the Washington 15-yard line. It took a lot of concentration and nimble dexterity for Staggers to pull in Hunter's pass. Staggers leaped high to snare the ball, which was gliding quickly out of bounds. He then had to somehow get both of his feet in bounds to make it a legal catch. He somehow managed to do so. It was certainly one of the best receptions that Staggers had made all year. The Over the Hill Gang defense would keep the Packers out of the end zone, however, so Green Bay settled for a 17-yard field goal from Chester Marcol, giving them a 3–0 lead.

Unfortunately for the Packers, their scoring for 1972 had officially reached its end, although they did not know it at the time. This was mainly due to the Redskins' strategy to keep five defensive linemen in the game. The tactic that Green Bay head coach Dan Devine believed that his opponent "would not dare use against us [again]"[7] was indeed being used against the Packers offense again, and this time, it proved to be much more successful than it had been in their earlier meeting in November. As a result, Washington head coach George Allen instructed his defense to keep employing it throughout the game until Devine could solve it. The brand new NFC Coach of the Year was never able—or willing—to do so. Devine tried to save face and deflect the blame after the game by telling reporters that "They [the Redskins defense] did some things differently, but nothing that surprised us."[8]

Allen's strategy worked to perfection by pulling linebacker Myron Pottios out of the lineup and replacing him with an extra defensive lineman. "We wanted to stop their powerful running game," acknowledged Allen. "That was the main idea behind it."[9]

The Redskin defense did just that, limiting MacArthur Lane to 56 yards rushing on 14 carries, and throttling John Brockington to a paltry nine yards on 13 carries. According to veteran Washington linebacker and team captain Jack Pardee, the Over the Hill Gang did not leave anything to chance.

"We sacrificed a man in the pass coverage," admitted Pardee, "but it was the right defense for a team like Green Bay."[10] Redskin defensive end Ron McDole concurred with Pardee's appraisal. "We stopped their run and that's what they do best," said McDole. "It was just inexperience [on the Packers' part], but you have to get every edge that you can."[11]

Like all game plans, studying the films of your upcoming opponent will give you ideas as to what will work and what will not, based in part on your own personnel and their unique abilities. The matchups along the line of scrimmage looked somewhat favorable for Washington, so George Allen had his team practice the five-man line all week long prior to the playoffs. "We worked on it this week and we felt that it could help us in this game," Allen stated. "This time it was beautiful."[12]

The main reason for the strategy's beauty was the successful play of the man who replaced Pottios on the Redskins' defense. Manny Sistrunk enjoyed a 10-year pro career as a defensive lineman from 1970 to 1979, but his time in the NFL was not spectacular by any means. He undoubtedly played the greatest game of his career, however, in this playoff game against Green Bay. Sistrunk constantly battered his way into the Packers' offensive backfield, keeping both Brockington and Lane from obtaining the inside yards that they were accustomed to getting during most of the regular season. Sistrunk rose his level of play when it was needed the most, and many of his teammates took notice of it.

"I think the five-linemen defense is a major reason we won the game," assessed veteran Redskins defensive tackle Diron Talbert, "and Manny is what made it so effective."[13] Sistrunk himself knew that he was a big cause for his team's victory, so when the throng of reporters visited his locker area and shoved their microphones in front of his face, he did not disappoint in offering his forthright opinion regarding his experiences in the game.

"I was mad and I was really breaking guys' heads," said the blunt

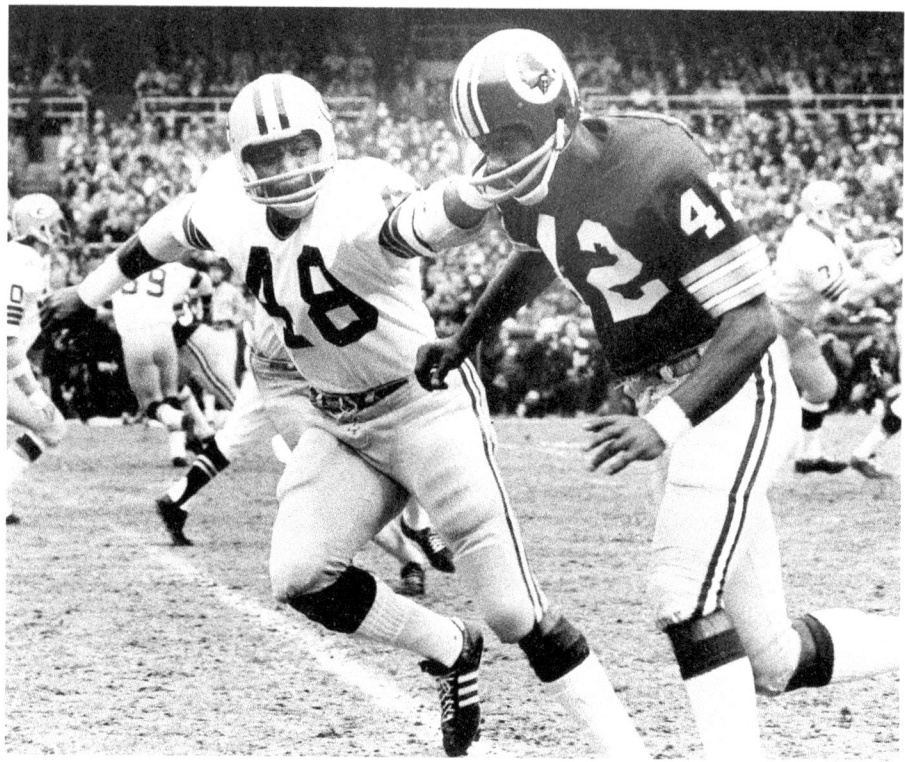

Green Bay cornerback Ken Ellis runs stride for stride with Washington wide receiver Charley Taylor during the Packers' 16–3 loss to the Redskins in the NFC divisional playoffs (AP Photo/Vernon Biever).

Sistrunk. "This was a money game. And any time you're playing with my money, I'm mad. I can whip any man that's made out of flesh and blood. I was knocking the bleep out of that center [veteran Packers center Ken Bowman]. I went around him and over him, but mostly through him."[14]

Washington's offense would go over the Green Bay defense immediately following Marcol's second quarter field goal. Following a 42-yard kickoff return by the Redskins' Herb Mul-Key, Washington completed a six-play drive in the Packer end zone. The fuzziness in Kilmer's head had by this time slightly receded, and on a play-action pass from the Green Bay 32-yard line, he spotted journeyman wide receiver Roy Jefferson streaking just a step in front of rookie Packer cornerback Willie Buchanon. Jefferson stretched as far as he could for the pass without horizontally diving for it, and caught it for the only touchdown of the game.

"The second the ball left my hand, I knew it was a touchdown," said Kilmer. "I had Roy for almost a touchdown on the same play earlier, but I lollypopped the ball and threw behind him."[15] According to pro football historian and author T.J. Troup, the Redskins "were setting up that play and were patient enough to wait to use it until the Packers defense was in the right alignment to insure its success."[16]

Jefferson described his moment of glory by confirming, "It was a play-action play. They [the Green Bay defense] were double-teaming on the weak side. I went back to the huddle and told Billy about it and he called the play. I just went inside and that was the touchdown."[17]

Washington scored again right before the end of the first half, when Redskin placekicker Curt Knight booted a 42-yard field goal. The third quarter would be a repeat of the first quarter, as both teams settled into a defense-driven repertoire. Neither offense was able to move the ball deep into their opponents' territory, as the game reverted to being played near midfield for most of the third quarter. Then in the fourth quarter, Kilmer drove Washington a little bit further than he had led them in the previous stanza. Curt Knight was again called on to perform his specialty, and he connected on a 35-yard field goal. The Redskins now owned a safe 13–3 lead. The Packers were being stymied on almost every play by Washington's defense during the second half. It was very depressing (at least for Packers fans) to watch, as the Green Bay offense was undeniably having its worst effort of the 1972 season. They could gain just one more first down before being forced to punt the ball back to the Redskins once again. Ron Widby's eighth and final punt of the season led to one more Washington drive, which once again resulted in another field goal by Knight, this one coming from 46 yards out. Green Bay's final offensive play of the season was a throw down the middle by quarterback Scott Hunter. Washington linebacker Chris Hanburger intercepted the errant toss, and what would be the Packers' only playoff game during the 1970s had officially ended. Washington 16, Green Bay 3.

The stories following that game are eerily similar, regardless of which player you talk to. The following story from John Brockington is just one representation of several other accounts that were voiced from the Packer players after their loss to the Redskins:

"After the 1972 season was over, I was chosen to play in the Pro Bowl," remembered Brockington. "And Chris Hanburger, one of the linebackers on that Redskins team comes up to me and says, 'Hey John! Why did you let us stay in that defense [the five-man defensive line] all game [long]?' He said, 'We came out because we knew that you [the Packers] had a great running game, so we came out in that five-man line to see what you we're going to do. We *never* expected you to *not* throw us out of that defense. But when you didn't try to challenge it, we *sat* in it.' They [the Redskins] didn't feel that Scott [Hunter] could throw well enough to beat them. But look who they had at quarterback. Billy Kilmer? He was no John Unitas.

"Bart Starr had told [quarterback] Scott Hunter, 'Okay Scott, if they [the Redskins] show that five-man line again, you get out of whatever play you're in, and you call the A option B circle.' That was a play where we [MacArthur Lane and John Brockington] circle out of the backfield, chip the linebackers, check the middle, then both of us go out in pass patterns. Whichever way the middle linebacker goes, that running back runs with him down the middle of the field, while the other running back cuts across the middle, with a big hole sitting in there. You can't stop it. They [the Redskins defense] cannot cover that pass, because they have one less linebacker. They've got to come out of that [five-man line] defense [to stop it]. But we didn't pass, and Scott could have hit that pass all day. But when we didn't do it [throw the ball] they [the Redskins defense] sat [in the five-man defensive line]. But we didn't do it, and it was embarrassing ... it was embarrassing, because we could have beat that team [the Redskins]. And they were beatable, because the Redskins' offense was very simple. They had Larry Brown, and a fullback [Charlie Harraway] to block for Larry Brown. They had [Roy] Jefferson and Charley Taylor [wide receivers] and [tight end] Jerry Smith. They only ran square-ins, quick slants, outs, and outs and ups. That was their whole passing scheme."[18]

Brockington's ire over losing that playoff game was indicative of most of his teammates, and his memories vividly draw bitter emotions ... even to this very day. Keep in mind that Dan Devine had for all intents and purposes stopped calling plays earlier in the year. Assistant coach Bart Starr was given those duties for most of the season. That situation changed sometime after Green Bay had won the NFC Central Division Title, and the team as a whole was destined to pay the price for another highly questionable Devine decision. Offensive guard Bill Lueck simply summarized the team's offensive strategy against Washington in the divisional playoff game as succinctly as anyone.

"It was one of those things where the coaches [meaning Dan Devine] said that 'We're just going to try to shove the ball down their throats.' That's what got us in trouble."[19]

"It was December 24th, Christmas Eve, and I'll never forget it," recalled Brockington. "Devine decides to coach that day. He had his little pad, his little chart out there with the plastic over it, and when the wind and the rain came you couldn't read the damn thing anyway. [He called] 30 Dive, 30 Dive. It was one of the most embarrassing games that I ever played in. I had 13 carries and nine yards. We never tried to get them [the Redskins] out of that [five-man line] defense. By the third quarter and [definitely] by the fourth quarter, Bart Starr had become totally disengaged. He was standing down at the 30-yard line looking in the stands. And [quarterback] Scott [Hunter] comes over to the sidelines [after the first series of the game] and said to Bart Starr, 'Coach, I thought...' And Bart stopped him right there and told him, 'Listen, I told you what to do.' But Scott got the word from Dan Devine that

10. Losing Too Soon

Quarterbacks coach Bart Starr (left) listens to head coach Dan Devine on the sidelines during the playoff game at Washington. This moment foretold the end to the Packers 1972 season, as Devine resumed the play calling duties from Starr, which eventually led to Green Bay's 16–3 defeat. Fred Carr (No. 53) is at left and Malcolm Snider (No. 67) is at right in the photograph (© Vernon J. Biever Photo).

he wasn't allowed to audible out of the play that Devine called. [Author's note: Hunter probably thought at first that Devine was okay with Starr having him change the plays at the line of scrimmage.] Even if he [Hunter] did the right thing and got the ball intercepted, or something like that, or a dropped pass, the Redskins would have stopped using that five-man defensive line. You know, disobeying an order [from Coach Devine] during a playoff game ... that wouldn't have been good for Scott. He didn't have that kind of clout."[20]

One has to consider the era in which this game was being played. Few were the players in the NFL who had the unabashed nerve to speak out against their coaches, and those players were more often than not sent packing in rapid fashion. The example of Duane Thomas comes to mind. Thomas was a star running back who helped the Dallas Cowboys win Super Bowl VI, but he did so amidst the shadow of sullen bitterness, which he directed towards the Dallas front office, who refused to renegotiate his contract. He also talked back to his coaches on occasion, and he refused to speak to most of his teammates all throughout 1971. Before the 1972 regular season began, he was traded to the San Diego Chargers, where he suited up for only one game, and where he never entered a huddle. He left the game unceremoniously after 1974, following a brief stint in Washington. Thomas' story was a vivid example of wasted talent, but the players on the 1972 Green Bay team knew that there were a number of similar stories to observe, where examples of even mildly disagreeing with a coach led to a premature dismissal from the sport. No player in his right mind in the early 1970s wanted to have such a mark on their resume.

Naturally, the question that comes to mind at this point involves Bart Starr and his sideline demeanor during the second half of that playoff game. Why did he refuse to say anything to Scott Hunter after that particular series of the contest, when the Green Bay play calling was in question?

"You know why. You know why," Brockington declared his answer to this author. "He [Starr] was on the sideline. He knew what Devine was doing. Dan Devine decided that he [and not Bart Starr] was going to coach that football game, and that was a freaking disaster, because that dumb idiot did not ... [pauses]. Look, the players have to play the game. The coaches can't play in a football game. The only thing that the coaches can do is put you in a position to win, and that he [Devine] did not do. He kept us running right into that five-man defensive line. By the end of the season, [Packers center] Kenny Bowman probably weighs 235 pounds. [Redskins defensive lineman] Manny Sistrunk is like 260–265 pounds. He [Sistrunk] wasn't a regular player, so he was fresh and rested. So [consequently] we got embarrassed."[21]

The Packers also endured embarrassment on another front. They had paid a statistical price for their lack of a passing game all season long, and because Devine chose not to throw the ball in the playoff game, it cost them a chance to advance further in the postseason. Offensive guard Bill Lueck would claim that "Our running game was over the line, but we had literally no passing game to speak of."[22]

If the team had a top-flight receiver in their lineup, that player might have drawn double coverage from the Redskins, thereby allowing the possibility of the Packers to run the ball more successfully. Regardless of such conjecturing, however, the press and virtually everyone else decided to correctly focus on Coach Devine's play-calling fiasco more than any other reason for the Green Bay defeat. Playing the role of the devil's advocate, could it be that the Redskins were simply a better team than the Packers on that day? Perhaps. But it did not matter. Had Dan Devine left the play-calling duties in the hands of Bart Starr, the Packers would certainly have had a better chance to defeat the Redskins. You will simply not find any former Packer player on the 1972 roster who will disagree with that statement. The price for winning the 1972 NFC Central Division Championship was having Coach Devine declare to his players in his own way that he was in charge of this team during the playoffs, irrespective of what anyone else thought or felt, or of the effect on his team's chances, because of his decisions. He simply refused to adapt his play-calling judgments in order to beat the Redskins. It was indeed a day for defeat.

As was previously stated by John Brockington, the most natural and obvious remedy to solving the Redskins' five-man defensive front was to throw the ball and throw it often, regardless of how open the receivers or setbacks were getting, or how many catches they were able to make. By increasing the amount of throws, the Green Bay offense would have eventually (probably before halftime or early in the third quarter at the latest) forced the Washington defense to remove that fifth lineman and replace him with another linebacker or another defensive back. The chess match would have then resulted in the Packers offensive scheme restoring its prized running attack into the forefront of their strategy, which had been their lifeblood all throughout the 1972 season. Scott Hunter could only complete 12 passes in 24 attempts for 150 yards against the Over the Hill Gang in the playoff game. It would seem obvious that by sometime in the second half of that contest, more throws downfield were needed and should have been called by Devine. But for some unknown reason, Devine stubbornly stuck with his floundering running strategy into the teeth of that five-man Redskin defensive line.

Prominent pro football author T.J. Troup observed the strategical situation in that particular playoff game rather well, and his stated opinion was founded within the all-important realm of common sense.

"If a defense like the Redskins takes something away from you, namely your prized running game," Troup said, "then you *have* to have an adjustment. The Packers did not make that adjustment. I feel that Dan Devine was overwhelmed by the playoff atmosphere in that game."[23]

The postseason stage may have been too big for Devine to deal with, and that could certainly be debated by pro football historians. But Devine's players were primed to play a great game against the Redskins. They were not in awe of Washington's talent on either side of the line of scrimmage. And their offensive play caller—quarterback coach Bart Starr—had forged a Hall of Fame career on leading his Packer teams of the 1960s to five world championships. Certainly he was not the least bit overwhelmed by the aura of a divisional playoff contest. But Coach Devine made a key play-calling decision, and the fortunes of the Packers changed abruptly.

Scott Hunter's memories of that game were naturally very similar to John Brockington's, as both men shared the misery of those moments from the same offensive backfield and huddle.

"The opening series they [the Redskins defense] went to their five-man [defensive] line," Hunter explained. "We were anticipating it, and Bart [Starr] said 'audible a throw weak [side] to [Packers setback] Mac [Lane] or to X [wide receiver Leland Glass].' If you look back at the game, I think on the opening series, we go straight down the field. I think I completed three, maybe four passes, throwing to the weak side against that five-man line. Because all they had was [Redskins linebacker] Chris Hanburger over there, and he couldn't cover Mac [Lane], and he couldn't get back into pass coverage to cover a split end [Glass or Carroll Dale]. So confidently, we went right down the field and kicked a field goal and took the lead 3–0 [author's note: Chester Marcol's field goal occurred early in the second quarter]. And I remember Bart's exact words when I came over to the sidelines. He said, 'If they [the Redskins defense] stay in that [the five-man defensive line], we're going to wear their tail out.' And the next thing I knew, Dan Devine takes over the play calling, and it all goes downhill from there [author's note: When Hunter described this particular moment in the game to me, I could audibly hear his voice tone slow down and soften somewhat, as if a cloud of depression slowed his speech. It was as if he was reliving the game, hoping for a different ending, but knowing that such was impossible. The frustration caused by that playoff loss still hurts the former Green Bay players, and being a Packers fan myself, I also felt that same frustration and disappointment, as I listened to his description of what might have been accomplished ... if a different decision was made by Coach Devine to allow Bart Starr to keep calling the plays on offense]."[24]

Upon discussing this particular moment with several Packers players and front office people, opinions varied as to exactly when Coach Devine decided to relieve Bart Starr of his play-calling duties. Some have said that Devine made the decision several days before the game. Others claim that the decision was made the night before the game. And still others believed that the decision was made five minutes before the opening kickoff. Regardless of when Devine took over the play calling for the playoff game at Washington, he was intensely stubborn about it, and getting him to change his mind was simply out of the question. As a result, his decision to call the plays instead of Bart Starr virtually ended any chance that Green Bay had of upsetting the Redskins on that day.

"I don't know what was said [between Coach Devine and Coach Starr] on the sideline," Hunter continued. "All I know is, I was on the field, and there was a change of a [play] call. And I looked over there and Devine was where Devine was, and Bart was about 15 yards down the bench with his arms crossed. I thought uh-oh. I came to the sideline after that series and went up to Bart and I said, 'What's going on?' And he says, 'Ask Coach Devine' or something like that. 'He's calling the plays now.'"

When asked if he (Hunter) went over to question Coach Devine what was going on, Hunter responded, "No, I already knew what was happening. You just kinda knew that this wasn't a good time for Coach Devine to be calling plays."[25]

The situation on the sidelines was impossible for any of the Packer players to avoid witnessing. The men were left to watch all of the confusion and

Veteran outside linebacker Dave Robinson gets instructions from head coach Dan Devine on the sidelines during the playoff game at Washington. Robinson never did see things the way that Devine saw them, however. Robinson was traded to the Redskins following this game (© Vernon J. Biever Photo).

the discord, but were unable to do anything to alter it. Offensive guard Bill Lueck described the scene by stating, "Our sideline was a mess. And that was from the very beginning of the game. I remember so clearly how frustrated Bart was. I mean here's a guy [Bart Starr] that knows ten times more football than Dan Devine would ever dream up. Bart was so frustrated. He just walked down to the end of the bench. He kept telling Dan that we have to throw the ball, but Dan didn't want to hear it."[26]

Dave Robinson was not in the mood to hear any excuses by the end of this playoff game. Moreover, the Packer linebacker did not know it at the time, but as he walked off the field at RFK Stadium on that grim and cloudy Christmas Eve, he had just played his last contest as a member of the Green Bay squad. He would soon be traded by Devine to ironically the same Redskins team that the Pack just lost to in the playoffs. He discussed his memories of his final game wearing Green and Gold, and of his subsequent trade to Washington, in an insightful interview in 2014:

"We went down to practice in North Carolina [just before the playoff game with the Redskins]," Robinson said, "and Dan decided that he was going to start coaching again. They [the Redskins] opened up the game with that five-man line. We were a running team. We had John Brockington and MacArthur Lane. And they [the Redskins] shut down the run. Scott Hunter is a decent quarterback. He wasn't a Bart Starr though. They [the Redskins] put too much pressure on him, and he succumbed [to the pressure].

"When they [the Redskins] brought me into Washington the next year, [Washington head coach] George Allen brought me in for my debriefing. The first thing he wanted to know was, 'what kind of plays did you have ready for that five-man line?' He just started laughing. He said, 'We [the Redskins] only started the game with that five-man line to see what kind of plays you [the Packers] had drawn up for it. The Packers looked confused, so [we] stayed there with that five-man line.' Going into that [playoff] game, I was the defensive captain, and I told Scott Hunter, '…you will win the game if you can score 20 points.' They [the Redskins] will not score 20 points against our defense, and they didn't. They [the Washington defense] shut us [the Green Bay offense] down."[27]

Reserve Green Bay quarterback Jerry Tagge witnessed all of this taking place, and he was probably just as dumfounded as everyone else on the Packers sideline. Tagge had better completion statistics in the November meeting against the Redskins than Hunter, but he (Tagge) did not take any snaps from center in the playoff game. It is impossible to say whether or not Tagge could have influenced the outcome of the game if he had seen some action, but he would have had to call the same plays that Hunter was forced to call.

Regardless of who was barking out the signals in the Packers' offensive backfield, however, the majority of the media's focus and scrutiny following Green Bay's loss was rightly centered on Devine, and his decision to stop Bart Starr from calling plays in the playoff game. When faced with the extra media attention that every team gets in the postseason, Devine tried his feeble best to shift or hide from the blame after the loss. He never did accept any fault for the defeat. His approach to this dilemma was in retrospect completely predictable, considering how he had dealt with the press all throughout his coaching career. Devine preferred instead to change the subject of the questioning. But just like Devine kept going back to running the ball up the gut in the playoff loss to the Redskins, so too did the reporters and sportswriters continue to redirect their questions back to the subject of Devine's faulty play calling, and why he decided against throwing the ball more often, especially in the second half.

Devine's plan to address the questions from the scribes was to spend a majority of the post-game interviews praising his players for what they did accomplish during 1972. It was a considerably nice thing to do, regardless of why he did it. And even though the media's and the public's attention quickly returned to Devine's play-calling decisions, the head coach could at least be somewhat commended for trying to console his defeated players.

A day of defeat. A trio of Packers come to a depressing acceptance of Green Bay's divisional playoff loss at Washington. Pictured from left to right are running back MacArthur Lane (No. 36), running back John Brockington (No. 42), and offensive guard (No. 62) Bill Lueck (AP Photo/Vernon Biever).

"That's about as hard as we can play," Devine said. "I couldn't ask for more [from the players and coaches], but it was a bitter pill. We got beat by a real good football team. We fully expected to win. The Redskin defense came up with the big play when they needed it. I said last year, after our last ball game, that we had anywhere from five to 10 guys [on our roster] who simply quit on us. Either they quit intentionally or they quit not knowing that they had quit. This year no way did anybody quit.

"We were a beat up team. [Wide receiver] Jon Staggers had a shoulder that went out during the game and he came back and played. We had things like that happening on the sideline. I finally had to take Staggers out at the end. His shoulder was completely dislocated. He had tears in his eyes and he begged me to let him stay in the game. Yes, I think we've got something started now."[28]

A couple of veteran leaders on the team agreed with their head coach. Wide receiver Carroll Dale stated, "You've got to profit from a game like this.

The best thing that you could say is that the younger guys have a lot—an awful lot—to look forward to."29

Such was the sentiment of NFL Films. In their highlight film on the 1972 Packers, the legendary narrator John Facenda declared, "The young Packers had flown their colors high, and their future was clearly championship gold, on a field of green."30 All-Pro Green Bay defensive tackle Bob Brown was also in profound agreement with the optimistic outlook for the team, and he summed up his feelings by declaring, "This game will carry us a long way. There is no doubt about it. The Pack Is Back."31

11
Proud to Be a Packer

The members of the 1972 Green Bay Packers have had a long time to think about that particular year, and to consider their thoughts as to what they accomplished. Their team has since been overshadowed by some great Packer teams in more recent decades. But in 1972, the Packers reclaimed a taste of glory that they had owned in the decade of the 1960s. The aura and the rejoicing of '72 would not last long, however. Clarence Williams' belief that "The Pack Is Back" unfortunately vanished almost as quickly as it appeared. The 1973 Green Bay team fell out of contention promptly, as they stumbled to a sub-par 5–7–2 record. The '74 squad finished with another losing record at 6–8. Dan Devine would resign as Packers head coach after the 1974 season to become the head coach of the Fighting Irish at Notre Dame University. He was replaced in 1975 by the legendary Bart Starr, who for the remainder of the decade could not bring Green Bay back into the playoffs. The reason for that failure, however, was mostly not Starr's fault. Devine had mortgaged the team's future by giving up five high draft choices to the Los Angeles Rams in order to obtain veteran quarterback John Hadl in 1974, who was already much past his prime. The rest of the 1970s thus recorded a forlorn Green Bay team, mired in mediocrity.

Nevertheless, the 1972 Packers are remembered by pro football historians today as a team that succeeded in a year when virtually no pro football expert predicted them to do so. They are the only Packers team to win a division title during the decade of the 1970s, and as the years go by, that accomplishment still stands out as quite an achievement for their former players. Statistically speaking, most of the men who donned a set of shoulder pads and a helmet for any team in the long lineage of NFL players, never got a chance to participate in a single playoff game. At least those players who took their stances for the 1972 Packers can say that they did play in a divisional playoff game, even though it did not turn out the way that they wanted. Despite their untimely loss to the Washington Redskins in the postseason, the men who comprised the 1972 Green Bay Packers could still be proud of their performance, as they look back on their collective history.

Teams that win the Super Bowl are naturally more remembered and honored than the teams that fail to earn the Vince Lombardi Trophy. But there has to be a reckoning for the teams who provide the league with an important story to tell. The 1972 Packers fall into that category. They were a team which faced and eventually which overcame the effects of a demanding and uncompromising head coach. They captured the NFC Central Division title, a division that was known at that time as the "Black and Blue Division," notable for the physical punishment that was annually distributed to all of the players in Chicago, Detroit, Minnesota, and Green Bay (the teams that were the members of the NFC Central Division). To survive and to win that division was an achievement in and of itself. The Green Bay team accepted the role of underdogs to start that '72 season. They would end that season with 10 wins, and three of their four losses were by a total of 12 points. That statistic is admirable by any of the league's standards, even today.

Like all of the men who have ever played in Green Bay, a measure of Packer Pride is a big part of their individual stories. It is a birthright of sorts ... a bona fide claim to a treasured legacy. Those Packer players in 1972 certainly own that Packer Pride. They own it through their impressive statistics, both offensively and defensively. They own it through their dedication to giving their all in every game. There were certainly no quitters on this roster, as Dan Devine had previously said following the team's loss to the Redskins in the playoffs. And that's precisely the type of roster that Dan Devine wanted to produce. They own it through their friendships and the brotherhood that each man had for his teammates. But also importantly, however, was the fact that they own Packer Pride from the victories and the '72 division title, which were won in spite of the internal strife that was meted out by Devine himself. No other Green Bay team—and perhaps no other NFL team—has ever had to deal with a similar situation. Such a state of affairs is enough to guarantee their spot in the storied and admired past of the Green and Gold. The men who were there, almost 50 years later, still speak glowingly of their past accomplishments, and of the town where they plied their gridiron trade in 1972. They are forever shrouded in the honor that they have earned while playing for the Packers. There should be an agreement that these former Packer players need to be and should always be regarded as a beloved part of the town.

"Green Bay, Wisconsin, was the ideal place for me," said cornerback Ken Ellis. "Because I came from a small town in Woodbine, Georgia, and I went to a small school in Southern University. I felt that if I had ended up in a big city like New York or Los Angeles, I probably would have gotten lost in the shuffle. We knew that with the team that we had [in 1972], that we were trying to measure up to the guys on the teams from the 1960s. It was just a tremendous honor to be a part of this organization.

"I regret that we didn't win more ball games. I felt that the fans deserved better than what they got from us overall, but we gave it our all. Playing football in general has taught me self-discipline, to be appreciative of what you do have, to help other people, and to give back."[1]

Every player from that 1972 team certainly gave back to each other. You often hear of stories where players on some teams are more like brothers than just teammates and acquaintances. The '72 Packer players were definitely a treasured fraternity. They played as one out on the field, and they supported each other no matter what. They also love the fact that they own a part of the story of Titletown.

"The camaraderie on that '72 team was tremendous," recalled star running back John Brockington. "I don't know how other teams were, but the Packers were unique because they're the Packers. Small town USA. And they're kind of a legendary team because of the small city. Titletown. The turf, the field had a name ... the frozen tundra.... Lambeau Field ... all that stuff played into the mystique of going to Green Bay. When I got there, there was a core of Packer players still there who were holdovers from the Lombardi era. Being here in this town after we finished practice many times we sat in the locker room and just talked. And we'd go to lunch and just talked. And [linebacker] Freddie Carr would go into those stories about what it was like to tackle Gale Sayers. And he [Carr] would say how 'Sayers would run sideways as fast as he could run forwards. And one of the defensive backs on our team would have him [Sayers] [penned in] by the sidelines by four or five feet, and Gale would still run past him for a touchdown.'

"And Kenny Bowman tells a story of when [Chicago Bears middle linebacker] Dick Butkus came into the league. He [Bowman] says, 'Let's just wipe this rookie's face [in the dirt] ... let's show him what it's like to be in the NFL.' And then Kenny paused and then said, 'I never touched him [Butkus] the whole game [Brockington heartily laughs].' He [Butkus] ran around him [Bowman], under him, and jumped over him. It was unbelievable. Butkus came into the league with such energy."[2]

It was more than just stories and anecdotes that the Packer players were trading back and forth with each other though. There were seven veteran Packer players on the 1972 roster who played for Vince Lombardi. Those men showed the leadership that they had learned from Lombardi by becoming an example to all of the rookies and the younger players on the team. They would repeat some of Lombardi's quotes in their efforts to inspire their youthful teammates. Then they would—by their own work ethic and actions during the practices and the games themselves—prove that they practiced what they preached. Those veterans were very prideful in their performance, and the rookies and youngsters on the 1972 team took notice of that, learned from their older teammates, and eventually became leaders themselves.

When discussing Packer Pride, John Brockington took a brief moment to gather his feelings. "It was heavy stuff for me," admitted the big halfback. "When I was in high school [in Brooklyn, New York], the quality and the football facilities were not the greatest. In Ohio [where Brockington went to college at Ohio State], they have great football programs. Same with Texas, Pennsylvania, Florida, California ... you know. So then I get to the pros, and I have all of this success, and I was like, holy smokes! And on [Packer] teams that weren't really competitive. I think that I broke the rookie rushing record in 1971 [he did], and I was Rookie of the Year, and first team All-Pro. And I went to the Pro Bowl. It was great.

Running back John Brockington once again led Green Bay in rushing in 1972 with 1,027 yards. He also scored eight rushing touchdowns in 1972 (AP Photo/Vernon Biever).

"Green Bay is just different. It's the closest thing that you can get to college football in the pros. It's just such an atmosphere around that team. It is magnificent. Because you know, it's a town where there's not a whole lot going on besides football there. But that [being] said, the enthusiasm that those fans have for that team is incredible. With the stadium ... what they've done there ... what they've created ... which wasn't the case when I was [playing] there. When I was [playing] there, people came for the football games, and then they left. Now, it's an experience. It's a destination point for people in the state [of Wisconsin], or even in Chicago, in Illinois, because the atrium is so beautiful. They have the [Packer] Pro Shop there, they have restaurants there, they have tours there. It's just wonderful to see what's going on up there. It's just a wonderful experience, and that's what Green Bay has done."³

It has been great for both players and fans in Green Bay for many decades. Just ask Packers offensive guard Bill Lueck, who was a key performer on the offensive line in 1972. The whole atmosphere of Green Bay won Lueck over.

"We [the Packer players] were all really close, and it was wonderful," Lueck said. "But the other thing that made it [playing in Green Bay] great was how different it is from other places. I got traded to the Philadelphia

Eagles after I had major knee surgery after my seventh year. I could tell a big difference between the two places [Philadelphia and Green Bay]. My wife and I always complemented the fans and the people of Green Bay. Packer fans are the greatest fans in the NFL.

"In my time spent with the Eagles, the fans would boo us, and maybe they deserved to boo us. But it [the situation in Philadelphia] just didn't have the camaraderie or the closeness that I saw in Green Bay. When I was in Green Bay, we would all hang out together. Even in the neighborhood where my wife and I had our house, we still to this day have contact with our old neighbors from that time. That's how close-knit everything was. It was a great place to live … except for the cold temperatures [chuckle]."[4]

When one visits the small city of Green Bay, Wisconsin, one views an unmistakable glimpse of the league's past. Green Bay today is truly representative of the atmosphere and the size of many NFL teams during the 1920s— the earliest years of the league. Several more NFL teams then began to move into larger cities a decade later, where more money and more fan support could enable those teams to survive the detrimental effects of the Great Depression, and then a decade after that, World War II. Today, Green Bay stands alone as the last of the "town teams." The players from every Packer squad since those of the 1920s all recognize and respect the lineage of the past. They all acknowledge and accept the traditions that have made both the town and the team special in the eyes of all who watch pro football. They all know that they are a part of that history, and a part of the stories of the past.

"You know, it's all about prestige being a Packer, all this tradition," said running back MacArthur Lane after helping the team win another division championship in 1972. "Man, we've got to put another flag in that stadium."[5] Many years later, Lane could still fondly recall what being a Packer meant to him. "I still think of it as something special," Lane said. "I enjoyed Green Bay. The atmosphere has to be right to have a winning ball club. I'm convinced of that.[6] It was a combination of the teammates and the camaraderie between the players. We had such a close group of players with the Packers. I got into winning. There was no selfishness at all. There was never any jealousy at all. We went to play football—that's all."[7]

Green Bay quarterback Scott Hunter certainly acknowledged and appreciated what Lane was referring to. Hunter had enjoyed success in college at the University of Alabama. He had been keenly immersed in the celebrated history of that institution. As soon as he joined the Packers in 1971, he got to experience a similar realm of tradition and honor. When asked if he was proud of his accomplishments in Green Bay, particularly in leading the team to a division championship in 1972, his answer was quite predictable.

"Oh very much so," Hunter confirmed. "It's like being a former Alabama quarterback. That's something to be proud of. You know I went on to play with Atlanta and on a couple more teams, but being in Green Bay ... that's such a special place. Special people, and a special stadium, the whole atmosphere of the whole state [of Wisconsin] ... it's just such a special place to play in. Of course coming from Alabama, with Coach [Paul 'Bear'] Bryant, it was like I went from one wonderful place to another."[8]

Packer Pride was and still is evident to notice in this group of athletes, and in particular in the way that the players talk about each other. They thought the world of each other, and they still do. They all realized that the only success that mattered involved the team as a whole. A championship could only be achieved if all of the men sacrificed all that they had for each other. The individual accolades and awards were fine and dandy, but they were certainly not the goal. Teamwork and brotherhood were the byproducts of all of the hard work and determination that the players gave to their sport and to each other.

The team's most celebrated star athlete—John Brockington—was the recipient of much of his teammates' praise. His rushing efforts put the Packers in the national headlines. They also helped to put the Packers at the top of the NFC Central Division standings. All of the applause and honors that he received were well earned.

"Just on sheer running ability," acknowledged veteran middle linebacker and future Hall of Famer Ray Nitschke, "I'd say he [Brockington] is as good as any running back Green Bay ever had."[9] Long-time Green Bay center Ken Bowman explained the worth of a man like Brockington in more detail. "Before Brock, we didn't have a power runner," admitted Bowman. "It doesn't help to gain four yards on a first down and five on the second unless you have a back who can come up on the third down and get one yard when you need it. A tough inside man makes all the difference in the world. You see a runner like him [Brockington] breaking his neck and it embarrasses you, really embarrasses you, to miss a block for him."[10] Fellow blocker Bill Lueck claimed that Brockington "could run through three or four guys at a time."[11]

Reserve Packers defensive back Charlie Hall got to know Brockington during the six years that they were teammates in Green Bay (1971–1976). His fondest memories of the "Crazed Camel" spoke to the passionate resolution of the man.

"He's unwilling to quit—on anything," Hall acknowledged during the 1970s. "At camp he spent hours after practice watching films of [former Packer great] Jim Taylor. He's never too tired to work some more. He has intense determination. I think he's going to become the greatest running back to ever play the game. Brock lives to excel."[12]

Perhaps the one man who knew John Brockington the best was the man who got in the three-point stance right alongside of him. MacArthur Lane came to Green Bay in the spring of 1972 with a hefty question mark surrounding him. No one was quite sure what to expect from him. By the end of the regular season, however, only an exclamation mark could be seen. Lane provided the powerful blocking that Brockington needed to be successful. Lane was also very successful carrying the ball in his own right in 1972, rushing for over 800 yards himself, and leading the Packers in receptions in that glorious year.

"I attributed a lot of his [Brockington's] yards to my blocking ability and his running," said Lane. "It made me feel good to be a part of his 1,000-yard seasons. In the passing game ... they threw me everything—long, short—because they had confidence I'd get open."[13] The always-modest Brockington naturally attributed his success to Lane. "I couldn't have gotten the thousand [yards] without Mac," admitted Brockington.[14] "It's the old mule and the young mule together," as Lane artistically described the dynamic duo during the 1972 season. "All we gotta do is run with that thing. We like each other. That's what makes it work so well."[15]

In much the same way that Brockington inspired the offense, cornerback Ken Ellis inspired the defense. Besides his stalwart play all season long in the defensive secondary, his critical 80-yard punt return for a touchdown at Detroit ignited the Packers and provided them with the most recognized turning point of 1972. Then in the wake of Ellis' shoulder injury that he sustained in the game at Washington on November 26, Ellis ignored the pain and the potential risk of further injury to suit up and play against Detroit the following week. It was a big game, one in which the winner would take over the ownership of the lead in the division near the end of the regular season. Ellis went on to produce another key performance in leading Green Bay to a big 33–7 victory over the rival Lions. He contributed two important interceptions in that contest, which helped to set up the Packer offense with excellent field position in Detroit territory.

"He [Ken Ellis] inspired us all," said veteran defensive tackle Bob Brown immediately after the win over Detroit. Keep in mind that Brown was a man who was well acquainted with inspiration, having played for Vince Lombardi. "I haven't seen a cornerback play a greater game [also note that Brown was a teammate of Hall of Fame cornerback Herb Adderley in the 1960s], especially considering the nature of his injury. It was a magnificent game, and he was just great."[16]

That splendid afternoon also bore witness to another tradition in this tradition-laden town ... the congratulations and support from the fans at Lambeau Field. "I didn't realize they [the fans] were [giving us] standing ovations until somebody told me," recalled veteran outside linebacker Dave Robinson following the victory over the Lions. "But I'll tell you this. I could tell our crowd was more vocal today and I was proud to be wearing the Green and Gold out there."[17] The game versus Detroit on December 3 would be Robinson's final home game in his 12-year pro career for the Packers, as he was traded to the Redskins following the 1972 season.

On this Packers team, the good feelings between teammates was impossible to overlook or ignore. What is interesting to note is that there were also some unique examples of good feelings and strong relationships between some of the players on the team and some of the assistant coaches as well. The relationship between the Packers' defensive backs and their defensive secondary coach Don Doll was one such relationship.

"It's good to have a better relationship than just coach-player," admitted star rookie cornerback Willie Buchanon. "It seems you get to know what he's thinking and more what's expected of you. I can sense this sometimes in him [Coach Doll], and he can sense it in me. Of course, our whole secondary is close. I guess you could say that we're Coach Doll's four adopted sons [smiling]."[18]

Doll would reciprocate his positive feelings for Buchanon, particularly near the end of the 1972 season, when the young cornerback was vying for the NFL Defensive Rookie of the Year award (which he eventually won).

"I'd like to see him get the rookie of the year honor," Doll said. "He's done some fine, fine things for us. I don't know who else [in the league] might be considered, but I think he certainly is very deserving. In that connection, I don't think there's one out of 26 teams in the league who wouldn't take him in a minute if they had the opportunity [author's note: The NFL only had 26 teams in 1972. The current number of teams is 32].

"He has great football sense. He's a pretty heady kid. Each week, you can go back to training camp and pertains to what's happening now, and he's pretty sure of what he's doing."[19]

The 1972 season began with few people really sure how things would turn out for the Packers. Many of the players were also doubtful as to how well the team would perform. One such man, rookie placekicker Chester Marcol, was in awe of his surroundings when he came to Green Bay. But he did not feel too unusual, based on the youthfulness on the team's roster.

"We had so many rookies and free agents on the team I don't think we realized we weren't supposed to win," admitted Marcol after the season ended. "Our success was totally unexpected.[20] It was really a dream season. I got to play in the Pro Bowl at age twenty-three; I was the only rookie on the National Football Conference team. The season ended in disappointment, but I had an amazing year. The points [that I scored] and the game-winning kicks were nice, but my leg strength on kickoffs was an important factor in our success, too. I kicked off seventy-five times in 1972 and recorded twenty-nine touchbacks. On the other forty-six kickoffs, the average return was just 20.3 yards, which meant opposing teams rarely started a drive from beyond their own twenty-yard line. The average return for all seventy-five of my kickoffs was just 12.3 yards."[21]

Chester Marcol's performance throughout the 1972 season became a reliable indicator of how successful the Packers were in that memorable year. It was undeniably his best year in pro football, and anytime that the Green Bay offense got fairly deep into their opponents' territory, the coaches knew that Marcol could be counted on to provide three points. That was a great feeling of confidence, and it basically meant that the team was going to have a chance to produce points and win most of their tougher, more competitive games. That confidence had not been seen in Green Bay since Super Bowl II (the last game that Vince Lombardi coached the Packers, and the last game that Don Chandler was Green Bay's placekicker).

During the time since the 1967 season, the Packers were forced to deal with mediocrity and failure. The championships that were earned during those victorious years of the 1960s were just a memory by the time that Dan Devine became the team's head coach in 1971. The 1972 season, however, offered the fans of Green Bay a great feeling of revival, a great feeling of hope for the future. The Packer fans had pride once again.

Many of the older Packer fans today still remember that 1972 season. Although only a small representation of the numbers of fans who were around during that year, a couple of Green Bay natives could still discuss with clarity the highs and lows of 1972, and the memories that the only Packers playoff team of the 1970s gave them. Robert Miller and Jonathon Schmidt were both born and raised in Green Bay, Wisconsin, in the early 1950s. They would become proud witnesses to the multitude of Packer victories in the 1960s, and to the images of success from the likes of players like Paul Hornung, Jim Taylor, Bart Starr, Herb Adderley, Willie Wood, and many others. They also observed Vince Lombardi's head coaching legacy, and the many scenes where Lombardi was carried off the field by his players after many important wins. Neither Miller nor Schmidt live in Wisconsin today, both having moved to a warmer southern state in their retirement ages. But both can readily recall the glory days of Lombardi's victorious dynasty, and then the disheartening days of the immediate years thereafter. The 1972 Packers gave both men an unmistakable feeling of hope that their beloved team was ready to relive those highly successful years in the 1960s, when Green Bay became Titletown, and when the Packers were firmly placed at the top of the pro football universe. Their insights into the '72 Packers are unique, and are proof positive that several decades of retrospective thought about the 1970s in the NFL have given them a higher opinion of the '72 Packer team than one might assume.

"We were rejuvenated by the success that the 1972 Packers had," said Miller in a 2018 interview. "We were overjoyed in fact. We had dealt with not winning and not going back to the playoffs for several years after Lombardi left. Then '72 came, and our Pack came back as they say, and got back to the playoffs. That was a great year. It was a very different team than Lombardi's teams. Yes, they still had a few of Lombardi's players on that team, but they also had a lot of new players. Many of those new players were rookies and younger players. We really weren't sure what to expect at the beginning of that year, but by mid-season, we knew [that] they had a chance. They were winning a lot of close games, and to me, that is the mark of a winner. Can you win the close, tight games? That team did."[22]

"What I remember most about the 1972 team was that they were not a great passing team," recalled Schmidt. "But their running game with Brockington and Lane was fantastic. It didn't matter who they played. They were able to run the ball against them. That would have made Lombardi proud, because he loved the running game."[23]

Dan Devine, the 1972 Packers coach, also instilled some pride. If not in the team, then certainly in the fans. They were selling and buying bumper stickers claiming, "Everything's Fine with Devine." Yes, the team lost to the Redskins in the playoffs, but most fans did not overtly blame Devine for the loss like his players did. Most fans felt that the Redskins were just a little bit better of a team with a better passing game. The Packer fans at that time were not privy to witnessing or hearing about the treatment that Devine gave to his players, or to the many unexplained strategical decisions that Devine made during the games, or to the questionable reasoning behind the player personnel decisions that Devine made to his roster. The fans never heard the derogatory comments that Devine centered on his players. That was an era of "keeping everything in the locker room," so the press did not hear too much about how Devine was running the team, at least not during most of 1972. The press over time, however, certainly got an inkling of how things were being dealt with regarding Devine and the players. That was obvious by 1974, when the disgruntled opinions of the players started to increase, and they were hard for the media to ignore. By the end of 1972, however, the fans were reinvigorated. They were optimistic and eager for 1973 to begin.

"We felt that there was no way that we were not going to at least go into the NFC Championship Game in 1973," opined Miller. "We knew that our younger guys had another year of experience under their belts. We knew that because we got taste of the playoffs again in '72, we would want a bigger taste of the playoffs in '73. But that didn't happen. That was when I started to question some of Devine's decisions.

"The '73 team had some bad injuries to some really important players, and that really hurt our chances. And our defense didn't do as well as they did in '72. But what really hurt was that our passing game did not improve at all in '73. So we were giving up more points, and we were scoring less points. It's hard to win a division title when you do worse statistically than you did in the previous year."[24]

The offense indeed did suffer in the 1973 season, scoring 102 less points than what was earned in 1972. But did the fans feel that they were doomed to what eventually happened during the remainder of the decade of the 1970s?

"No, we always had ... and we *still* always have ... faith that our team will succeed," said Schmidt. "Every year we feel this way. But when we look back to the end of the seventies, we realize that the '72 team was the only team to make the playoffs during that decade. We're born optimists. We would rather celebrate the victories, instead of think too much or too long at the defeats. After all, the Packers are *our* team. Many of us are shareholders. They'll always be *our* team. Win or lose, we are with them. It's our tradition in Green Bay. We'll always be with them."[25]

Packer Pride as we have seen is instilled in the players on the team. But it is also instilled in all of the fans of the team—as evidenced from the statements of Robert Miller and Jonathon Schmidt—regardless of where they live. Those confirmations and affirmations are practically endless among the Packer Backers, for well over several decades. It really flourished in earnest during the era of Vince Lombardi's tenure as head coach, and it continues to this day. In 1972, that pride was personified in the family atmosphere that the players had for each other, and that the fans had for the team. There are many stories of how the fans have bestowed their love for the team over the years, and vice-versa. From hundreds of fans volunteering to shovel snow off of the playing surface and in the stands at Lambeau Field in winter, to hundreds more joining in cheering for the team each day during summer training camp, to the community involvement that all of the players partake in to raise money for local charities. It is not uncommon to see both current and former Packer players visiting unhealthy kids on a regular basis in local hospitals. The fans and the team are inseparable.

Talk to any former Green Bay player, and they will all echo the sentiments of how honored they were to be a part of the team, and to be loved by the town and its people.

"Throughout my playing days here, and prior to that and after that, the Packers fans have been extremely loyal," said former Green Bay safety Jim Hill. "They come out in all kinds of conditions and all kinds of adversity."[26]

Some of the stories from the 1972 Packers are indicative of the stories that players from any era in Green Bay will tell you. The 1972 Packers were a special team, however, as they own the honor of being the only Packer team during the 1970s to go to the playoffs. They did their best for a town filled with special people. They were a team that is too oft forgotten in the long lineage of Green Bay championship teams, but they are a team that is well

Defensive tackle Bob Brown prepares a delicacy for the team. Brown was considered one of the best gourmet cooks on the Packers squad (AP Photo).

worth remembering and commemorating. Those players all look back to that memorable season and revel in winning many of those tough games. But they also revel in just the day-to-day atmosphere that they experienced, and in many ways nurtured, as they worked their way to claiming the NFC Central Division title.

"That team was a great team and we had great morale," remembered former outside linebacker Dave Robinson. "We had a team meeting. What we needed [during our mid-season slump] was more team parties. [Veteran defensive tackle] Bob Brown was a chef of sorts, and we had a big cookout at his house. We came in, played cards. [Cornerback] Kenny Ellis liked to eat raccoons, and Bob looked all around for raccoons. We finally got some. To make a long story short, we decided that a raccoon was a good luck symbol, and so every week we started eating raccoons. More and more guys came to the dinners, and before you knew it, every hunter in northeastern Wisconsin was hunting raccoons for us [author's note: Once Packer fans get wind of something that their team wants or needs, they go out of their way to accommodate the team even if their desire was for the delicacy of raccoons. It has been that way for generations, and it remains so today. The Packers are—after all—*their* team].

"A true story: Bob Brown had his car stolen at practice. He left the keys in it. Someone stole his car, drove to Minneapolis and ran out of gas, and parked it in a hospital parking lot and walked away from it. Bob got the car back and opened up the trunk. He had [inside the trunk] his attache with his two Super Bowl rings in it ... and six carcasses of raccoons."[27]

12
A Legacy Remembered

Lambeau Field in Green Bay, Wisconsin, looks very different today than it did in 1972. In that year, the stadium was a simple rectangular bowl, with only one level of seats (aluminum benches, actually) gently sloping and surrounding the playing field. It had a four-story press box, which was only roughly about 25 yards in length above the middle of the playing surface behind the Packers bench area. Lambeau Field in 1972 was indeed a far cry from what it eventually became in a few more decades and with a few more additions and renovations. Today's modern facility and its beautiful atrium, Packer Hall of Fame Museum, restaurants and souvenir shops, and climate-controlled luxury suites, stand as a testament to the team's progress and growth over the years. Many players who suited up for the Green Bay Packers in 1972 make a visit back to their old stomping grounds every few years or so, and they all marvel at how incredible and grand the site looks today. Through the long train of years, the players of the past will inevitably look down on the natural grass football field, and will recollect their time and their deeds running on that very field, now such a long time ago. Invariably and sadly, those Packers of 1972 will often think of falling just short of achieving the ultimate reward in the sport—winning a Super Bowl championship.

They need not feel too depressed, however. They had survived a very tumultuous season and had earned a division title when nobody thought that they could. And that is more than a lot of teams and a lot of players throughout the history of the NFL can lay claim to. The details of the story of the 1972 Green Bay Packers did not appear to me until many years after the fact. In 1972, I was just a kid enjoying watching pro football on television, many days before the now hugely popular ESPN and NFL Network 24-hour programming came into existence. To me, the '72 Packers were just another playoff team that lost their first-round playoff game. Little did I know back then of the many stories behind the headlines.

In reality, the players who comprised the roster of that team were some of the finest men around at that time. As I found out through my research and by talking to some of them personally, I adamantly feel that they still are. They were (and are) chock-filled with integrity, courage, kindness, and a strong desire to be the best that they could (and still can) be. They met each other in an unusual and in some cases an unfair situation in 1972, and yet they still did their best to overcome their state of affairs and to win in spite of what their head coach was saying or doing on any given day. In the midst of their shared experiences, they gelled as a team, and quickly became more of a family than a team of individual athletes. Quarterback Scott Hunter described their team in the term of "a oneness."[1] I had never heard it put that way before, but that is a perfect description of the '72 Packers. Their friendships were born from the shared sacrifices that each of them made for the good of the team.

If you've reached this part of the book, then you probably won't believe this next statement, but the good of the team was also probably what Packers head coach Dan Devine might have been thinking about in his own decisions and attitudes. We will never know for sure (Devine passed away in 2002). Devine—like all head coaches—wanted to win football games and championships. His methods to accomplish those goals, however, were certainly much different than most of his coaching contemporaries. Inspiring his players was probably one of Devine's objectives throughout 1972, but the means that he employed to do so were assiduously questionable. Playing mind games and deriding and verbally embarrassing several players in front of the rest of the squad rarely inspires high school and college players, let alone professional players in the NFL. There are definitely better ways to inspire a team, regardless of the level of competition. One coach can build his team up by proclaiming his faith every day in their abilities. Other coaches present a business-like presence that displays an air of knowledge, intelligence, and confidence. Still others, when things go wrong, accept all of the blame, and refuse to criticize their players. These methods usually go a long way in instilling a player's respect for his coach.

How much does a coach's reputation count for garnering his players' respect? That can be a debatable question. Consider this comparison: Vince Lombardi ranted, yelled, and threatened to cut his players from the team during his time in Green Bay. So did Devine. Yet Lombardi's players would run through a brick wall for him, and often played hard for him, in spite of enduring injuries which have sidelined lesser men. Many of those players who are still alive today still think fondly of Lombardi, even over six decades since the glory years that they spent in Titletown.

It is highly doubtful that any of the 1972 Packers would think of Dan Devine in terms of endearment. Why the difference? What did Lombardi give his players (besides five world championships) that Devine could not or did not? Maybe it all boiled down to simple respect. The men respected Lombardi. The men who played for Mike Holmgren certainly respected him. I cannot say that the men who played for Devine respected him or not. That is a question that only they can answer, and it is not as simple of a question as you might think. That is possibly because the players on that Packers team respected each other so much, that they may not have ever really thought about the respect—or the lack of respect—that they had for their head coach. They were simply too focused on not letting their teammates down. Maybe they considered such a topic a simple afterthought, when compared to the sacrifices that they made for each other. The Green Bay players in 1972 would certainly have run through a brick wall for each other. Their story is indeed an inspiring one.

Dan Devine's story, in contrast, is indeed an unfortunate one. I had heard a lot of derogatory comments directed at him through the years since the 1970s, and I really did not know how to accept them. I tried to consider the sources of those comments before I lent credence to them. Many comments were repeated by several people who knew Devine quite well, while others were articulated from just passing acquaintances of the man. Positive or uplifting comments were very few. I was somewhat perplexed. How could someone as a pro football coach—indeed *any* pro football coach—be thought of in such a bad way by so many people?

So part of my efforts in writing this book was to purposefully search for opinions in favor of Devine and his actions, in the hopes of balancing the scales of sorts, and in the hopes of making this book more of an objective look back at the 1972 Packers, with all sides and all convictions represented. I did not want this to be a book specifically about Dan Devine, however. I wanted it to be a book about the 1972 Packers. Through my research, however, what I discovered was that the team and Devine were inseparably connected to each other. I simply could not pull apart the two entities, and the more that I thought about it, the more that I realized that I should not try to separate the team and their head coach. They were both enmeshed in a situation that neither were able to do anything about. The Packer players could not and would not quit and remove themselves from their teammates, as the positive feelings that they had for each other and for the game was far too strong. And Dan Devine would not change the way that he coached football. Even years later when he went back to coaching college football, Devine still led his Fighting Irish players at Notre Dame in the same fashion that he managed the Packers.

The fashion in which the 1972 Packers won games was also unique on many different levels. According to the research-oriented pro football historian and author T.J. Troup, there was never any one thing that stood out in any one particular contest where people could take a long, hard look, and

12. A Legacy Remembered 185

come up with a definitive answer as to why or how Green Bay won a division title in 1972. Most observers would conclude that the Pack won with Brockington and Lane toting the pigskin, and to an extent, that is true. But other teams in 1972, such as Miami with Larry Csonka, Mercury Morris, and Jim Kiick, were more feared for their ability to cram the ball right down an opposing defense's throat than the Packers were. There were also several teams with rushing tandems which also earned a good share of headlines during that season. Those teams included the Cleveland Browns (with Leroy Kelly and Bo Scott in the backfield), the San Francisco 49ers (with Ken Willard and Vic Washington in the backfield), the Atlanta Falcons (with Art Malone and Dave Hampton in the backfield), the Detroit Lions (with Steve Owens and Altie Taylor in the backfield), the Dallas Cowboys (with Calvin Hill and Walt Garrison in the backfield), the Washington Redskins (with Larry Brown and Charlie Harraway in the backfield), and the Pittsburgh Steelers (with Franco Harris and John Fuqua in the backfield).

Where Brockington and Lane stood in the midst of all of the other outstanding running duos in the league did not really matter much, however, especially when compared to the team's wins and losses. Some unique statistics that really shed some degree of light on how Green Bay won their games stood out by the time that 1972 ended. For example, the punt return squad did incredibly important and outstanding work. Green Bay punt returners brought the ball back on punts 25 times for 364 yards, which equated to a punt return average of 14.56 yards per return. That meant that the Packers often started many of their drives in decent to good field position. Green Bay also did not throw the ball that much, but when they did, they were quite effective. Packer quarterbacks and their targets rang up just over 15 yards per completion, meaning that every Green Bay player who caught a pass moved the yardsticks downfield for first downs. So the answer as to what the main ingredient was in accruing victories in 1972 could have been many different ingredients, each featuring a variety of success when the Packers most needed big plays, on both the offensive and defensive sides of the ball.

Speaking of defense, it was there where the team made some really important strides towards obtaining victories. While the running game was earning most of the headlines, the defensive unit was quietly but systematically performing at championship levels throughout the 1972 season. Let's start with pass defense. That unit limited their opponents to a meager seven touchdown passes all season long, which was easily the best mark in the entire league. The aforementioned defensive secondary of Willie Buchanon, Ken Ellis, Al Matthews and Jim Hill was rightly credited for this outstanding statistic, but they were only one part of that accomplishment. The defensive line of Bob Brown, Clarence Williams, Alden Roche and Mike McCoy put enough pressure on opposing quarterbacks to limit them to a total of only

2,146 yards passing all season long, the second-best mark in the NFC. It gets even better. The Green Bay run defense was almost as formidable as their pass defense. Linebackers Fred Carr, Dave Robinson, Jim Carter, Ray Nitschke and others limited opposing running backs to a meager 3.4 yards per rushing attempt, which turned out to be the lowest mark in the entire league. When your foes cannot gain ground running the ball in a game and in an era where running the ball was still the accepted standard way that most coaches employed to advance the pigskin downfield, you know that you are doing something right. The defense also recovered 19 of their opponents' fumbles in 1972, the highest number in the NFC. Clearly, the Packers' defense had as much to do with the team's victory total as did the offense.

It did not take me too long in the throes of my research regarding this unique Packers team to become more and more interested in them. But it was much more than just statistics that intrigued me. The human element was also apparent, and I needed to follow it wherever it led me. The strong and simple trait of honesty guided my efforts with this book. I accepted what the players were telling me as the truth into their remembrances of the past. Despite how badly I wanted some of the players to say some nice things about Dan Devine, only two that I know of did (offensive lineman Francis Peay and running back MacArthur Lane). The vast majority of players were not pleased with how their head coach handled the team in 1972, but there was not much that they could do about it. Those who did voice their displeasure with Devine would be sent out of Green Bay in quick fashion. Coach Devine simply wanted to rid the team—his team—of any vestige of the players who played for the iconic Packers legend, Vince Lombardi. Devine knew that he could not trade or cut all of those veteran players overnight, but he sure did try. For those veterans, playing for Devine must have been sheer hell, considering all of the success that they enjoyed while playing for Coach Lombardi.

But on the other hand, I tried to put myself in Devine's shoes. How could he compare to Lombardi and the Lombardi image? He simply could not. Nor could any coach. Lombardi is generally accepted by every knowledgeable pro football expert and fan as the greatest coach in NFL history. Devine would have been well advised to just be his own man, and not worry about the team's past or what Lombardi accomplished. Unfortunately, Devine's own ego would not allow for such an outlook on things, and it was his ego which proved to be his own undoing. Devine coached the Packers in 1973 and 1974, and neither of those two teams were able to achieve what the 1972 Packers team accomplished.

More digging led to more opinions and more different ways to look at the past. Some unnamed people who represented the Green Bay corporate officers would several years later indirectly feel that giving Devine the multiple titles of head coach *and* general manger was a mistake. One of those jobs was probably tough enough to manage, much less both positions. Other random notions from at least one of that same body of decision makers, which included men such as Dominic Olejniczak (President), Richard Bourguignon (Vice President), John B. Torinus (Secretary), Fred N. Trowbridge Sr. (Treasurer), an Executive Committee of seven men, and a group of dozens of Board of Directors, were in agreement with Devine's wishes to make a clean break from the Vince Lombardi era, regardless of how the veteran players felt. I never found any direct quotes from anyone supporting this belief, so I only include it here in this epilogue to give voice to the possibility of differing opinions on the matter. Still others professed that Devine succeeded in 1972 because he hired some good assistants, then let them do their job without much interference. Well, Devine certainly interfered with Bart Starr's play calling in the divisional playoff game at Washington on December 24, 1972, which was enough proof to lay at least some measure of doubt as to that belief. Finally, a few opinions even suggested that Devine was an excellent recruiter of overall talent, a sentiment that very few of his players would have found favor with. If you really wanted to play devil's advocate with Devine and his coaching of the Packers from 1971 to 1974, you could look at a surprising result: Devine had a better winning percentage as Green Bay head coach (.481) than the iconic Packer hero Bart Starr (.406). But you could also come to grips with those figures by correctly stating for a needed perspective that Starr coached for five more years in Green Bay than did Devine.

I tried to take in everything that I researched and everything that I was told with as much credulity as possible. I decided to employ a two-part plan in writing this book. First, I was determined to let the players speak their minds as my guide, and in doing so, I was left with objectivity. It was the key to this whole effort. I took a backseat, and I just listened to the players. It is their memories that make this story a special one. My next step was an introspective one. I admitted the fear of becoming too close to the narrative, because I was (and still am) a Packers fan myself, and because I have experienced working for several bosses in my own life who possessed identities that were similar to Dan Devine's. I asked myself, "How truthful are you to the subject? Can you ignore your own opinions well enough to just write the truth?" In the end, I had to divorce my personal opinions and rely first and foremost on what the players were telling me. They were there. I was not. They saw it all, heard it all, and lived it all. I did not. The reader has to decide for himself or for herself how honest my efforts were.

It is important to note that this is not a complete book about the 1972 Packers. Many of my interview requests from the surviving team members went unanswered. Some former players have sadly passed away, and some others told me that they were not interested in participating in the project.

Only several of the players were willing to be interviewed, and to them I am very grateful. There are undoubtedly many more stories and anecdotes from the voices that I did not hear which have yet to be discovered or discussed, but which are still very important to adding to this incredible story.

What are the lessons that we learned from the 1972 Packers? Is there anything that we can glean from what those players went through to impact our own lives? I am guessing that every single one of us has at one time or another had to deal with a difficult or an incompetent boss at least once in our lives. How did we deal with those situations? Did we get upset enough to quit? Did we keep our mouths shut and just tolerate the situation? Did we take out our anger and disgust at the situation on the ones we love when we got home from work? Did we confront our boss and risk getting fired? How do we respond to this type of adversity?

We at times look on professional athletes as better or greater than ourselves, mostly because they are famous and because we observe their success on television and in the stadiums. But here is a fact that you don't realize until you get older: Professional athletes are normal people. They are faced with the same trials and tribulations that we all experience in our daily lives. They are faced with the same possibilities of success or failure with every decision that they make. They have to cope with problems, come to a realization of their own faults and shortcomings, and try to minimize the adverse actions that their own egos lead them to.

The 1972 Green Bay Packers had to consider all of these things as they dealt with the situation that they faced with their head coach, Dan Devine. Every man on the team was an individual, and every man made his own decisions as to how he would act or respond to any particular situation at practices, during film study, or on game day. The solution to their situation involved unity. The 1972 Packers decided to bond together by confiding in each other, by talking over their issues with each other and supporting each other, by celebrating their victories with each other, and by playing like hell every Sunday.

Those three hours on Sunday afternoons in the fall of 1972 were a much needed remedy to their problems. It was their escape from dealing with the ego of their head coach, even though he—Dan Devine—would be standing just a few short yards away from them all the time. Those three hours on those Sunday afternoons gave the Packer players an opportunity to excel by blasting into their opponents at the line of scrimmage, by throwing the ball accurately and catching it with skill and style, by running to daylight with the ball and by sprinting downfield to make a tackle on special teams. That was what they felt comfortable and justified in doing, and the football field was where they felt a strong sense of support and brotherhood from all of their teammates. The snap of the ball initiated an immediate response among all of the players on that team that had absolutely nothing to do with their head coach. The snap of the ball gave every man on that team a chance to make a key play and to succeed. The 1972 Green Bay Packers were a special group of individual men, but more importantly, they were a team in the truest sense of the word. They were very united and very determined in all of their efforts.

What the 1972 Packers did in their specific story is not to be regarded as a primer of possible answers for our own questions regarding our own lives unless we as individuals think that their decisions and their resolve can serve as a blueprint in our own particular situations. But what that team did stands out as an example of what *can* be accomplished when a group of men want to win badly enough in spite of their unfavorable state of affairs. As a result, the 1972 Packers *did* succeed. They won a division title against difficult odds and against a toilsome personal situation with their boss every single day that they came to work. They deserve to be remembered in Titletown and indeed honored by all Packer fans and NFL fans for that accomplishment. So forget them not. They were the 1972 Green Bay Packers ... the Champions of the NFC Central Division.

Appendix A: The Players

The individual facts and basic information of the men who comprised the 1972 Green Bay Packers roster are as unique as the men themselves. Some made key plays during that epic year, while others served as role players who were called upon to perform a specific duty. Some players were starters, while others were reserves. Regardless of what part they played, however, they were all important in one way or another in helping to make the 1972 Packers the NFC Central Division Champions. Below is a brief account of each of the players.

Ken Bowman, Center. Bowman was counted on greatly to provide the team with some semblance of established wisdom and experience on the offensive line in 1972. Bowman came into the league back in 1964, and was present to participate in some of the greatest years in Green Bay's history, during Vince Lombardi's tenure as head coach. Bowman earned an NFL Championship ring in 1965, and two World Championship rings in 1966 and 1967. In the famous Ice Bowl NFL Championship Game versus Dallas in 1967, Bowman helped Jerry Kramer to block Dallas defensive tackle Jethro Pugh, which enabled Packer quarterback Bart Starr to sneak into the end zone for the winning touchdown.

Center Ken Bowman anchored the Packers offensive line in 1972. Bowman's ability to stay healthy and start every game for the team was vital for the Green Bay rushing attack to succeed (courtesy the Green Bay Packers).

In 1972, Bowman's blocking, particularly in the game at Minnesota on December 10, enabled Green Bay's run-oriented offense to control that contest in the second half en route to the Packers' 23–7 division-clinching victory. In that game, Bowman was tasked with helping to uproot All-Pro Vikings defensive tackle Alan Page, a chore that few centers were ever successful performing. But Bowman was able to do it often enough to pry open room for running backs John Brockington and MacArthur Lane, whose runs controlled the second half of that game. Bowman was a hard-nosed type of performer, and it was common to see him leaving a game after the final gun banged up and bleeding from his battles in the trenches. Bowman played 10 years in the NFL, all of which were in Green Bay.

John Brockington, Running Back. Brockington was anointed as the most important and most dynamic player on the 1972 Packers. Although only in his second year in the league, the burly and bruising runner assumed the role as a team leader despite his youth. Every man on the squad looked up to Brockington, and he responded with 1,027 rushing yards and eight rushing touchdowns, despite being keyed on by every opposing defense. Brockington was mostly an inside runner, gaining the majority of his yards in between the tackles. But the big back (6-foot-1, 225 pounds) brought much more than just his inside running abilities to the team. He was also a devastating blocker for fellow runner MacArthur Lane, and his pass-catching abilities were grossly underrated. Brockington caught 19 passes for 243 yards in 1972, which ranked second on the team. Watching game films of Brockington during his early years gives viewers a look at a man who required at least two defenders to bring him down on virtually every one of his carries. Most impressively, Brockington utilized peerless second efforts while running the ball to gain extra yards after he was initially hit, which in turn provided the Packers with numerous first downs. Brockington played nine years in the NFL. He also played briefly for the Kansas City Chiefs at the end of his pro career.

Bob Brown, Defensive Tackle. Just as Ken Bowman provided the Packers with needed experience on the offensive line, so too did Bob Brown give the defensive line a good dose of wisdom and knowledge in 1972. Brown's main talent was stopping the run, but he was also quite difficult to block while he rushed opposing passers. Brown's size (he stood out at a robust 6–5, 260) provided an obvious problem for opposing offensive linemen, as he constantly pushed them backwards into the passing pocket, which in turn disrupted many offensive plays. Brown was named to the United Press International's All-Conference team in 1972. He joined the Packers in 1966, and was a member of the Super Bowl I and II championship teams. Brown played a total of 11 years in the NFL, including briefly for the Cincinnati Bengals and the San Diego Chargers.

Willie Buchanon, Cornerback. The impact that Willie Buchanon had on the Green Bay pass coverage unit was immediate and vital to helping the team win 10 games in 1972. The gifted rookie from San Diego State was given a lot of responsibility from his very first game, and he did not disappoint. Buchanon virtually shut down some of the best wide receivers in the sport in 1972, and he was a co-leader of interceptions on the team with four. He also led the team with three opposing fumble recoveries in 1972. Buchanon just seemed to get better as he went along, gaining experience every week. He learned through regular film study the tendencies of opposing wide receivers. Through daily practice, he honed his skill to a sharp edge, learning how to get the best angle to defense a pass, and how to bait wide receivers into thinking that they are open (when they were not). He had great athletic ability and speed, both of which are critical if one wants to succeed in the NFL as a cornerback. He was named the Defensive Rookie of the Year in the NFL in 1972. Buchanon played 11 years in the NFL, including his final four years in the league as a member of the San Diego Chargers.

Fred Carr, Outside Linebacker. Fred Carr provided the team with a rough and tumble performance from his outside linebacker position in 1972. Carr was easily one of the hardest hitters on the defense, and many opposing offenses simply ran the ball in the opposite direction when playing against Green Bay. Carr was equally adept at dropping back in pass coverage as he was in forcing a running play and making tackles at the line of scrimmage. Carr was a demonstrative, animated, and excitable man on the field. In short, he was an intimidating force on the Packers defense. He was certainly not afraid of contact, as he loved to hit any member of an opposing offense who got in his way of the ball carrier. He made his most memorable hits on opposing running backs, however. Carr made one of the key plays of the 1972 season on December 10, when he tracked down Minnesota setback Bill Brown, recovered Brown's ensuing fumble, then returned the ball deep into Vikings territory. That play turned that important game around for the Packers, and ignited them to a 23–7 triumph and a division championship. Carr played 10 years in the NFL, all in Green Bay.

Jim Carter, Middle Linebacker. Carter took over the esteemed middle linebacker position from veteran Ray Nitschke, and gave the team a consistent effort all throughout the 1972 season. Opposing offenses declared with their actions that they were going to avoid the outside edges of Green Bay's defense, believing that Carter would be the weakest of the three starting linebackers (Dave Robinson and Fred Carr being the other two). Carter did not seem to mind the extra attention that opposing offenses were giving to him, however. He hit opposing runners just as hard in the fourth quarter of games as he did in the first quarter. Carter was most adept at reading what his foes were trying to do on any given play, and being at the right spot to help make the play. Naturally, the more he played, the more experience he got. He did a pretty fair job at stopping the forward progress of some of the best runners in the league. Few were the running backs who broke a Jim Carter tackle in 1972. Carter played eight years in the NFL, all in Green Bay.

Middle linebacker Jim Carter learned his craft from future Hall of Famer Ray Nitschke. Carter was a hard hitter, but he also was a quality pass defender. Like many Packers starters, Carter also spent time on several of the squad's special teams units (courtesy the Green Bay Packers).

Tommy Crutcher, Linebacker. Crutcher was one of those key reserve players that every team needs in order to be successful. Like most of the defensive reserves, Crutcher was an important special teams player, covering kickoffs and punts throughout the 1972 season. He gained a lot of practical experience as a player for the great Vince Lombardi during the late 1960s. He was a member of Green Bay's Super Bowl I and II championship teams. Crutcher played eight years in the NFL, including two seasons (1968 and 1969) as a member of the New York Giants.

Carroll Dale, Wide Receiver. Carroll Dale provided the 1972 Green Bay receiving corps with their most experienced wide receiver. He unselfishly displayed to the young receivers on the team how to practice, how to devote one's time studying film and charting opponent tendencies, and how to read opposing defensive

Veteran wide receiver Carroll Dale was playing in his final year with the Packers in 1972. His experienced leadership was vital to Green Bay's offense, and he was very important in passing on to the younger pass catchers on the team his knowledge of how to beat a defensive back's coverages. Dale averaged 19.8 yards per reception in 1972. Despite wearing jersey No. 81 in this photograph, Dale wore jersey No. 84 throughout 1972 (courtesy the Green Bay Packers).

backs and work in coordination with the quarterback. Because the Packers were primarily a running team, the Green Bay passing game did not get too many chances to display their abilities. Nevertheless, whenever Dale went out on a pass pattern, he was often double-teamed, due to his advanced knowledge and experience over that of his younger counterparts at the receiver position. Dale averaged 19.8 yards per catch, however, and kept many of Green Bay's offensive drives moving downfield with catches that gave the team first downs. He was a member of the 1965 Green Bay NFL Championship team, and a member of the Super Bowl I and II Packer teams. Dale played 14 years in the NFL, including five years in Los Angeles for the Rams (1960–1964), and one year (1973) as a member of the eventual NFC Champion Minnesota Vikings.

Dave Davis, Wide Receiver. Dave Davis was one of those young wide receivers who benefited from the tutelage gained from listening and watching his older teammate, wide receiver Carroll Dale. Davis did not see much action early in the 1972 season, but as the year wore on, head coach Dan Devine inserted him increasingly more often in the lineup. Davis had good speed for a pass catcher, and as the final games of the 1972 season came about, he was also helpful in blocking downfield for Green Bay's running backs. Green Bay quarterbacks coach Bart Starr eventually tried to take advantage of Davis' speed by using the flanker on several reverse runs later in the 1972 season, with fair results. Davis played four years in the NFL, including a year each for the Pittsburgh Steelers and the New Orleans Saints at the end of his pro career.

Ken Ellis, Cornerback. Ken Ellis was a key defensive back for the Packers in 1972. Just as Willie Buchanon was able to handle an opposing wide receiver man-on-man, so too was Ellis able to do the same on the opposite side of the Green Bay pass defense. Ellis earned first team All-Pro honors in 1972, as well as first team All-Conference honors. Ellis made his mark by playing tight coverages to opposing pass catchers in one-on-one situations. This in turn allowed the other Packer defensive backs ample opportunities to play more intricate zone defenses, knowing that Ellis had single-handedly curtailed the potential success of some pretty fair wide receivers across the league, week in and week out. Ellis co-led the team with four interceptions in 1972. He also provided Green Bay with what was generally accepted as the biggest play of the year with his 80-yard punt return for a touchdown against division rival Detroit on *Monday Night Football* on October 16, which spurred the Packers to a key 24–23 victory. Ellis also provided his teammates with a needed jolt of momentum against the Lions on December 3, when he intercepted two big passes in the rematch between the two clubs. Those important plays led Green Bay to a 33–7 rout over their division rivals, thereby opening the door to the division title for the Packers with a win over Minnesota the following week. Ellis intercepted a total of 22 passes during his 13 years of service in the NFL. He also scored five touchdowns off of interception returns during his pro career. Ellis also played for the Houston Oilers, the Miami Dolphins, the Cleveland Browns, the Detroit Lions, and the Los Angeles Rams.

Len Garrett, Tight End. Garrett was pressed into service in the wake of Rich McGeorge's season-ending injury in the second week of the regular season. Many football observers believe that the position of tight end is one of the most difficult to play, and to be thrust into a starting role in that position in the NFL was quite a challenge for Garrett. Like most young players, however, he grew into the job, and got better as the 1972 season went along. He only caught four passes that year, but he was typically not used as a primary passing target. Rather, Garrett was expected to block for the Packer running game, and he did that rather well, as evidenced by Green Bay's team rushing mark of 2,127 yards. Garrett played five years in the NFL, including a short stint in both New Orleans and San Francisco.

Paul Gibson, Safety, Wide Receiver. Gibson played in only one game for the Packers in 1972. He was originally thought to be used as a wide receiver, and he was listed on the team roster as such. But in reality, he was used primarily as a backup defensive back to fill in behind the other backup defensive backs on the team. Naturally, like all rookies, he was first and foremost a special teams player. He played only one year in the NFL, and became a member of the International Track Association in 1974.

Gale Gillingham, Offensive Guard. Gillingham was a consensus All-Pro guard entering the 1972 season. He was a very good pass blocker, but he was a superior run blocker, pile driving opposing defensive linemen and linebackers down in a most abrupt fashion. He was also an outstanding blocker when pulling out and leading Green Bay runners on end sweep runs. Some of the holes in the line of scrimmage that Gillingham created were wide enough for even the slowest of ball carriers to run through. Gillingham unfortunately became the victim of one of head coach Dan Devine's most ridiculous decisions, which called for Gillingham to move to the defensive line in 1972, in a position that he had never played before. Gillingham suffered an untimely season-ending leg injury soon after he made the switch, and was sadly never really the same again. Devine's experiment to move Gillingham failed, and it served as one of the first noticeable examples that showed that the head coach simply did not know what he was doing when it came to making decisions regarding the team's personnel. To his credit, however, Gillingham fought back hard to come back, and was awarded with All-Conference recognition in 1974. He was a member of Green Bay's Super Bowl I and II championship teams. Gillingham played 10 years in the NFL, all with the Packers.

Leland Glass, Wide Receiver. Glass was drafted by the Packers in the eighth round out of the University of Oregon. He was signed mostly to provide some needed speed to the position, but he was called upon to do so much more. Green Bay used virtually all of their receivers at one time or another throughout the 1972 season. Glass was soon relied upon to come through big on dozens of pass patterns. What he had going for him was his youth, and his opponents' question marks. There was not a whole lot of information available about him. Nor was there much film on what he was capable of doing on the field. As a result, his opponents could not really prepare for him as much as they would for a more seasoned receiver. Glass caught the winning touchdown pass in the *Monday Night Football* game at Detroit on October 16. He had set up the Lions defense by running deep patterns throughout much of the game, being used by the Green Bay offense as mostly a decoy. But on his winning scoring reception, Glass broke off of his deep pattern to run a down-and-out pattern, which fooled the Detroit defensive secondary just long enough to give him enough open room to catch the ball in the corner of the end zone. Glass played only two years in the NFL, both with Green Bay. The 1972 season was his best, as he played in every game that year, and in which he caught 15 passes for 261 yards.

Charlie Hall, Cornerback. Hall was a reserve defensive back who filled in nicely for the Packers on the various special teams units in 1972. Hall was often counted upon to be one of the first players downfield along the far edges of the field to make the tackle on both punt and kickoff coverage teams. This he did rather well, especially towards the end of the season, when Green Bay's special teams units really started to help the team immensely in the division-clinching game at Minnesota on December 10, and in the playoff game at Washington on December 24. Hall played six years in the NFL, all with Green Bay.

Bill Hayhoe, Offensive Tackle. Hayhoe was one of the tallest offensive tackles in the league in 1972, standing 6-foot-8. He used that size to counter opposing defensive ends, who seemingly were getting taller as each year went by. Hayhoe was a key man on Green Bay's offensive line, as he helped to seal off the edge of the opposing defenses for the Packers' sweep runs. It is hard to gauge the performance of an offensive tackle, but two statistics which point to Hayhoe's success are noteworthy. Green Bay gained a total of 2,127 rushing yards in 1972, and the Packer quarterbacks were sacked only 17 times in 1972, one of the lowest marks in the league. Hayhoe played five years in the NFL, all with Green Bay.

Larry Heffner, Linebacker. Heffner was drafted in the 14th round by the Packers out of Clemson University, and as such, he was the lowest-round draft selectee to make the team in 1972. He was a reserve linebacker who saw action in only two games in 1972. Like all rookies, he would serve mostly on the special teams units. He would see more game action on his later years with the team than he did in 1972. Heffner played four years in the NFL, all with Green Bay.

Jim Hill, Safety. Jim Hill was obtained in a trade with the San Diego Chargers, and his addition to the team greatly solidified Green Bay's defensive secondary. He came to the Packers with three years of pro experience under his belt, and it was this experience that he imparted to the younger members of the Packer secondary. Hill was somewhat of a reliable traffic cop on passing plays, directing the other secondary members where to go, what zones to cover, etc. He was also a very good tackler on running plays, and he was called upon to perform that duty on a constant basis. Added to all of this was the fact that Hill was a co-leader of the team with four interceptions in 1972. He played seven years in the NFL, completing his pro career for the Cleveland Browns in 1975. Hill went on to become a television sports broadcaster in California following his pro football career, and he would even come back to Lambeau Field to broadcast Packer games for CBS-TV.

Dick Himes, Offensive Tackle. Himes was called upon to provide the Packer offense with veteran leadership from the offensive tackle position. Like his counterpart on the opposite side of the line (Bill Hayhoe), Himes was expected to keep outside pass rushers from annihilating Green Bay's quarterbacks. Also like Hayhoe, Himes adeptly opened holes for the likes of John Brockington and MacArthur Lane all throughout the 1972 season, particularly on the famous Packer sweep runs. Himes played for 10 years in the NFL, all of which were with the Packers.

Bob Hudson, Running Back. Hudson was a sixth-round draft choice by the Packers in 1972. He saw most of his action on the various special teams units during the 1972 season, returning 11 kickoffs for 247 yards (a 22.5-yard average). Two of his kickoff returns against Dallas on October 1 went for a total of 79 yards (a 39.5-yard average). But towards the end of the year, Hudson also got several chances to fill in for John Brockington, when those late-season games in December against Detroit and New Orleans were winding down, and when the outcome of both of those contests had already been decided. He carried the ball 15 times for 62 yards in 1972. Hudson played three years in the NFL, and concluded his pro career in 1974 as a member of the Oakland Raiders.

Kevin Hunt, Offensive Tackle. Hunt saw action in only three games in the 1972 season. He was signed as a free agent in 1972, and served as a backup to both Bill Hayhoe and Dick Himes on the offensive line. Hunt played seven years in the NFL, and he would later play for the New England Patriots, the Houston Oilers, and the New Orleans Saints.

Scott Hunter, Quarterback. Hunter ran the Packer offense for most of the 1972 season. Still only a youngster himself (he was only in his second pro season in 1972), Hunter shouldered a large amount of responsibility to help the fortunes of the team. While it was true that many of his plays involved handing the ball off to John Brockington and MacArthur Lane, Hunter was also counted upon to surprise opposing defenses with timely passes, coming in both short and long distances. Hunter received tutelage from Green Bay quarterbacks coach Bart Starr, himself a five-time world champion quarterback. The knowledge that Hunter obtained from Starr was immensely helpful to the young signal caller. Hunter led the Packers in both touchdown passes and passing yards in 1972. His interception total went down from 17 in 1971 to nine in 1972. That statistic alone was very important in helping the team's offense improve greatly during the 1972 season. Hunter was what one would term as a journeyman quarterback, going from team to team during his career. He would play seven years in the NFL, including stints after his time in Green Bay with the Buffalo Bills, the Atlanta Falcons, and the Detroit Lions.

Dave Kopay, Running Back. Every NFL team needs quality backup players, especially during the early 1970s, when the roster limits were smaller in number than they are in today's pro game. Dave Kopay served in that role for the Packers during the 1972 season. He carried the ball 10 times in 1972 for 39 yards, and like Bob Hudson, he saw mop-up duty for starters John Brockington and MacArthur Lane towards the end of the season. Kopay also played on several of Green Bay's special teams units, most notably on the punt coverage unit. Kopay played nine seasons in the NFL, the 1972 season being his last. He also played for the likes of the San Francisco 49ers, the Detroit Lions, the Washington Redskins, and the New Orleans Saints.

Bob Kroll, Safety. Kroll saw action in five games during the 1972 season, mostly on the special teams punt and kickoff coverage units. Thanks to the overall health of Green Bay's starters in the defensive secondary, Kroll was not used too much in reserve of players like Jim Hill and Al Matthews. Kroll played only one year in the NFL.

Pete Lammons, Tight End. Lammons was picked up by Coach Devine in the wake of Rich McGeorge's season-ending injury in the early stages of the 1972 season. Lammons brought championship pedigree to the team, having been a starter for the 1968 World Champion New York Jets. Lammons also brought some needed experience to the tight end position, which he shared with youngster Len Garrett. Lammons contributed just one reception during the 1972 season, but he was extremely helpful in blocking for the Packer rushing attack. Lammons played seven seasons of pro football. The 1972 season was his final year in the NFL.

MacArthur Lane, Running Back. Lane could possibly be called the most important offensive player on the Packers team in 1972. His ability in opening holes for fellow runner John Brockington were extremely vital to Green Bay's offensive production, and for Brockington's second straight 1,000-yard season in 1972. Moreover, Lane also contributed 821 rushing yards of his own from the fullback position, giving the team a one-two punch when toting the pigskin. Lane also possessed very deceptive speed, and he was able to employ it in some really tight spots where there was not much running room to be found. But it was in pass receiving out of the backfield where Lane truly excelled. He led the Packers with 26 receptions in 1972, and he averaged 11 yards per reception. Lane was relied upon heavily by the likes of quarterback Scott Hunter, who was more than happy to call his number in the huddle. By going out on pass patterns, Lane immediately drew at least one defender to him, which often opened up more room for Brockington to run with the ball. Lane came to the Packers in a trade with the St. Louis Cardinals. He would play for 11 years in the NFL, including several seasons in Kansas City to conclude his pro career.

Bill Lueck, Offensive Guard. Lueck was a consistent run blocker who did great work opening holes for the likes of John Brockington and MacArthur Lane all throughout the 1972 season. Seldom getting any fanfare, Lueck was a solid performer who was counted upon by the Green Bay coaches and his teammates alike to perform one of the toughest duties of all in pro football—opening up holes in the line of scrimmage against opposing teams that were expecting the Packers to run the ball on almost every play. This he did quite well, as evidenced by how dominating Lueck and the rest of the Green Bay offensive line performed in the playoff-clinching victory at Minnesota on December 10. Lueck played eight years in the NFL, his first seven of which were with the Packers. He played his final year in 1975 with the Philadelphia Eagles.

Chester Marcol, Kicker. Marcol was drafted in 1972 by Dan Devine to solve the Packers' numerous kicking problems, which went on for several years before 1972. Marcol provided an immediate boost to point scoring on the team, as he himself led the entire NFL in scoring in his rookie year with 128 total points. Marcol connected on 33 field goals in 1972, and was perfect on 29 conversion kicks in 1972. He never did enjoy as good of a season during the remainder of his pro football career as he did in 1972, but he was still a solid placekicker all throughout his time in the league. Marcol played 11 seasons in the NFL, including a little over a year in Houston. If Marcol had not been kicking for the Packers in 1972, it is questionable if they would have made the playoffs that year.

Al Matthews, Safety. Matthews was probably the least-noticed member of the Green Bay starting defensive secondary in 1972. Nevertheless, his performance that season was vital in solidifying that unit, which permitted a league-low of only seven opposing touchdown passes all year. Matthews gelled with cohorts Willie Buchanon, Jim Hill and Ken Ellis to become one of the most formidable defensive secondaries in the NFL in 1972. Matthews chipped in with two interceptions during that season. He was also called upon on a regular basis to force opposing running plays and help to make tackles at or near the line of scrimmage. Matthews played for eight years in the NFL, the first six of which were in Green Bay. His final two pro seasons were in Seattle and in San Francisco.

Mike McCoy, Defensive Tackle. McCoy was a mountain of a man who teamed up with fellow defensive tackle Bob Brown to form one of the most formidable inside run-stopping tandems in the league in 1972. McCoy stood 6-foot-5, and weighed 284 pounds, which was huge for interior linemen during the early 1970s. Few were the opposing running backs who could obtain a wealth of ground yardage running in between their center and offensive tackle when faced with the specter of Mike McCoy filling up those holes. It was not uncommon for McCoy to take up and occupy two blockers on many plays, which enabled the other Green Bay defensive linemen to penetrate into the opponent's passing pocket. McCoy played for 11 years in the NFL. Toward the end of his career, he also played for the Oakland Raiders and the New York Giants.

Rich McGeorge, Tight End. McGeorge was one of the biggest and most reliable tight ends in the NFL throughout his nine-year career, each year of which was spent in Green Bay. He possessed great hands and was extremely hard to tackle, often bouncing off of defenders who attempted to bring him down. Unfortunately, McGeorge was injured in the second week of the 1972 season, which diminished the weapons that quarterback Scott Hunter had to use in the team's short passing attack. Had McGeorge been healthy throughout 1972, there is no telling how much improved Green Bay's passing numbers might have been that year, and how many more victories the Packers might have accrued.

Ray Nitschke, Middle Linebacker. The venerable Ray Nitschke led the Green Bay defense during their glory years of the 1960s. He enjoyed participating in every Packer championship season throughout that decade. In 1972, he was called upon to play a supportive and backup role, which he did very well. Nitschke willingly gave sagacious advice to his fellow defensive teammates all season long. His 34-yard pass reception off of a blocked field goal attempt against the Saints on December 17 was one of the most surprising plays of the year. Nitschke played for 15 seasons in the NFL, all with Green Bay. He was enshrined in the Pro Football Hall of Fame in 1978.

Frank Patrick, Quarterback. Patrick saw mop-up duty in two games in 1972, completing one pass in four attempts. Patrick played three seasons in the NFL, all in Green Bay. The 1972 season was his final year in the league. He was drafted in the 10th round of the 1970 NFL Draft by the Packers.

Francis Peay, Offensive Tackle. Peay suited up for six games for Green Bay in the 1972 season, serving as a backup offensive lineman. Peay played for Packer head coach Dan Devine while both were at the University of Missouri. Peay played for nine years in the NFL, including stints in New York for the Giants, and in Kansas City for the Chiefs.

Dave Pureifory, Defensive End. Pureifory was a sixth-round draft selection by the Packers in 1972, and he became a steady and often spectacular defender for the team. Pureifory was equally adept at playing the defensive tackle position as well as his slated defensive end position. He was also extremely important for the Packers on their special teams punt and kickoff coverage units. In those duties, it was his job to blast into the blocking wedges and remove an opposing returner's blockers in a most abrupt and conclusive way. Pureifory's 260-pound frame and better than average speed for a defensive lineman enabled him to perform his various roles quite well. Pureifory played 11 years in the NFL, including short tours of duty in Cincinnati and in Detroit.

Dave Robinson, Outside Linebacker. Robinson was a team leader who excelled at his position, and whose experience really helped the Green Bay defense become one of the league's best throughout the 1972 season. Robinson was big, quick, and agile, and like fellow linebacker Fred Carr, he would make plays all over the field. He could not only thwart opposing rushing plays, but he could also drop back into pass coverage as fast as any outside linebacker in the league. Moreover, Robinson could also blitz from the outside extremely well. Robinson intercepted two passes in 1972. He was also one of the surest tacklers in the pro game all throughout his pro career. He regularly disseminated his knowledge and experience to all of his younger teammates, which in turn aided their efforts immensely in 1972. Robinson played 12 years in the NFL, the last two of which were for the Washington Redskins. He was enshrined in the Pro Football Hall of Fame in 2013.

Alden Roche, Defensive End. Roche came to the Packers in 1971 after playing his rookie season in Denver. He was a quality pass rusher that every team needs from the outside defensive end position. When teamed with Clarence Williams on the other side of Green Bay's defensive line, Roche was a formidable foe for any offensive tackle to handle. Roche's main weapon was his quickness off of the snap of the ball, something that every top-notch defensive end needs in order to be effective in the NFL. He played a total of nine seasons in pro football, including his final two years as a member of the Seattle Seahawks.

Malcolm Snider, Offensive Guard. Snider came to the team via a trade with the Atlanta Falcons in 1972, and he immediately provided the Packers with outstanding play from his guard position. Snider was tasked with what many would consider to be an impossible chore—filling in for All-Pro guard Gale Gillingham in the wake of his season-ending injury. Snider was very successful by all accounts in this labor, as he regularly opened interior holes for the likes of John Brockington and MacArthur Lane. Snider played in every game during the 1972 season, providing the offensive line with emergency stability throughout the year. He played six years in the NFL.

Defensive end Alden Roche excelled as a pass rusher for the 1972 Packers, but he was also greatly relied upon by the team for his run-stopping abilities. The Green Bay pass rush was one of the best in the league in 1972, and the consistent efforts of Roche were a main reason why (courtesy the Green Bay Packers).

Jon Staggers, Wide Receiver. Staggers was one of several plug-in wide receivers that Dan Devine used in an effort to open up the team's passing attack in 1972. He was acquired from the Steelers after playing his first two years in Pittsburgh in 1970 and 1971. Staggers caught eight passes for 123 yards for the Packers in 1972, which equated to a 15.4-yards-per-catch average. He made a great diving catch off of a deflection for a touchdown against the Chicago Bears on October 8, which led to a 20–17 Green Bay win. Staggers was also a very important punt and kickoff returner for Green Bay. His 85-yard punt return for a touchdown against Houston on November 19 was the longest punt return of the season for the Packers. Staggers played for six years in the NFL, his final season coming in 1975 with the Detroit Lions.

Jerry Tagge, Quarterback. Jerry Tagge came to the Packers as a first-round draft choice from the National Champion Nebraska Cornhuskers in 1972. He was a big quarterback (6–2, 220), cut in the mold of Chicago's Bobby Douglass. Like Douglass, Tagge was a running quarterback, and also like Douglass, he had a very strong throwing arm. He was slated to serve as a backup to starting quarterback Scott Hunter, but he always prided himself on being as prepared as possible, in the event that Hunter sustained any injuries. This is exactly what happened on November 12, 1972, when Tagge replaced the injured Hunter in a tough 23–17 victory at Chicago. By all accounts, Tagge did a fair job with this difficult task on that day, as he led the Packers offense to obtain some vital first downs in the fourth quarter to preserve the win. Tagge saw action in a total four games in 1972, completing 10 passes for 154 yards and zero interceptions. He played three seasons in the NFL, all in Green Bay.

Ike Thomas, Cornerback. Thomas was obtained in 1972 with a trade from Dallas, and was used most often as a reserve for fellow cornerback Ken Ellis. Thomas also used his speed and his elusiveness as a kickoff returner, which he did rather well. He returned 21 kickoffs in 1972 for the Packers, worth 572 yards, which equated to a team-leading 27.2-yard average. He also contributed an 89-yard kickoff return against Houston on November 19, 1972. Thomas played four years in the NFL. His final year was in 1974 as a member of the Buffalo Bills.

Vernon Vanoy, Defensive Tackle. Vanoy saw duty in 13 games in 1972, filling in on selected plays for both Mike McCoy and Bob Brown. He had the best game of his life on October 1, as he sacked Dallas quarterback Craig Morton three times in Green Bay's 16–13 upset victory over the defending world champion Cowboys. Vanoy played three years in the NFL for three different teams (the New York Giants, the Packers, and the Houston Oilers).

Ward Walsh, Running Back. Walsh only saw action in two games in 1972, serving as a backfield reserve and a special teams player. He did not have any carries or pass receptions in 1972. He played only two years in the NFL, the first of which was for the Houston Oilers.

Ron Widby, Punter. Widby came to the Packers fresh off of a world championship as a member of the 1971 Dallas Cowboys. Widby punted 65 times in 1972 for a 41.8-yard punting average. His longest punt traveled 64 yards. But Widby was an athlete in this sport, and he was called upon by the Packers to do more than just punt the ball. He also threw the ball twice in 1972, both times with successful results. One of those throws went for a touchdown to wide receiver Dave Davis against Houston on November 19 (a 23–10 Green Bay win). Widby also served as the Packers' holder on field goal and extra point conversion attempts. Widby played six years in the NFL.

Clarence Williams, Defensive End. Williams was nicknamed "The Big Cat" by his teammates. He certainly was big, standing 6-5, 255. He was a great pass rusher, and he sacked Minnesota quarterback three times in Green Bay's division-clinching victory over the Vikings on December 11, 1972. This was probably the best game he ever played, but throughout his pro career, Williams played well enough to be very troublesome to many opposing blockers. He was a quick and rangy defensive end, and he also took advantage of numerous opponent mistakes. Williams returned a fumble against the Bears for a critical touchdown on October 8, 1972 (a 20–17 Packers victory). Williams played eight years in the NFL, all with the Packers.

Perry Williams, Running Back. Williams played in every game for the 1972 Packers, serving mostly as a special teams performer on the punt and kickoff return and coverage units. Late in the year, he had a chance to carry the ball more than any other reserve running back on the team, especially against Detroit on December 3, and at New Orleans on December 17 (both Green Bay victories). Williams toted the ball 33 times for 139 yards (a 4.2-yard average) in 1972. Williams played six years in the NFL. His final year in the league was in 1974 with the Chicago Bears.

Cal Withrow, Center. Withrow played in every game during the 1972 season for the Packers. He saw duty mostly as a special teams player, but he also served as veteran center Ken Bowman's backup. Withrow spent much of his on-field time in Green Bay as the team's long snapper for punts, and on occasion the snapper for field goal and extra point conversion placements. Withrow played five years in the NFL, including one season in San Diego (1970) and one season in St. Louis (1974).

Keith Wortman, Offensive Guard. Wortman was drafted in the 10th round by the Packers in the 1972 NFL Draft. He played in 13 games during his rookie season, mostly on special teams. He utilized his rookie year wisely by learning the nuances and techniques of his position, which enabled him to have a good pro career. Wortman played 10 years in the NFL, the final six of which were in St. Louis, where he was a part of one of the best offensive lines in the league during the latter part of the 1970s.

Appendix B: Roster and Statistics

1972 Green Bay Packers

No.	Name	Age	Pos.	Wt	Ht	College
57	Ken Bowman	30	C	230	6'3"	Wisconsin
42	John Brockington	24	RB	225	6'1"	Ohio St.
78	Robert Brown	33	RDT	260	6'5"	Arkansas-Pine Bluff
28	Willie Buchanon	22	LCB	190	6'0"	San Diego State
53	Fred Carr	26	RLB	238	6'5"	Texas-El Paso
50	Jim Carter	24	MLB	235	6'3"	Minnesota
56	Tommy Crutcher	31	LB/FB	229	6'3"	Texas Christian
84	Carroll Dale	34	WR	200	6'2"	Virginia Tech
47	Dave Davis	24	WR	175	6'0"	Tennessee St.
48	Ken Ellis	25	PR	190	5'10"	Southern
88	Len Garrett	25	TE	230	6'3"	New Mexico Highlands
41	Paul Gibson	24	WR	195	6'2"	Texas-El Paso
68	Gale Gillingham	28	G	255	6'3"	Minnesota
46	Leland Glass	22	WR	185	6'0"	Oregon
21	Charlie Hall	24	DB	193	6'1"	Pittsburgh
77	Bill Hayhoe	26	LT	258	6'8"	University of Southern California
51	Larry Hefner	23	LB	230	6'2"	Clemson
39	Jim Hill	26	FS	190	6'2"	Texas A&M-Kingsville
72	Dick Himes	26	RT	244	6'4"	Ohio St.
23	Bob Hudson	24	RB	210	5'11"	NE State (OK)
64	Kevin Hunt	24	T/G	260	6'5"	Doane
16	Scott Hunter	25	QB	205	6'2"	Alabama
40	Dave Kopay	30	RB	218	6'0"	Washington
44	Bob Kroll	22	DB	195	6'1"	Northern Michigan
86	Pete Lammons	29	TE	230	6'3"	Texas
36	MacArthur Lane	30	RB	220	6'1"	Utah St.
62	Bill Lueck	26	LG	250	6'3"	Arizona
13	Chester Marcol	23	K	190	6'0"	Hillsdale

No.	Name	Age	Pos.	Wt	Ht	College
29	Al Matthews	25	SS	190	5'11"	Texas A&M-Kingsville
76	Mike McCoy	24	LDT	284	6'5"	Notre Dame
81	Rich McGeorge	24	TE	235	6'4"	Elon
66	Ray Nitschke	36	MLB	235	6'3"	Illinois
10	Frank Patrick	25	QB	225	6'7"	Nebraska
71	Francis Peay	28	OT	250	6'5"	Cameron, Missouri
75	Dave Pureifory	23	DE	260	6'1"	East. Michigan
89	Dave Robinson	31	LLB	245	6'3"	Penn State
87	Alden Roche	27	RDE	255	6'4"	Southern
67	Malcolm Snider	25	RG	251	6'4"	Stanford
22	Jon Staggers	24	WR	185	5'10"	Missouri
17	Jerry Tagge	22	QB	220	6'2"	Nebraska
37	Ike Thomas	25	KR	193	6'2"	Bishop
73	Vern Vanoy	26	DT	275	6'8"	Kansas
26	Ward Walsh	24	RB	213	6'0"	Colorado
20	Ron Widby	27	P	210	6'4"	Tennessee
83	Clarence Williams	26	LDE	255	6'5"	Prairie View
31	Perry Williams	26	RB	219	6'2"	Purdue
58	Cal Withrow	27	C	240	6'0"	Kentucky
65	Keith Wortman	22	G/T	260	6'2"	Nebraska

1972 Schedule and Results

Preseason

August (3–1)	Result	Record	Attendance
5 G-Cincinnati Bengals	W 24–14	1-0-0	56,263
12 at Miami Dolphins	W 14–13	2-0-0	75,332
19 at Houston Oilers	L 3–20	2-1-0	46,460
27 M-Chicago Bears W	10–7	3-1-0	47,222

September (1–1)	Result	Record	Attendance
2 G-St. Louis Cardinals	L 10–31	3-2-0	56,263
9 M-Kansas City Chiefs	W 20–0	4-2-0	47,281

Regular Season

September (1–1)	Result	Record	Attendance
17 at Cleveland Browns	W 26–10	1-0-0	75,771
24 G-Oakland Raiders	L 14–20	1-1-0	56,263

October (3–2)	Result	Record	Attendance
1 M-Dallas Cowboys	W 16–13	2-1-0	47,103
8 G-Chicago Bears	W 20–17	3-1-0	56,263
16 at Detroit Lions	W 24–23	4-1-0	54,418
22 M-Atlanta Falcons	L 9–10	4-2-0	47,967
29 G-Minnesota Vikings	L 13–27	4-3-0	56,263

November (3–1)	Result	Record	Attendance
5 M-San Francisco 49ers	W 34–24	5-3-0	47,897

12 at Chicago Bears	W 23–17	6-3-0	55,701
19 at Houston Oilers	W 23–10	7-3-0	41,752
26 at Washington Redskins	L 16–21	7-4-0	53,039
December (3–0)	**Result**	**Record**	**Attendance**
3 G-Detroit Lions	W 33–7	8-4-0	56,263
10 at Minnesota Vikings	W 23–7	9-4-0	49,784
17 at New Orleans Saints	W 30–20	10-4-0	65,881

Playoffs

December (0–1)	**Result**	**Record**	**Attendance**
24 at Washington Redskins	L 3–16	0-1	53,140

Notes: The "G" in front of specific opponents means that the game was played at Lambeau Field in Green Bay, Wisconsin. The "M" in front of specific opponents means that the game was played at Milwaukee County Stadium in Milwaukee, Wisconsin.

Team Offensive Stats	Team Defensive Stats
Points Scored: 304	Points Allowed: 226
Total Yards: 3,539	Total Yards Allowed: 3,474
Total Plays: 798	Total Opposing Plays: 812
Yards Per Play: 4.4	Yards per Play Allowed: 4.3
First Downs: 195	First Downs Allowed: 209
Pass Completions: 101	Pass Completions Allowed: 174
Pass Attempts: 237	Passes Attempted: 340
Total Passing Yards: 1,412	Total Passing Yards Allowed: 1,957
Total Passing Touchdowns: 7	Total Passing Touchdowns Allowed: 7
Interceptions: 9	Interceptions: 17
First Downs By Passing: 72	First Downs By Passing Allowed: 109
Rushing Attempts: 544	Rushing Attempts: 443
Total Rushing Yards: 2,127	Total Rushing Yards Allowed: 1,517
Total Rushing Touchdowns: 17	Total Rushing Touchdowns Surrendered: 14
Yards Per Rushing Attempt: 3.9	Yards per Rushing Attempt Allowed: 3.4
First Downs By Rushing: 109	First Downs By Rushing Surrendered: 85

Passing Statistics

Scott Hunter: Played in 14 Games. Started 14 Games. Completed 86 passes in 199 attempts. Completion Percentage was 43.2 percent. Total Passing Yards was 1,252 yards. Threw for 6 touchdowns and 9 interceptions. His longest pass completion was for 49 yards. His passer rating was 55.5. He was sacked 13 times for 86 yards in losses.

Jerry Tagge: Played in 4 Games. Started 0 Games. Completed 10 passes in 29 attempts. Completion percentage was 34.5 percent. Total passing yards was 154 yards. Threw for 0 touchdowns and 0 interceptions. His longest pass completion was for 31 yards. His passer rating was 52.9. He was sacked 3 times for 27 yards in losses.

Frank Patrick: Played in 2 Games. Started 0 Games. Completed 1 pass in 4 attempts. Completion percentage was 25 percent. Total passing yards was 9 yards. Threw for 0 touchdowns and 0 interceptions. His longest pass completion was for 9 yards. His passer rating was 39.6. He was sacked 1 time for 11 yards in losses.

MacArthur Lane: Played in 14 Games. Started 14 Games. Completed 2 passes in 2 attempts. Completion percentage was 100 percent. Total passing yards was 19 yards. Threw for

0 touchdowns and 0 interceptions. His longest pass completion was for 10 yards. His passer rating was 106.2. He was sacked 0 times for 0 yards in losses.

Ron Widby: Played in 14 Games. Started 0 Games. Completed 2 passes in 2 attempts. Completion percentage was 100 percent. Total passing yards was 102 yards. Threw for 1 touchdown and 0 interceptions. His longest pass completion was for 68 yards. His passer rating was 158.3. He was sacked 0 times for 0 yards in losses.

Jon Staggers: Played in 11 Games. Started 0 Games. Completed 0 passes in 1 attempts. Completion percentage was 0.0 percent. Total passing yards was 0 yards. Threw for 0 touchdowns and 0 interceptions. His passer rating was 39.6. He was sacked 0 times for 0 yards in losses.

Rushing Statistics

John Brockington: Played in 14 Games. Started 14 Games. Rushed for 1,027 Yards on 274 Carries. Rushing Average was 3.7 Yards Per Carry. Scored 8 Rushing Touchdowns. Longest Run From Scrimmage was 30 Yards. Averaged 73.4 Yards Per Game Rushing. Fumbled the Ball 4 Times.

MacArthur Lane: Played in 14 Games. Started 14 Games. Rushed for 821 Yards on 177 Carries. Rushing Average was 4.6 Yards Per Carry. Scored 3 Rushing Touchdowns. Longest Run From Scrimmage was 41 Yards. Averaged 58.6 Yards Per Game Rushing. Fumbled the Ball 6 Times.

Perry Williams: Played in 14 Games. Started 0 Games. Rushed for 139 Yards on 33 Carries. Rushing Average was 4.2 Yards Per Carry. Scored 0 Rushing Touchdowns. Longest Run From Scrimmage was 14 Yards. Averaged 9.9 Yards Per Game Rushing. Fumbled the Ball 1 Time.

Scott Hunter: Played in 14 Games. Started 14 Games. Rushed for 37 Yards on 22 Carries. Rushing Average was 1.7 Yards Per Carry. Scored 5 Rushing Touchdowns. Longest Run From Scrimmage was 15 Yards. Averaged 2.6 Yards Per Game Rushing. Fumbled the 5 Ball Times.

Bob Hudson: Played in 12 Games. Started 0 Games. Rushed for 62 Yards on 15 Carries. Rushing Average was 4.1 Yards Per Carry. Scored Rushing 0 Touchdowns. Longest Run From Scrimmage was 17 Yards. Averaged 5.2 Yards Per Game Rushing. Fumbled the Ball 1 Time.

Dave Kopay: Played in 14 Games. Started 0 Games. Rushed for 39 Yards on 10 Carries. Rushing Average was 3.9 Yards Per Carry. Scored Rushing 0 Touchdowns. Longest Run From Scrimmage was 20 Yards. Averaged 2.8 Yards Per Game Rushing. Fumbled the Ball 1 Time.

Jerry Tagge: Played in 4 Games. Started 0 Games. Rushed for -3 Yards on 8 Carries. Rushing Average was -0.4 Yards Per Carry. Scored 1 Rushing Touchdowns. Longest Run From Scrimmage was 2 Yards. Averaged -0.8 Yards Per Game Rushing. Fumbled the 0 Ball Times.

Leland Glass: Played in 14 Games. Started 14 Games. Rushed for 13 Yards on 2 Carries. Rushing Average was 6.5 Yards Per Carry. Scored 0 Rushing Touchdowns. Longest Run From Scrimmage was 13 Yards. Averaged 0.9 Yards Per Game Rushing. Fumbled the 0 Ball Times.

Dave Davis: Played in 10 Games. Started 0 Games. Rushed for 0 Yards on 2 Carries. Rushing Average was 0.0 Yards Per Carry. Scored 0 Rushing Touchdowns. Longest Run From Scrimmage was 7 Yards. Averaged 0.0 Yards Per Game Rushing. Fumbled the Ball 0 Times.

Jon Staggers: Played in 11 Games. Started 0 Games. Rushed for -8 Yards on 1 Carry. Rushing Average was -8.0 Yards Per Carry. Scored 0 Rushing Touchdowns. Longest Run From Scrimmage was -8 Yards. Averaged -0.7 Yards Per Game Rushing. Fumbled the Ball 2 Times.

Receiving Statistics

John Brockington: Made 19 Receptions for 243 Yards. Made 12.8 Yards Per Reception. Caught 1 Touchdown Pass. Longest Reception was for 48 Yards.
MacArthur Lane: Made 26 Receptions for 285 Yards. Made 11.0 Yards Per Reception. Caught 0 Touchdown Passes. Longest Reception was for 49 Yards.
Dave Kopay: Made 3 Receptions for 19 Yards. Made 6.3 Yards Per Reception. Caught 0 Touchdown Passes. Longest Reception was for 9 Yards.
Leland Glass: Made 15 Receptions for 261 Yards. Made 17.4 Yards Per Reception. Caught 1 Touchdown Pass. Longest Reception was for 31 Yards.
Dave Davis: Made 4 Receptions for 119 Yards. Made 29.8 Yards Per Reception. Caught 1 Touchdown Pass. Longest Reception was for 68 Yards.
Jon Staggers: Made 8 Receptions for 123 Yards. Made 15.4 Yards Per Reception. Caught 1 Touchdown Pass. Longest Reception was for 48 Yards.
Carroll Dale: Made 16 Receptions for 317 Yards. Made 19.8 Yards Per Reception. Caught 1 Touchdown Pass. Longest Reception was for 48 Yards.
Len Garrett: Made 4 Receptions for 66 Yards. Made 16.5 Yards Per Reception. Caught 0 Touchdown Passes. Longest Reception was for 21 Yards.
Rich McGeorge: Made 4 Receptions for 50 Yards. Made 12.5 Yards Per Reception. Caught 2 Touchdown Passes. Longest Reception was for 23 Yards.
Pate Lammons: Made 1 Reception for 19 Yards. Made 19.0 Yards Per Reception. Caught 0 Touchdown Passes. Longest Reception was for 19 Yards.
Ray Nitschke: Made 1 Reception for 34 Yards. Made 34.0 Yards Per Reception. Caught 0 Touchdown Passes. Longest Reception was for 34 Yards.

Kickoff Returns and Punt Returns

Ike Thomas: Had 21 Kickoff Returns for 572 Total Yards. Averaged 27.2 Yards Per Kickoff Return. Longest Kickoff Return was for 89 Yards.
Jon Staggers: Had 11 Kickoff Returns for 260 Total Yards. Averaged 23.6 Yards Per Kickoff Return. Longest Kickoff Return was for 39 Yards. Had 9 Punt Returns for 148 Yards. Averaged 16.4 Yards Per Punt Return. Longest Punt Return was for 85 Yards. Scored 1 Touchdown on a Punt Return.
Ken Ellis: Had 1 Kickoff Return for 10 Total Yards. Averaged 10.0 Yards Per Kickoff Return. Longest Kickoff Return was for 10 Yards. Had 14 Punt Returns for 215 Yards. Averaged 15.4 Yards Per Punt Return. Longest Punt Return was for 80 Yards. Scored 1 Touchdown on a Punt Return.
Bob Hudson: Had 11 Kickoff Returns for 247 Total Yards. Averaged 22.5 Yards Per Kickoff Return. Longest Kickoff Return was for 55 Yards. Had 1 Punt Return for 0 Yards. Averaged 0 Yards Per Punt Return. Longest Punt Return was for 0 Yards. Scored 0 Touchdowns on a Punt Return.
Len Garrett: Had 1 Kickoff Return for 0 Total Yards. Averaged 0 Yards Per Kickoff Return. Longest Kickoff Return was for Yards.
Bob Kroll: Had 1 Kickoff Returns for 23 Total Yards. Averaged 23.0 Yards Per Kickoff Return. Longest Kickoff Return was for 23 Yards.

Dave Robinson: Had 1 Kickoff Returns for 20 Total Yards. Averaged 20 Yards Per Kickoff Return. Longest Kickoff Return was for 20 Yards.
Perry Williams: Had 1 Kickoff Returns for 9 Total Yards. Averaged 9 Yards Per Kickoff Return. Longest Kickoff Return was for 9 Yards.
Keith Wortman: Had 1 Kickoff Returns for 0 Total Yards. Averaged 0 Yards Per Kickoff Return. Longest Kickoff Return was for 0 Yards.
Leland Glass: Had 1 Punt Return for 1 Yard. Averaged 1 Yard Per Punt Return. Longest Punt Return was for 1 Yards. Scored 0 Touchdowns on a Punt Return.

Kicking

Chester Marcol: Kicked 33 Field Goals. Attempted 48 Field Goals. Field Goal Percentage was 68.8 Percent. Longest Field Goal was for 51 Yards. Kicked 29 Extra Points. Attempted 29 Extra Points. Extra Point Percentage was 100 Percent. Scored 128 Total Points.

Punting

Ron Widby: Punted 65 Times for a Total of 2714 Yards. Averaged 41.8 Yards Per Punt. Longest Punt was for 64 Yards. Had 2 Punts Blocked.

Defense

Interceptions and Fumble Recoveries

Ken Ellis: Intercepted 4 Passes for 106 Yards in Returns. Longest Return was for 40 Yards. Scored 1 Touchdown on an Interception Return. Recovered 2 Opponents' Fumbles.
Willie Buchanon: Intercepted 4 Passes for 62 Yards in Returns. Longest Return was for 26 Yards. Scored 0 Touchdowns on Interception Returns. Recovered 3 Opponents' Fumbles.
Jim Hill: Intercepted 4 Passes for 37 Yards in Returns. Longest Return was for 21 Yards. Scored 0 Touchdowns on Interception Returns. Recovered 1 Opponent Fumble.
Al Matthews: Intercepted 2 Passes for 8 Yards in Returns. Longest Return was for 8 Yards. Scored 0 Touchdowns on Interception Returns. Recovered 2 Opponents' Fumbles.
Dave Robinson: Intercepted 2 Passes for 10 Yards in Returns. Longest Return was for 7 Yards. Scored 0 Touchdowns on Interception Returns. Recovered 1 Opponent Fumble.
Jim Carter: Intercepted 1 Pass for 0 Yards in Returns. Longest Return was for 0 Yards. Scored 0 Touchdowns on Interception Returns. Recovered 1 Opponent Fumble.
Fred Carr: Recovered 2 Opponents' Fumbles.
Clarence Williams: Recovered 2 Opponents' Fumbles.
Bob Brown: Recovered 1 Opponent Fumble.
Bob Kroll: Recovered 1 Opponent Fumble.
Mike McCoy: Recovered 1 Opponent Fumble.
Alden Roche: Recovered 1 Opponent Fumble.
Ike Thomas: Recovered 1 Opponent Fumble.
Cal Withrow: Recovered 1 Opponent Fumble.

Scoring Summary

Chester Marcol: 128 Points. **John Brockington:** 54 Points. **Scott Hunter:** 30 Points. **MacArthur Lane:** 18 Points. **Ken Ellis:** 12 Points. **Rich McGeorge:** 12 Points. **Jon Staggers:** 12 Points. **Willie Buchanon:** 6 Points. **Carroll Dale:** 6 Points. **Dave Davis:** 6 Points. **Leland Glass:** 6 Points. **Jerry Tagge:** 6 Points. **Clarence Williams:** 6 Points. **Bob Brown:** 2 Points.

Chapter Notes

Preface

1. Quote from an unnamed Lambeau Field tour guide on July 9, 2016. Simply by stating that she was instructed on her tours to ignore Green Bay's history during the 1970s, could not help but illicit me to inquire why she said this, and to explore the Packers of the 1970s even more.
2. Ray Nitschke, as told to Robert W. Wells, *Mean on Sunday: The Autobiography of Ray Nitschke*, Black Earth, Wisconsin: Prairie Oak Press, 2001, 267. Many famous pro football players of the 1970s would write and publish their memoirs. Nitschke's book ranks as an underappreciated gem.
3. Bob Rubin, *Green Bay's Packers Return to Glory*, Englewood Cliffs, New Jersey: Prentice-Hall, Inc., 103. According to pro football historian and author T. J. Troup, Packers head coach Dan Devine "should have chauffeured MacArthur Lane around Green Bay for all that Lane did for the Packers offense in 1972." Lane was a multitalented and needed addition to the Green Bay offense.

Chapter 1

1. Bob Oates, "'New Lombardi?' No, Simply 'Old Devine,'" *The Sporting News*, July 31, 1971, 56. At the end of every NFL season, every pro coach goes through a period of self-introspection. What went right? What went wrong? How can I improve? Dan Devine was no different.
2. Lee Remmel, "I'm Certainly Not Discouraged," *Green Bay Packers 1972 Yearbook*, Volume 13, 1972, 5. Green Bay's 4–8–2 record in 1971 may have given new head coach Dan Devine a sour taste in his mouth, but to his credit, he quickly went about doing the things that he felt were needed to improve upon that record in 1972.
3. *Ibid*. The wet and soggy turf in the 1971 season opener against the New York Giants might have been listed as a possible cause for Devine's accident. His leg was probably firmly planted in the mud, so when Hyland's upper body dove into Devine's leg, Devine's shoes got stuck in the mud, resulting in a cracked bone in Devine's leg. Also, Devine was probably not paying attention to Hyland heading right for him, because he was likely watching where the ball was going.
4. *Ibid*., "Buchanon Sparkles in Pack Camp," *Green Bay (WI) Press-Gazette*, April 9, 1972. Willie Buchanon turned out to be a godsend for the 1972 Packers. His ability to shut down opposing passing attacks was the main cause for the Packers' defensive resurgence.
5. Gene W. Hintz, "Room for Improvement," *Green Bay Packers 1972 Yearbook*, Volume 13, 1972, 20. Few pro head coaches were willing to start a rookie player during the early 1970s, especially at a key position such as cornerback. Devine's willingness to start Willie Buchanon right from his first pro game was due to a couple of factors. One, he knew that Buchanon was talented enough to handle the pressure. And two, he really did not have much of a choice, as the Packers defensive secondary desperately needed someone to play the position.
6. *Ibid*. On-the-job training was (and still is) a most certain way to see how well a young player will perform in the NFL. By the time that the 1972 preseason was through, the Green Bay coaching staff knew full well that Willie Buchanon was ready for the rigors of the regular season.
7. *Ibid*. Green Bay defensive backs coach Don Doll probably was praying the night before the NFL draft that the Packers would select Willie Buchanon, assuming that he was

still available when the time came for head coach Dan Devine to make his first selection. Buchanon was the answer to Doll's prayers.

8. Len Wagner, "The Three Best." *Green Bay Packers 1972 Yearbook*, Volume 13, 1972, 27. As it turned out, quarterback Jerry Tagge learned quite a bit in 1972, even though he only saw action in four games. By 1973, he was ready to compete for the starting job.

9. *Ibid.*, 29. The Ice Bowl game—the famous 1967 NFL Championship Game in 13-degree below zero temperature, is still celebrated in Green Bay, and probably always will be. You can visit the Packers Hall of Fame and Museum in Lambeau Field and see numerous exhibits detailing that historic game.

10. *Ibid.* Probably more than any other reason why the Packers won 10 games in 1972 was because of the success of their rookie placekicker, Chester Marcol. He kicked key field goals in each of the Packers' four wins that were achieved by less than a touchdown.

11. Chester Marcol with Gary D'Amato, *Alive and Kicking: My Journey Through Football, Addiction and Life*, Stevens Point, Wisconsin: KCI Sports Publishing, 2011, 46. There is never anything so certain as the uncertainty of the annual NFL draft. Green Bay's selection of Chester Marcol in the second round of the draft was wise, because another team probably would have chosen him by the end of the third round. Credit head coach Dan Devine for realizing the team's kicking problem and doing something productive about it.

12. Terry Bledsoe, "Marcol's Kicking Gift Turned a Loser into a Winner." *Milwaukee Journal*, August 4, 1973. There never is an accepted plan for every team as to which players are roommates. Every team goes by its own ideas. Some players request whom they wish to room with for away games. Some players room together based on their positions on the field. For example, defensive linemen might room with other defensive linemen.

13. *Ibid.* It sure did not take head coach Dan Devine too long to realize that his selection of placekicker Chester Marcol in the 1972 NFL Draft would be a good one.

14. James Green (Director), 1972 Green Bay Packers Highlight Film, *The Year the Pack Came Back*, NFL Films, Ed Sabol (Executive Producer). NFL Films produces annual highlight films for every NFL team. Many from the decade of the 1970s were some of the best and most iconic films that the company has ever created.

15. Interview with T. J. Troup, March 24, 2018. Troup felt that "all the stars aligned" for the Green Bay defensive secondary in 1972. Even though Willie Buchanon and Ken Ellis received more attention and media scrutiny, the steady performance of Jim Hill really solidified the unit.

16. Interview with John Brockington, June 23, 2017. Brockington's response to the move of All-Pro offensive guard Gale Gillingham to the defensive line was warranted. Gillingham helped greatly to pave the way for Brockington to become the first rookie runner since 1934 to eclipse the 1,000-yard rushing mark in 1971.

17. Interview with Cliff Christl, July 8, 2016, in Green Bay, Wisconsin. With Jerry Kramer now a member of the Pro Football Hall of Fame, the comparison between he and Gillingham has become somewhat moot. Had Gale Gillingham not been injured early in 1972, however, there is no telling how many more wins the Packers would have attained in the 1972 season. There is also the possibility that Gillingham might also be in the Hall of Fame himself, had he enjoyed an injury-free career. Finally, a completely healthy Gillingham might possibly have rendered the Redskins' use of a five-man defensive line in their playoff game against Green Bay useless.

18. Interview with John Brockington, June 23, 2017. Gillingham impressed his teammates so much in practices that they could not wait to see him "destroy people" in the actual games.

19. George Bozeka (Ed.), *The 1966 Green Bay Packers: Profiles of Vince Lombardi's Super Bowl I Champions*, Jefferson, North Carolina: McFarland, 2016, 165. Every veteran player on the 1972 Packers was a team leader in his own right. Those veterans who played for Vince Lombardi—like Gillingham—would demonstrate their leadership in so many tangible ways, both in practices as well as in games.

20. *Ibid.* Part of the price of having Dan Devine for a head coach. A really bad decision that made absolutely no sense, and the resulting injury to one of the team's best players.

21. Glenn Miller, "Devine Seeks a Win—and Gets It," *Madison (WI) State Journal*, August 6, 1972, 50. Preseason games in the NFL are a mixed blessing. With six exhibition games in 1972, a pro coaching staff really had plenty of time to gauge the talents and abilities of the rookies on their roster. The fact that Dan Devine decided to play most of his starting players for most of the first preseason game does not make any sense, either today or back in 1972. It was an unnecessary risk of injury to those starters for games that did not count in the actual league standings.

22. Associated Press, "Rookie-Saturated Packers Embarrassed by 20–3 Loss," *Sheboygan (WI) Press*, August 21, 1972, 23. Dan Devine wasted no time in trimming his roster before the official cutdown dates. A dropped pass here, a missed block there, and that rookie

would be gone. Second chances to impress Devine were rare.

23. Chester Marcol with Gary D'Amato, *Alive and Kicking: My Journey Through Football,* Addiction and Life, Stevens Point, Wisconsin: KCI Sports Publishing, 2011, 50. Few rookie placekickers ever came into the NFL with more self-confidence than what was displayed by Chester Marcol in 1972.

24. Associated Press, "Devine Orders Double Drill after Packer Defeat," *Ironwood (WI) Daily Globe,* September 5, 1972, 15. It has always been better for a team to make its mistakes during the preseason games. No team, not even the defending Super Bowl champions, are immune from making mistakes in the summer.

25. *Ibid.* Rookies at the 1972 Packers training camp may have had a pretty fair chance to make the team, if for no other reason than Dan Devine wanted to get rid of some of the older veterans, thereby opening up several roster spots.

26. Bud Lea, "Donny Tells of Rift with Devine," *Milwaukee (WI) Journal Sentinel,* February 23, 1972, 1. Donny Anderson was a fan favorite in Green Bay, and many of them were upset and somewhat angry when they heard that he was traded by Dan Devine to the St. Louis Cardinals.

27. *Ibid.,* 3. Lane was unceremoniously suspended by the St. Louis Cardinals for the final game of the 1971 season. In order to earn that suspension, Lane publicly criticized team vice president William V. Bidwill because of a salary dispute.

Chapter 2

1. Interview with Dave Robinson, June 5, 2014, in Berea, Ohio. Veteran Packers linebacker Dave Robinson confirmed a lot of the rumors and stories that I had heard over the years but was unsure as to their legitimacy. Dan Devine's jealousy of Vince Lombardi's legacy was nearly impossible for Devine to conceal, however.

2. Lee Remmel, "Personality Parade," *Green Bay Press Gazette,* November 29, 1972. Willie Buchanon's alma mater, San Diego State, made it their mission to get as many of their football players ready to play in a pro-style offense and defense. Buchanon entered the NFL with plenty of intelligence and ability, and when combined with the knowledge that he gained in college, he would become a "can't miss" pro prospect.

3. Interview with John Brockington, June 23, 2017. Like most—if not all—of the players on that 1972 Packers team, Brockington had nothing but praise for all his teammates.

4. Interview with Scott Hunter, September 20, 2017. One must figure that the Packers passing statistics in 1972 would have been much better had tight end Rich McGeorge not gotten injured in the second week of the regular season.

5. Lee Remmel, "Marcol Finds Himself in Packer Record Book after Just One Game," *Appleton (WI) Post-Crescent,* September 18, 1972, 8. A blocked field-goal attempt in the first game which was returned for an opposing touchdown would have rattled most kickers. Not Chester Marcol. His four field goals and his two extra-point conversions provided the margin of victory for Green Bay over Cleveland in the 1972 season opener.

6. Chester Marcol with Gary D'Amato, *Alive and Kicking: My Journey Through Football,* Addiction and Life, Stevens Point, Wisconsin: KCI Sports Publishing, 2011, 51.

7. Lee Remmel, "McGeorge Makes Dream Come True," *Appleton (WI) Post-Crescent,* September 18, 1972, 8. Throughout his pro football career, Rich McGeorge was always able to sneak into the defensive secondary unnoticed and open for a timely pass. His big size (6–4, 235 pounds) always made it quite remarkable that opposing outside linebackers or safeties would ignore him so much when he ran his pass patterns.

8. *Ibid.* All NFL coaches from the early days of the pro game have tried their best to expose as little of their game plans as possible, especially during the preseason. Dan Devine was no different.

9. *Ibid.,* Lee Remmel, "Marcol Finds Himself in Packer Record Book after Just One Game," *Appleton (WI) Post-Crescent,* September 18, 1972, 8. Marcol would keep his wits about him in many games throughout 1972. His accurate kicking was the difference in at least four Packer victories that season.

10. *Ibid.,* Lee Remmel, "McGeorge Makes Dream Come True," *Appleton (WI) Post-Crescent,* September 18, 1972, 9. Winning the first regular season game of the year is always good, regardless of which team you are talking about. The victory over Cleveland was a positive jolt for the team.

11. Interview with Scott Hunter, September 20, 2017. The play that Hunter describes was the first tangible regular-season example of how much MacArthur Lane would be helping out the Packers offense in 1972. Lane was a big man with speed, excellent blocking ability, and great hands. He was just as dangerous catching the ball as he was running with the ball and pass and run blocking.

12. Interview with T. J. Troup, March 24, 2018. Bart Starr knew that opposing defenses

would key on stopping Green Bay's rushing attack, so sneaking one or both of his setbacks out of the backfield on pass patterns would be occasionally needed to cause those opposing defenses to worry about being burned by such a move.

13. Mark Shapiro, "Raiders Got Some Help," *Madison (WI) State Journal*, September 25, 1972, 31. Oakland Raiders safety Jack Tatum was simply in the right place at the right time. There was no Packers player in position to catch him as he sprinted down the sidelines.

14. Ibid. Quite simply, the referees should have blown their whistles and signaled dead ball the moment the ball hit the grass. It was clearly a muff, not a fumble.

15. Ibid. To say that one play caused Green Bay to lose to Oakland in Week 2 is a bit of a stretch, but that one play was certainly the margin of the Raiders' victory. Draw your own conclusions.

16. Mike O'Brien, "Packers Question Officials on 2 Big Plays," *Fond du Lac (WI) Reporter*, September 25, 1972, 21. There was nothing worse for a head coach in pro football to experience than what Dan Devine experienced following Green Bay's loss to Oakland. Devine received a letter from the league office several days after the game stating that he was correct in arguing a blown call by the referees, and that Jack Tatum's touchdown should not have counted. In essence, the league admitted their mistake, but there was nothing that could be done to rectify or change the final score.

17. Ibid. Packers assistant coach and defensive coordinator Dave "Hog" Hanner was probably one of the few people in Lambeau Field that day who knew that a muffed ball was not allowed to be advanced by the recovering team.

18. Ibid. Lane did not take any steps with complete control of the ball. He was taking steps, but the ball was never fully in his grasp. The film confirms this.

19. Interview with Scott Hunter, September 20, 2017. To his credit, Hunter was willing to take at least some of the blame for the results of the play. But the fact remains that Lane should have caught and secured Hunter's pitchout.

20. Ibid. If there was any further proof that this was not going to be Green Bay's day, the pass interference call on rookie cornerback Willie Buchanon would have provided it. Bad breaks in the NFL sometimes come in bunches, and usually at the most inopportune times.

21. Ibid. Both the defender and the receiver are allowed to go for the ball once the ball is in the air. That is exactly what Buchanon did. In today's pass-happy NFL, the play would have been ruled an incomplete pass. Any bumping between the two players that might have occurred would have been ruled "incidental contact."

22. Lee Remmel, "Buchanon Crestfallen," *Green Bay (WI) Press-Gazette*, September 25, 1972. Buchanon would also admit after the game that he kept telling the officials that Biletnikoff was pushing off on him throughout the game in order to get open.

23. Ibid. Receivers and cornerbacks—regardless of their perceived guilt—will always proclaim their innocence to the referees. It has been this way for years. And so it shall ever be.

24. Mark Shapiro, "Injuries Slowed Pack," *Madison (WI) State Journal*, September 25, 1972, 31. Devine and the rest of the Packers coaches were probably praying that losing two big cogs in their offense versus the Raiders—Gale Gillingham and Rich McGeorge—would be the end of the injuries that the Packers would sustain in 1972. Undoubtedly, the loss of those two key players for the remainder of the year would be difficult to overcome, but Green Bay somehow was able to do just that.

25. Ibid. Oakland head coach John Madden was certainly prophetic, even as early as the second week of the 1972 regular season.

Chapter 3

1. Interview with Scott Hunter, September 20, 2017. The Green Bay-Dallas rivalry actually started in the 1960s when former assistant coaches with the New York Giants—Tom Landry and Vince Lombardi—each had the opportunity to become head coaches in the NFL. During the 1960s, the Packers and the Cowboys played in several great games, epitomized by the historic Ice Bowl contest for the 1967 NFL Championship.

2. Ibid. Many pro teams in the 1970s played in what was known as "multi-purpose stadiums," meaning that both football and baseball teams from one city would share a stadium. Such was the case with the Packers in 1972, whenever they played a game in Milwaukee County Stadium. During the Major League Baseball season, the Milwaukee Brewers baseball team would play their home games in the same stadium.

3. Interview with John Brockington, June 23, 2017. When he came into the league in 1971, John Brockington was probably the closest reincarnation of the great Jim Brown that the NFL had ever seen at that time. He had speed, brute force, desire, power, good hands ... virtually everything that a runner needs to be successful.

4. Mark Shapiro, "Defense Stymies Cham-

pions, 16–13," *Madison (WI) State Journal*, October 2, 1972, 29. As is the case with most competitive games where the opponents match up quite evenly, a key mistake can often produce the cause for a victory. In the game against Dallas, it was the Cowboys who made the key mistake(s).

5. Ralph Trower, "Devine Says Packer Win Great Team Effort," *Racine (WI) Journal Times*, October 2, 1972, 26. The victory over Dallas was crucial to the Packers. Not only was it against the defending world champions, but it was also against a conference team, which would be helpful if the Packers were trying to make the playoffs (based on the league's tie-breaking procedures). Most importantly, the win over Dallas gave Green Bay's young squad a lot of needed confidence.

6. Ibid. Once a relatively unknown player—like Green Bay's Vernon Vanoy—has a big day, he no longer becomes unknown. Upcoming opponents saw the films of what Vanoy did versus the Cowboys and prepared adequately for him. Vanoy would never again throughout the rest of his short career have a bigger game than what he had against Dallas on October 1, 1972.

7. Ibid. Stunting (looping) your defensive linemen is a tactic that all teams use. The key to stopping it is to have a very intelligent and prepared offensive line. Unfortunately for the Cowboys, their offensive line never adequately adjusted to what the Green Bay defensive line was doing in the game.

8. Ibid. The best friend that a defensive backfield ever had was a strong pass rush, as evidenced by what happened against Dallas. The pressure on Dallas quarterback Craig Morton forced him to throw quicker and/or more inaccurately than he wanted to. The result was some key interceptions by the Green Bay defensive backs.

9. Ibid. The win over Dallas was certainly a big confidence booster for the youthful Packers.

10. Tom Drolshagen, "QBs: Study in Contrasts," *Kenosha (WI) News*, October 9, 1972, 17. In reality, each game that the Packers played against the Bears in 1972 could have been won by Chicago. Both teams were very evenly matched.

11. Gene W. Hintz, "Packers Stagger Home," *Kenosha (WI) News*, October 9, 1972, 17. The 1972 Packers would rely on a different player in each game to make a big play or two. In the first regular-season game against Chicago, it was reserve Green Bay wide receiver Jon Staggers who stepped up and helped the team to a big victory.

12. Tom Drolshagen, "QBs: Study in Contrasts," *Kenosha (WI) News*, October 9, 1972,

17. Chicago quarterback Bobby Douglass would eventually go on to play quarterback for the Green Bay Packers in 1978.

13. Ibid., 17. Douglass's record of 968 rushing yards for a quarterback in 1972 was eventually broken by Atlanta Falcons quarterback Michael Vick in 2006. But Vick had two extra regular-season games with which to earn his record of 1,039 yards.

14. Chester Marcol with Gary D'Amato, *Alive and Kicking: My Journey Through Football*, Addiction and Life, Stevens Point, Wisconsin: KCI Sports Publishing, 2011, 52. For being a little guy (Marcol only stood six feet tall and weighed 190 pounds), he sure had a strong kicking leg, particularly early in his career.

15. Gene W. Hintz, "Packers Stagger Home," *Kenosha (WI) News*, October 9, 1972, 17. Winning close games, regardless of the opponent, is generally regarded as the most noteworthy key to a successful season for any team.

16. Tom Drolshagen, "QBs: Study in Contrasts," *Kenosha (WI) News*, October 9, 1972, 17. The Packers-Bears rivalry is one of the greatest in NFL history. The hitting that occurs when those two teams get together, even today, is legendary.

17. Gene W. Hintz, "Packers Stagger Home," *Kenosha (WI) News*, October 9, 1972, 17. Hard hitting often leads to fumbles, regardless of the teams involved. A big key to winning a Bears-Packers game is holding on to the ball.

18. Tom Drolshagen, "QBs: Study in Contrasts," *Kenosha (WI) News*, October 9, 1972, 17. Even though they were without the services of All-Pro offensive guard Gale Gillingham for the remainder of the 1972 season, the Green Bay offensive line was really doing well in the early stages of the year.

Chapter 4

1. Tex Maule, "Green Bay Turns with the Tide," *Sports Illustrated*, October 30, 1972, 32. Detroit cornerback Lem Barney would eventually become a Hall of Famer in 1992.

2. Larry Paladino, "Packers Take Lead with 24-23 Squeeze Past Lions," *Eau Claire (WI) Leader Telegram*, October 17, 1972, 25. Coming from behind to win a game is a common denominator of all winning teams.

3. Associated Press, "Brilliant Packer Rally Tips Lions," *Racine (WI) Journal Times*, October 17, 1972, 33. Long punt returns—like the one turned in by Ken Ellis against the Lions on *Monday Night Football*—can sometimes be determined with the first two or three steps that the returner makes upon catching the

punt. Those first few steps can cause the coverage teams to make a mistake. A brief moment of indecision can sometimes cost a team a touchdown.

4. *Ibid.* In the 1970s, most teams did not have a punt or kick returner who only returned punts or kickoffs. Players back then had multiple positions on a team. Green Bay's Ken Ellis was first and foremost a starting cornerback, but he also did double duty by returning punts.

5. *Ibid.*, "Packers Win; Hold Division Lead," *Freeport (IL) Journal-Standard*, October 17, 1972, 9. Many people went to bed when the Lions took a 17-7 halftime lead over the Packers on *Monday Night Football*. Those folks missed a great Green Bay comeback.

6. Associated Press, "Brilliant Packer Rally Tips Lions," *Racine (WI) Journal Times*, October 17, 1972, 33. Ellis's prediction spoke of a bravado that had not been heard in Green Bay in years. His confidence was probably shared by most of his teammates, especially after the great comeback win over the Lions.

7. Don Kowet, "What Has Four Heads, Eight Arms, Eights Legs, & Plays for Green Bay?" *Sport Magazine*, November, 1973, 74. Besides the points supplied from the kicking foot of Chester Marcol and the vital addition of MacArthur Lane to the team's offense, no other part of the team was as responsible for Green Bay's 1972 division title than the play of the defensive secondary.

8. *Ibid.*, 82. It did not take too long before Packers opponents started to throw the ball away from cornerbacks Willie Buchanon and Ken Ellis. The two quickly became one of the most formidable cornerback combinations in the entire NFL.

9. *Ibid.*, 75. Much to his great credit, Green Bay defensive back coach Don Doll did not do too much too soon to overwhelm his young secondary. He wanted them to stay confident, and let their own natural abilities form the foundation for their success. In 1972, the Packers defensive backs played better than anyone—even Coach Doll—could have ever expected.

10. Interview with T. J. Troup, November 10, 2017. If a defensive secondary is to be successful, they have to work very well together, and their coordination together has to be top notch. The 1972 Green Bay defensive secondary accomplished this high level of communication and coordination through 14 regular season games.

11. Interview with Scott Hunter, September 20, 2017. Packers quarterbacks Scott Hunter and Jerry Tagge could not be blamed for quite a few of their respective incompletions, as many of those failed passes occurred when their receivers simply dropped balls that were laid into their hands perfectly by the quarterbacks. But Hunter was incorrect in his belief that his wide receiver, Leland Glass, beat Lem Barney on the winning touchdown reception. Glass, in fact, beat Rudy Redmond on the game-winning score.

12. Tex Maule, "Green Bay Turns with the Tide," *Sports Illustrated*, October 30, 1972, 32. Reserve wide receiver Leland Glass was pressed into a starter's role thanks to several injuries at that vital position. He dropped a lot of passes during the year, but he also gained a lot of confidence with each reception that he made.

13. *Ibid.* No football team can win without a good quarterback. Scott Hunter filled the bill for the 1972 Packers. He managed to stay healthy for most of the year, and his abilities and youthful exuberance helped to make the Packers a competitive team.

14. *Ibid.*, 35. Packers assistant coach Bart Starr was a godsend for quarterbacks Scott Hunter and Jerry Tagge. In the early 1970s, there was no better quarterback coach in the league than Starr, and both of Green Bay's young signal callers tried to soak up as much of Starr's knowledge as possible.

15. *Ibid.*, 32. Scott Hunter probably gave more credence to what assistant coach Bart Starr was trying to impress upon him, because both men graduated from the University of Alabama. That familiarity breeds respect and trust, two things that Hunter certainly had for Starr.

16. Associated Press, "Brilliant Packer Rally Tips Lions," *Racine (WI) Journal Times*, October 17, 1972, 33. Young football teams usually have emotion as their most recognizable trait. The 1972 Packers were an emotional group to be sure, as evidenced by their excitement upon starting the season with a 4-1 record.

17. Interview will Bill Lueck, January 25, 2018. For the younger players on the team, the thought of having a 4-1 record to start the 1972 season would certainly provide them with a reason to celebrate, and perhaps become too overconfident. The veteran players on the team did their best to keep the rookies and the younger players from getting too overconfident.

Chapter 5

1. Tom Drolshagen, "Hampton Running with Confidence," *Kenosha (WI) News*, October 23, 1972, 21. Dave Hampton was a great multi-talented running threat when he played for Green Bay from 1969 to 1971. He was also a very good punt and kickoff returning threat.

2. *Ibid.* Even in the 1970s, you did not want

to give your opponent a reason to have some measure of momentum. Packers head coach Dan Devine gave his former running back, Dave Hampton, such a reason by cutting him following the 1971 season, and that action eventually resulted in one of Hampton's best games of the year against his old team.

3. United Press International, "Refs Rile Devine again," *Kenosha (WI) News*, October 23, 1972, 21. The Atlanta game was a very close contest that could easily have been a Packers win. One play can often be the difference in a close game. The penalty against Green Bay linebacker Fred Carr certainly did not help the Packers' efforts in this game.

4. Interview with Scott Hunter, September 20, 2017. The rain that day was unceasing, and the resulting mud meant that the players' footing was questionable at best.

5. Mark Shapiro, "Marcol Keeps His Cool," *Madison (WI) State Journal*, October 23, 1972, 37. None of Chester Marcol's teammates placed any blame on him for the team's loss to the Falcons. They all knew that Marcol kicked three successful field goals in the game, which amounted to all the points that the Packers scored on this rainy and muddy day.

6. Bill Dwyre, "Marcol's Moment of Drama," *The Milwaukee (WI) Journal*, October 23, 1972, 18. The wet weather also caused many pass receivers to drop passes. It was indeed a difficult day to handle the ball.

7. Mark Shapiro, "Marcol Keeps His Cool," *Madison (WI) State Journal*, October 23, 1972, 37. The prevailing wind on the day of the Atlanta game was blowing to the southeast at 10 miles per hour, so it, was not really much of a factor for either team's kicking game.

8. Bill Dwyre, "Marcol's Moment of Drama," *The Milwaukee (WI) Journal*, October 23, 1972, 18. Perhaps no other position on a football team is more apt to suffer from a shattered psyche than that of placekicker. One missed kick can affect a kicker for the remainder of a game, or even for a season. To his great credit, Chester Marcol never let a missed kick affect him in a detrimental way.

9. *Ibid.* Bob Brown's statement was indicative of the feelings that Marcol's teammates had for the rookie placekicker.

10. Associated Press, "Officials Draw Dan's Ire," *Fond du Lac (WI) Reporter*, October 23, 1972, 14. Prior to the current days of instant replays helping the officials make the right call, the referees on the field were the final arbiter when it came to deciding what happened on every play. Every few years when the referees made what was considered an incorrect call, the league office would send the team that suffered from an erroneous referee call an apology letter, confirming that the referees were wrong, and that they will try better the next time. In the example with the Packers versus the Raiders on September 24, the referees *should* have known that no one can advance a muff. But they did not, hence the letter that Devine describes.

11. United Press International, "Refs Rile Devine again," *Kenosha (WI) News*, October 23, 1972, 21. When pressed by the reporters, Coach Devine went into further detail regarding the bad call and how its detrimental effects could hurt his team in the standings.

12. *Ibid.* Sometimes a coach or a player can go too far when criticizing an official especially if the criticism is made public through the media. When that happens, the league office will usually impose a monetary fine on that person.

13. Tex Maule, "Green Bay Turns with the Tide," *Sports Illustrated*, October 30, 1972, 32. Atlanta running back Dave Hampton was a former teammate of Bart Starr's, and he knew what he spoke of. Starr turned out to be the glue that held the Packers offense together throughout the 1972 season. Starr's play calling proved to be critical to the team winning 10 games in 1972.

14. *Ibid.*, 31. Both Green Bay running backs John Brockington and MacArthur Lane received plenty of praise from their opponents throughout the 1972 season. They were the best running duo in the NFC in 1972.

15. *Ibid.*, 32. Opposing coaches such as Atlanta's Norm Van Brocklin also had a lot of respect for Brockington, Lane, and the rest of the Packers. The opposing coaching staffs around the league spent countless hours watching and dissecting film of the Green Bay offense as they made their upcoming game plans.

16. Dave Grey, "Vikes Turn Breaks into Touchdowns for Win," *Oshkosh (WI) Daily Northwestern*, October 30, 1972, 7. In a game where Green Bay needed one or two big plays, they could not get them. Instead it was their opponent—the Vikings—who got them. Minnesota was the more experienced team on this day, and the Packers' lack of experience showed in their loss to the Vikings.

17. Ralph Trower, "Viking Rally Defeats Packers 27–13," *Racine (WI) Journal Times*, October 30, 1972, 41. Minnesota free safety Paul Krause was probably one of the savviest defensive backs in the history of pro football. He is still—four decades after his retirement—the owner of the most career interceptions in NFL history (81).

18. Mike O'Brien, "Interceptions Turn Tide Vikings' Way," *Fond du Lac (WI) Reporter*, October 30, 1972, 20. Paul Krause made a career out of baiting quarterbacks into throwing into

the zone that he was covering. On his game-breaking interception and touchdown, he managed to keep out of John Brockington's view, and benefitted from the traffic in front of him to disguise himself from Green Bay quarterback Scott Hunter's vision.

19. Ralph Trower, "Viking Rally Defeats Packers 27–13," *Racine (WI) Journal Times,* October 30, 1972, 41. Veteran Minnesota quarterback Fran Tarkenton won fame as a scrambler, but it was his ability to read defenses which separated him from many of his contemporaries. Few quarterbacks in the late 1960s and most of the 1970s was as adept at fooling an opposing defense as Tarkenton.

20. Interview with Scott Hunter, September 20, 2017. Like most young quarterbacks (Hunter was only in his second pro year in 1972), he was prone to making mistakes. But his enthusiasm and athleticism more than made up for his miscues in 1972, as evidenced by Green Bay's 10 victories.

21. Todd Mishler, *Cold Wars: 40 Years of Packer-Viking Rivalry,* Black Earth, Wisconsin: Prairie Oak Press, 2002, 49. Every now and then, Devine would do something out of his usual character, and stand behind his players after they made a mistake or two. Had he done more of that, he may have received more overall respect from the players on his roster.

22. Ralph Trower, "An Interesting Race Now: Devine." *Racine (WI) Journal Times,* October 30, 1972, 41. Packers fans might have felt a tinge of optimism from the way that the team started the 1972 season, with four wins in their first five games. But a team so young was bound to have some setbacks along the way. It was quite reassuring to hear that the players still had plenty of confidence, even after a two-game losing streak.

23. Interview with John Brockington, June 23, 2017. John Brockington's opinion that the season was still young, and that even though the team had just lost two straight games, the time to panic was not yet at hand, was also shared by the rest of his teammates.

Chapter 6

1. Interview with Scott Hunter, September 20, 2017. You might want to call it fate, or possibly very good fortune. No matter how you describe it, the players on the 1972 Packers blended very well together right from the start of the preseason. Scott Hunter only had one year of pro experience, but he spared no effort for his teammates, and they loved the example of leadership that he displayed. It was as if this team had played together for years.

2. Mark Shapiro, "Brock Proudly Pleased," *Madison (WI) State Journal,* November 6, 1972, 19. John Brockington and his teammates bought in to the goal that no one man wins the game, but the team wins the game. Probably due to the unusual situation that was going on with Coach Devine, the players and the assistant coaches drew more strength within each other, and supported each other on a higher level, because they were rarely getting such support from their head coach.

3. Interview with John Brockington, June 23, 2017. Coach Devine would regularly show the Packers players films from his University of Missouri team (where Devine had coached prior to going to Green Bay). This trend was rather unsettling to the players, who knew that the pro ranks were filled with much better athletes than Devine coached in college. Devine would have been better off to accept Brockington's advice and leave the Lombardi legacy alone. Instead, Devine tried to eradicate the Lombardi legacy, an impossible task which was insulting to Green Bay's inheritance of pro football history.

4. Interview with Dave Robinson, June 5, 2014, in Berea, Ohio. Before you think that Dave Robinson had an axe to grind with Dan Devine, you need to keep in mind that Robinson and veterans like him were used to winning and were used to being treated fairly, as they were while playing for Vince Lombardi. Robinson was man enough and a team leader enough to play hard for any coach. But when he saw the many injustices that came with Devine, he had to say something, if for nothing else than to keep his own self-esteem intact. Like most of the players who played for Lombardi, Devine would soon get rid of Robinson.

5. Interview with John Brockington, June 23, 2017. In every successful organization, building up your players or employees will almost always aid their morale, and produce successful results for everyone involved. Dan Devine never seemed to learn this simple fact, but he is not alone. There are many thousands of bosses in American society and in American industries today who have developed a work environment of bitterness, anger, fear, threats and degradation. Those types of bosses rarely succeed, and the businesses that employ such people in leadership positions inevitably see a high turnover rate among the rank and file employees. People and players realize that life and athletic careers are too short, and no one wants to be miserable at their places of employment. Even though Devine drafted John Brockington, he still felt that the best way to motivate his star running back was to tear down his self-

confidence. Devine's efforts in doing so only lengthened the gulf between himself and his players.
 6. Interview with Frank D'Agostino, February 14, 2017. As evidenced by this story, honesty did not appear to be one of Dan Devine's strong suits. Devine simply did not spend much time watching films of his team or of his upcoming opponents. The practice of watching and dissecting film would often make the difference between winning and losing in the sport of football, and most coaching staffs throughout the league recognized and accepted this as fact.
 7. Lee Remmel, "I'm Certainly Not Discouraged," *Green Bay Packers 1972 Yearbook*, Volume 13, 1972, 6. I have not read anything which points to any possible bipolar problem for Dan Devine. But sometimes, when one reads some of his quotes, one must consider that he had some sort of problem. Perhaps it is simply a case of thinking more of himself than what he actually was or had achieved. He would not be the first coach to boast of his abilities and/or successes, and he certainly was not the last. At the very least, Dan Devine was delusional in regard to some coaching matters. Very few—if any—Packers would describe Devine as being "on top of things."
 8. Interview with Bill Lueck, January 25, 2018. Lueck was one of the unsung heroes on the Packers offensive line. He led many a sweep for the likes of John Brockington and MacArthur Lane. While those two running backs rightly deserve plenty of praise, the members of the Green Bay offensive line achieved remarkable exploits all throughout 1972.
 9. Lee Remmel, "I'm Certainly Not Discouraged," *Green Bay Packers 1972 Yearbook*, Volume 13, 1972, 6. By the middle of 1972, most of the Green Bay players were sick and tired of hearing about Devine's coaching exploits at the University of Missouri, and of the achievements of his college players. So much so, that apparently an unnamed and uncorroborated source among the Packers players was once claimed to have said—off the record—that if one of his kids ever wanted to attend the University of Missouri, he would remove that child from his will.
 10. Interview with Dave Robinson, June 5, 2014, in Berea, Ohio. John Brockington was the type of football player who did not need any external examples of motivation. He was simply motivated by his own desire to be the best running back that he could possibly be. Coach Devine's methods of humiliating Brockington were certainly not welcomed by Brockington or by anyone else on the team.
 11. *Ibid.* Dan Devine's foolish comparison of any average running back to John Brockington was laughable back in the early 1970s. Today, it still sounds ridiculous, considering the fact that Brockington was the first rusher in NFL history to gain over 1,000 yards in each of his first three seasons.
 12. *Ibid.* It is really no big surprise that a coach with so many faults as Dan Devine would also include being nit-picky to those imperfections as well. Sometimes, laughter from any situation was the only avenue that the players could use to keep their sanity.
 13. *Ibid.* Having a popular veteran on the team like Dave Robinson was important in so many ways. Besides his knowledge, experience, and athleticism on the field, Robinson's willingness to point out to the rest of the players the multitude of Devine's shortcomings and incorrect statements was probably equally as significant, but it really was not needed all that much. The players would see and hear Coach Devine for themselves and make their own judgments. Robinson's rebuttals no doubt angered his head coach greatly. But they were really Robinson's only available method of standing up to Devine. He attempted to correct the false and/or exaggerated stories that Devine was responsible for, so that the rest of the team could see Devine for who he really was ... an egotistical man who wanted his players to think that he (Devine) was a great coach, and that his past exploits at the University of Missouri should have been honored by his Packers players. Robinson's willingness to speak his mind would eventually get him traded to Washington. Nevertheless, Robinson should be lauded for his attempts at being a whistle-blower.
 14. *Ibid.* Dave Robinson was a consensus All-American as a collegiate at Penn State University from 1960 to 1962. He is a member of both the College Football Hall of Fame and the Pro Football Hall of Fame.
 15. *Ibid.* As the weeks of the regular season went on, Devine's decision to "leave the team alone" might be believed by some folks, in retrospect, to be a possible key to the winning streak that the Packers went on as they drove towards a 1972 division title. Leaving the defense alone may have been the best thing that could happen to the Green Bay defense, especially when considering how much youth dotted the defensive roster at that time. Coach Devine could have really messed up those young players' minds if he had insisted on coaching them himself on an individual basis.
 16. Interview with Bill Lueck, January 25, 2018. Lueck's confirmation of Dave Robinson's remarks confirmed to me how poor of a motivator Dan Devine really was. It also confirmed to me how unified the Packer players were with

each other as they dealt with the difficult situation that they were faced with in 1972.

17. Discussion with Cliff Christl, September 4, 2018. Christl stands apart as one of the foremost experts on Packers history. If anyone would have uncovered definitive facts that Dan Devine purposefully "quit" on the team, Christl would have been the person to find that information. Nothing but opinions from some of the players would ever be voiced, however, regarding Devine "quitting" on the team.

18. Interview with Dave Robinson, June 5, 2014, in Berea, Ohio. Robinson's disagreements with Devine and his methods made this a story worth writing about. Devine's poor player evaluations were accepted in retrospect as fact during his years as both a pro and college head coach.

19. Interview with Scott Hunter, September 20, 2017. It must have been quite disconcerting for a young quarterback like Hunter to discover that his team's head coach did not possess the elemental strategical knowledge of the game. It is inexcusable for a pro coach to be ignorant of the basics of formations and strategy. Even today, it is hard to fathom how Dan Devine could have ever reached the level of a pro head coach without this background knowledge.

20. Interview with Bill Lueck, January 25, 2018. It would probably be rare—even in 1972—to find a high school coach who does not know how to draw up a football play on a chalkboard, much less a professional football coach.

21. *Ibid.* Hunter said that in a very raspy Southern voice, as he tried his best to imitate the voice of his former college head coach. Author's Note: He did a pretty good job imitating Coach Paul "Bear" Bryant.

22. Interview with Chuck Lane, July 8, 2016. Chuck Lane worked for the Packers throughout the Vince Lombardi years. He worked very hard during those years, but he got a front row seat to experience one of the greatest historical chapters in NFL history with Lombardi. Lane's years with Dan Devine were sadly not as happy or victorious.

23. *Ibid.* In all fairness, many NFL teams decided not to draft Joe Montana. Former San Francisco head coach Bill Walsh knew talent when he saw it, however. They teamed up to make the 49ers world champions several times in the 1980s. Today, both Montana and Walsh have a bust in Canton, Ohio, at the Pro Football Hall of Fame.

24. Associated Press, "Lane Reveals Secret: 'These Cats Love Each Other,'" *Appleton (WI) Post-Crescent*, December 11, 1972, 20. The players on the 1972 Packers had to rely on each other, due mainly to the lack of support that they were getting from their head coach. It did not take long for the players to form a very strong bond with each other.

25. *Ibid.*, "Packer Loyalty Noted by Devine; Robinson Lauds Play of Williams," *Appleton (WI) Post-Crescent*, December 11, 1972, 15. One could argue that the Packers players *were* loyal to their head coach. Most people did not hear stories about how Devine ran the team until after he left Green Bay following the 1974 season.

26. Mark Shapiro, "It Started With A Loss," *Madison (WI) State Journal*, December 11, 1972, 17. Dan Devine desperately wanted to rid the Green Bay roster of players who did not buy into his methods of coaching, or who he did not draft or trade for. The top players on Devine's chopping block were those who played for the legendary Vince Lombardi.

27. Lee Remmel, "I'm Certainly Not Discouraged," *Green Bay Packers 1972 Yearbook*, Volume 13, 1972, 7. It was not unusual for a head coach to bring in some of his former assistant coaches to his new team. It has been going on for years, and it still happens today. Familiarity and/or success from past shared ventures will lead a head coach to try to repeat such instances with people that he knew well. Dan Devine was very willing to bring to Green Bay some of his former assistant coaches from the University of Missouri.

28. *Ibid.*, 7. It stands to reason that the 1972 Packers would do better in the standings than the 1971 Packers, who won only four games. If there was going to be an improvement in the number of victories, then Dan Devine was more than willing to take credit for it. The increased number of wins in 1972 gave Devine a legitimate reason to feel that he did a better job of coaching over what he did the previous year.

29. *Ibid.* Dan Devine certainly wanted to keep the veteran players who were productive for him, but he nevertheless had a firm desire to fill his roster with players whom he thought would be loyal to him. If he detected a disloyal player, he tried his best to trade him. In a way, the situation resembled any work environment, where a boss brings in people who will kiss the boss's backside, regardless of how well that person does their job, or regardless of how distasteful it looks to the other employees. Devine was therefore no different than any other boss, as he was prone to playing favorites.

30. *Ibid.* None of Devine's players wanted the reputation of being a difficult player to coach or to work with. But Devine could label them as such. It was not really blackmail, but it could be interpreted as being so. Knowing Devine's character, it is not out of the realm of

possibility. He could quite possibly make things tough for those players. Devine might decide to contact front office people across the league and smear the player(s) in question, especially if he had a grudge against the player(s). Those front office people might thus be dissuaded from bringing any of Devine's former players onto their teams. It would be a really dirty and punitive thing to do, and it is strictly conjecture, but if anyone would actually do it, Dan Devine would be that person.

31. Bob Rubin, *Green Bay's Packers Return to Glory*, Englewood Cliffs, New Jersey: Prentice-Hall, Inc., 1973, 22. Just as players such as Dave Robinson, Ken Bowman and Ray Nitschke were loyal to Vince Lombardi, so Francis Peay was loyal to Dan Devine.

32. *Ibid.*, 22. Coaches have for generations searched for ways to motivate their players. Dan Devine was no different. This example was one of Devine's most creative.

33. *Ibid.* The television cameras rarely caught Devine spewing out a vocal tirade along the sidelines. Most of the time he appeared to be very stoic.

34. Lee Remmel, "I'm Certainly Not Discouraged," *Green Bay Packers 1972 Yearbook*, Volume 13, 1972, 7. Devine probably said this because he wanted people to believe that he was humble and modest. In fact, he was a very egotistical man.

35. Bob Rubin, *Green Bay's Packers Return to Glory*, Englewood Cliffs, New Jersey: Prentice-Hall, Inc., 1973, 24. See the above notes 21 and 24.

Chapter 7

1. Ralph Trower, "Viking Rally Defeats Packers 27–13," *Racine (WI) Journal Times*, October 30, 1972, 41. The Green Bay offense was not very intimidating in 1972, primarily because their passing game was one of the worst in the league. The Packers could account for only 1,412 total passing yards in 1972, which was the second-lowest total in the entire league. They were just not designed to score a lot of points, because they had no real game breakers at the wide receiver position, and because their best tight end—Rich McGeorge—was injured in the second week and sidelined for most of the regular season.

2. Interview with Dave Robinson, June 5, 2014, in Berea, Ohio. Even those players who were apt to give Dan Devine the benefit of the doubt eventually started to dislike some of the things that their head coach was saying to the team.

3. *Ibid.* Sometimes, the players' senses of humor was all that they had to combat the insults and the degradations that came from Devine.

4. Interview with John Brockington, June 23, 2017. John Brockington gets too little credit when it comes to offensive strategy. He knew very well what was happening out on the field. He was known mostly as a bullish runner, but he could also catch a key pass when counted upon. Because the Packers did not have a great passing game, few players on the San Francisco defense paid any attention to Brockington as he snuck out of the backfield to run a pass pattern.

5. Interview with Scott Hunter, September 20, 2017. Ample proof that the less that Dan Devine knew what was going on, the better. Of course, Devine was never going to deflect any credit for something good that the team achieved. The Jerry Rice reference was to the legendary former 49ers wide receiver, a Hall of Famer and generally considered by most experts to be the greatest wide receiver in pro football history.

6. United Press International, "49ers Rally Falls Short," *Eureka (CA) Times Standard*, November 6, 1972, 14. Few—if any—defenders were able to bring John Brockington down with a simple arm tackle. If he had a running head start, it would not be uncommon to see prospective defenders bounce off him as he charged through their feeble tackling attempts.

7. Ralph Trower, "Pack Still Tops, Win 34–24," *Racine (WI) Journal Times*, November 6, 1972, 45. Like all teams, the Packers had a few plays that always seemed to work well. They could not use a play like this one often, however, because opposing defenses would get too used to seeing it on film. But if you used it two or three times a season, it had a pretty good success rate.

8. Associated Press, "Pack Uses 34–24 Win over SF to Keep Pace with Lions," *Wisconsin Rapids Daily Tribune*, November 6, 1972, 27. Perhaps Dan Devine was caught up like everybody else in the big victory over the 49ers, but here he interjects a moment of honesty with the print media. The truth is that the less that Devine interfered with his assistant coaches' decisions, the better for the team's fortunes.

9. Associated Press, "49ers' Rally Falls Short Against Pack," *Oxnard (CA) Press Courier*, November 6, 1972, 27. San Francisco head coach Dick Nolan led the 49ers to three straight NFC Western Division titles in 1970, 1971, and 1972.

10. Interview with Dave Robinson, June 5, 2014, in Berea, Ohio. Robinson's story was just one example that was indicative of the mind games that Dan Devine would play with his players and with his assistant coaches. Good

communication is key to any successful enterprise, and it starts at the top. If the person at the top is not a good communicator, there will probably be failure in some aspects of the said enterprise. The specific incident that Robinson describes in this quote actually occurred in the third quarter in the game against the 49ers on November 5, 1972. It has to be noted that Robinson laughed heartily at the retelling of this story, specifically with Clarence Williams's "Thank God you're here!" remark.

11. Ralph Trower, "Pressure Is Finally Off Packer Secondary," *Racine (WI) Journal Times*, November 6, 1972, 45. Based on Dave Robinson's description of this incident, Dan Devine was in denial of accepting the blame for the faulty defensive lineup. Instead, Devine deflected the blame. As the team's head coach, he had the final say in who started and who did not. But in true Devine fashion, he passed the blame off to the rest of his assistant coaches.

12. *Ibid.*, 45. San Francisco wide receiver Gene Washington made a career out of beating the league's best cornerbacks. Green Bay rookie cornerback Willie Buchanon correctly used the lessons that he learned from Washington throughout his career. Many outstanding wide receivers such as Minnesota's John Gilliam, Cleveland's Frank Pitts, and Dallas's Bob Hayes were each shut down by Buchanon in 1972.

13. *Ibid.* San Francisco wide receiver Gene Washington would lead the league in touchdown receptions in 1972 with 12.

14. Lee Remmel, "Personality Parade," *Green Bay (WI) Press-Gazette*, November 29, 1972. Many of Willie Buchanon's teammates came over to him that day and gave him their confidence. Keep in mind that Buchanon was a rookie, but he was having a spectacular season in 1972. He seldom was beaten by any wide receiver. It was no shame to have been beaten by the likes of the 49ers' Gene Washington.

15. Associated Press, "49ers' Rally Falls Short Against Pack," *Oxnard (CA) Press Courier*, November 6, 1972, 27. San Francisco quarterback Steve Spurrier did an admirable job of replacing veteran quarterback John Brodie in 1972. Spurrier started nine games in place of the injured Brodie that season. Spurrier also led the team in touchdown passes (18) and passing yardage (1,983) in 1972.

16. Associated Press, "Pack Uses 34–24 Win Over SF to Keep Pace with Lions," *Wisconsin Rapids Daily Tribune*, November 6, 1972, 27. The more that San Francisco quarterback Steve Spurrier threw the ball, the more familiar the Packers defensive backs got with defending those throws.

17. *Ibid.*, 27. One must give Steve Spurrier some credit. The 49ers quarterback knew that the Packers' pass coverage was the strongest aspect of their defense, yet he continued to throw the ball against Green Bay. No other opposing passer attempted more throws in a game against the Packers in 1972 than Spurrier.

18. Ralph Trower, "Pack Still Tops, Win 34–24," *Racine (WI) Journal Times*, November 6, 1972, 45. Green Bay cornerback Ken Ellis accounted for four interceptions in 1972. He was also named as a first-team All-Pro in 1972.

19. Associated Press, "Pack Uses 34–24 Win over SF to Keep Pace with Lions," *Wisconsin Rapids Daily Tribune*, November 6, 1972, 27. Had Ken Ellis not scored on his fourth-quarter interception versus the 49ers, Brockington and the Green Bay offense would have undoubtedly ran out the clock with their typical power surges into the heart of the San Francisco defensive line.

20. Ralph Trower, "Pack Still Tops, Win 34–24," *Racine (WI) Journal Times*, November 6, 1972, 45. The Packers would lose four regular-season games and one playoff game in 1972. Of those five combined losses, Green Bay owned the lead in every single game.

21. *Ibid.*, 45. After interviewing Hunter in 2017 and hearing his recollection of his touchdown pass to John Brockington against the 49ers, one has to wonder how many other times that Dan Devine was unsure of which play was being called by assistant coach Bart Starr.

22. *Ibid.* Legendary Green Bay middle linebacker Ray Nitschke was enshrined in the Pro Football Hall of Fame in 1978. He was also named as the Most Valuable Player in the 1962 NFL Championship Game. Keeping Nitschke on the 1972 Packers roster was important, because the younger players on the team really needed to absorb his wealth of knowledge.

23. Ray Nitschke, as told to Robert W. Wells, *Mean on Sunday: The Autobiography of Ray Nitschke*, Black Earth, Wisconsin: Prairie Oak Press, 2001, 267. Dan Devine's treatment of Ray Nitschke was difficult to understand. He spoke highly of the veteran middle linebacker, yet he kept him on the bench for most of the 1972 season. Because Nitschke played for the Packers during the Lombardi era, Devine was naturally interested in getting rid of him. However, Devine probably knew that Nitschke would retire at the end of the 1972 season, and he figured that there would be little interest from any other team in trading for him, so Devine kept Nitschke on the team. Nitschke, for his part, did not publicly condemn Devine, but he disagreed with him in regard to not being named the starting middle linebacker for much of the year.

24. Ralph Trower, "Packers Lose Statistics but Win Game 23–17," *Racine (WI) Journal*

Times, November 13, 1972, 33. The Packers-Bears rivalry is the longest continuing rivalry in NFL history. Every year, regardless of the records of those two teams, a bruising encounter always occurs between Green Bay and Chicago.

25. Joe Mooshil, "Tagge Helps Pack Turn Back Bears, 23-17," *Eau Claire (WI) Leader Telegram*, November 13, 1972, 34. Back in 1972, there were no rules that protected a quarterback's well-being. Helmet-to-helmet hits were commonplace, and so were the resulting concussions.

26. *Ibid.*, 34. It was indeed fortunate for the Packers that Devine drafted Jerry Tagge. While it is true that quarterbacks were more durable in 1972 than they are in today's NFL, it is also true that the defensive players who are trying to hit today's quarterbacks are much bigger, faster, and stronger than the defensive players of the 1970s. To his credit, Devine realized that the rookie (Tagge) would need his support, so he gave it to him.

27. *Ibid.* The plight of a backup quarterback is akin to a relief pitcher in baseball. You never know when you will be called upon to play, so you better be as prepared as possible to play when called upon. Against the Bears, Tagge showed a lot of poise, and helped the Packers win a really tough game.

28. Ralph Trower, "Jerry Tagge Was Ready," *Racine (WI) Journal Times*, November 13, 1972, 33. In retrospect, either Dan Devine or Bart Starr should have informed Tagge at halftime whether he would start at quarterback to begin the third quarter. Keeping a rookie quarterback guessing about his status is never a good thing. It leads to doubt and indecision. Fortunately for Green Bay, Tagge kept his confidence in his abilities in this particular situation.

29. *Ibid.*, 33. Jerry Tagge came into the NFL with a lot of potential and a lot of raw athletic ability. That is why he was drafted so high (in the first round) by the Packers in 1972.

30. *Ibid.* Opposing defenses will almost always blitz their linebackers when facing an untested rookie quarterback. The Green Bay offensive line was prepared for this, but in a way, so was Tagge. The young signal caller had a large frame (6-2, 220), meaning that he was going to be tough for a defensive player to bring down.

31. Ralph Trower, "Packers Lose Statistics but Win Game 23-17," *Racine (WI) Journal Times*, November 13, 1972, 33. For their part, the Green Bay defense knew that they had to make a big play in order to preserve the victory. Chicago quarterback Bobby Douglass was probably the toughest quarterback to sack in the entire league in 1972. So if the Packers were going to sack Douglass, they would probably have to send a linebacker on a blitz to his (Douglass's) blind side, which is exactly what happened.

32. *Ibid.*, 33. Chicago quarterback Bobby Douglass set an NFL record for rushing by a quarterback in 1972 with 968 yards. That record no longer stands, but the threat of Douglass running with the ball was much more feared by opposing defenses than when he was throwing the ball.

33. *Ibid.* A strong-armed quarterback is a necessity for most teams today. But in 1972, not too many of those quarterbacks were playing pro football. The quarterbacks with the strongest throwing arms in the league in 1972 included Bobby Douglass (Bears), Joe Namath (Jets), Terry Bradshaw (Steelers), Daryle Lamonica (Raiders), and Roman Gabriel (Rams).

34. *Ibid.* The Packers were very fortunate in 1972 that they were able to find a way to win most of the tight contests in which they were involved. Both of their victories over the Chicago Bears that year could easily have been won by the Bears. A key play here or there eventually turned the tide of momentum for the Packers.

35. Joe Mooshil, "Tagge Helps Pack Turn Back Bears, 23-17," *Eau Claire (WI) Leader Telegram*, November 13, 1972, 34. Conversely, the Bears were unable to make many key plays in many of their games during the 1970s. They were always a tough, physical team. But they were often prone to making mistakes, which cost them many games.

36. *Ibid.*, 34. Dan Devine believed that the team's statistics would take care of themselves. The only statistic that mattered was points scored at the end of the game.

37. Lee Remmel, "Marcol Delivers Return Message," *Green Bay (WI) Press-Gazette*, November 13, 1972, B-2. On occasion, several special teams coaches instructed their coverage men to go after the opposing kickers on kickoffs. Chester Marcol was one player that Dan Devine definitely did not want to lose to an injury in 1972. He was just too vital when it came to scoring and deep kickoffs for the team.

38. *Ibid.*, B-2. Even though he played most of his career for a losing team, Chicago middle linebacker Dick Butkus was not about to give up any edge—however small—to any of his opponents. Butkus is generally regarded by most pro football historians today as the game's greatest middle linebacker ever.

39. *Ibid.*, B-1. Green Bay placekicker Chester Marcol highlighted his rookie season in 1972 by providing the winning field goals in a preseason win over the Bears, and in both regular-season wins over Chicago.

40. Associated Press, "Special Teams Do Job for Green Bay," *Fond du Lac (WI) Reporter*, November 20, 1972, 27. A long punt return, like the one that Green Bay's Jon Staggers delivered against the Houston Oilers in 1972, was very important to helping the Packers grab the lead and momentum against their opponents. A big special teams play can often change the course of a game. A player on any special teams unit gets their desire measured most visibly and most often, as it takes a complete willingness to sacrifice your physical health on most special teams coverage and return units. Staggers was just the type of player who could be relied upon to make a big catch on offense or return a punt or a kickoff for a long distance on special teams. He could do a lot of things well for the Packers. Everybody on the 1972 Green Bay team contributed in one way or another to the success of the team, as Staggers exemplified at Houston.

41. Associated Press, "Houston Gambled—And Lost," *Fond du Lac (WI) Reporter*, November 20, 1972, 27. Some teams will go through an entire season without getting a long punt return. Fortunately for the 1972 Packers, Jon Staggers had the speed and elusiveness with which to take a punt back a long distance.

42. Ibid., 27. Houston head coach Bill Peterson had a couple of similarities to Green Bay head coach Dan Devine. Both men had coached a college team before becoming a head coach in the NFL, and both men should have kept coaching a college team instead of coaching in the NFL. Peterson is generally regarded as one of the worst head coaches in modern NFL history. His head coaching record was a dismal 1–18.

43. Associated Press, "Pass Completion Eases Negative Thoughts," *Appleton (WI) Post-Crescent*, November 20, 1972, 5. Green Bay punter Ron Widby was also the team's holder in 1972. Anytime that a fake punt is tried, it needs to surprise your opponent. Because of this fact, most teams don't try to use a fake punt more than once or twice in a season. Some teams never try to use a fake punt. The risk of failure is just too great.

44. Associated Press, "Special Teams Do Job for Green Bay," *Fond du Lac (WI) Reporter*, November 20, 1972, 27. Green Bay wide receiver Dave Davis was thrust into the lineup on a regular basis, especially during the latter part of the 1972 season. The Packers receiving corps was in a state of flux throughout the year, due partly to untimely injuries, and to a lack of overall speed at that position. Davis would account for only four receptions in 1972.

45. Ibid., 27. By the midpoint of the 1972 season, Packers running back John Brockington was not fooling anyone. The entire league took notice of his exploits as the Rookie of the Year in 1971. The first half of 1972 saw him continue to gain yards and deliver punishing bruises to defenders. Houston, like most teams, realized that the Green Bay passing game was not as good as their running game. Hence, the Oilers decided to focus their attention on stopping the Packers ground game, and in particular, John Brockington.

46. United Press International, "Lane Great as Fill In," *Kensoha (WI) News*, November 20, 1972, 26. Green Bay fullback MacArthur Lane was very similar to his running mate in the backfield, John Brockington. Both men were students of the game. On Lane's touchdown run at Houston, he was smart enough to quickly change his direction. Lane's maneuverability helped to cause the score to occur.

47. Associated Press, "Special Teams Do Job for Green Bay," *Fond du Lac (WI) Reporter*, November 20, 1972, 27. Lane's method of playing, as Devine intimated, was an all-out style, where he would pound defenders to a point where those defenders would—by the fourth quarter of most games—rely on trying to arm tackle Lane instead of lowering their shoulders into Lane's churning legs. For every bruise or pinched nerve that Lane got, he probably gave out two to his would-be tacklers.

48. Lee Remmel, "'Big Play' Packers Retain Division Lead," *Appleton (WI) Post-Crescent*, November 20, 1972, 5. Green Bay special teams coach Hank Kuhlmann was brought to the team by head coach Dan Devine. Kuhlmann was an assistant coach for Devine at the University of Missouri.

Chapter 8

1. Leonard Shapiro, "Packers Grumble as Tagge Replaced Hunter," *Madison (WI) Capital Times*, November 27, 1972, 17. You have to wonder if the penalty for speaking your mind to the press was so ingrained into the players by Dan Devine, that by the middle of 1972, the players were fearful to say anything that could be construed as criticism. Those penalties might involve being benched, traded, or financially fined by the team. If a player like starting quarterback Scott Hunter was unwilling to voice his displeasure at the time, you can imagine that most of the other players on the 1972 Packers were as well.

2. Ibid., 17. Sometimes in the NFL, players say things in the heat of battle. After the first game against the Redskins in 1972, John Brockington was probably enduring the pit of frustration with the decisions that Dan Devine was

making. Green Bay would lose twice to Washington that season, and both of those losses were winnable games. Just like an NFL coach could get fined by the commissioner for publicly criticizing a referee, so too could a Packers player be fined for publicly criticizing a coach's decision.

3. Interview with Scott Hunter, September 20, 2017. Scott Hunter's freak accident was indeed unfortunate. But at least he only missed the remainder of the regular-season game at Washington. He managed to be healthy enough to play the following week against Detroit.

4. Leonard Shapiro, "Packers Grumble as Tagge Replaced Hunter," *Madison (WI) Capital Times*, November 27, 1972, 17. For a quarterback with hardly any pro experience, Jerry Tagge did pretty well against the Redskins. He managed to keep the game close, and he kept his poise throughout in the face of the Redskin blitzes. By 1973, Tagge would see even more action as a starter.

5. Associated Press, "QB Problem Evident in Loss to Redskins," *Fond du Lac (WI) Reporter*, November 27, 1972, 24. It did not take long for the Washington coaches to realize that Ken Ellis was taken out of the game due to injury. Ellis was probably the best man-to-man cover cornerback on the Packers in 1972. Reserve Green Bay cornerback Ike Thomas was instantly targeted by the Redskins offense.

6. Ibid., 24. Washington wide receiver Charley Taylor actually started his pro career as a running back but was eventually moved to a more natural position. Taylor would lead the NFL in receiving in 1966 and 1967. He would eventually be enshrined in the Pro Football Hall of Fame in 1984.

7. Associated Press, "Redskins' Pass Attack Topples Packers, 21–16," *Madison (WI) Capital Times*, November 27, 1972, 17. Opponents of the 1972 Green Bay club may have seen them on film, but until they faced them on the field, they really could not tell for sure how improved the Packers were. Veteran Washington quarterback Billy Kilmer got a taste of how competitive the Packers were in the two games that he faced them in 1972.

8. Associated Press, "QB Problem Evident in Loss to Redskins," *Fond du Lac (WI) Reporter*, November 27, 1972, 24. Washington head coach George Allen was naturally not 100 percent sure that his team would face Green Bay in the 1972 playoffs, but he was the type of coach who left no stone unturned in preparing the Redskins just in case. In that regard, Coach Allen was a much better coach and a much more thorough coach than Dan Devine.

9. Leonard Shapiro, "Packers Grumble as Tagge Replaced Hunter," *Madison (WI) Capital Times*, November 27, 1972, 17. Coach Devine really had no other option at this point of the game at Washington. Keeping Hunter on the field would have risked further injury, something that no one on the team was in favor of. Despite the change in quarterbacks, the game plan remained the same. Hunter was a better passer than Tagge, but Tagge was a better runner/scrambler than Hunter.

10. Ralph Trower, "Packer Wounded Ignore Injuries," *Racine (WI) Journal Times*, December 4, 1972, 33. It was simply amazing how well the Green Bay defensive backfield performed in 1972. Despite their youth and overall inexperience, they overcame the odds (and various injuries) to surrender only seven touchdown passes all regular season long. That team record will likely never be broken.

11. Ibid., 33. Fortunately for the Packers, Kenny Ellis was able to convince Dan Devine that he could play well enough to help the team in their game on December 3 against the Lions. Indeed, his interceptions led to two important Green Bay touchdowns.

12. Mike O'Brien, "Packers Manhandle Lions in 33-7 Win," *Madison (WI) Capital Times*, December 4, 1972, 17. Ken Ellis had willingly delivered the sacrifice to his teammates by playing against Detroit while still being injured. The brotherhood of the team had taken strong root, and every player was willing to sacrifice his health for his teammates, as evidenced by Ellis's actions.

13. Interview with Scott Hunter, September 20, 2017. Effective game clock management is a very important strategical part of the game that few coaches ever seem to master. The average fan can get annoyed beyond belief when their team is trying to run down the clock, yet the center snaps the ball with more than five seconds still remaining on the play clock. Green Bay quarterback Scott Hunter's anecdote shows that he was well aware of what he needed to do in order to use up the clock and put his team in the best position to defeat Detroit.

14. Ralph Trower, "Packer Wounded Ignore Injuries," *Racine (WI) Journal Times*, December 4, 1972, 33. Pro football's offensive strategy in the 1970s for the most part favored running the ball over passing it. Most offensive coaches preferred to put a greater emphasis on the running game. As a result, there were less passes thrown by quarterbacks across the league, hence there were fewer interceptions recorded.

15. Ibid., "Packers Have Fun, Destroy Lions, Take Lead," *Racine (WI) Journal Times*, December 4, 1972, 33. Green Bay linebacker Fred Carr was probably one of the most athletic players on the 1972 team. He possessed the attributes of speed, quickness, strength, and the

smarts needed to play the linebacker position. Moreover, Carr showcased a meanness on game day that few defenders in the league could rival. Carr was named to the All-Conference team in 1972.

16. *Ibid.*, 33. Green Bay running back John Brockington knew that he had two more regular season games left in which to eclipse the 1,000-yard rushing mark. The odds of him doing so were very good, and he eventually did accomplish that feat in the Packers' next game.

17. *Ibid.* Dave Kopay was a journeyman special teams player who only rarely got to see some action at running back for the five different teams that he played for in his nine-year career. The 1972 season was his final year in the league.

18. *Ibid.* Coach Devine was undoubtedly relieved to have won a one-sided game for a change. Before the second game versus Detroit, the 1972 Packers had won their previous seven games by an average of just a little over seven points per game. Beating the Lions by 26 points with just two games left in the regular season was a blessing for the Pack.

19. *Ibid.* Veteran Green Bay defensive tackle Bob Brown had lived through the years during the Lombardi era when the Packers had a killer instinct and finished their games with a flurry of scoring and a dominating performance by their defense. Then Brown lived through the years of 1968 to 1971 when the Packers had very much difficulty in winning rivalry games against the teams in their own division. When 1972 came around, Brown got a chance to see the team succeed once again, and he was no doubt joyful for it. Giving up a shutout very late in the second game against Detroit, while scoring 33, was not a big letdown for Brown and the rest of the Packers. By this time in the 1972 season, they definitely felt like they could win the NFC Central.

20. *Ibid.* Veteran Green Bay linebacker Dave Robinson knew quite well from his many years of experience that it is easier for a team to hold on to a big lead against an opponent, than it is to come back from a big deficit. The more points that the Packers could score against the Lions in the early minutes of the game, the better.

21. *Ibid.* Detroit head coach Joe Schmidt was a Hall of Fame linebacker for the Lions for 13 seasons during the 1950s and 1960s.

22. *Ibid.*, "Packer Wounded Ignore Injuries," *Racine (WI) Journal Times*, December 4, 1972, 33. Green Bay probably knew that Detroit would try to pick on cornerback Ken Ellis, to test how well he could play with his injury. Ellis and defensive backfield coach Don Doll prepared for such attention, and their efforts proved fruitful. Ellis had one of his best games of the 1972 season on December 3 against the Lions.

23. *Ibid.*, 33. Green Bay safety Jim Hill was not the only Packers player huddled by the sideline heaters on that day. Many players would be congregating around those heaters during the game versus the Lions, and they were probably wishing that the team had employed several more of those heaters as well.

24. *Ibid.*, "Packers Have Fun, Destroy Lions, Take Lead," *Racine (WI) Journal Times*, December 4, 1972, 33. It was probably too cold for Green Bay center Ken Bowman and the rest of his teammates to relax long enough to take their foot off the gas against the Lions. They just never relented in this victory.

25. *Ibid.*, 33. Packers head coach Dan Devine said the right thing following his team's 33-7 win over Detroit. He definitely did not want his players feeling even the least bit overconfident, with the Minnesota Vikings on the horizon the following week.

26. *Ibid.* Veteran Green Bay linebacker Dave Robinson had seen far too many times how a team can get caught up in a victory, only to perform poorly the following week. Robinson was probably one of the more pragmatic members of the team.

Chapter 9

1. Todd Mishler, *Cold Wars: 40 Years of Packer-Viking Rivalry*, Black Earth, Wisconsin, Prairie Oak Press, 2002, 38. The Green Bay public relations director in 1972 was Chuck Lane. He described the team's rookie cornerback Willie Buchanon as being "very bright." Buchanon's willingness and aplomb to discuss with Coach Devine the wearing of gloves at Minnesota—while providing a reasonable rationale for doing so—might have looked to some as sheer genius. In reality, Buchanon probably just needed to lend Devine some small measure of his own common sense regarding the matter. Former Hall of Fame Pittsburgh Steelers head coach Chuck Noll had a saying that he used often to describe such a situation. When faced with making a similar decision, Noll simply said "whatever it takes." A couple of side notes: Buchanon was somewhat mistaken regarding his memory of the second game versus Detroit. He did not intercept any passes in that contest, so he probably just mistook that game for a game in cold weather where he did intercept a couple of passes. Dan Devine probably agreed to Buchanon's request because of the exceptional play all year long from his rookie cornerback, and from the fact

that he virtually shut down every Detroit receiver in the second game versus the Lions.

2. *Ibid.*, 176. NFL Films is replete with motion picture images of propane heaters spewing out fire during many late-season games at Metropolitan Stadium. The Vikings' field crew actually employed two different methods of keeping their playing field from freezing on game days. Besides the wheeled carts with flames shooting out of them were two 60-yard tarpaulins, each of which covered the field from sideline to sideline, and from the opposite end lines to the midfield stripe. Several openings in the tarps would allow for hot-air heaters to blow hot air underneath onto the thawing field. They sort of resembled a couple of giant rectangular inflatable bounce houses at carnivals, where youngsters go inside and are propelled to bump into each other as they jump up and down.

3. Interview with John Brockington, June 23, 2017. Charlie Hall was a reserve cornerback and a regular on the Green Bay special teams coverage units.

4. Interview with Scott Hunter, September 20, 2017. It may be a coincidence, but Hunter enjoyed a much more productive second half in the game at Minnesota with a sweatshirt underneath his jersey.

5. Mark Shapiro, "The Pack IS Back, 23-7," *Madison (WI) State Journal*, December 11, 1972, 17. Sometimes words are just words. Sometimes they can provide some sense of inspiration to a team. The Packers players certainly exhibited the "poise" that they needed in order to win the division-clinching game at Minnesota on December 10.

6. *Ibid.*, "Pack's Mules Showed Vikes," *Madison (WI) State Journal*, December 11, 1972, 18. The Packers running backs focused their attention on not fumbling so much, that they gained only a combined net total of 56 ground yards in the first half at Minnesota. In the second half of the game, they had more luck finding open holes in the line of scrimmage. They ran for 158 more net rushing yards in the second half of the game.

7. Bob Rubin, *Green Bay's Packers Return to Glory*, Englewood Cliffs, New Jersey, Prentice-Hall, Inc., 112, 115. Clarence "Big Cat" Williams had the game of his life at Minnesota on December 10, 1972. Besides his three sacks of Vikings quarterback Fran Tarkenton, his pass rushing efforts helped to limit the famous scrambler to just 11 completions and 118 passing yards.

8. Associated Press, "Packer Loyalty Noted by Devine; Robinson Lauds Play of Williams," *Appleton (WI) Post-Crescent*, December 11, 1972, 15. That pass interference penalty was one of the few mistakes that Green Bay cornerback Ken Ellis was guilty of all season long.

9. Interview with Scott Hunter, September 20, 2017. Hunter's self-confidence was warranted. He had destroyed a pretty strong Detroit defense just a week before the game at Minnesota, and the Vikings defense was certainly not having their usual dominating year in 1972. So Hunter had good reason for displaying confidence in his and in his team's abilities.

10. Interview with John Brockington, June 23, 2017. The cold weather usually worked in favor of the Vikings in those days, because they played in those elements much more than most other teams. But the Packers played in cold weather too on a regular basis up in Wisconsin, and that proved to be the great equalizer in the game at Minnesota on December 10.

11. Associated Press, "John Brockington and MacArthur Lane: Two 'Mules' Who Form the Perfect Team," December 16, 1972. MacArthur Lane's ability to cut back against the grain in very rapid fashion was rarely seen by runners as big as he was (6–1, 220).

12. *Ibid.*, "Packers Capture Division Title," *Appleton (WI) Post-Crescent*, December 11, 1972, 20. Lane definitely had a better second half in the game at Minnesota than he did in the first half. Lane accumulated only 23 rushing yards in the first half against the Minnesota defense. He improved on that by running for 76 yards in the second half.

13. *Ibid.*, 20. Green Bay placekicker Chester Marcol and Minnesota placekicker Fred Cox each missed one field goal on this day. But Marcol managed to connect on his three other field-goal attempts in the game. Cox never got another chance to attempt a field goal.

14. *Ibid.* Green Bay linebacker Fred Carr never stopped hustling on the play. His quick reaction enabled him to snare Brown's fumble cleanly on one bounce. It proved to be the turning point of the game, as the Vikings would continue to turn the ball over three more times from that point onward.

15. Mark Shapiro, "Pack's Mules Showed Vikes," *Madison (WI) State Journal*, December 11, 1972, 18. Scott Hunter's confidence was contagious for the whole Packers team at Minnesota, especially in the second half of the game, where the Packers just continued to pour it on the Vikings. That fourth quarter at Minnesota was probably the most dominating quarter of the 1972 season for the Packers offense.

16. Interview with T. J. Troup, November 10, 2017. Sometimes, you can't coach a player's natural-born talents. Rookie Green Bay cornerback Willie Buchanon played so well at

Minnesota, one might have thought that he was *born* to be a pro cornerback.

17. Associated Press, "Packers Capture Division Title," *Appleton (WI) Post-Crescent*, December 11, 1972, 20. If an instant replay official from today were to rule on Willie Buchanon's second interception at Minnesota down the far sideline, he would undoubtedly rule it an incomplete pass. Buchanon dropped the ball, and he clearly did not possess it for a long enough period of time before dropping it. But in 1972 there was no instant replay official in the NFL, much to Buchanon's and the Packers' benefit.

18. Mark Shapiro, "Pack's Mules Showed Vikes," *Madison (WI) State Journal*, December 11, 1972, 18. The Minnesota front four had an outstanding year in 1971, but not so much in 1972. The Green Bay offensive line and running backs simply ran the ball right down their throats in the second half of their December 10 contest at Minnesota.

19. Associated Press, "Packers Capture Division Title," *Appleton (WI) Post-Crescent*, December 11, 1972, 20. For all of his greatness throughout his Hall of Fame career, Minnesota defensive tackle Alan Page could be incited to frustration, as evidenced by his outburst against the Packers in 1972, and by his outburst in the Vikings' loss to Miami in Super Bowl VIII in January 1974.

20. *Ibid.*, 20. Green Bay rookie cornerback Willie Buchanon certainly made his share of big plays against the Vikings at Minnesota, intercepting two key second-half Fran Tarkenton passes.

21. *Ibid.* In the fourth quarter of the game at Minnesota, the Vikings were trailing by more than a touchdown, a situation which forced their necessity to pass. The NFC's best defensive secondary (Green Bay's) was more than ready for them to do so.

22. Interview with T. J. Troup, March 24, 2018. Green Bay quarterback coach Bart Starr had the faith in his convictions and his decisions. He had seen and experienced enough in pro football to know that his plan to run the ball would work against the Vikings.

23. Mark Shapiro, "Pack's Mules Showed Vikes," *Madison (WI) State Journal*, December 11, 1972, 18. The athleticism and determination that the Green Bay defense exhibited versus Minnesota's offense was spectacular. They did not get down on themselves while trailing at halftime. Instead, they just got more motivated to shut down the Vikings in the second half, which they did. Minnesota quarterback Fran Tarkenton simply had to throw the ball by the fourth quarter, and defenders like Green Bay linebacker Dave Robinson were ready to disrupt Tarkenton's throws.

24. Todd Mishler, *Cold Wars: 40 Years of Packer-Viking Rivalry*, Black Earth, Wisconsin: Prairie Oak Press, 2002, 141. Clarence "Big Cat" Williams was lined up against Minnesota offensive tackle Ron Yary. Williams beat the future Hall of Famer to sack Vikings quarterback Fran Tarkenton three times in the game, which ranks as one of the best games ever against Yary, a consensus All-Pro.

25. *Ibid.*, "It Started with a Loss," *Madison (WI) State Journal*, December 11, 1972, 17. This is definitely one of the greatest quotes ever which describes the 1972 Green Bay Packers. It speaks to the desire, the dedication, and the brotherhood of the players in their quest for victory.

26. Todd Mishler, *Cold Wars: 40 Years of Packer-Viking Rivalry*, Black Earth, Wisconsin: Prairie Oak Press, 2002, 142. Like all great power runners, John Brockington seemed to get stronger with more carries in the second half of most games. It is a beautiful thing to watch—a power runner like Brockington simply wearing an entire defense down, all the while keeping the opposing offense on the bench as the game clock wears down with every successive first down.

27. Interview with Scott Hunter, September 20, 2017. The John Brockington run that Packers quarterback Scott Hunter described actually occurred in the second quarter of the December 10 game at Minnesota, not in the fourth quarter as Hunter stated. Given the fact that it has been more than 45 years since that game, Hunter's recollections regarding many individual offensive plays during the 1972 season is nevertheless still quite astounding.

28. Mark Shapiro, "Pack's Mules Showed Vikes," *Madison (WI) State Journal*, December 11, 1972, 18. The Green Bay offensive line probably knew that they were going to focus on power runs throughout the second half at Minnesota. There was to be very few deceptive draw or counter plays during the third and fourth quarters. Packers offensive play caller Bart Starr wanted the offense to do what they did best—run the ball straight ahead into the guts of the Minnesota defense. So Starr called straight ahead runs and basic off-tackle runs on a regular basis in the second half of Green Bay's 23–7 division-clinching victory over the Vikings.

29. Associated Press, "Packers Capture Division Title," *Appleton (WI) Post-Crescent*, December 11, 1972, 20. It is said that championships in football are rarely won in December … they are usually won with the sacrifices and sweat in the heat of July and August in training camp.

30. Mark Shapiro, "Pack's Mules Showed

Vikes," *Madison (WI) State Journal,* December 11, 1972, 18. Green Bay quarterback Scott Hunter's teammates had full faith and confidence in his abilities to put the first game versus Minnesota behind him, even as the Packers were trailing the Vikings at halftime of the second game against the Norsemen (as the Minnesota team was often called). Hunter proved worthy of their trust, as he led his team to 23 unanswered points in the second half to win the game and the NFC Central Division title.

31. Associated Press, "Packers Capture Division Title," *Appleton (WI) Post-Crescent,* December 11, 1972, 20. Most of the younger players on the Packers, such as safety Jim Hill, would never again win a division title during their careers after 1972, so the win over the Vikings on December 10, 1972, was certainly a moment to savor and remember.

32. Mark Shapiro, "It Started with a Loss," *Madison (WI) State Journal,* December 11, 1972, 17. This statement represents in all its fullness the paradox that was Dan Devine. Degrading his players to their faces in weekly practices, yet praising them to the press after a big win. This statement is a wonderful commentary which pays homage to his players after a glorious victory over an archrival. And still, one must temper the good feelings from this comment, because of all that Devine did and said to hurt the mental psyche of his team throughout the 1972 season. It was almost as if there were two head coaches in Devine, one good and one bad. Readers should draw your their conclusions. The Green Bay players indeed have drawn theirs.

33. Associated Press, "New, Old Celebrate Packers' 23-7 Win Over Purple Gang," *Dubuque (IA) Telegraph Herald,* December 11, 1972, 15. Hall of Fame middle linebacker Ray Nitschke was a team player, and even though he did not play much in 1972, he was always willing to lend his help, advice, and support to all of his Packer teammates. It was a wonderful way for the great Nitschke to retire from the game—as a division champion.

34. "John Brockington and MacArthur Lane: Two 'Mules' Who Form the Perfect Team," December 16, 1972. Lane rushed for 821 yards on 177 carries in 1972, equating to 4.6 yards per carry. Lane averaged 58.6 yards per game rushing. He played in every game during the year.

35. *Ibid.* Lane was overjoyed that he was finally a member of a division champion in 1972. Indeed, it was largely through his efforts that the Packers managed to win the NFC Central in 1972.

36. Associated Press, "New, Old Celebrate Packers' 23-7 Win over Purple Gang," *Dubuque (IA) Telegraph Herald,* December 11, 1972, 15. It is a credit to Lane and Brockington and the rest of the Packers that they were somehow able to keep their winning momentum going all throughout the 1972 season. Key victories in close games over their division rivals like Chicago and Detroit boosted team morale, and big wins over perennial playoff teams like Dallas, San Francisco, and Minnesota helped the Packers players to realize that they belonged at the top of the divisional standings.

37. Interview with John Brockington, June 23, 2017. Former Green Bay public relations director Chuck Lane surmised that those players who carried Dan Devine off the field after beating Minnesota may have been the guys who were trying to renegotiate their contracts.

38. Jerry Estill, "Packers 'Stumble' to Win Over Saints, 30-20," *Madison (WI) Capital Times,* December 18, 1972, 19. Almost every team in pro football history has one or two games in a season (or more) where they play a bad game. The 1972 Packers can be excused for playing below par against the Saints in the final regular season game of the year. Green Bay had just won their first division title, and the game at New Orleans on December 17 would not affect their playoff standing in any way. Moreover, quite a few younger and inexperienced Packers players would see quality playing time against the Saints, so there was a natural expectation for the Green Bay success rate at New Orleans to be at least a shade below normal.

39. Jim Turner, "Pack Just Missed 2 Coveted Records," *Madison (WI) Capital Times,* December 18, 1972, 19. Veteran Green Bay middle linebacker Ray Nitschke should be applauded for his instinctual awareness regarding the play. Chalk it up to his experience. He knew that once Chester Marcol's kick was blocked, he had to either block someone, or find an open space to receive a potential pass. He chose the latter, and it paid off big for the Packers.

40. Lee Remmel, "Packers Achieve Best Record Since 1966," *Appleton (WI) Post-Crescent,* December 18, 1972, 15. While inspiring his teammates with his pass reception, he undoubtedly also gave them quite a laugh with the play.

41. *Ibid.,* "'Old Times' for Nitschke," *Appleton (WI) Post-Crescent,* December 18, 1972, 15. To be fair to Green Bay's Chester Marcol, the placekicker stood only 6-0, and weighed only 190 pounds. If anyone on that play was going to get "buried," it would have been Marcol.

42. Jim Turner, "Pack Just Missed 2 Coveted Records," *Madison (WI) Capital Times,* December 18, 1972, 19. Pro football teams today spend many hours each week practicing special teams situations. During the early 1970s,

the various special teams (punt and kickoff returns and coverage, field goal and extra point blocking units, etc.) were little more than an afterthought in the realms of pro coaching. As a result of this, when a special teams play succeeded, the success was much more due to pure luck than actual strategy and execution.

43. Associated Press, "Blocking Was Fundamental to Pack's Conquest," *Madison (WI) State Journal*, December 18, 1972, 20. In all the years that the New Orleans Saints have been playing pro football (since 1967), they undoubtedly have never scored a touchdown as easy as the one that Richard Neal scored against the Packers on December 17, 1972. You can see the play on NFL Films' Week 14 weekly program, *This Week in Pro Football*, or on the Saints' 1972 highlight film entitled *Spirit of the Saints*, written and directed by James Green.

44. Lee Remmel, "Packers Achieve Best Record since 1966," *Appleton (WI) Post-Crescent*, December 18, 1972, 15. I don't know it for sure, because I couldn't find any photos depicting the moment, but I think that it is a fair bet that Green Bay head coach Dan Devine ground down at least two millimeters of enamel between the upper and lower bridges of his teeth while watching his team play against the Saints in the final regular season game of 1972.

45. Chester Marcol with Gary D'Amato, *Alive and Kicking: My Journey Through Football*, Addiction and Life, Stevens Point, Wisconsin: KCI Sports Publishing, 2011, 55. Chester Marcol's performance in 1972 turned the fortunes for the Packers around a complete 180 degrees. The points scored by field goals and extra points combined in 1971 were a woeful 74 points. A year later, Marcol alone accounted for 128 points, which led the entire league in scoring.

46. Jim Turner, "Pack Just Missed 2 Coveted Records," *Madison (WI) Capital Times*, December 18, 1972, 19. Chester Marcol's confidence—for a rookie—cannot be understated. He learned the secret to successful placekicking early, which was simply to never dwell on a missed kick, except to aid in planning for how you will correct your miss with your next attempt.

47. Ibid., 19. One important reason for the record of fewest touchdown passes surrendered that the Green Bay secondary earned in 1972 had nothing to do with their defense. Packers running backs John Brockington and MacArthur Lane used up so much time on their offensive scoring drives throughout the year, that the opposing offenses just did not get that much time to have the ball. As a result, that lack of time of possession indirectly led to a lesser amount of actual passes thrown, which certainly aided the Green Bay defensive secondary in their quest for a team record.

48. Lee Remmel, "Packers Achieve Best Record Since 1966," *Appleton (WI) Post-Crescent*, December 18, 1972, 15. Given some time to examine statistics and game film, every coach in the league—for the most part—simmers down a bit and becomes more even-tempered, even after a loss. Devine simply tried to look at the bright side after his team's performance at New Orleans.

49. Associated Press, "'Can't Help Thinking About Washington,' Declares Jim Carter," *Appleton (WI) Post-Crescent*, December 18, 1972, 15. Every team that makes the playoffs wants to enter the postseason at a rising or peaking level. While it is true that the Packers won their final regular-season game against the Saints, it is also true that they looked quite sloppy in doing so. No witnesses of that game—including New Orleans defensive lineman Richard Neal—would describe Devine's team as "peaking" after the win over New Orleans on December 17, 1972.

Chapter 10

1. Interview with John Brockington, June 23, 2017. John Brockington had gained 42 yards rushing against the Redskins in their first meeting on November 26. If he knew at that time what his rushing totals would be in Green Bay's next meeting at Washington in the playoffs, he would have undoubtedly reached a high level of incredulousness and/or complete disgust.

2. Bob Greene, "Redskin Ambush of Packers Nicest Present for Allen," *Monroe (LA) News Star*, December 25, 1972, 22. Washington head coach George Allen was definitely not afraid to tweak a certain element in strategy if he felt strongly enough that it could help his team. Such was the case with the five-man defensive line that the Redskins employed against the Packers. Just because it did not work well enough in their first meeting, it did not mean that it would not work well enough in their second meeting in the divisional playoffs. Coach Allen felt that the new alignment could work well throughout the game if it was used vigorously enough, not just in a few plays as was the case in the first meeting between the two teams.

3. Interview with Dave Robinson on June 5, 2014, in Berea, Ohio. Robinson offered this story to primarily point out how little effort Dan Devine gave in preparing the Packers for their playoff game versus Washington.

4. Interview with Scott Hunter, September 20, 2017. Despite Hunter's optimism, the Pack-

ers to a man did not think beyond their divisional playoff game at Washington on December 24. They knew that none of their hopes for playing in Super Bowl VII would have been realized if they did not beat the Redskins first.

5. Mark Shapiro, "It Started With a Loss," *Madison (WI) State Journal*, December 11, 1972, 17. Again, this is yet another example of Packers head coach Dan Devine voicing support for his team in the press, in the hopes of giving them confidence. As things turned out, however, Devine's actions and game day decisions in the playoff contest at Washington did much to destroy his players' confidence.

6. Stanton Greene, *The Green Bay Packers—The Dan Devine Years 1971-1974*, NorthernWriter.com Publishing, 2015, 139. Veteran Washington quarterback Billy Kilmer was probably one of the gutsiest men to ever play the game. It is quite incredible that he was able to shake off the combined hit that he took from Green Bay's Clarence Williams and Alden Roche.

7. Interview with Dave Robinson on June 5, 2014, in Berea, Ohio. See note 3 above.

8. Bob Greene, "Redskin Ambush of Packers Nicest Present for Allen," *Monroe (LA) News Star*, December 25, 1972, 22. Dan Devine's stubborn folly of not preparing for Washington's five-man defensive line was responsible for costing the Packers the potential victory. But a bigger cause of Green Bay's loss to the Redskins was the fact that Devine was unwilling to allow Bart Starr to continue to call the offensive plays in that game as he had done so all season long. Starr would definitely have had quarterback Scott Hunter throw the ball in the face of that five-man defensive line, and that move would have ultimately helped the Packers much more than Devine's plan of just running the ball straight ahead on virtually every play. Devine never outwardly or publicly accepted any of the blame for the 1972 playoff loss to Washington.

9. Mike Lucas, "Redskins Beat Packers at Own Game—Defense," *Madison (WI) Capitol Times*, December 26, 1972, 51. Washington head coach George Allen had to have felt a sense of relief that Dan Devine never changed his offensive game plan, especially in the second half. It was almost as if Allen was playing chess against Devine, but Devine was wearing a blindfold.

10. *Ibid.*, 51. Veteran Redskins linebacker Jack Pardee did not comment about this in the press, but in his strategical and analytical mind, he *had* to have questioned the Packers' offensive strategy in the face of the extra lineman on his team's defensive line.

11. *Ibid.* Veteran Washington defensive lineman Ron McDole was quite magnanimous following his team's playoff victory over the Packers. But it was actually not Green Bay's inexperience which hurt the Packers that much. Rather, it was Dan Devine who derailed the Packers' chances to advance to the NFC title game.

12. Associated Press, "Late-Game 'Miracles' for Pro Playoffs," *Monroe (LA) News Star*, December 25, 1972, 22. Proof that practice makes perfect. The Redskins took the time in practice to make sure that their five-man defensive line would succeed against Green Bay in the playoffs. In contrast, Dan Devine did not spend any time worrying about Washington's five-man defensive line. That disregard proved to be Green Bay's undoing.

13. Kenneth Denlinger, "Over-the-Hill Redskins Undermine Packers," *The Sporting News*, January 6, 1973, 20. Veteran Washington defensive tackle Diron Talbert stated the obvious—shutting down the Green Bay rushing attack was the key to the Redskins' 16–3 victory over the Packers. The five-man defensive line was the key to stopping John Brockington and MacArthur Lane.

14. *Ibid.*, 20. Without a doubt, Washington's playoff win over Green Bay in 1972 was the greatest game and the most memorable game that Manny Sistrunk had ever and would ever play.

15. *Ibid.* Roy Jefferson's touchdown really did a lot of damage to Green Bay's psyche. No one expected that the Redskins would achieve any decent amount of success against the most formidable segment of the Packers team, their defensive secondary.

16. Interview with T. J. Troup on October 27, 2017. An important key to Roy Jefferson's touchdown was also the veteran savvy of Redskins quarterback Billy Kilmer, who may have lulled the Green Bay defense into a guessing game as to his intentions on the critical play. The Packers guessed wrong, and Kilmer's scoring pass to Jefferson proved to be the winning points.

17. Bob Greene, "Ambushing Defense Leads Washington," *Charleston (SC) Daily Mail*, December 25, 1972, 21. The other Redskins wide receiver, future Hall of Famer Charley Taylor, was also double-teamed by the Packers defensive secondary during the game. Pro football is a strategical chess match, and it is also a guessing game. You will see many different risks being taken in the course of any pro football game. The Redskins took some risks against the Green Bay defense, and enough of them paid off in a big way, including Jefferson's touchdown.

18. Interview with John Brockington, June

23, 2017. Green Bay assistant coach Bart Starr had designed a well thought-out plan to beat the Washington defense. He had done the required preparation. But head coach Dan Devine proved to be the monkey wrench in Starr's designs. John Brockington could have had the game of his life against the Redskins in the 1972 playoffs, but Devine's pulling of the plug of Starr's play calling ended Brockington's hopes, and the hopes of all of his teammates.

19. Interview with Bill Lueck, January 25, 2018. When a defense knows exactly what play you are doing to run, most teams will try to change the play. Dan Devine refused to change plays, however, and he refused to allow his quarterback (Scott Hunter) to call audibles (changes to the play that was called) at the line of scrimmage prior to the snap of the ball. In short, Devine's stubbornness and his ego cost the Packers the game.

20. *Ibid.* Photos of Bart Starr during the course of the playoff game at Washington shows the visage of a prideful man who had been immersed in what was probably the most frustrating chapter of his pro football career. Regardless of how much he tried to reason with Dan Devine, he simply could not convince the head coach to change his mind regarding the offensive play calling. Hunter's confusion over what was going on along the Green Bay sideline was the obvious result of the friction that occurred between Devine and Starr. It was one of the worst moments of the 1970s for the Packers.

21. *Ibid.* John Brockington is a proud man, and an accomplished man. He was also a football superstar. There was no easy way for me to ask him about this playoff loss to Washington without asking him about Devine's stubbornness. Almost 50 years after that game, the hurt of losing still remains for Brockington. But the hurt of losing the way that they lost hurts much more, because it simply did not have to end that way. Dan Devine should have swallowed his pride, and he should have allowed Bart Starr to continue calling the offensive plays. It is important to note that Green Bay may have still lost to Washington in the 1972 playoffs, but if they did, they would have been better able to deal with it years later, knowing that they lost with no arrows left in their quivers. The Packer players are thus rightly without blame for their bitterness so many years later.

22. Interview with Bill Lueck, January 25, 2018. Green Bay guard Bill Lueck and his fellow offensive linemen were not to be faulted for the lack of air yardage accumulated by the team in 1972. The Packers did not have a breakaway threat at the wide receiver position. But what could have been the big reason why Green Bay's passing game did not measure up to its running game is simply because the running game was so very successful with the likes of John Brockington and MacArthur Lane carrying the ball. Those two men churned out yardage and used up much of the clock on many long and sustained scoring drives. As a result, the Packers focused their play calling on the running game.

23. Interview with T. J. Troup, March 24, 2018. Troup believed in the genius play calling abilities of Green Bay assistant coach Bart Starr. He believed—as do many—that this was certainly a winnable game for the Packers.

24. Interview with Scott Hunter, September 20, 2017. Green Bay quarterback Scott Hunter and running back John Brockington would both agree that the key to solving the Washington defense in the playoff game was to employ simple short passes to the Packer running backs coming out of the backfield. Such a move would have quickly forced the Redskins to remove their fifth defensive lineman and replace him with another linebacker. Green Bay head coach Dan Devine was unwilling to do this, however. As a result, he was outcoached by Washington's George Allen, and everybody (except maybe Devine himself) knew it. If Hunter had actually changed one of Devine's plays in the game to one of those short passes, he would have probably been benched for insubordination by his head coach for the remainder of the game.

25. *Ibid.* Besides trying to figure out the utter confusion that was going on along the Packers sideline, Hunter was left with a feeling of disgust. He knew that he was virtually powerless to do anything about the situation. As stated in the previous note, if he had tried to call an audible, Devine would have benched him, and may even have cut him from the team after the game. Such were the possible (and some would agree probable) results of disobeying Coach Devine.

26. Interview with Bill Lueck, January 25, 2018. Green Bay offensive guard Bill Lueck had to be scratching his head as to what he was witnessing on the Packers sideline. He was not alone. Several photos from that playoff game of the Green Bay players show their facial expressions of forlorn disgust.

27. Interview with Dave Robinson on June 5, 2014, in Berea, Ohio. For a veteran player who was so used to winning while playing for the great Vince Lombardi, this playoff loss to Washington had to be extremely galling to linebacker Dave Robinson. His anecdote here is yet another note of truth as to how the Redskins defeated the Packers on December 24—

the willingness to change their plans during the course of the game in order to achieve success.

28. Associated Press, "Packers Shake Off Loss, Look to Future," *Fond Du Lac (WI) Reporter*, December 26, 1972, 20. The veteran players on the Green Bay squad undoubtedly expressed to the younger players on the team how difficult it is to make the playoffs, and how difficult it is to win in the playoffs. The younger players took those words to heart, and they played their hearts out against the Redskins in the 1972 divisional playoffs. Every player on the team knew that they might not make it to the playoffs again, so they (as evidenced by Jon Staggers's efforts) gave it their all and then some.

29. *Ibid.*, "Pack Looks Forward to New Dynasty," *Madison (WI) Capital Times*, December 26, 1972, 51. The Christmas Eve loss to the Redskins would turn out to be Carroll Dale's final game in a Green Bay uniform. Devine shipped him off to Minnesota the following year, and he concluded his illustrious NFL career with a loss in Super Bowl VIII, as a member of the 1973 NFC Champion Minnesota Vikings.

30. NFL Films, "The Year the Pack Came Back," written and directed by James Green; executive producer Ed Sabol, 1973. NFL Films would produce a highlight film for each pro football team from the late 1960s to the present day. If you ever watch the Green Bay 1972 highlight film, writer and director James Green credits Dan Devine as the man "most responsible" for the Packers' winning season. I and a great majority of Packer players would certainly disagree with that sentiment.

31. Associated Press, "Packers Shake Off Loss, Look to Future," *Fond Du Lac (Wisconsin) Reporter*, December 26, 1972, 20. Following the end of the 1972 NFL season, bumper stickers proclaiming THE PACK IS BACK could be seen all throughout Wisconsin.

Chapter 11

1. Interview with Ken Ellis, March 23, 2014, *Alumni Spotlight* by Interviewer Vic Ketchman on Packers.com. Young Green Bay cornerback Ken Ellis followed his outstanding All-Pro season of 1972 with another super season in 1973 and 1974. Ellis was named to the All-Pro team in each of those years as well.

2. Interview with John Brockington, June 23, 2017. "Packer Pride" begins with the stories. Every player gets to hear the stories of the past and of the players of the past. He then—all throughout his years with the team—envisions the day when future Packers will tell their younger teammates about his exploits. It is a special feeling that all former Packers hold dear to their hearts. All-Pro Green Bay running back John Brockington soaked up the stories from his rookie year in 1971, and he quickly carved his own niche into the legends of the Packer gridiron. Today, every Green Bay rookie hears about the masterful achievements of the likes of John Brockington.

3. *Ibid.* What separated Green Bay running back John Brockington from other running backs in the NFL was his perseverance. Following his Rookie of the Year season of 1971, Brockington went on to gain over 1,000 yards rushing in 1972 and 1973 as well, even as opposing defenses were keying on stopping him first and foremost, due to Green Bay's lackluster passing game. The town of Green Bay has grown up some since the days of Vince Lombardi, but it is still a small town compared to the other NFL cities. Lambeau Field, however, has grown so much that it now has a seating capacity of just under 81,000, which is 25,000 more than the 56,000 seats that were filled by Packer fans in the late 1960s during the Lombardi era.

4. Interview with Bill Lueck, January 25, 2018. Packers offensive guard Bill Lueck's relationships with his neighbors in Green Bay was certainly not uncommon. Many players from that era became close friends with their non-football-playing neighbors. Every summer in Green Bay, the neighborhood kids let the players ride their bicycles from the locker room to the practice field, a sentimental tradition that is not duplicated anywhere else in the NFL.

5. Mark Shapiro, "Pack's Mules Showed Vikes," *Madison (WI) State Journal*, December 11, 1972, 18. To the casual outside observer, Packers running back MacArthur Lane appeared to be rather bullish and brusque at times. When you get to know him, however, you discover that quite the opposite is true. Lane fell in love with Green Bay, its traditions, and with the Packers fans as soon as he became a Packer in 1972. And Packers fans reciprocated that love from the first day that Lane donned a Packers jersey. The NFC Central Division championship that Lane helped the Packers win in 1972 was the only championship that he was a part of in his 11-year pro football career.

6. Todd Mishler, *Cold Wars: 40 Years of Packer-Viking Rivalry*, Black Earth, Wisconsin: Prairie Oak Press, 2002, 142. The atmosphere that Lane speaks of came to the Packers almost overnight, and even though they did not have a high level of talent at every position, they certainly had enough talent to win a lot of tough, competitive games in 1972.

7. Jerry Polling, "MacArthur Lane Could Do It All," *Packer Report*, October 9, 1989, 13.

The 1972 Green Bay Packers probably knew that they were not going to get a lot of notice or national publicity anyway, playing in the smallest television market in the entire NFL. They certainly did know, however, that the more games they won, the more attention from the media they would draw. Most players who reach the level of the professional ranks in football know and believe that the success of the team is everything. Individual honors mean nothing when compared to team honors. Every Packers player in 1972 believed that fact within the very core of their hearts and minds.

8. Interview with Scott Hunter, September 20, 2017. Even though Scott Hunter did not reach the level of fame as a quarterback at the University of Alabama compared to fellow Crimson Tide alums Bart Starr, Joe Namath and Ken Stabler; or the level of fame in Green Bay as future Packers Brett Favre and Aaron Rodgers, Hunter was the perfect team player for the 1972 Packers. He recognized and accepted his role as a game manager, and despite his youth, he learned well under Starr how to follow and execute a pro game plan. Today, Hunter may not be the first person that you think of when you think of former Alabama or Green Bay quarterbacks, but he owns both of those cherished and honored labels nevertheless, and he is rightly proud of both.

9. Bob Rubin, *Green Bay's Packers: Return to Glory*, Englewood Cliffs, New Jersey: Prentice-Hall, Inc., 1973, 97. Hall of Fame Green Bay middle linebacker Ray Nitschke should know what he is talking about here. He was a teammate of fellow Hall of Fame Packers running backs Jim Taylor and Paul Hornung.

10. Ibid., 97. Legendary Green Bay head coach Vince Lombardi once said that "football is first and foremost a running game; that will never change." In 1972, pro football still was a running game, and the Packers' offensive game plans were geared to feature a bullish runner like John Brockington, who could and usually did get the tough inside yards when Green Bay needed them most.

11. Interview with Bill Lueck, January 25, 2018. Green Bay offensive guard Bill Lueck was one of the better and underrated pulling guards in the NFL in 1972. Watching films of him from that season, he led the likes of John Brockington and MacArthur Lane on many sweeps. He rarely missed blocks on those sweeps and pitchouts. Lueck should have received All-Pro or at least All-Conference mention in 1972.

12. Ibid. Green Bay reserve defensive back Charlie Hall played his best brand of football in 1972 as the season wore on. In the decisive 23–7 win at Minnesota on December 10, Hall made several key tackles on the special teams punt and kickoff coverage units, which forced the Vikings to begin many of their offensive possessions from deep in their own territory.

13. Jerry Polling, "MacArthur Lane Could Do It All," *Packer Report*, October 9, 1989, 13. Besides having confidence in MarArthur Lane's ability to get open on pass routes, the Green Bay coaches also had confidence in his ability to catch the ball. Lane led the Packers in pass receptions in 1972 with 26 catches.

14. Bob Rubin, *Green Bay's Packers: Return to Glory*, Englewood Cliffs, New Jersey: Prentice-Hall, Inc., 1973, 102. Like all great running backs, Brockington knew that his greatness could only flourish if he had people blocking for him. It was true in 1972, and it is still true today.

15. Ibid., 102. The NFC backfield duo of John Brockington and MacArthur Lane rivaled the AFC backfield trio of Larry Csonka, Jim Kiick, and Mercury Morris of Miami. No NFC backfield was better than Brockington and Lane in 1972.

16. Ibid., 130. In virtually every game of the 1972 season, a different Packer player would inspire the rest. Sometimes, several players would do so. You do not win 10 of 14 regular season games in the NFL without some measure of inspiration. Green Bay cornerback Ken Ellis tied for the team lead in interceptions in 1972 with four.

17. Ralph Trower, "Packers Have Fun, Destroy Lions, Take Lead," *Racine (WI) Journal Times*, December 4, 1972, 33. Many years after his retirement, Hall of Fame Packers linebacker Dave Robinson confided to this author that he really wanted to finish his career at Green Bay, but head coach Dan Devine clearly wanted him gone as quickly as possible. Robinson finished his pro football career as a member of the Washington Redskins after the 1974 season.

18. Lee Remmel, "Personality Parade," *Green Bay (WI) Press Gazette*, November 29, 1972. Having a couple of quality cornerbacks on the roster made Green Bay defensive secondary coach Don Doll look good. Willie Buchanon and Kenny Ellis were two of the best coverage guys in the league in 1972.

19. Ibid. Green Bay cornerback Willie Buchanon did indeed fulfill assistant coach Don Doll's hopes by winning the prestigious defensive Rookie of the Year award in 1972.

20. Chester Marcol with Gary D'Amato, *Alive and Kicking: My Journey Through Football, Addiction and Life*, Stevens Point, Wisconsin: KCI Sports Publishing, 2011, 53. As Green Bay placekicker Chester Marcol hinted at, the influx of eight rookies on the Packers 1972 roster gave a tremendous boost to the team's overall level of enthusiasm all year long.

21. *Ibid.*, 55. As his recitation of his statistics show, rookie Green Bay placekicker Chester Marcol was very aware of his level of performance all throughout 1972. He knew what areas of kicking needed improvement.

22. Interview with Robert Miller on January 24, 2018, in Nashville, Tennessee. When the 1972 Packers began the season with a 4–1 record (which included a win over the defending Super Bowl champion Dallas Cowboys), Miller knew that 1972 was going to be a special year for all Packers fans.

23. Interview with Jonathon Schmidt on January 24, 2018, in Nashville, Tennessee. The great Vince Lombardi stressed running to perfection a bunch of simplistic off-tackle runs, sweeps, and straight up the middle dive runs. The 1972 Packers went back in time to excel at many of those same running plays.

24. Interview with Robert Miller on January 24, 2018, in Nashville, Tennessee. The 1973 Packers did not become complacent. They wanted to win as much as the '72 Packers. But there were far more injuries to key personnel in '73, and head coach Dan Devine certainly did not become a better coach in 1973. His indecision on who to start at the quarterback position crippled any chance for the Green Bay offense to succeed.

25. Interview with Jonathon Schmidt on January 24, 2018, in Nashville, Tennessee. Indeed, Packers fans are some of the most loyal fans in the league. And regardless where they live, they still support the Packers, win or lose. They bleed Green and Gold.

26. Jim Hill, CBS-TV game broadcast, Tampa Bay versus Green Bay, Lambeau Field in Green Bay, on December 1, 1985. Former Green Bay safety Jim Hill would become a sports broadcaster in Los Angeles after his pro playing days were over.

27. Interview with Dave Robinson on June 5, 2014, in Berea, Ohio. Many teams since the 1960s enjoy team get-togethers. They build team chemistry, and they help to produce and bond friendships that will last for a lifetime. It is quite doubtful, however, if any team in NFL history but the 1972 Packers ever invited a bunch of dead raccoons to their team parties.

Chapter 12

1. Interview with Scott Hunter, September 20, 2017. Green Bay quarterback Scott Hunter's very apt description of the 1972 Packers served quite well as the reason for their greatness. See note 1 in Chapter 6.

Bibliography

Articles

Newspaper articles appear in chronological order by author.

Associated Press. "Rookie-Saturated Packers Embarrassed By 20-3 Loss." *Sheboygan (WI) Press*, August 21, 1972, 23.
_____. "Devine Orders Double Drill After Packer Defeat." *Ironwood (MI) Daily Globe*, September 5, 1972, 15.
_____. "Conservative Approach Benefits Raiders." *Fond du Lac (WI) Reporter*, September 25, 1972, 22.
_____. "Mistakes Help out Green Bay to Victory Over Dallas, 16-13." *Bryan (TX) Eagle*, October 2, 1972, 13.
_____. "Packers Pass to 20-17 Victory Over Chicago." *Ironwood (MI) Daily Globe*, October 9, 1972, 11.
_____. "Bad Bounce Beats Bears." *Ironwood (MI) Daily Globe*, October 9, 1972, 11.
_____. "Packers Win; Hold Division Lead." *Freeport (IL) Journal-Standard*, October 17, 1972, 9.
_____. "Brilliant Packer Rally Tips Lions." *Racine (WI) Journal Times*, October 17, 1972, 33.
_____. "Falcons in Ball Control Play to Edge Pack, 10-9." *Madison (WI) Capital Times*, October 23, 1972, 13.
_____. "Officials Draw Dan's Ire." *Fond du Lac (WI) Reporter*, October 23, 1972, 14.
_____. "Old Cliche Applies to Minnesota." *Fond du Lac (WI) Reporter*, October 30, 1972, 20.
_____. "49ers' Rally Falls Short Against Pack." *Oxnard (CA) Press Courier*, November 6, 1972, 27.
_____. "Pack Uses 34-24 Win over SF to Keep Pace with Lions." *Wisconsin Rapids Daily Tribune*, November 6, 1972, 27.
_____. "Special Teams Do Job for Green Bay." *Fond du Lac (WI) Reporter*, November 20, 1972, 27.
_____. "Houston Gambled—And Lost." *Fond du Lac (WI) Reporter*, November 20, 1972, 27.
_____. "Pass Completion Eases Negative Thoughts." *Appleton (WI) Post-Crescent*, November 20, 1972, 5.
_____. "Vanoy Wasn't Aware of Head Slaps." *Appleton (WI) Post-Crescent*, November 20, 1972, 7.
_____. "Redskins' Pass Attack Topples Packers, 21-16." *Madison (WI) Capital Times*, November 27, 1972, 17.
_____. "QB Problem Evident in Loss to Redskins." *Fond du Lac (WI) Reporter*, November 27, 1972, 24.
_____. "Allen Impressed by Packers." *Fond du Lac (WI) Reporter*, November 27, 1972, 24.

Bibliography

____. "New, Old Celebrate Packers' 23-7 Win Over Purple Gang." *Dubuque (IA) Telegraph Herald*, December 11, 1972, 15.

____. "Pack Wins Division; Dolphins Beat Giants to Equal NFL Record." *Dubuque (IA) Telegraph Herald*, December 11, 1972, 15.

____. "Packer Loyalty Noted by Devine; Robinson Lauds Play of Williams." *Appleton (WI) Post-Crescent*, December 11, 1972, 15.

____. "Lane Reveals Secret: 'These Cats Love Each Other.'" *Appleton (WI) Post-Crescent*, December 11, 1972, 20.

____. "5,000 Welcome Packers Home." *Racine (WI) Journal Times*, December 11, 1972, 34.

____. "John Brockington and MacArthur Lane: Two 'Mules' Who Form the Perfect Team." December 16, 1972.

____. "Blocking Was Fundamental to Pack's Conquest." *Madison (WI) State Journal*, December 18, 1972, 20.

____. "Pack Just Missed 2 Coveted Records." *Madison (WI) Capital Times*, December 18, 1972, 19.

____. "'Can't Help Thinking About Washington,' Declares Jim Carter." *Appleton (WI) Post-Crescent*, December 18, 1972, 15.

____. "Late-Game 'Miracles' for Pro Playoffs." *Monroe (LA) News Star*, December 25, 1972, 22.

____. "Pack Looks Forward to New Dynasty." *Madison (WI) Capital Times*, December 26, 1972, 51.

____. "Packers Shake Off Loss, Look to Future." *Fond Du Lac (WI) Reporter*, December 26, 1972, 20.

Bledsoe, Terry. "Bumper Stickers Right: Packers Are Back." *Milwaukee (WI) Journal*, December 11, 1972, 13.

____. "Marcol's Kicking Gift Turned a Loser into a Winner." *The Journal*, August 4, 1973.

Denlinger, Kenneth. "Over-the-Hill Redskins Undermine Packers." *The Sporting News*, January 6, 1973, 20.

Drolshagen, Tom. "QBs: Study in Contrasts." *Kenosha (WI) News*, October 9, 1972, 17.

____. "Hampton Running with Confidence." *Kenosha (WI) News*, October 23, 1972, 21.

____. "Big John Starts Smokin.'" *Kenosha (WI) News*, November 6, 1972, 23.

Dwyre, Bill. "Marcol's Moment of Drama." *Milwaukee (WI) Journal*, October 23, 1972, 15, 18.

Estill, Jerry. "Packers 'Stumble' to Win Over Saints, 30-20." *Madison (WI) Capital Times*, December 18, 1972, 19.

Greene, Bob. "Redskin Ambush of Packers Nicest Present for Allen." *Monroe (LA) News Star*, December 25, 1972, 22.

____. "Ambushing Defense Leads Washington." *Charleston (SC) Daily Mail*, December 25, 1972, 21.

Grey, Dave. "Vikes Turn Breaks into Touchdowns for Win." *Oshkosh (WI) Daily Northwestern*, October 30, 1972, 7.

Hawley, Tom. "Green Bay's Front Four Isn't Fancy." *Madison (WI) State Journal*, October 2, 1972, 29.

Hendricks, Martin. "Gillingham Survived Some Tough Packers Years." Special to Packer Plus, *Milwaukee (WI) Journal Sentinel*, August 31, 2011.

Hintz, Gene W. "Room for Improvement." *Green Bay Packers 1972 Yearbook*, Volume 13, 1972, 19-20.

____. "Packers Stagger Home." *Kenosha (WI) News*, October 9, 1972, 17.

Kowet, Don. "What Has Four Heads, Eight Arms, Eights Legs, & Plays for Green Bay?" *Sport Magazine*, November 1973, 74-82.

Langenkamp, Don. "Fate Switched Sides." *Oshkosh (WI) Daily Northwestern*, October 30, 1972, 7.

Lea, Bud. "Donny Tells of Rift with Devine." *Milwaukee (WI) Journal Sentinel*, February 23, 1972, 1, 3.

Lucas, Mike. "Redskins Beat Packers at Own Game—Defense." *Madison (WI) Capital Times*, December 26, 1972, 51.

Maule, Tex. "Green Bay Turns with the Tide." *Sports Illustrated*, October 30, 1972, 31–35.
Meyers, Jeff. "John Brockington: Is He Another Jim Brown?" *Football Digest*, March 1972, 42–43.
Miller, Glenn. "Devine Seeks a Win—and Gets It." *Madison (WI) State Journal*, August 6, 1972, 50–51.
———. "Packers Humiliate Kansas City, 20–0." *Madison (WI) State Journal*, September 9, 1972, 48.
———. "Oakland Delays Verdict, 20–14." *Madison (WI) State Journal*, September 25, 1972, 31–32.
Mooshil, Joe. "Tagge Helps Pack Turn Back Bears, 23–17." *Eau Claire (WI) Leader Telegram*, November 13, 1972, 34.
———. "Devine Not Concerned: 'We Kept Getting Out of Trouble.'" *Eau Claire (WI) Leader Telegram*, November 13, 1972, 34.
Oates, Bob. "'New Lombardi?' No, Simply 'Old Devine.'" *The Sporting News*, July 31, 1971, 56.
O'Brien, Mike. "Packers Question Officials on 2 Big Plays." *Fond du Lac (WI) Reporter*, September 25, 1972, 21.
———. "Hampton Instrumental in Atlanta Win." *Fond du Lac (WI) Reporter*, October 23, 1972, 14.
———. "Interceptions Turn Tide Vikings' Way." *Fond du Lac (WI) Reporter*, October 30, 1972, 20.
———. "Packers Manhandle Lions in 33–7 Win." *Madison (WI) Capital Times*, December 4, 1972, 17.
Paladino, Larry. "Packers Take Lead with 24–23 Squeeze Past Lions." *Eau Claire (WI) Leader Telegram*, October 17, 1972, 25.
Poling, Jerry. "MacArthur Lane Could Do It All." *Packer Report*, October 9, 1989, 13, 20.
Remmel, Lee. "I'm Certainly Not Discouraged." *Green Bay Packers 1972 Yearbook*, Volume 13, 1972, 4–7.
———. "Buchanon Sparkles in Pack Camp." *Green Bay (WI) Press-Gazette*, April 9, 1972.
———. "McGeorge Makes Dream Come True." *Appleton (WI) Post-Crescent*, September 18, 1972, 8–9.
———. "Marcol Finds Himself in Packer Record Book After Just One Game." *Appleton (WI) Post-Crescent*, September 18, 1972, 8–9.
———. "Buchanon Crestfallen." *Green Bay (WI) Press-Gazette*, September 25, 1972.
———. "Marcol Delivers Return Message." *Green Bay (WI) Press-Gazette*, November 13, 1972, B-1, B-2.
———. "'Big Play' Packers Retain Division Lead." *Appleton (WI) Post-Crescent*, November 20, 1972, 5.
———. "Personality Parade." *Green Bay (WI) Press-Gazette*, November 29, 1972.
———. "Packers Achieve Best Record Since 1966." *Appleton (Wisconsin) Post-Crescent*, December 18, 1972, 15.
———. "'Old Times' for Nitschke." *Appleton (WI) Post-Crescent*, December 18, 1972, 15.
Shapiro, Leonard. "Packers Grumble as Tagge Replaced Hunter." *Madison (WI) Capital Times*, November 27, 1972, 17.
Shapiro, Mark. "Devine Sees Hard Work as Pack Cure." *Madison (WI) State Journal*, September 4, 1972, 35.
———. "Raiders Got Some Help." *Madison (WI) State Journal*, September 25, 1972, 31–32.
———. "Injuries Slowed Pack." *Madison (WI) State Journal*, September 25, 1972, 31.
———. "Defense Stymies Champions, 16–13." *Madison (WI) State Journal*, October 2, 1972, 29.
———. "Marcol Keeps His Cool." *Madison (WI) State Journal*, October 23, 1972, 37.
———. "Brock Proudly Pleased." *Madison (WI) State Journal*, November 6, 1972, 19.
———. "The Pack IS Back, 23–7." *Madison (WI) State Journal*, December 11, 1972, 17.
———. "It Started with a Loss." *Madison (WI) State Journal*, December 11, 1972, 17.
———. "Pack's Mules Showed Vikes." *Madison (WI) State Journal*, December 11, 1972, 18.
Trower, Ralph. "Devine Says Packer Win Great Team Effort." *Racine (WI) Journal Times*, October 2, 1972, 26.

_____. "Devine Reflects on Big Win." *Racine (WI) Journal Times*, October 2, 1972, 28.
_____. "Viking Rally Defeats Packers 27–13." *Racine (WI) Journal Times*, October 30, 1972, 41.
_____. "An Interesting Race Now: Devine." *Racine (WI) Journal Times*, October 30, 1972, 41.
_____. "Pack Still Tops, Win 34–24." *Racine (WI) Journal Times*, November 6, 1972, 45.
_____. "Pressure Is Finally Off Packer Secondary." *Racine (WI) Journal Times*, November 6, 1972, 45.
_____. "Packers Lose Statistics but Win Game 23–17." *Racine (WI) Journal Times*, November 13, 1972, 33.
_____. "Jerry Tagge Was Ready." *Racine (WI) Journal Times*, November 13, 1972, 33.
_____. "Packers Have Fun, Destroy Lions, Take Lead." *Racine (WI) Journal Times*, December 4, 1972, 33.
_____. "Packer Wounded Ignore Injuries." *Racine (WI) Journal Times*, December 4, 1972, 33.
United Press International. "Refs Rile Devine Again." *Kenosha (WI) News*, October 23, 1972, 21.
_____. "49ers Rally Falls Short." *Eureka (CA) Times Standard*, November 6, 1972, 14.
_____. "Lane Great as Fill In." *Kensoha (WI) News*, November 20, 1972, 26.
_____. "Widby Nervous About Pass." *Kensoha (WI) News*, November 20, 1972, 26.
Wagner, Len. "The Three Best." *Green Bay Packers 1972 Yearbook*, Volume 13, 1972, 25–29.
Zagorski, Joe. "Jim Carter: Former Packer Put Problems Behind Him." *Packer Report*, August 10, 1987.
_____. "Season of Change: The 1972 Packers." *The Coffin Corner*, Volume 10 Annual, 1988.

Books

Bozeka, George (Ed.). *The 1966 Green Bay Packers: Profiles of Vince Lombardi's Super Bowl I Champions*. Jefferson, NC: McFarland, 2016.
Devine, Dan with Steele, Michael R. *Simply Devine: Memoirs of a Hall of Fame Coach*. Champaign, Illinois: Sports Publishing Inc., 2000.
Goska, Eric. *Green Bay Packers: A Measure of Greatness*. Iola, Wisconsin: Krause Publications, 2003.
Greene, Stanton. *The Green Bay Packers—The Dan Devine Years 1971-1974*. NorthernWriter.com Publishing, 2015.
Marcol, Chester with D'Amato, Gary. *Alive and Kicking: My Journey Through Football, Addiction and Life*. Stevens Point, Wisconsin: KCI Sports Publishing, 2011.
Mishler, Todd. *Cold Wars: 40 Years of Packer-Viking Rivalry*. Black Earth, Wisconsin: Prairie Oak Press, 2002.
Nitschke, Ray as told to Wells, Robert, W. *Mean on Sunday: The Autobiography of Ray Nitschke*. Black Earth, Wisconsin: Prairie Oak Press, 2001.
Rubin, Bob. *Green Bay's Packers: Return to Glory*. Englewood Cliffs, New Jersey: Prentice-Hall, Inc., 1973.
Zagorski, Joe. *The NFL in the 1970s: Pro Football's Most Important Decade*. Jefferson, NC: McFarland, 2016.

Yearbooks

Green Bay Packers 1972 Yearbook. Daley, Art and Yuenger, Jack. Green Bay, Wisconsin.
Green Bay Packers 1973 Yearbook. Daley, Art and Yuenger, Jack. Green Bay, Wisconsin.

Magazines

Prolog: The Official National Football League Annual for 1971. New York: NFL Properties, 1971.

Prolog: The Official National Football League Annual for 1972. New York: NFL Properties, 1972.
Prolog: The Official National Football League Annual for 1973. New York: NFL Properties, 1973.

Editorials

Buckli, Ron. *Eau Claire Leader-Telegram*, August 29, 1972, 11A.
Kuenster, John. *Football Digest*, March 1973, 4–7.

Interviews

John Brockington, June 23, 2017.
Jim Carter, May 14, 1987.
Cliff Christl on July 8, 2016, in Green Bay, Wisconsin, and September 4, 2018.
Frank D'Agostino, February 14, 2017.
Ken Ellis, March 23, 2014. *Alumni Spotlight* by Interviewer Vic Ketchman on Packers.com.
Chuck Lane, July 8, 2016, in Green Bay, Wisconsin.
Bill Lueck, January 25, 2018.
Robert Miller on January 24, 2018, in Nashville, Tennessee.
Dave Robinson on June 5, 2014, in Berea, Ohio.
Jonathon Schmidt, on January 24, 2018, in Nashville, Tennessee.
Bart Starr on September 27, 1990, in Philadelphia, Pennsylvania.
T. J. Troup on October 27, 2017, November 10, 2017, and March 24, 2018.

Videos

1972 Green Bay Packers Highlight Film. *The Year the Pack Came Back*. NFL Films. Green, James (Director). Sabol, Ed (Executive Producer).
1972 New Orleans Saints Highlight Film. *Spirit of the Saints*. NFL Films. Green, James (Director). Sabol, Ed (Executive Producer).
This Week in Pro Football, 1972 Weeks 1–15. NFL Films. Ringe, Buzz and Morcom, Dave (Directors). Ryan, Bob, Green, Jim, Tuckett, Phil and Adams, Mike (Editors). Sabol, Ed (Executive Producer).

Television

Hill, Jim. CBS-TV game broadcast, Tampa Bay versus Green Bay, Lambeau Field in Green Bay (WI), on December 1, 1985.

Index

Adderley, Herb 175, 177
Air Force Academy 94
Alderman, Grady 137
Aldridge, Lionel 6, 18, 93
Alexander, Willie 110, 114
Allen, George 116, 120, 152–153, 157, 166, 227, 232–234
Anderson, Donny 6, 26, 44, 91, 93, 215
Appleton (Wisconsin) 23, 215, 222, 226, 229–232, 238–240
Army 47
Atkinson, George 36–37
Atlanta Falcons 17, 19, 67, 97, 109, 185, 199, 203, 207, 217
Austin-Straubel Airport 146

Barney, Lem 53–54, 62, 217–218
Bass, Mike 156
Beasley, John 133, 138
Bell, Bill 69
Bengston, Phil 5, 7, 15, 35
Biletnikoff, Fred 37–38, 216
Black and Blue Division 66, 95, 146, 170
Blanda, George 35, 37
Bourguignon, Richard 187
Bowman, Ken 47, 64–65, 69, 84, 100, 129, 158, 162, 171, 174, 191–192, 205–206, 223, 228
Bratkowski, Zeke 21, 50–51, 93
Brockington, John 8, 19–22, 24, 26, 31, 34–35, 37–39, 42–45, 49–50, 53, 55, 58, 67, 69, 71, 75–77, 79, 82–83, 86, 92, 95, 99–101, 105–106, 110, 113–114, 117–119, 123–127, 132–137, 141–143, 145–146, 151, 153, 157, 159–160, 162–163, 166–167, 171–172, 174–175, 178, 185, 192, 198–200, 203, 206, 209–211, 214–216, 219–221, 223–224, 226, 228–236, 239–240, 242
Brooklyn, New York 172
Brown, Bill 74, 136, 193
Brown, Bob 6, 27, 46–47, 70, 103, 114, 128, 156, 168, 175, 180–181, 185, 192, 201, 204, 211, 219, 228

Brown, Larry 115, 117–118, 160, 185
Bryant, Bobby 76
Bryant, Paul (Bear) 90, 124, 174, 222
Buchanon, Willie 8, 14–15, 27, 30, 34, 37, 42, 46, 50, 60–61, 81, 103, 134, 137–138, 140, 148, 150, 158, 176, 185, 193, 195, 201, 206, 211, 213–216, 218, 224, 228–230, 236
Buoniconti, Nick 154
Butkus, Dick 109, 171, 225
Butler, Bill 149
Butler, Skip 112

Carr, Fred 27, 30, 50, 69–70, 110, 116, 125, 136, 149, 161, 186, 193, 202, 206, 211, 219, 227, 229
Carter, Jim 6, 27, 50, 73, 108, 112, 116, 125, 139–140, 149, 186, 193–194, 206, 211, 232, 239, 241–242
Central Park 13
Charles, John 111
Chicago Bears 21, 23, 36, 47, 84, 86, 101, 171, 203, 205, 207–208
Christl, Cliff 20, 89, 214, 222, 242
Cincinnati Bengals 21, 192, 207
Clemons, Craig 106
Cleveland Browns 2, 30, 185, 196, 198, 207
Cleveland Municipal Stadium 29
Cochrane, John (Red) 44
Cockcroft, Don 32
Crutcher, Tommy 110, 194, 206
Csonka, Larry 151, 185, 236

Dale, Carroll 6, 26, 58, 73–74, 107, 117, 155, 164, 167, 194–195, 206, 210–211, 235
Dallas Cowboys 17, 21, 38–40, 42–43, 46, 76, 111, 123, 161, 185, 204, 207, 237
Darden, Thom 34
Davis, Ben 34
Davis, Butch 27
Davis, Dave 26, 49, 111–112, 114, 119, 195, 204, 206, 209–211, 226
Dawson, Len 24

Index

Detroit Lions 40, 51, 59, 70, 76, 101, 109, 121, 130–131, 185, 196, 199, 203, 207–208
Devaney, Bob 16
Devine, Dan 3–8, 11–24, 26–31, 33–40, 45–53, 55, 58–60, 63–64, 66–68, 70–71, 73–74, 76–77, 80–95, 98–99, 101–109, 111, 114, 117–122, 127–132, 143–147, 149–157, 160–167, 169–170, 177–178, 183–184, 186–188, 195–196, 199–200, 202–203, 213–216, 219–228, 231–241
Doll, Don 7, 15, 60, 176, 213, 218, 228, 236
Dotsch, Rollie 7, 44, 105, 148

Eischeid, Mike 75
Ellis, Ken 27, 38, 57, 59–61, 81, 103–105, 119, 122, 124–125, 128, 133, 140, 151, 153, 158, 170, 175, 185, 195, 201, 204, 206, 210–211, 214, 217–218, 224, 227–229, 235–236, 242
Elon 26, 32, 207
Essex House 13–14

Facenda, John 168
Farmer, George 50
Favre, Brett 3, 236
Federspiel, Joe 147
Feller, Happy 148
Finkelstein, Mo 83
Fischer, Pat 117, 119
Fond du Lac (Wisconsin) 23, 216, 219, 226–227, 235, 238–240
Fritsch, Toni 42, 45
Funchess, Tom 114
Fuqua, John 185

Garrett, Len 50–51, 140, 196, 199, 206, 210
Garrison, Walt 45–46, 185
Gibron, Abe 50, 108, 110
Gibson, Paul 25, 196, 206
Gilliam, John 133, 137, 140, 224
Gillingham, Gale 19–20, 38, 44, 65, 67, 81, 154, 196, 203, 206, 214, 217
Glass, Leland 26, 34, 49, 54, 58–59, 62, 76, 99, 114, 163, 197, 206, 209–211, 218
Grabowski, Jim 6
Great Depression 173
Green, Bobby Joe 106
Green, Cornell 41, 43–44
Gregg, Forrest 6
Griese, Bob 154
Gunn, Jimmy 107
Gustafson, Bert 7

Hadl, John 169
Hall, Charlie 27, 106, 132, 137, 174, 197, 206, 229, 236
Hampton, Dave 6, 19, 67–68, 71, 93, 185, 218–219
Hanburger, Chris 159, 164
Hand, Larry 55, 125
Hanner, Dave (Hog) 7, 15, 36, 88–89, 102, 216

Harraway, Charlie 118, 160, 185
Harris, Franco 185
Harrison, Jim (Jimmy) 48–50, 84, 106
Hart, Doug 6, 12, 93
Harvard University 47
Hayes, Bob 42, 46, 224
Hayes, Woody 83
Hayhoe, Bill 113, 135, 197–198, 206
Hefner, Larry 27, 206
Heisman Trophy 16, 53, 101
Henderson, John 133, 140
Hilgenberg, Wally 76, 137
Hill, Calvin 42, 185
Hill, Jim (Jimmy) 18–19, 27, 37, 45, 50, 56, 60–61, 73, 81, 103–104, 106, 122, 124, 129, 137, 144, 179, 185, 198–199, 201, 206, 211, 214, 228, 231, 237
Hillsdale College 17, 33, 206
Hilton, John 57
Himes, Dick 65, 148, 198, 206
Hollway, Bob 91
Holmgren, Mike 1–2, 83, 184
Horn, Don 6, 15
Hornung, Paul 8, 33, 113, 177, 236
Houston Astrodome 22, 110–111, 114
Houston Oilers 22, 109, 115, 196, 199, 204, 207–208, 226
Hudson, Bob 45, 198–199, 206, 209–210
Humphrey, Claude 71
Hunt, Kevin 198, 206
Hunter, Scott 16, 21, 24–26, 31–38, 41, 43, 49–50, 52–56, 58–59, 62–64, 69, 73–76, 79, 90, 95, 98–100, 105–107, 113, 117, 120–121, 123–127, 132, 134–138, 141–143, 145, 148, 150, 154–156, 159–164, 166, 173, 183, 199–201, 204, 206, 208–209, 211, 215–216, 218–220, 222–223, 226–227, 229–230, 232–234, 236–237, 240
Hutson, Don 150
Hyland, Bob 12, 213

Ice Bowl 16, 123, 154, 191, 214, 216

Jefferson, Roy 118, 120, 158, 233
Jessie, Ron 53, 59, 128
Jeter, Bob 6, 93
Jordan, Lee Roy 41–43

Kansas City Chiefs 24, 192, 202, 207
Kelly, Leroy 30, 33, 185
Kiick, Jim 151, 185, 236
Kilmer, Bill (Billy) 115, 118–120, 155–156, 158–159, 227, 233
Knight, Curt 119, 159
Kopay, Dave 128, 199, 206, 209–210, 228
Kosins, Gary 109
Kowet, Don 60, 218, 239
Kramer, Jerry 20, 33, 64, 191, 214
Krause, Paul 75–76, 134–135, 142–143, 219, 241

Kroll, Bob 27, 124, 137, 199, 206, 210–211
Kuhlmann, Hank 7, 114, 226

Lambeau, Curly 1, 3
Lambeau Field 3, 9, 12, 16, 21, 23, 41, 48, 51, 72–73, 77, 97, 122–123, 146, 154, 171, 175, 179, 182, 198, 208, 213–214, 216, 235, 237, 242
Lammons, Pete 107, 145, 199–200, 206, 210
Landry, Greg 53–54, 56, 59, 124–125, 127
Landry, Tom 45
Lane, Chuck 90–91, 222, 228, 231, 242
Lane, MacArthur 8, 26, 31, 33–37, 39, 43, 49, 51, 53–55, 58, 67, 71, 76, 84, 91–92, 95, 97, 99, 110, 113–114, 118–119, 123, 126, 134–141, 144–145, 151, 157, 160, 163–164, 166–167, 173–175, 178, 185–186, 192, 198–200, 203, 206, 208–211, 213, 215–216, 218–219, 221–222, 226, 229, 231–236, 239–242
Larsen, Gary 76
Lombardi, Vince 1, 3, 5–7, 28–29, 35, 44–45, 48, 65, 76, 81, 83, 85–86, 94, 98, 106, 113, 117, 123, 135–136, 144, 152, 170–171, 175, 177–179, 183–184, 186–187, 191, 194, 213–216, 220, 222–224, 228, 234–237, 240–241
Lombardi Avenue 29, 83
Lucci, Mike 53
Lueck, Bill 38, 64, 76, 85, 89–90, 100, 113–114, 135, 160, 162, 165, 167, 172, 174, 200, 206, 218, 221–222, 234–236, 242

Madden, John 35, 38, 216
Madison (Wisconsin) *State Journal* 22, 214, 216–217, 219–220, 222, 229–233, 235, 239–240
Malone, Art 69, 185
Manhattan (New York City) 13
Mann, Errol 54, 56, 58
Manning, Archie 149–150
Marcol, Chester 17, 23, 31–34, 42, 45, 49, 51, 56, 59, 68–70, 73–74, 101, 104, 107, 109, 116, 119–120, 124, 128, 134, 136–137, 140, 147–151, 156, 158, 164, 176–177, 200–201, 206, 211, 214–215, 217–219, 225, 229, 231–232, 237, 239–241
Matthews, Al 27, 33, 42, 45, 47, 50, 60–61, 69, 104, 119, 136–137, 140, 185, 199, 201, 207, 211
Maule, Tex 62, 217–219, 240
McCoy, Mike 27, 70, 108, 185, 201, 204, 207, 211
McCullough, Earl 56
McDole, Ron 116, 157, 233
McGeorge, Rich 26, 31–33, 38, 196, 199, 201, 207, 210–211, 215–216, 223, 240
McNally, Art 36
Metropolitan Stadium 130–131, 144, 229
Miami Dolphins 42, 66, 96, 196, 207
Miller, Glenn 22, 214
Miller, Robert 177, 179, 237, 242

Milwaukee Brewers 41, 43, 216
Milwaukee County Stadium 23–24, 43, 67–68, 97, 99, 208, 216
Minnesota Vikings 40, 72–77, 80, 97–98, 101, 114, 121, 127, 129–142, 144, 146, 150, 192–193, 195, 204, 207–208, 219, 228–231, 235–236, 240
Mitchell, Jim 55
Monday Night Football 53, 55–56, 64, 76, 195, 197, 217–218
Moore, Jerry 84, 106
Morris, Mercury 151, 185, 236
Morton, Craig 41–42, 46, 204, 217
Mul-Key, Herb 158
Munson, Bill 128
Myers, Tommy 148

Navy 47
Neal, Richard 149–150, 232
Nelsen, Bill 29–30, 33
New England Patriots 199
New Orleans Saints 146–150, 195, 199, 202, 205, 208, 231–232, 239, 242
New York City 13, 17–18
New York Giants 12, 29, 41, 194, 201–202, 204, 213, 216, 239
New York Jets 17, 121, 150, 199, 225
NFL Draft 6, 12–15, 17, 202, 205, 213–214
Nitschke, Ray 6–7, 27, 102, 105–106, 144–145, 147–148, 174, 186, 193–194, 201–202, 207, 210, 213, 223–224, 231, 236, 240–241
No-Name Defense 22
Noel, Bob 132
Nolan, Dick 101, 103, 223
Noonan, Karl 22
Notre Dame University 91, 94, 169, 184, 207
Nunley, Frank 99

Ohio State University 8, 83
Olejniczak, Dominic 187
Orange Bowl 11, 16, 22, 87, 94
Orange Bowl Stadium 11, 94, 154
Osborn, Dave 139
Oshkosh (Wisconsin) 23, 219, 239
Over-the-Hill Gang 233, 239
Owens, Steve 53, 185

Page, Alan 75, 139–140, 192, 230
Pardee, Jack 157, 233
The Parkettes 72–73, 75, 77
Parks, Dave 150
Pastorini, Dan 22, 110, 114
Patrick, Frank 50, 202, 207–208
Peay, Francis 38, 94, 186, 202, 207, 223
Penn State University 87–88, 207, 221
Peppler, Pat 13–14
Percival, Mac 49–51
Peterson, Bill 112, 226
Phipps, Mike 29, 33
Pinder, Cyril 49–50, 106

Pitts, Elijah 93
Pitts, Frank 30, 224
Polonchek, John 7
Pottios, Myron 157
Potts, Charlie 57
Pro Football Hall of Fame 20, 64, 85, 105, 202, 214, 221–222, 224, 227
Pugh, Jethro 191
Pureifory, Dave 27, 202, 207

Rasmussen, Wayne 55
Redmond, Rudy 58–59, 218
Reed, Oscar 73
Rice, Bob 139
Rice, Jerry 100, 223
Robert F. Kennedy (RFK) Stadium 119, 152, 155, 165
Robinson, Dave 6, 27, 29, 48, 83, 85–90, 95, 98, 101–102, 108, 128–129, 141, 153–154, 165, 175–176, 180, 186, 202, 207, 211, 215, 220–224, 228–230, 232–234, 236–237, 239, 242
Robinson, Paul 111
Roche, Alden 16, 27, 108, 155, 185, 202–203, 207, 211, 233
Rodgers, Aaron 3, 236
Rodgers, Johnny 16
Rozelle, Pete 13, 71
Rubin, Bob 94, 213, 223, 229, 236, 241

St. Louis Cardinals 8, 23–26, 44, 67, 91, 113, 144, 200, 205, 207, 215
Saint Norbert's College 17, 84
San Diego Chargers 8, 18–19, 61, 161, 192–193, 198, 205
San Diego State University 8, 14, 193, 206, 215
San Francisco 49ers 2, 87, 91, 97, 99–106, 154, 185, 196, 199, 201, 207, 222–224, 231
Sanders, Charlie 53
Sayers, Gale 86, 171
Schmidt, Joe 128, 228
Schmidt, Jonathon 177–179, 237, 242
Schnelker, Bob 84
Scott, Bo 185
Scott, Clarence 32
Seattle Seahawks 2, 201, 203
Sheboygan, Wisconsin 23, 214, 238
Sherk, Jerry 32
Shy, Don 50, 106
Simpson, Mike 99, 101
Sistrunk, Manny 157–158, 162, 233
Skorich, Nick 29
Smith, Charlie 37
Smith, Jerry 119, 160
Smith, Ron 51
Snider, Malcolm 19, 52, 56, 67, 75, 113, 135, 161, 203, 207
Soldier Field 109
Southern University 170, 206–207

Spurrier, Steve 101, 103–105, 224
Staggers, Jon 26, 49, 51, 56, 58, 110–111, 114, 119, 133, 151, 156, 167, 203, 207, 209–211, 217, 226, 235
Starr, Bart 3, 7, 15–16, 25, 34–35, 58–59, 62–64, 71, 88–89, 95, 98–100, 105, 117, 119, 124, 127, 134, 141, 152–153, 160–166, 169, 177, 187, 191, 195, 199, 215, 218–219, 224–225, 230, 233–234, 236, 242
Staubach, Roger 41
Super Bowl VI 38, 42, 161
Super Bowl VII 78, 96, 154, 233
Super Bowl VIII 230, 235

Tagge, Jerry 16–17, 21–22, 26, 31, 50, 98, 107–108, 117–119, 121, 149, 166, 203–204, 207–209, 211, 214, 217–218, 225–227, 240–241
Talbert, Diron 157, 233
Tarkenton, Fran 48, 74, 76, 129, 133–134, 137–141, 220, 229–230
Tatum, Jack 36, 216
Taylor, Altie 53–54, 125, 127, 185
Taylor, Bruce 99
Taylor, Charley 120, 158, 160, 227–228, 233
Taylor, Jim 8, 113, 174, 177, 236
Taylor, Joe 49
Texas A&M–Kingsville 18, 206
Thomas, Duane 161–162
Thomas, Ike 21, 38, 107, 110, 119–120, 128, 204, 207, 210–211, 227
Tiger Stadium 53, 62, 64
Torinus, John B. 187
Treml, Al 84
Troup, T.J. 19, 35, 60–61, 137, 141, 150, 159, 163, 184, 213–215, 218, 229–230, 233–234, 242
Trowbridge, Fred N., Sr. 187
Tulane Stadium 147
Turner, Cecil 107
Turner, Jim 149, 231–232

University of Alabama 63–64, 90, 123–124, 173, 218, 236
University of Michigan 47
University of Minnesota 6, 206
University of Missouri 5, 11, 82, 84, 88, 94, 202, 207, 220–222, 226
University of Nebraska 16, 118, 207

Van Brocklin, Norm 71, 219
Vanderbundt, Skip 99–101
Vanoy, Vernon 47, 204, 207, 217, 238
Villapiano, Phil 37
Vince Lombardi Trophy 1, 170
Voigt, Stu 134

Walker, Wayne 54
Walsh, Ward 204, 207
Walton, Larry 53
Warfield, Paul 154

Washington, Gene (San Francisco) 103–105, 224
Washington, Vic 100, 185
Washington, D.C. 152
Washington Redskins 84, 96, 115–121, 146, 152–167, 169, 175, 185, 187, 197, 199, 202, 208, 221, 227, 232–234, 239
Weaver, Charley 53
Weaver, Herman 56–57
Weger, Mike 53, 56, 125
West, Charlie 133, 135
White, Ed 137
Widby, Ron 21, 33, 38, 69, 104, 111–112, 116, 129, 139, 147–149, 159, 204, 207, 209, 211, 226, 241
Wilcox, Dave 101
Willard, Ken 185
Williams, Clarence (Big Cat) 27, 48, 59, 69, 99, 102, 133, 141, 148, 155–156, 169, 185, 202, 204–205, 207, 211, 222, 224, 229–230, 233, 239
Williams, Perry 57, 127, 205, 207, 209, 211
Williams, Travis 6
Winner, Charlie 91
Winston, Roy 76, 136
Withrow, Cal 205, 207, 211
Wood, Willie 93, 177
Woodbine (Georgia) 170
World War II 173
Wortman, Keith 205, 207, 211
Wright, Jeff 74
Wright, Nate 73–74

Yale University 47

Zofko, Mickey 57, 124

www.ingramcontent.com/pod-product-compliance
Ingram Content Group UK Ltd.
Pitfield, Milton Keynes, MK11 3LW, UK
UKHW041936140426
5217IPUK00014B/513